LABOR ARISTOCRACY

MASS BASE of SOCIAL DEMOCRACY

H. W. Edwards

Second Edition

Second Edition Print ISBN 979-8-9887747-7-8
EBook ISBN 979-8-9887747-3-0
Library of Congress Control Number: 2024916401

First Edition, Aurora Press, Stockholm, 1978.
ISBN 91 7252 013 2

Second Edition Published by
Estuary Press
472 Skyline Drive
Vallejo, CA, 94591

Cover Designed by Paul Richards. Cover Art by Brigada Orlando Letelier BOL, printed in Mission Gráfica, c. 80s.

Second Edition is produced by Paul David Richards, Hodee Edwards' (1914-2012) son, with permission from Teddy Hultberg, formerly of Aurora Press.

Notes on changes to the text. I have omitted her Appendices from this edition. They are available in the first edition on the web (https://archive.org/details/edwards-labor-aristocracy-1/mode/1up). I have left her footnotes as they appear in the first edition. I have also let stand the English spelling of words as they appear in the first edition which was written in London and first published in Sweden. Her preface to the first edition is at the end of the book. I take responsibility for all errors that may have remained into the text.

Dedication

This book is a tribute to and a token of love for my beloved young comrades in Ghana, and for their contemporaries everywhere in Black Africa.

"I consider it a hindrance to basic change that a decisive section of the world proletariat can allow itself to enjoy, and will defend to the death, privileges which (a) hide its own exploitation and (b) derive from the blood, sweat and tears of proletarian brothers and sisters in the Third World."

H. W. Edwards, from her Preface.

Contents

List of Tables

Labor Aristocracy

Editor's Preface by Paul Richards

Why a New Edition of "Labor Aristocracy"

Estuary Press is proud to offer the publication of a second edition of H. W. Edwards' 1978 book *The Labor Aristocracy, Mass Base of Social Democracy*. Publishing a second edition of my mother's book 46 years after its first edition is the result of the prophetic nature of her critique of the labor aristocracy. By defining the material base of the western labor aristocracy, she provided a necessary element for explaining how and why western populations continue to support imperialist policies like the genocide in Gaza and the bloody conflict in the Ukraine. The base of this repulsive situation lies in the history of the 20th century. Hodee's book delves deeply into these origins from her standpoint as an American Marxist who lived in Africa. She focuses on the role of racism and social democracy in bringing about western popular support for colonialism.

The notion of a labor aristocracy really says it all. Aristocracies have always existed at the pleasure of the king and loyally served his interests. Western popular support for our monstrous wars arises from the fact that our material prosperity is inextricably tied to the superprofits of colonial and neo-colonial exploitation of the nations of the what is now called the global south. Imperialist superprofits accrued by US multinational corporations are the material base of western prosperity. Corporations are the new kings of the capitalist world. The labor aristocracy grew out of this unequal economic system and owes it allegiance and its prosperity to its corporate masters no less than aristocracies of old owed their loyalty to the king. History works its way in the subconscious of the passing generations as we reproduce ancient ways in the modern world. If we are ever to crawl out of this nightmarish reality, we must turn on the lights to expose exactly what we are dealing with. And seeing the material base of western support for racism, war and imperialism is an integral part of the picture.

H. W. Edwards and I shared an extensive correspondence in the 1960s and 70s during the writing of her book when she lived in Ghana and London. Then decades and generations of life swept us apart. I lost our correspondence and her book sank into the back of my mind until long after she was gone. Fate intervened when the original publishers of her book, Aurora publishers, turned up in my email and sent me rare copies of her books. Aurora had been out of business for 20 years when this happened.

In the 1970s, H. W. Edwards was a long time Marxist even though she was no longer associated with any particular vanguard party. Her ideas referenced the long forgotten and suppressed world of polemical debates that included the Sino-Soviet dispute. She wrote in Marxist terms and she based much of her thinking on Lenin's "Imperialism, the Highest Stage of Capitalism". Yet, her book was not just a regurgitation of old ideas. It wasn't another debate between rival factions of the fractured white western left. It was the view from the dark bottom, from the outside, from the colonial hinterland of imperialism.

Hodee's focus on the Marxist dialog that she witnessed in her 14 years in the Communist Party may seem misplaced to many unfamiliar with it. Yet, I believe it is true that the demise of the left in the western world flows in part from the way that this dialog unfolded. Hodee takes up the dialog again in 1978 to reveal the path that western radicalism took leading up to its present situation as an irrelevant minority. Her critique is a necessary part of future dialogues exposing how mainstream narratives have silenced opposition to colonialism within the empire.

On the way to publishing this second edition of the Labor Aristocracy, I re-examined another long lost piece of her writing from our 1988 Frank family reunion which had brought together her mother's side of our family. Hodee's mother's maiden name was Frank. The reunion organizers solicited biographical statements from all the attendees and put together the "Frank Family Reunion Book" in Burlington Vermont in August, 1987. Most attendees wrote nice little paragraphs or even a page or two. Hodee wrote a 50 page essay for the Reunion book that went into the file cabinet and sat there for decades. Now reading it again, I found answers to my question of what motivated her to write *Labor Aristocracy*. I published her 1988 autobiographical essay in a 150 page book now available from Estuary Press called *Autobiography 1988*.

Her autobiography illuminated the path she had taken in writing the *Labor Aristocracy*. She covered her childhood in Boston, her flight from her wealthy Jewish family, her radicalization at Radcliffe and Bryn Mawr colleges where she majored in physics ("because it was hard.") She became on open Communist on both campuses. Right after college, she married my father, Harvey Richards, a Communist Party member who worked as an organizer with the WPA (FDR's New Deal agency). They moved to the West Coast in 1940 where she continued her radical journalism that had started back east as a student. She covered war news for the Daily People's World under a man's name, as L.C. Shepard. She liked the L.C. part best. Sounds like Elsie. Her marriage to my dad ended in 1946 when I was 2. Then she married another CP member, my step father, George Edwards, in 1948. He was African American and soon along came a daughter, my sister, Eva Edwards.

Hodee and George had a stormy marriage and a rough time being harassed by the FBI in the racist anti-communist economic world of the San Francisco Bay Area during the 1950s. Just as I graduated high school in 1961, George and Hodee, along with Eva, moved to Ghana, West Africa. He was a plumber who teamed up with other African American electricians and building trades workers to relocate to Ghana to help contribute their skills to the first independent African country inaugurating the post colonial epoch that is still unfolding today. They joined W. E. B. DuBois and Shirley Graham who had moved to Ghana shortly before in October, 1961. George had met DuBois back in the 1930s when George was a bootlegger plying his trade at the Cotton Club in NYC. They had a history. Hodee soon took up her journalism trade again in Ghana covering things like the creation of fishing cooperatives by market women to bring more protein into the diets of ordinary Ghanaians. In the process she met the young African revolutionaries around Nkrumah who were battling against the forces of neo-colonialism who were trying to take Ghana back from its new independence.

In 1966, just days after the coup that overthrew Nkrumah, I visited her and spent two months in Ghana. Our plane landed in Accra where we were met by armed soldiers dressed in green fatigues who escorted us across the tarmac into the passengers terminal. Later, I met a few of her revolutionary friends and even went to a luncheon put on by the market women of a fishing cooperative. The most memorable part of that lunch was the hot pepper that blew my mind and caused my face to turn even redder, much to the amusement of the Ghanaians watching me intently around the table.

During my visit I first learned of my mother's involvement with the writing of Nkrumah's book *Neo Colonialism, the Last Stage of Imperialism*. She wrote chapter 18, entitled "The Mechanisms of Neo-Colonialism." Her young Ghanaian friends who were meeting with Nkrumah told her that her chapter received praise from Nkrumah and was included verbatim in the book. She and all the other contributing writers never received credit for their work. In Hodee's case, she was cautioned to remain silent about it because of the political issues involved if it became known that a white woman communist writer was helping Nkrumah.

My sister was 12 and 13 years old when Hodee was writing her chapter of *Neo-Colonialism*. Hodee sent her to the library in Accra repeatedly when Eva went there from their home in Kumasi to visit friends. She had to find specific statistical numbers from books like the most recent Statistical Atlas of the USA, for Hodee's research. Hodee became completely invested in supporting the African revolution and was close personally with the young revolutionaries supporting Nkrumah. So Nkrumah's overthrow in the coup of 1966 hit her hard, motivating her to begin writing the *Labor Aristocracy*. What better way to support her new friends and the cause of the African revolution than to take up the fight against US imperialism on her own home turf? And what question was more compelling than trying to understand how and why the people of the USA and other western countries had come to support imperialist policies in the 20th century, and now the 21st century?

With her radical Marxist world view, she focused on the story of how Marxists had underestimated and ignored the impact of colonialism on the people of the US and Europe, creating the largest labor aristocracy the world has ever known. Not only did Western populations not oppose these policies, but they actually supported them in more ways than one. I saw this personally in the 1960s when my whole generation signed up and went off to war in Vietnam, dying in the tens of thousands. And over the decades since that war ended in 1973, I have continued to witness the expanding influence of the imperialist narrative on the minds of my generation and those that have followed. As the world moves towards global warming and species extinctions on an unprecedented level, the time has come to look more deeply into what keeps us glued to the lies of the deep state.

Labor Aristocracy, second edition is offered as part of this new look into the roots of our problem.

Labor Aristocracy

INTRODUCTION
by Hodee Edwards

The theme of this book is that Social Democracy, for all that it developed what Lenin called a "petty bourgeois ideology", only came into its own with, and will die only with the destruction of, the Western labour aristocracy, whose continued existence forms its material basis, and whose needs it serves.

Lenin had first exposed and documented imperialism's chief characteristic as its parasitism.[1] He had shown that such parasitism consists primarily in the production of a ceaseless stream of super-profits which, once capitalism has developed into imperialism, become indispensable; and which the ruling class then, as its own "life insurance", shares with "its own" working class, creating among them "a labour aristocracy".

Without apology, this text subscribes to that entire analysis and holds it -- if possible — truer today than in Lenin's time (in how ever varied new forms and however diversifiedly now expressed). But it was precisely this feature of the system which, in a kind of "Freudian" economic "loss of memory", virtually all Marxists" forgot".

For example, a number of eminent Marxists in the 30s made blatantly wrong predictions about Social Democracy: Georgi Dimtroff, of Reichstag Fire Trial fame, who subsequently became first President of the Bulgarian Socialist Republic; R. Palme Dutt, Indian author of *Fascism and Social Revolution*, leading figure of the British Communist Party; and Palmiro Togliatti, late head of the Italian Communist Party. All these had publicly proclaimed in the mid-30s the early "revolutionisation" of Europe's Social Democratic masses under the guidance of Communists specifically dedicated to that purpose. This illusion-ridden vision is still around, still bedazzling those who claim to be "the real Marxists"; only now, instead of "the general crisis" alone and glittering in its generality, it takes the form of the May 1968 events in France, most recent manifestation that capitalism is, indeed, in a general crisis which it cannot cure.

If, however, the parasitism of imperialism of which Lenin spoke is recalled and analysed in its current - vastly expanded forms, it reveals as so much poppycock all talk of any "world-shaking" role by the current Western proletariat; and it also thumbs its nose at any attempts to discuss "neo-capitalism" or "neo-imperialism": the vigorous manhood of the system Lenin so accurately examined[2] has merely yielded to the same system's old age, with clear evidence of senility now setting in.

That is, analysis - such as this text hopes to offer - based on Lenin's major work on imperialism clearly reveals that the imperialist system cannot, and will not, survive the achievement of genuine (meaning economic) freedom by colonial peoples on a scale broad enough to create a massive dent in ruling class super-profits, and to destroy unequal exchange. This is the meaning of Indonesia, Brazil et al and Vietnam: the imperialists know what they are about, and those who want "in" on that knowledge need only watch imperialist and revisionist maneuvers in and affecting the misnamed "Third World".

So, in the end, both in the 30s and now in reference to France, Italy, Germany and elsewhere, the Social Democratic masses do not become "revolutionised". Rather, the Social Democratic "machine" gobbles up - ideologically, at least — the self-styled Communists, including Palme Dutt and Togliatti in their day, and the "New Left" and plenty of "mighty Maoists" in ours.

The cited wrong forecasts (then and now) make it obvious that something must be missing from these Marxists' estimates of Social Democracy. In Africa, this proved to be a serious matter; an investigation had to be started.

Basically, the conclusion reached was that the Marxists in question had never carried far enough their own first study of Social Democracy. For reasons which it is hoped the body of the text will clarify, they preferred to rest on Lenin's 1916 analysis, which defined Social Democracy merely as "the principal social (not military) prop of the bourgeoisie."[3] They ignored the fact that Lenin, pioneer analyst, necessarily generalised.

Had they, however, applied his generalisations to the phenomenon as it developed in their own epochs, they would have discovered, as we hope to do in the text, the inner "secrets" of Social Democracy which might have enabled them to deal with it more adequately.

But because they did not pursue the subject further than, at the latest, 1940, they began losing their original understanding of the system as a whole; and then, of all its parts. They were not prepared for what really happened; could not adjust to reality, explain it or find the proper political response to it among workers they were supposed to be leading. Rather, they entirely misjudged the developmental direction of those whom collectively they defined as "the working class in the main capitalist countries", and continued talking of as "the proletariat". Furthermore, they cast the latter as "hero" in their annual doom prophecies, whereby the entire imperialist system, as a result of its undeniable general crisis, was imminently to collapse.

When the system defied them, as it still does again and again, "recovering" from each "paralytic stroke" delivered by the advance of its own inner contradictions; when Western workers refuse to live up to the "poverty-stricken" and "revolutionised" image built up for them, and fail to support the struggles for freedom of their "class brothers in colonies", these Marxists respond by urging the election of "Communists" to parliament. And when such elections actually occur in some countries — or when some Western cities actually elect "Communists" to "power" for decades (Waldeck Rochet, for instance) — instead of socialism, as promised, the result has been only to keep the great monopolies and their administrations precisely from folding up.

Why? What has been wrong? Has Marx been disproved, now at last? What happened to capitalism's "grave-diggers"?

Answers to these questions have existed all along – in Lenin's cited work.[4] There, Lenin had provided criteria, some of which is possible to apply to current statistics. Restudying these would have revealed the direction in which the West was really moving, powered precisely by the system's parasitism.

Social Democrats and racists have a big stake in concealing the spread of parasitism. But Marxists have an even bigger one in exposing it. A re-analysis of Social Democracy, therefore,

> a) clarifies the phenomenon itself;
> b) reveals in detail why the Marxists of the 30s were unable to make correct predictions about it;
> c) confirms, from an entirely different approach, the Chinese diagnosis of today's main contradictions,[5] main center of revolution, and main direction of current history; but
> d) casts considerable doubt on a recent Chinese contention that the Western metropoles today, particularly as exemplified in the May 1968 events in France, are either "on the verge of revolution", or that the Western proletariat is as yet any main agent "shaking" the moribund system.

To such re-analysis the text now turns.

Section A:

Background

Labor Aristocracy

1. Political Mothballs or Pertinent Politics?

On Saturday, April 20, 1968, a British Tory named Enoch Powell startled not only his parliamentary colleagues but a good portion of the world when he voiced the existing virulent racialism of his own society.

On Tuesday, April 23, 1968, at least a thousand British dockers staged England's first political strike in a long while - supporting Enoch Powell.

Only the day before, a staid London daily had editorially called Mr. Powell's effort "An Evil Speech", and dubbed it "a political action". It charged that

> "it was an arranged occasion, carefully scripted, carefully planned... a clear challenge to Mr. Heath's (Shadow Prime Minister's) leadership. . . (he) had to dismiss Mr. Powell in order . . . to clear the Conservative Party of complicity in Mr. Powell's racialism . . . are there really so many Conservative members who go all the way not only with Mr. Powell's views, but also with his language?"[1]

Six days later, a leading weekly paper printed a study of the entire phenomenon, leading off with a quote from "a race relations officer", who said that:

> "Enoch Powell's speech has suddenly made racial prejudice look respectable. Coming from a member of the Tory Shadow Cabinet (he had been Shadow Defense

> Minister - H.W.E.), people can't help taking it as some kind of authority to let rip with 'anti-nigger' words.[2]

London dockers corroborated him in action, at the same time illuminating the entire situation. The London weekly noted what it called a "curious" fact:

> only four coloured men are employed in the thousands-strong dock labour force, and these are only acceptable because they are second generation. Dock work is a family ... affair and it can be hard for a white worker to join the force unless he is 'known'."[3]

In a word, the dockers were not responding to local stimuli, but to something more general. The OBSERVER noted:

> "Like the dockers' demonstration, the token strikes elsewhere have been spontaneous and usually started by people who are not normally politically active. They were small but wide spread in the Midlands. They affected breweries, radiator and car component factories, and engineering works of all kinds. "[4]

More revealing were actions and reactions of leaders of some unions involved.

First, a divisional officer for Number 3 docks group of the Transport and General Workers' Union (familiarly known as "the T & G") knew nothing of what was going on till "tipped off that there was trouble in his parish". He "and another official" rushed off "to try to preach the union's official policy of no discrimination", but to no avail. By 11.30 a.m. of the 23rd, "all but 21 of the 3000-odd West India Dock workers had decided on a pro test". Many of those interviewed were surprised at "the speed and spontaneity of the action".

While the OBSERVER stated that "there were no ring-leaders", it named one, whom it described colourfully, as well as by saying that he was "active in the Labour Party".

One well-known Communist and union leader did, the OBSERVER sneered, "manage a squawk of protest":

> "With five colleagues, he issued a circular – 'in their personal capacities' – protesting against the racial demonstration."[5]

But, commented the weekly,

> "dockers ridiculed (this Communist) attempt to PREVENT a strike. They had decided the race issue was worth the loss of anything from £5 to £8 for a day's work."[5]

All union officials interviewed, said the OBSERVER, "are deeply embarrassed by last week's events". Of course! Those events went contrary to union policy. Significantly, one "ex-T & G official" told the paper that

> "every year the head office gets a lot of resolutions for the union s annual conference from branches all over the country which are strongly colour prejudiced... the senior officers of the union, not least the General Secretary himself... see to it that none of them comes up for debate."[6]

So, the dichotomy between union policy and membership practice has been perpetuated by those appearing to espouse policy, perhaps picturing this as the means for doing so.

Another union official, divisional officer of the Association of Scientific, Technical and Managerial Staffs, had received threatening phone calls from members of his own organization because of his letter to the Midland press criticising Enoch Powell's speech.

Puzzled this unionist:

> "I fail to understand this. What else can this be but naked racialism? We are supposed to be a left-wing union."

Well might the poor man exclaim in bafflement! He is among that majority who have not forgotten the great fanfare with which Harold Wilson had been ushered into the highest seat of British Government at the end of 1964.

When, some twenty days later, the "liberal peace candidate" Lyndon Baines Johnson was catapulted into Presidential prominence in the USA., in the contest with Barry Morris Goldwater, these joyful peans were augmented from across the sea.

Both events, thanks to illusions and forgetfulness, had generated hopes on the African continent: "NOW things will surely change! NOW Africa will be able better to fight colonialism." A sigh of relief went up over the world, which settled back for a long lull. Only certain Cassandras of the Orient (and elsewhere) refused to withdraw earlier warnings about all such "men of peace".

By the last week in April, 1968, the London OBSERVER could quote the general secretary of the Pakistani Workers' Association "which has the support of some 10,000 Pakistani workers in the Midlands" as saying:

> "We have lost faith in the British Trade Union movement. The dockers have confirmed our suspicions."7

Simultaneously, the general secretary of the Indian Workers' Association predicted "separate unions" for coloured workers "in the near future". He added that such an eventuality would "be bad for the principle of . . . unionism".8

But the Labour Government itself had contributed to this disillusionment by its odd idea of "anti-colonialism": Congo Kinshasa, British Guiana, Southern Rhodesia, South Africa, Malaysia, Aden - sacrificed in quick succession on the altar of political expediency. Lyndon Johnson's even stranger version of "peace" quickly popped up in North and South Vietnam, at Stanleyville, Santo Domingo, in Indonesia and all over Africa.

While the shock to many was severe, illusion persisted broadly. For, eulogies uttered even by certain Marxists lauded "good" "sincere" and "truly radical" individuals included in the British Labour Government of late 1964, people who had long since declared their intentions of "doing right" by workers both "at home" and in the colonial areas.

Actually, their "goodness", supplemented by the deeds they did, demonstrated that the course of Social Democracy (like that of any other material phenomenon in this material world) proceeds independently of the will, intelligence or intentions of individuals.

This was not the first time that "Labour" parties had shown the same schism between words and deeds. Those words obtain for them the authority to perform their deeds. And events have shown that even once-hard-bitten Communists are still being taken in, and - some say – now contributing to the pervasive illusions contained in Social Democracy's words.

The world, however, still includes Marxists who remain tough. One of the most famous of them not long ago declared:

> "Marxist philosophy holds that the law of the unity of opposites is the fundamental law of the universe... Between the opposites in a contradiction, there is at once

unity and struggle, and it is this that impels things to move and change.

"Contradictions exist everywhere, but they differ in accordance with the different nature of different things. In any given phenomenon or thing, the unity of opposites is conditional, temporary and transitory, and hence relative, whereas the struggle of opposites is absolute."[9]

What "contradictions" is this successful revolutionary talking about?

In 1957 and again in 1960, Marxists – some of them by then a bit less case-hardened than previously – met in Moscow and, despite developing differences in their ranks, managed a unanimous answer to this question.

They enumerated as "the fundamental contradictions in the contemporary world" those between "the socialist camp and the imperialist camp;

". . . the proletariat and the bourgeoisie in the capitalist countries;
". . . the oppressed nations and imperialism; and
". . . among imperialist countries and among monopoly capitalist groups."[10]

Having thus set them out, they elaborated on them in 25 points. But among the first comments preceding exposition of the " points" was this:

"These contradictions and the struggles to which they give rise are interrelated and influence each other. Nobody can obliterate any of (them) or subjectively substitute one for all the rest.
" It is inevitable that these contradictions will give rise to popular revolutions, which alone can resolve the m."[11]

In Point No. 8, the world's Marxists officially further declared:

> "The various types of contradictions in the contemporary world are concentrated in the vast areas of Asia, Africa and Latin America; these are the most vulnerable areas under imperialist rule and the storm centres of world revolution dealing direct blows at imperialism. . .
>
> "The national democratic revolution in these areas is an important component of the contemporary proletarian world revolution... pounding and undermining the foundations of the rule of imperialism and colonialism... "In a sense, therefore, the whole cause of the international proletarian revolution hinges on the outcome of the revolutionary struggles of the people in these areas, who constitute the overwhelming majority of the world's population."[12]

Here is precisely the rock on which the less "stern" among self-styled Marxists have stubbed a collective toe. For, as the cited document noted,

> "Certain persons now go so far as to deny the great international significance of the anti-imperialist revolutionary struggles of the Asian, African and Latin American peoples, and, on the pretext of breaking down the barriers of nationality, colour and geographical location, are trying their best... not to break (these) down... but to maintain the rule of the 'superior nations' over the oppressed nations. It is only natural that this fraudulent 'theory' is rejected by the people in these areas."[13]

But matters are much more serious even than this:

"It is impossible for the working class in the European and American capitalist countries to liberate itself unless it unites with the oppressed nations and unless those nations are liberated. Lenin rightly said,

> 'The revolutionary movement in the advanced countries would be a sheer fraud if, in their struggle against capital, the workers of Europe and America were not closely and completely united with the hundreds upon hundreds of millions of 'colonial' slaves who are oppressed by capital.'"[14]

It is at this point that Enoch Powell and the British dock workers enter the picture. Powell, the Right-wing, openly-racist Tory spokesman for monopoly capital, finds "spontaneous" and wide spread support from thousands of English rank-and-file union embers. Their "Labour" Government, and Labour and Communist officials, publicly deploring, are completely powerless to stop the exhibition. In fact, sober reflection suggests that they were, at least objectively, "accessories after the fact".

Here is how, seemingly suddenly, the above epitomization of England's scene reveals the crucial overall importance not only to England but to today's world of understanding the role, nature, origins and history of Social Democracy.

Where does the latter fit into the pattern of world contradictions[10] officially postulated by world Marxists? What effect has it had on revolution: in colonies? "at home"? Why was a "Labour" man leading the London dockers in their openly racist strike?

Only a thorough restudy of Social Democracy, from its beginnings through current events, can provide answers.

2. Social Democracy Defined

To discuss anything intelligently, we must first define it. What, then, is Social Democracy?

Before World War I, Lenin used the words referring to revolutionary working class organisation in Russia and elsewhere. Can this be done today?

In 1914, the Second International, then comprising all Socialist Parties whether "right" or "left," split over whether or not to support "one's own" bourgeoisie in "the war to end war". Those who stayed with the Second International turned nationalist and chauvinist, indulging in an orgy of "patriotism." Typically, the "patriots" wound up at war's end vastly improved in their material conditions. After the formation of the Third International, those who practiced "proletarian internationalism" began calling themselves "Communists", leaving the title "Social Democracy" to those who had discredited it.

The British writer, R. Palme Dutt, has noted that

> "It should be explained that the term 'Social Democracy' is here used only to cover ... post-1914 Social Democratic Parties which subsequently united to form the post-war Second International or 'Labour and Socialist International'. It should be further noted that the policy of Social Democracy is here used only to denote the policy of collaboration with capitalism as preached and practiced by the post-war Second International."[1]

The definition in the following pages will follow Dutt's time boundary: Social Democracy will be considered a phenomenon that post-dates the First World War, although its roots obviously extend much further back into the history of modern political movements.

To what "phenomenon" are we referring, precisely, when we say "Social Democracy"?

— Palme Dutt calls it class collaboration. Is this the whole of it? Between whom, for example, does collaboration occur?

— Social Democracy has also frequently been called reformism.[2] Is this its definition? Is "reformism" the same as "class collaboration"?

— In some places – like Scandinavia or England – there are mass parties which call themselves Social Democratic or Labour. Are such parties required by the definition of Social Democracy? If no such parties exist - as in the United States or South Africa – is Social Democracy thereby non-existent in those places?

— For a long time, Social Democracy covered its leaders and/or its policies with "the mantle of Karl Marx". Either Social Democrats claimed to be "the real Marxists" or they said they were "improving on Marx". Is a claim to being the heir of Marx still a criterion of Social Democracy?

A dialectical materialist approach in answering such questions requires a preliminary examination of Social Democracy's material – especially, economic – base. Lenin has offered an unequivocal description thereof:[3]

As we shall see, (see Chapter 3, below) at the stage of imperialism, the capitalist world had become divided into "usurer" and subjugated nations. "Usurer nations" began to derive their main economic resources from the export of capital, which was soon to bring in super-profits "obtained over and above the profits which capitalists squeeze out of their 'own' country". Now, the oligarchs who cull super-profits from "overseas" investments constitute a tiny minority of population, world-wise and in their own strongholds. Their ability to continue reaping the benefits of owning society's means of production depends on relative tranquility, especially in their own back yard. For that reason, modern imperialist rulers have conceded in action that sharing their swag as a divisive measure is far cheaper for them than would be losing it altogether to a possibly united class enemy superior in number. Out of their super-profits, therefore, they bribe a section of "home" workers to create a labor aristocracy, whose existence is an economic necessity for the ruling class in the world's industrial centers.

Lenin analysed the labor aristocracy itself, whom he called "the labor lieutenants of the capitalist class", as "the labor leaders and upper stratum" of workers in metropolitan countries, those

> "bourgeoisified workers ... who are quite philistine in their mode of life, in the size of their earnings, and in their entire out look."[3]

These particular workers, he went on, form

> "the principal prop of the Second International and the principal SOCIAL (not military) PROP OF THE BOURGEOISIE."[3]

But the Second International derives from an organization originally set up to create Socialism – i.e., from an originally revolutionary outfit. In fact, in 1917 did not its Russian off-shoot commit real revolution that refused to die down? Who could assess the "reliability" of the proletariat anywhere in those dangerous years?

Here was a job for jugglers of ideology, capable on the one hand of sounding "revolutionary" enough to hide their real betrayal in supporting "their own" bourgeoisies in imperialist war; and, on the other, of leading down the political garden path any hot headed followers of "wrong" examples.

Social Democracy – of the post-1914 bourgeoisified variety – was the obvious candidate for such a post. It stepped into its role with an aplomb developed from previous decades of rehearsal.

The ideological prompter came in, moreover, with perfect timing behind those post-war goodies at first promised as bonus on "victory" in "the war to end war"; and then delivered, beginning in the "allied" countries with the US in the lead.

From then on, the Second International was busy all over the world – and as a Second World War followed the First, a world labor aristocracy took hold in the West, its leading contingent soon shifting from Britain to the United States.

Clearly, then, the economic base of Social Democracy is the labor aristocracy in industrialised countries. Even more specifically, it is those who, in one way or another, keep the Second International alive. Hence, organizations, ideology or individuals who serve such a group must be included in Social Democracy's armory.

Conversely, Social Democracy's main function must be to serve the interests of metropolitan labor aristocracies within the bounds of the capitalist system, a service clearly of primary value to the ruling class.

(Naturally, this is not to say that Social Democracy was founded with the proclaimed goal of "maintaining capitalism forever". Rather, originally, its political ancestors constituted a trend in the working class. Their first, main appeal to workers lay in their announced intention of abolishing an unjust system, an intention their off-spring still often pretends to harbor.)

If so, then Social Democracy is clearly revealed as part and parcel of contradiction between the bourgeoisie and the proletariat in capitalist lands.

But what part is it? And how does it fit into the world picture?

Plainly, the same evaluation – "of primary importance to the modern ruling class" – applies to all major "acceptable" economic, political and social bodies in any society ruled by a minority. Therefore, establishing that Social Democracy serves "its own" ruling class by no means clarifies its specific function within the system – as proved in the erroneous predictions made by Marxists who thought otherwise.

As capitalism became more and more parasitic through growing dependence on revenue from "overseas", its ability to bribe with ever-bigger inducements more and more of "its own" workers made it therefore necessary for the bribed now to insist on the continued influx to the "home" country of super-profits, fountain head of its own "super-wages", the quid pro quo of its support for the system. In this way, an ever-larger portion of the working class in capital-exporting nations, as long as and because they accept the system, become committed to continued colonialism, the source of imperialism's major super profits: the more decadent imperialism becomes, the more militant the anti-colonial liberation movement grows, both as cause and result, further threatening the already-moribund status quo, the more colonialism becomes indispensable to the existing comfort of labor aristocracies inside the system.

The specific task of Social Democracy – in the process, indispensable to the ruling class, of ensuring capitalism's survival – is to act as a political mechanism for maintaining the constant flow of super-profits to the "mother" country. Here is how, while acting for the labor aristocracy, Social Democracy serves the bourgeoisie as its "principal SOCIAL (not military) PROP".

In performing that service, however, Social Democracy can only hide, not resolve, the basic contradiction it exists to combat: whether they know it or not (and for some time they have not known it), the more the bribed workers support the system for the comforts it gives them, the more they, willy-nilly, are exploited by "their own" bosses, a fact disguised by the ten-fold greater exploitation of colonial workers.

Overlooking such reasoning caused Marxists a few decades ago to miss the mark grossly in assessing Social Democracy's future and led to the absence of any effective countervailing ideology. In turn, that lack has enabled Social Democracy, by inducing the labor aristocracy to close its eyes to its own basic working class role in industrialized countries, to cause ever-growing numbers of metropolitan workers to act against those very working class interests which Marx had declared the only basis for solving the world's problems. Rather, with its enormous - in many countries, automated — productivity, that labor aristocracy enriches the bourgeoisie it supports better and faster than the bourgeoisie enriches it. No wonder monopolists willingly pay a price they can afford for services rendered. For, by bribing it, the ruling class merely uses the labor aristocracy as a buffer between itself and those whom, with the uncanny class instinct of minority rulers on the decline, it recognizes as its main enemies: the numerically far greater "lower stratum of the proletariat" in world hinterlands.

The corollary is that, when the contradiction between the ruling class and the main, hinterland, proletariat reaches a critical point. Social Democracy, in siding with the ruling class, unhesitatingly sacrifices as much of "its" labor aristocracy as necessary to ensure the safety of the system. Such a procedure is under way in Britain now. Yet it is a fact conveniently forgotten - with a little assistance from pundits of both the bourgeoisie and Social Democracy - in order to avoid considerable trouble.

Labor aristocracy support for its own main class enemy has successfully put off revolution in industrialized areas - and else where - many times. Far from being the result of evil individuals or misleaders, this has rather come about because the system it self, of which Social Democracy is an inseparable part, has evoked a new, inner but subordinate, contradiction inside the imperialist system. This is a temporary contradiction. Nevertheless, for the time being, the internal systemic main contradiction between the working class in metropolitan areas and their "own" ruling class has been obscured by this artificially-induced but no less real contradiction between the working class in imperialist nations and those who fundamentally are really their class brothers in the world's subjugated areas. This has occurred to the great cost of the "lower stratum" of the world proletariat . . . and eventually, to that of the bribed, as well.

Social Democracy's aim is to make this situation "permanent".

How is such a contradiction to be dealt with?

The answer is a main target of this text.

In the foregoing context, it is now possible to examine specific features of Social Democracy:

1. Class collaboration. Obviously, as induced by Social Democracy, this occurs between the labor aristocracy and the imperialist bourgeoisie of the industrialised countries.

Is this all there is to it?

It is a fully-documented[1] matter of record that Social Democracy is inseparable from the rise of Fascism. In various countries, the leading spokesmen of Social Democracy have either paved the path to power for Fascism, or have themselves taken part in Fascist governments. In either case, Social

Democratic Parties have "when necessary" shot down "their own" workers. (Later in the text (Chapter 14, Page 132), a new look at Fascism will explain why. Also explained later: WHY Social Democracy acted in this particular way in some countries while not even taking on mass form in others; WHY Marxist predictions of the imminence of naked Fascist power inside certain Western "democracies" failed to materialize.)

For definitive purposes, it need only be noted here that Social Democracy, via its policy of class collaboration, is invariably connected with Fascism.

2. Reformism. Palmiro Togliatti, late head of the Italian Communist Party, used the terms "Social Democracy" and "reformism" interchangeably. For example:

> "... the basis for the development of reformism in the ranks of the working class is to be found in the fact that the bourgeoisie . . . is in a position to corrupt a section of the working class.[2]

That "corrupt" or bribed "section of the working class" is, of course, the labor aristocracy. But is reformism confined to Social Democracy?

In capitalist countries like the US, aren't there out-and-out bourgeois parties which espouse reformism? What about the US Democratic Party under Franklin Delano Roosevelt? Was it also "Social Democratic"?

First, such bourgeois parties of reform do not directly fulfill Lenin's qualification of "prop" for the Second International.

Second, and more important: bourgeois reform parties are based upon and run by a section of the bourgeoisie itself in its own class interests. This is so whether or not their platforms make promises to or "in the interests of" workers. In this case, gains for workers are by-products of activities and aims.

On the other band, Social Democratic parties, whose memberships always consist mainly of workers, are operated by the labor aristocracy in the name of labor. In their case, support for the bourgeoisie is the (indispensable) by-product.

(It is not intended to infer that membership, support or other factors are immutable characteristics. Memberships of such parties, while still mainly working class, have been declining rather massively of late. Support for such parties, while still – as for all major parties under "bourgeois democracy" – working class, is now about one-third traceable to the middle class. The candidates of such parties are being drawn more and more from non-working class sources.[4])

Reformism, therefore, is an element of Social Democracy, but not its totality. To take it as its totality would blur the basic motive for its specific support for colonialism. Similarly, reformism is not the same as, but only one form of, class collaboration: another is the one where Social Democracy shoots down "its own" workers. In general, the latter type is more broadly expressed in aiding Fascism to power under some conditions and/or participating in Fascist rule.

3. The mass base. Must its ideology have a mass political base in order for the whole phenomenon to qualify as Social Democracy?

While the answer is negative, Social Democracy and its function cannot be understood until the TEST is applied whether a given situation produces a mass base for Social Democracy or not.

Applying that test will be shown to clear up a number of questions never before examined, yet of close relevance to the meaning and purpose of Social Democracy and its relationship to colonialism.

Furthermore, our analysis will bring out the following facts, which must be included in any definition of Social Democracy:

— If there is NO mass base, one of TWO possibilities is indicated:

a) Confrontation: the given labor aristocracy is enjoying the benefits of a colonialism whose subjects are in its midst, in which case RACISM emerges openly, and Social Democracy ceases to be organisationally needed; or
b) Colonialism or Semi-Colonialism: the territory under consideration has, from having served as a source of super-profits, produced no labor aristocracy of its own, leaving no suitable soil in which to cultivate a LOCAL mass base for Social Democracy.

—If there IS a mass base, it proves the existence of colonialism without confrontation. That is, the given labor aristocracy is enjoying the benefits of a colonialism NOT IN ITS MIDST.

So, the test of a mass base acts as a watershed between those sectors of world labor for whom organized Social Democracy is necessary and those for whom it is either a frill (racists) or a foreign export designed to serve alien interests (colonial or semi-colonial peoples).

The test of a mass base is inextricable from the definition of Social Democracy, despite the fact that a mass base is not, per se, a criterion for Social Democracy.

4. The mantle of Karl Marx. Mass parties of Social Democracy in industrialized countries arose in an ideological atmosphere

where the name of Karl Marx was always invoked as the ultimate authority for policy. Yet today, most such parties have discarded this custom. In fact, the only avowed supporters of the Second International still claiming to be Marxists live in colonial or semi-colonial areas.

Today, even references to socialism are not necessary to qualify an ideology or party as Social Democratic. What is needed is an alleged tie to labor; or, at least, some type of demagogy.

5. Is Social Democracy an ideology? Since the labor aristocracy of industrialized nations economically active "overseas" is its material base, Social Democracy requires a policy of class collaboration as a by-product of its alleged support for "labor's interests".

On this basis, any ideology, espoused by labor aristocracies and/or their spokesmen in labor's ranks, which claims to be specifically in labor's interests, and which requires for this purpose collaboration with "its own" (or any other) bourgeoisie, is a Social Democratic ideology. Since such an ideology coincides with that of the Second International, whether or not the espousing body or spokesmen formally acknowledge the tie, it is necessarily a reinforcement for that organization and therefore qualifies as its "prop".The role and/or function of such an ideology would be assessed through the test of a mass base.

The content of the ideology is petty-bourgeois. The essence of the latter is vacillation and "tailism". Lenin put it the following ways:

> "The proletariat fights for the revolutionary overthrow
> of the imperialist bourgeoisie; the petty bourgeoisie
> fights for the reformist 'improvement' of imperialism,
> for adoption and SUBMISSION to it.

> "The main thing the Socialists fail to understand and what constitutes their ... captivity to bourgeois prejudices and their political treachery to the proletariat, is that in capitalist society, as soon as there is any serious intensification of the class struggle on which it is based, there cannot be any middle course between the dictatorship of the bourgeoise and the dictatorship of the proletariat. All dreams about some third course are merely the reactionary lamentations of the petty bourgeoisie."[5]

A comprehensive definition of Social Democracy should now be possible:

Social Democracy, which (whether this is revealed sooner or later) is inseparable from the development of Fascism, is a political entity post-dating the First World War, with ideas undistinguishable from those of the Second International, being espoused by "labor leaders" and/or their spokesmen in labor's ranks, and claiming to be primarily "in labor's interests".

Although, like any major acceptable trend in a society, it serves the ruling class in general, its specific economic base is the labor aristocracies of industrialized countries, whence it is objectively committed to continued colonialism because the labor aristocracy relies on (indeed, exists only because of) a share of super-profits, its own super-wages and other bribes.

Its program includes: class collaboration as a by-product of "policy in labor's interests"; an element of reformism (making capitalism "work better"); and some sort of demagogy, usually referring to labor but not necessarily mentioning socialism.

In addition, fully to define it, the test of the mass base must be applied to Social Democracy to determine its precise function. The outcome will be one of these possible alternatives, all related to its commitment to colonialism:

A. There IS a mass base for Social Democracy because the colonial subjects are not living amidst the given labor aristocracy;

B. There is NO mass base because

1) the colonial subjects live in the midst of the given labor aristocracy (as in the US or South Africa), in which case RACISM tends to replace Social Democracy, which thereby becomes a "political frill;" or

2) the territory itself involves colonial subjects, who produce no labor aristocracy and hence cannot produce any mass manifestation of Social Democracy. In this case, Social Democracy, if it appears, is a FOREIGN EXPORT serving METROPOLITAN labor aristocracies.

A definition may be applied to any situation.

Application of this one will follow detailed study of Lenin's analysis of Social Democracy, with special reference to its current applicability.

3. The Origins of Social Democracy

Lenin's Analysis

In the early thirties of this century, Marxists wrote frequently about Social Democracy. Since then, however, the Left has had little to say about it. Why? Had Social Democracy departed from this world? Had its significance lessened?

In this writer's opinion, the reason for the lull is that earlier Marxist diagnoses of Social Democracy, important though they were, fell short of truth.

Marxists who studied Social Democracy made signal contributions by laying bare that ideology's splitting effect on the working class. They revealed how, in certain industrialized countries, such splitting had in practice prevented what once seemed to be "growing revolution." They illumined Social Democratic hypocrisy, documented its specific results, its methods, and showed the role it played as catalyst for Fascism's success.

Yet, like any scientists, they were hemmed in by what facts were available at the time. Certainly some facts appeared to support their analysis. "Hindsight is marvelous", runs a well known saying.

Nonetheless, thirty years of actual events do offer a vantage point from which to examine what, with all due respect, can be shown to be the insufficiencies of earlier Marxist analyses of Social Democracy.

The fact is that Lenin had actually provided all the tools needed, even in the 30s, for complete understanding of Social Democracy and its functions. We have summarized his findings as follows:

"Private property based on the labor of the small proprietor, free competition, democracy, all the catchwords with which the capitalists and their press deceive the workers and the peasants, are things of the distant past. Capitalism has grown into a world system of colonial oppression and of the financial strangulation of the overwhelming majority of the population of the world by a handful of 'advanced' countries . . .[1]

"The international split of the whole working-class movement is now quite evident (the Second and Third Internationals) . . . What is the economic base of this world historical phenomenon?

"Precisely the parasitism and decay of capitalism which are characteristic of its highest historical stage of development, i.e., imperialism. . . . Capitalism has now singled out A HANDFUL (less than one-fifth at the most 'generous' and liberal calculation) of exceptionally rich and powerful states which plunder the whole world simply by 'clipping coupons'. Capital export yields an income of eight to ten billion francs per annum, at pre-war prices and according to pre-war (World War I - H.W.E.) bourgeois statistics. Now, of course, they yield much more.

"Obviously, out of such enormous SUPER-PROFITS (since they are obtained over and above the profits which capitalists squeeze out of the workers of their 'own' country) it is possible to bribe the labor leaders and the upper stratum of the labor aristocracy. And the capitalists of the 'advanced' countries are bribing them . . . in a thousand different ways, direct and indirect, overt and covert.

"This stratum of bourgeoisified workers, or the 'labor aristocracy', who are quite philistine in their mode of life, in the size of their earnings and in their entire outlook, is the principal prop of the Second International, and in our days, the principal SOCIAL (not military) PROP OF THE BOURGEOISIE. For they are the real AGENTS OF THE BOURGEOISIE IN THE WORKING CLASS MOVEMENT, the labor lieutenants of the capitalist class, real channels of reformism and chauvinism...

"Unless the economic roots of this phenomenon are understood and its political and social significance is appreciated, not a step can be taken toward the solution of the practical problems of the Communist movement and of the impending social revolution ."[2]

Lenin's comments on the ideas in the above summary are also instructive. He began by noting that "insufficient importance" had been attached to the parasitism "characteristic of imperialism". Capitalist monopoly, he stressed, caused the entire imperialist economy to have a tendency toward stagnation, expressed by unused capacity, suppressing patents, etc. Monopoly also retards development internationally through "the monopoly ownership of very extensive, rich or well-situated colonies".

Imperialism, he noted, is "an immense accumulation of money capital in a few countries", leading to

"the extraordinary growth of a class, or rather, of a stratum of rentiers, i.e., people who live by 'clipping coupons', who take no part in any enterprise whatever, whose profession is idleness. The export of capital, one of the most essential economic bases of imperialism, still more completely isolates the rentiers from production and sets the seal of parasitism on the whole country that lives by exploiting the labor of several overseas countries and colonies."3

He reinforced this point by quoting bourgeois economists to prove that

> "the income of the rentiers is five times greater than the income obtained from the foreign trade of the biggest 'trading' country in the world! This is the source of imperialism and imperialist parasitism."4

The result had been that

> "the world has become divided into a handful of usurer states and a vast majority of debtor states."5

The consequences for the working class movement Lenin described thus:

> "The rentier state is a state of parasitic decaying capitalism and this circumstance cannot fail to influence all the social-political conditions of the countries concerned, in general, and the two fundamental trends in the working class movement, in particular."6

A leading British economist of the day, J. A. Hobson, is quoted on the connection between imperialism and interests of financiers, Hobson talked of

> "groups of financiers, investors, and political and business officials draining the greatest potential reservoir of profits the world has ever known (Asia and Africa) in order to consume it in Europe,7

> "While the directors of this definitely parasitic policy are capitalists, the same motives appeal to special classes of

> the workers. In many towns most important trades are dependent upon government employment or contracts..."8

Discussing the bribery of the " lower classes", the English economist also recorded

> "the reckless indifference with which Great Britain and other imperialist nations are embarking on a (policy where by) most of the fighting by which we have won our.. Empire has been done by the native."9

Lenin comments that

> "Imperialism, which means the partition of ,the world, and the exploitation of other countries. .. which means high monopoly profits for a handful of very rich countries, creates the economic possibility of bribing the upper strata of the proletariat, and thereby fosters, gives shape to, and strengthens opportunism."10

He also pointed out that

> "The percentage of the productively employed population to total population is declining"11

in imperialist countries themselves. Lenin defined these "upper strata of the proletariat" as they were "at the beginning of the twentieth century", they furnish, he declared,

> "the bulk of the membership of the cooperatives, of trade unions, of sporting clubs and of numerous religious sects. To this level is adapted the electoral system which... is ... 'sufficiently restricted to exclude the lower stratum of the proletariat proper'."12

Evidence of this trend in the working class movement during the epoch of imperialism lies in

> "the decline in emigration from imperialist countries and the increase in immigration into these countries from the more backward countries where lower wages are paid."[13]

Concluding his analysis of the "labor aristocracy", Lenin quotes Engels on the same subject.

First: from a letter to Marx dated October 7, 1858:

> "The English proletariat is actually becoming more and more bourgeois, so that this most bourgeois of all nations is apparently aiming ultimately at the possession of a bourgeois aristocracy and a bourgeois proletariat ALONGSIDE the bourgeoisie. For a nation which exploits the whole world this of course is to a certain extent justifiable."[14]

Second: a letter to Karl Kautsky, dated September 12, 1882:

> "You ask me what the English workers think about colonial policy. Well, exactly the same as they think about politics in general. There is no workers' party here, there are only Conservatives and Liberal-Radicals, and the workers gaily share the feast of England's monopoly of the world market and the colonies. "[15]

The question now arises: Does Lenin's description of parasitism apply to today's world? Later chapters will try to answer this question, through certain others related to it:

    — Is the modern imperialist economy still parasitic?
    — What are the distinguishing features of the modern

bourgeoisie?

— Class collaboration under modern conditions: its forms and shapes?

— Fascism today: is it in power anywhere, and if so, in what form?

— The modern labor aristocracy: who is it and where is it found?

— Does Social Democracy have a mass base in today's world?

Where? Why?

But before we can answer such questions, it will be necessary to look specifically into Social Democracy a bit further.

4. The Methods of Social Democracy

At the Sixth Congress of the Comintern in Moscow (July through September 1928), Social Democracy was high on the agenda. There Ercoli – Palmiro Togliatti, late head of the Italian Communist Party – made his detailed report on "Social Democracy and the Colonial Question", to which reference has already been made. (See Chapter 2, Note 2).

Known before his death for a belief the Italy's workers would vote "their own" capitalism out of existence, Ercoli in this early speech masterfully exposed Social Democracy, demonstrating the real unity of its theory and practice.

His report will be studied in detail both for the many positive lessons it contains, as well as because its short-comings create pointers for today.

Most instructive is Togliatti's documentation of Social Democracy's specific record in, and policy toward, colonies. A summary of his documentation is essential context for all the discussion which follows:

IN SYRIA, whose "complete independence" the Second Inter national had once demanded, the French Socialist Party voted for the war appropriations for imperialist expeditions, during which French generals massacred the populations of Damascus and other towns.

IN INDONESIA, the Dutch Socialists warned "their" government that a revolt was coming; and once it came, not only did they "not defend in parliament this bloody revolt", they severely condemned the spirit of the revolt "whether it originated in Moscow or Canton". When mass death sentences brutally suppressed the revolt, Dutch Socialists boasted of disapproving only death sentences " merely for propaganda". That is, they approved death for workers and peasants who "gave cause", i. e., who revolted.

IN AFRICA, the record of British Social Democracy is too long to be covered in less than a book. The specific story of the Clement Atlee Labour Government from 1945 to 1951 has, however, been given in detail by Jack Woddis.[1]

IN SUDAN, the Labour Government sent warships to terrorize the population, instructing British authorities to "do everything necessary to maintain order".

IN KENYA, the Atlee Government record by itself is enough to damn Social Democracy once and for all. At Mombasa in 1947, the African Workers' Federation and the Railway Staff Union called a general strike for higher wages and lower house rents. They were joined by hotel, shop and domestic workers. And what happened?

> "The Colonial Office under the Labour Government acted with the same ruthlessness as under any Tory Government. Police and troops were called in, the strike was suppressed, and the President of the African Workers' Federation, Chege Kibachia, was banished without trial to a remote village in Northern Kenya."[1]

At Uplands Bacon Factory in September 1947, when another strike broke out the police were again called in. They fired on the workers: 3 dead, 22 arrested, including 20 sentenced to two years at hard labour.

In September 1948, Makhan Singh, Secretary of the Labour Trade Union of East Africa, organised a Cost of Living Conference. Delegations came from more than 16 trade unions and associations, representing more then 10,000 African and Asian workers. The Labour "leaders" of Britain arrested Singh and deported him.

During 1949 and 1950, new legislation was introduced into Kenya, of which the following six were typical:

1) A Wage-Freezing Bill, "The Compulsory Trade Testing and Wage Fixing Scheme";

2) A Trade Union Registration Ordinance;

3) A "Slave Labour" Bill, introducing forced labour at starvation wages;

4) A Deportation Ordinance, giving Government increased power to deport;

5) A law banning strikes in "essential services": all the Governor had to do to make any strike illegal was to add its industry to "essential services";

6) The already-existing Emergency Powers Ordinance was amended to increase the Governor's powers.

The result, Woddis declared, was a series of attacks on Kenya's trade unions, including the arrest of leaders of the East African Workers' Federation, of the East African T.U.C., and an eventual ban on the latter on pretext that "it was not registered".

IN NIGERIA, official Social Democratic policy resulted in the shooting of coal miners at Enugu in 1949. 7,500 miners had struck for higher pay, allegedly a common Social Democratic demand. Outcome? 21 dead, 50 wounded. In the ensuing mass counter demonstrations, further repressions and wholesale arrests took place.

IN TANGANYIKA, strikes occurred in 1948 at Port Tanga, and in 1950 at Dar-es-Salaam, the latter involving the Dock Workers' Union. The Labour Government promptly outlawed the union, confiscating all its funds and property, and arrested and imprisoned its leaders, During the same period, the leadership of African Cooks' and Washermans' Union of Tanganyika was removed as "unsatisfactory".

IN GHANA, a demonstration of unemployed ex-servicemen ended when police fired on it, killing three, In 1949 and 1950, a general strike as last push to independence saw mass arrests, including Dr. Kwame Nkrumah and others later part of Ghana's first African Government.

The colonial record of Harold Wilson's Labour Government since 1964 is written in the names of countries it betrayed: Congo Kinshasa, Aden, Malaysia, British Guiana, South Africa, Southern Rhodesia, Southwest Africa, Bechuanaland – and on and on.

Furthermore, these examples form a pattern by which Social Democracy in power fully reveals its real colonial policy: as in Wilson's present Government, it does all in its power to make a mockery of such political independence as colonial countries had achieved despite all interference.

Brutality, both economic and military, is the major weapon of Social Democracy's colonialism, exactly the same as – if not worse than – ANY imperialist government. Togliatti himself called attention to this, saying that all super-exploitation of colonial peoples is done by

> "methods of unheard-of brutality... the result of which is the undermining and at times the complete destruction of tribes and even whole races, which frequently takes place where the plantation regime is introduced . . . the destruction of great masses of human beings."

Actually, brutal measures by Social Democracy against colonial peoples are quite logical considering what they accomplish for the metropolitan labor aristocracies whom Social Democracy represents. Precisely because the Labour Government had destroyed all attempts by colonial workers to improve their living standards, it could be recorded that

> "The economic position in Britain improved in 1952 because there was a world-wide fall in the price of food and raw materials which benefited the British economy."[2]

What the author neglected to add was that colonial economies depend heavily for their incomes precisely on "the price of food and raw materials", and the benefit to the British economy resulted because colonial economies had been rendered more lopsided than before.

SUCH brutality never seems to upset the Western Left nearly as much as the selfsame instrument turned against "its own" workers in the streets "at home", when for some reason or other the colonial cushion has either been removed by military defeat or not attained because of later arrival by the specific ruling class on the capitalist world scene.

Yet, surely it must be clear by now that Social Democracy will use brutality as one effective modus operandi wherever necessary to ensure continued super-profits. Even though new forms of colonialism have had to be devised to meet the advance of the Liberation movement throughout the subjugated areas of the world, the casualties go on; brutality escalates.

5. The Theoretical Pretensions of Social Democracy

An important corollary of the Social Democratic record is that its "theory" and its practice have always been one, a fact Togliatti reported. Dissecting its allegedly "theoretical" pronouncements invariably reveals policy indistinguishable from imperialism's.

Nevertheless, Social Democracy still encourages the widely-held belief that some sort of separate "theory" exists on which the Second International bases its various less objectionable activities (the others are not mentioned in polite society – i. e., in the ranks of Social Democratic spokesmen).

In his speech, Ercoli examined and exposed these pretensions to "theory." Social Democracy, said he, always had had a colonial policy

> "which consisted in allying itself with or directly participating in the colonial enterprises of the bourgeoisie."

The colonial attitude before World War I of those who were to become the post-1914 Social Democrats found expression in a number of Socialist Congresses: at Paris in 1900; at Amsterdam, 1904; and at Stuttgart, 1907.

Summed up, the pre-World War I colonial position of these gatherings consisted of following main planks:

1) Verbal condemnation of colonisation and its "existing methods."

2) Recognition of the possibility of improving the system of imperialist domination in colonies by certain "reform for the natives", to be supported by "good socialists".

3) Substituting the "right of self-administration" for the more basic right of self-determination.

At the Stuttgart Congress, for example, Karl Kautsky, most "left" of such Socialists, hemmed and hawed on colonial liberation: the possibility was "doubtful", it was by no means "simple", and even if it could be agreed that it should take place, the question as to how would have to be discussed "later." Kautsky said:

> "The idea of emancipation of the colonies is a sort of border idea which shows us the course to be followed, but it is not a practical proposition for the immediate application of which we must work."[1]

He suggested that the colonies wait for the "socialist revolution" "automatically" to liberate them. Meantime, he concluded,

> "the right of the natives (sic!) to self-administration must be extended as rapidly as possible."[1]

In a word, imperialism's own position on "colonial freedom"!

Following World War I, with the emergence of modern Social Democracy, the earlier colonial policy outlined above was strengthened and more plainly articulated. If at one time, Social Democrats had hesitated to show' their true colours about colonialism, by 1928 that reluctance was gone. For, Togliatti noted, at the Brussels Congress of the Second International in that year, Social Democracy displayed "its attitude on colonial questions without any embarrassment whatsoever". Quite naturally! They had become "teachers" to "their own" bourgeoisies on how best to prevent colonial revolution. They began by jettisoning Karl Marx. They continued by openly proclaiming the policy of class collaboration.

In fact, following World War I, Togliatti said,

> "the Social Democrats have become colonial politicians.
> They recognise the possession of colonies as something
> which their countries could never renounce and that,
> when their country has no colony it is up to them to
> demand a colony for it in a more or less open manner.
> In this field, there is not a single Social Democratic Party
> which is an exception."[1]

And Togliatti's survey of various countries confirmed his diagnosis:

IN FRANCE, the Socialist Party always voted all credits for colonial enterprises. In December 1927, at a French Socialist Party Congress, it was stated that without colonies, "the post-war problems cannot be solved". In 1928, a resolution drawn up by a French Socialist named Zyromski averred that

> "nothing would more contradict socialism than the
> acceptance of certain narrow, petty and egoistic
> individualism. Socialism ... cannot tolerate self-sufficient
> nationalism, and the intervention of higher economic
> countries constitutes the corollary of its principles."[1]

IN HOLLAND, the Socialist Party didn't even discuss the need for colonies; it was interested only in the method by which colonies should be ruled. Naturally, for it, "the interests of international humanity set up limits to the right of free determination" , such that on the practical level "separation of Indonesia from the Netherlands" was not its slogan.

Here, the labour aristocracy equates itself to "international humanity", whose interests then "naturally" supersede such mundane petulance as "the right of free determination" for those whose misery serves such lofty "international humanity".

IN GERMANY, Social Democrats, for instance at the Berne Conference in 1919, openly protested the fact that Germany had been deprived of colonies. At the Marseilles Congress, through

R. Hilferding, it demanded colonies for Germany. This demand was still being repeated in 1928. In 1966, it is being quietly exercised by expanding West German penetration of Africa, Asia and Latin America.

IN ITALY, in 1928, the Social Democrats passed a resolution protesting against the distribution of colonies in the Treaty of Versailles. A fresh settlement of the colonial problem was demanded, taking into account Italian capitalism!

IN BRITAIN, the Labour Government of Ramsay MacDonald (1929-1931) rejected all demands to it by the Zaghloul Government of EGYPT, which were : for England to withdraw her troops, economic and political "advisers" ; and for freedom of the Suez Canal.

The British labour aristocracy's program, drawn up in 1918, said that

> "the Labour Party is against the egoistic conception of 'non-intervention' in the affairs of the various countries of the British Empire."

And why? Because the Labour Party considered it its duty

> "To defend the rights of British citizens who have over seas interests."[1]

Finally,

> "as for this community of races and peoples of different colours, religions and different stages of civilization which is called the British Empire, the Labour Party is in favour of its maintenance."[1]

That Labour Party was not fooling when it declared that the right of self-determination was not applicable to any of the British colonies, and subsequent Labour Governments drove home the assertion at the point of a bayonet.

Even THE LEAGUE OF NATIONS, that great World War I "achievement" in "world cooperation", declared that "the civilised countries" have the right to "determine the fate" of "the others".

All these activities Togliatti traced to what he called their "theoretical sources". Those, he said, had roots in Social Democracy's "idea" that, since capitalism was "historically inevitable", therefore, it must be assisted in every way to spread over the globe.

But, said Togliatti, this was a vulgarisation of Marx's position on the historically progressive nature of bourgeois revolutions, and of his postulate that the form of production and organisation of capitalist society are the "objective pre-conditions for the formation of Communist society".

It was vulgarisation because, to stop at this meant omitting Marx's concomitant and inseparable position that the development of society and its forces of production do not proceed peacefully, but dialectically and in a revolutionary way. What Social Democracy was leaving out, he said, was precisely Marx's central thesis of class struggle as the motive force of history. The baby having thus been tossed out, the bath water followed when Dutch Social Democrats "pioneered" a "theory" about how economic exploitation of colonies was not tied to their political domination from afar. According to them,

> "a clear distinction between the economic and political aspect which exists in the life of a colonial society offers the possibility of participation in the struggle of emancipation of the natives (sic!) from an international point of view."[1]

Social Democracy showed the way for modern neo-colonialism!

At Brussels in 1928, Social Democracy as a whole followed through on the Dutch start with a resolution saying that Socialists were against "political domination" over colonies in principle, but they "left open" the question of "economic domination" (which Ercoli commented "is stronger, more perceptible, and burdensome, and on the basis of which political domination develops").

From there it was but a step to claiming that

> "colonial policy ...has opened up access to the natural resources of the backward countries, has developed production and modern means of transportation in these countries and has thus very greatly increased the basis of raw materials for world economy and promoted the development of the international division of labour.[1]

Precisely! Togiatti commented on this frank exposition that

> "every system of colonisation... is determined in its form and in its development by the internal requirements of the colonising country, and that those requirements are in strict and irreconcilable contradiction to the economic development of the colonised country."[1]

That was why, he explained, capitalism relentlessly drained away colonial resources, exhausting supplies with no regard for the effect on population. He added that

> "Countries which were formerly renowned for their fertility, such as India and even China, were condemned to periodically recurring crop failures... Everywhere the creation of a class of landless and wretched peasant is taking place as well as the progressive pauperisation of the great mass of the workers. "[1]

Labor Aristocracy

Worse than merely not developing the forces of production in its colonies, industrial capitalism distorted these economies, preventing any real economic progress; in fact, literally for centuries draining away the material basis for it. Even where certain industries did develop in colonial territories they never in any way eased the super-exploitative nature of the colonial economy.

Ercoli stressed that

> "the aim of capitalism in general is not to develop the forces of production, but to pocket the greatest possible profit for each capitalist and for each individual capitalist country."[1]

Figures from Indo-China in 1928 supported the speaker's contention that "no capitalist enterprise offers such great profits as a colonial enterprise".

Today's statistics show his contention truer than ever. For in stance, a leading apologist and self-offered mentor for a more "sensible" US imperialism has noted that, in the United States,

> "foreign investments account for ...with armaments, 50% of the profits of industrial corporations... In 1960, the 20 industrial corporations with the largest profits obtained 33.7% of the profit of all industrial corporations . . . the 20 largest military contractors obtained 49% of all prime contracts. In 1957, the 20 industrial corporations receiving the most profits from foreign investments obtained 69.3% of the profit of all industrial corporations from this source . . . If the rising trends in military and foreign investment profits continue, in the near future military and foreign business combined will definitely provide over 50% of the total profits of the industrial giants. In fact, that point may have been passed already in 1962."[2]

Such facts make much clearer today than in 1928 the inseparable connection between colonialism (or neo-colonialism) and WAR as the twin basis of the dying imperialist world system. To retain its slipping hold on life, imperialism cannot do without "its colonies in fact". To ensure those "colonies in fact", it is being drawn into ever-spreading wars which, in turn, prime its clogging economic pump and reinforce the struggle for world division and redivision.

More than ever, its "overseas" activities alone hold dying imperialism to life. Colonies are clearly an inseparable part of the imperialist system as a whole as long as it lasts. This point underlies a small book with a huge sock by a French economist: "The fact that imperialism entails an essential internal contradiction between exploiting countries and those that suffer exploitation does not destroy its unity; on the contrary, its unity is created by this contradiction without which it would not be imperialism ...both groups are essential parts of the imperialist system - that is what makes imperialism what it is."3 (See Chapter 1, Note 1.)

Inescapable is the corollary that the destruction of the colonial portion of imperialism's economy will be the destruction of imperialism itself. In this way, Liberation is pin-pointed as the main pivot in the current phase of world revolution. Commented Togliatti in prophetic words:

> "This, then, is the real danger for Social Democracy, the approaching colonial revolution."1

Small wonder, then, that colonies should be that specific portion of the capitalist system which Social Democracy protects!

6. Marxist Predictions about Social Democracy in the 1930's

Communist failure to tie Social Democracy's colonial record even to its general function as upholder of capitalism had at least one fairly immediate result: predictions by Marxists in the 30s about Social Democracy's future fell flatter than a bride's cake.

What, specifically, were those predictions? How and why did they fail?

The grand-daddy of them all was one by Georgi Dimitroff, remarkable defendant in the infamous Reichstag Fire Trial of Hitler Germany's early days. Defeating intended legal murder by transforming his accusers into accused, Dimitroff survived his trial to become first president of the Bulgarian Socialist Republic.

Between July 25 and August 20, 1935, in speeches to the Seventh World Congress of the Comintern[1], he had summarised his own experience of Fascism, postulating how the working class and its vanguard should overthrow it where it existed and prevent its success elsewhere.

His ground-breaking analysis illumined the decay of bourgeois democracy during the twilight of imperialism.

While scrutinising Fascism, Dimitroff found it necessary to discuss Social Democracy:

> "Comrades, in view of the tactical problems confronting us, it is very important to give a correct reply to the question of whether Social Democracy at the present time is still the principal bulwark of the bourgeoisie, and if so, where. "[2]

To his own question, he replied:

> "It must be borne in mind that in a number of countries the position of Social Democracy in the bourgeois state, and its attitude towards the bourgeoisie, have been undergoing a change.

> "In the first place, the crisis has thoroughly shaken the position of even the most secure section of the working class, the so-called labor aristocracy, upon which, as we know, Social Democracy relies for support. This section, too, is beginning more and more to revise its views as to the expediency of the policy of class collaboration with the bourgeoisie.

> "Second ... the bourgeoisie in a number of countries is it self compelled to abandon bourgeois democracy and resort to the terroristic form of its dictatorship, depriving Social Democracy not only of its previous position in the political system of finance capital but also, under certain conditions, of its legal status, persecuting and even suppressing it.

> "Third, under the influence of the lessons learned from defeat of the workers in Germany, Austria and Spain, a defeat which was largely the result of the Social Democratic policy of class collaboration with the bourgeoisie, and, on the other hand, under the influence of the victory of Socialism in the Soviet Union as a result of the Bolshevik policy and the application of living, revolutionary Marxism, the Social Democratic workers are being revolutionised, and are beginning to turn to the class struggle against the bourgeoisie.

> "The joint effect of all this has been to make it increasingly difficult, and in some countries actually

impossible, for Social Democracy to preserve its former role of supporting the bourgeoisie."[2]

In a major Left work of the 1930s, Palme Dutt had undertaken to bolster Dimitroff's vivisection with Fascism's and Social Democracy's actual records. Studying conditions at various historical periods of the working classes in advanced countries, he had noted that

> "Liberalism enjoyed one last blooming in the earlier or pre-war period of imperialism ... The super-profits of imperialism provided the means in the imperialist countries to endeavour to buy off the revolt of the advancing workers with a show of meager concessions to a minority. "[3]

After World War I – at least in the victorious countries – expansion continued of these "meager concessions to a minority." But, after the Wall Street crash of 1929 signaling the onset of the general crisis of capitalism, Dutt recorded a new development:

> "With the rising colonial revolts, the basis of imperialism began to weaken. The stream of super-profits diminished . . . (leading to) the cutting down and withdrawal of concessions already granted."[3]

Here, surely, was the harbinger of imperialism's actual demise, the world Left inferred, and a corresponding euphoria enveloped it. Nor was it surprising. The objective situation certainly appeared to support to the hilt their optimism: A united front pact between the French Socialist and Communist Parties had been signed on July 27, 1934, leading rapidly to the fall of the pro-Fascist Doumergue-Tardieu Cabinet. In Austria, the illegal Communist Party had become a mass organisation, absorbing Left Social Democratic and certain other elements, to found a United Socialist Party. In Italy, in the Saar and in Spain, similar developments were taking place.

On the other hand, Dutt was forced to report, significantly, that "the British Labour Party and a number of other Social Democratic parties ... actively opposed the united front and even developed extended disciplinary measures to prevent its realisation.[3]

In October 1934, a meeting between representatives of the Communist and Socialist Internationals was held; it was felt to augur great things. But in November,

> "the Executive of the Second International at Paris, after a four-days' debate, by a narrow margin rejected the proposal of the united front and broke off negotiations. Nevertheless, the strength of the united front was such that the ban of the Second International on the united front for its separate sections had to be lifted; and a minority declaration of seven parties was issued in support of the united front.[3]

In a preface to the third edition of his book in August 1935, Dutt added that

> "Since the book originally appeared, many new developments have taken place, among the most important of which are the new processes taking place in the Social Democratic parties, offering hopes of a healing of the split in the working class and of the passing over of the majority of the workers to the revolutionary cause."

7. Why the Predictions Failed

If the correctness of any analysis is measured by the accuracy of the predictions to which it gives rise, then it must be noted that neither the Communist-forecast "decisive struggles" not its "united front of the working class" materialised after all.

What is more, the preceding false predictions of what they would accomplish lulled Marxist vigilance, weakened self-reliance in the movements of the oppressed peoples, and supported a misinterpretation, continuing to this day, of the real role on the world revolutionary scene of the Western working classes.

What material factors had Dimitroff and Dutt omitted from their analyses to cause such an outcome?

When establishing his criteria for judging Fascism, Dutt had simply ignored imperialist parasitism, although he had noted:

"The 'democratic freedom' of Western imperialism has been built on the foundation of colonial slavery."[1]

As general conditions favouring the growth of Fascism, Dutt had listed:

> "1) intensification of the economic crisis and of the class struggle;
>
> "2) widespread disillusionment with parliamentarism;
>
> "3) the existence of a wide petit-bourgeoisie, intermediate strata, slum proletariat, and sections of the workers under capitalist influence;
>
> "4) the absence of an independent class-conscious leader ship of the main body of the working class."[2]

(It is interesting that nearly all these conditions exist in England as these words are being written, May-June, 1968.)

Dutt documented these "general conditions", and concluded that Fascism was the

> "characteristic instrument of finance-capital which can be brought into play in the most highly-developed industrialised countries when the stage of crisis and of the class struggle requires it."

Just when was that?

Dutt had an answer:

> "Its success or failure, as in every country, depends on the degree of preparedness and militant resistance of the proletariat."

At this contention, history has thumbed its nose. For instance, what better indication of the "degree of preparedness and militant resistance of the proletariat" can there be than its closeness to revolution? Don't facts suggest that revolution in that epoch was almost at hand in Italy and Spain, and that it certainly was closer in Germany, vanquished, than in Britain, the US, or even France? If Dutt were correct, why did Fascism not attain power where the proletariat was least "ready"? Obviously, the upheavals of the day did not have the content the Marxists attributed to them. Or else those Marxists were overlooking something big.

Within a remarkably short period after Dutt's analysis, it became clear that Western workers were blithely ignoring Left advise to "place no faith in the 'democratic institutions' of such countries." Forgetting the great struggles of the 30s, the Western proletariat year after year abandoned itself to the blandishments of exactly those "institutions": for example, elections from 1940 through 1964 in Britain, the U.S. and elsewhere in the West showed anything but "widespread disillusionment with parliamentarism." Understandably, for parliamentarism was again rewarding its faithful. (See Table 11, which shows a constant increase in both absolute numbers and percentage of eligibles voting in the US.)

To be fair, Dutt did try to protect his own rear when he said:

> "All this is not to argue that Fascism must necessarily develop and conquer in Western countries."

As things turned out, here at least he came close to prophecy. Fascism actually did conquer some Western countries but not others, despite Dutt's and other Marxists' belief that it was an imminent danger even in the West's "great democracies." Despite the ferment of the post-Crash decade and the onset of capitalism's general crisis, the Western "democracies" did not, after all, turn inward on "their own" working classes; they did not, as predicted, institute Fascism "at home".

What decided which countries Fascism conquered?

Marxists had proven that imperialist war was fought for division or redivision of colonial spoils. In 1918, the defeated — Germany, Austria, etc. — had been deprived of their colonies. More: those colonies had been redistributed. At the stroke of a pen in Versailles, the vanquished had thus been cut off completely from their former "stream of super-profits", while the "Allies" (who were, of course, the "great democracies") were cut in on a new, additional source. Military victory against Germany had thus ensured imperialism's top dogs of a new lease on life.

Equally, military defeat had forced German imperialism and its associates either to find new outlets for their export capital or to turn inward against "their own" working classes. Hitler's cry for "lebensraum" accurately recorded that, for imperialism, "room" in which to "live" was synonymous with "room" into which ever more – monopolised capital could expand – and that for German capital expansion was indistinguishable from life itself. Somebody was going to have to supply the economically-choking vanquished with necessary "air." During the great depression, with the First World War too recent to be revived as the usual solution, only one obvious and available outlet existed: "one's own" working class.

Countries like Hungary, Czechoslovakia, Poland and their like offer examples of what happens when, having reached the stage where capital export has become essential, a capitalist country has no foreign outlet for it. Germany, Austria and Spain demonstrate a corollary: what happens when a developing capitalist economy is deprived of such an outlet. In both cases, the ruling classed did, in fact, turn inward as their "solution".

Yet, oddly enough, while these examples were actually arising, Lenin's warning was scarcely dead on the historical air:

> "unless the economic roots of this phenomenon (that is, overseas financial activities as the specific source of imperialist parasitism - H. W. E.) are understood and its political and social significance is appreciated, not a step toward the solution of the practical problems of the Communist movement and of the impending social revolution can be taken."[3]

This prophecy has been fulfilled. Uttered in 1921, it had already indicated that "success or failure" for imperialism depended on the growth of parasitism, expressed as ever-widening pools of man-power and resources to be super-exploited by metropolitan monopolies.

If, then. Fascism was a specific stage of imperialism, where else could its "success or failure" lie?

History supports the observation that Fascism has in fact been exercised by imperialism against Western peoples only if they are about to be forced into the role of a "source of super profit", either to replace a lost, or to substitute for a never achieved, colonial empire. As long as real colonies, territorial or economic, exist, imperialism is "safe".

For these reasons, any conclusion in 1935 about "imminent Fascism" which did not document this crucial factor was bound to come to grief. International imperialism in the "democracies" still has room to maneuver, to "solve" its difficulties at the expense of peoples in colonial or neo-colonial areas. (Today, direct super-exploitation has ceased to be necessarily the main form of imperialist parasitism. But the principles enunciated in these pages remain the same.)

The system's central pillar remains that vast colonial labor reservoir, available for super-exploitation.

Fascism's "success or failure" inside Western "democracies" could simply not be accurately forecast in the way the Marxists of the 30s tried to do it.

Obviously from the foregoing reasoning, too. Fascism's absence in "democracies" cannot be attributed to "greater benevolence" or "understanding" or, despite their inner conflicts on other issues, to any "differences in interest" among ruling classes or between one section of a given bourgeoisie and another when it comes to preserving their system.

Although Marxist analyses of Fascism had dealt with Social Democracy, they did not, in the writer's opinion, fully analyse the connection between the two. They merely chronicled it, showing that wherever Fascism triumphed, Social Democracy paved the way for it. As "explanation", they contented themselves with repeating Lenin's 1916 formula that Social Democracy was "the principal bulwark of the bourgeoisie" ; without applying his criteria to the conditions of their own day, they could offer no satisfactory explanation for the failure of their predictions and simply dropped the whole subject.

From a historical vantage point three decades later, it now appears that those Marxists could have seen that – if the Western labor aristocracy under the impact of the great depression was indeed "revising its views as to . . . class collaboration" – the bourgeoisies in pivotal Western countries still had a couple of aces up their sleeves. Blinded by glittering generalities, Marxists got those aces slipped over on them. By leaving out of account the ruling class vector, Dimitroff simply drew wrong conclusions about Western labor's real direction in his day.

When he had said that "the position of Social Democracy in the bourgeois state, and its attitude toward the bourgeoisie, have been undergoing a change", he had based himself on a firm material foundation: the crisis, he had said, has "thoroughly shaken the position of the . . . labour aristocracy." Surely the general crisis of capitalism is a solid enough cornerstone for such a prediction? Unfortunately, Dimitroff had relied not just on the crisis, but on a crisis to which he envisaged only one solution: namely, revolution. It proved a serious and costly underestimation of imperialist parasitism.

Social Democracy did not undergo any major change, either in its "position in the bourgeois state" or in its "attitude toward the bourgeoisie". Nor could it. Moreover, Lenin had already predicted as much. "It may be argued", he had said,

> "that of the (leaders of Social Democracy), some will return to the revolutionary socialism of Marx. This is possible, but it is an insignificant difference in degree, if we take the question in its political, i.e., in its mass aspect. Certain individuals among the present social-chauvinist leaders may return to the proletariat: but the TREND

> can neither disappear nor 'return' to the revolutionary proletariat ...

> "We have not the slightest grounds for thinking that these (Social Democratic) parties can disappear BEFORE the social revolution. On the contrary, the nearer the revolution approaches, the stronger it flares up . . . the greater will be the role in the labour movement of the struggle between the revolutionary mass stream and the opportunist-philistine stream."[4]

Those who did not know of, or forgot, such words missed the deduction that, because of its tie with colonialism (implicit in its need for super-wages), Social Democracy had to change tactics when a colonial empire seemed in danger. Its eye remained where Marxists should have kept theirs: on the state of imperialism's "stream of super-profits." Social Democracy admirably adapted its tactics to the varying levels of that stream: as long as that kept flowing in, super-wages were sure to follow.

So, although the labor aristocracy was, for the time being, "thoroughly shaken by the crisis", it was far from "revising its views" about class collaboration itself. Actually, Dimitroff had said only that the labor aristocracy was

> "revising its views about the expediency of the policy of class collaboration."

The operating word was "expediency". If imperialism is forced to withdraw its bribes, polite class collaboration becomes, indeed, no longer expedient: some new form is required. This was where Fascism came in. And it served its purpose. In noting that the bourgeoisie could no longer afford democracy at home, and so had turned to "the terroristic form of its dictatorship," Dimitroff had been reporting fact. But this had little to do with what became of Social Democracy. For, both he and Dutt, the latter in irrefutable detail, had proved that this dictatorship generally did not deprive Social Democracy of its "position in the political system" or even of its legal status except in individual cases. Dutt had documented instance after instance where Social Democracy took part in that "terroristic form" of imperialism's dictatorship.

In this, once it is admitted that its aim is to ensure the continued flow of super-wages to the labor aristocracy, Social Democracy was merely logical. That flow must come from whatever source is available.

In the light of current events, it can only be concluded that Dimitroff must have been motivated by an understandable wish when he suggested that Western workers had learned from the defeat of their class brothers in places like Germany. He was generalising too soon from working class actions of his day when he added that USSR success was revolutionizing Western Workers. If anything, his diagnosis was carried out in reverse.

Within a very short historical period thereafter, led by the shining example of Franklin Delano Roosevelt in victorious, soon-economically-rampant America, a veritable cascade of glittering bribes again began flowing into American working class pockets with effects soon to mock Dimitroffs theses. Restive workers in the U.S. were given on an increasingly grand scale a substantial stake in the status quo. The gift, accompanied by odes of virtually unchallenged praise for a system which makes such things possible, successfully, if temporarily, obscured the fact that even the bribed labor aristocracy is exploited. Marxists like Dimitroff had seen the exploitation, but had grievously underestimated how big a stake in the status quo could be raised, as well as the primacy, enormity and soporific effect "at home" of super-exploitation abroad. They had failed to foresee what a large sector of the Western proletariat were eventually to be bought over, serve alien class aims, thereby to keep alive a system which Marxist analysts of the 30s claimed was on its last legs.

Far from being unable, as Dimitroff had concluded, to maintain its allegedly former role of supporting the bourgeoisie, opportunism was soon rewarded for its police role during tight times by a new stream of super-wages at a level far higher than before. And, for its officials, lucrative Government posts opened up in ever-larger numbers.(In 1934, British TUC officials were represented on six Government committees; in 1949, on 60; in 1954, on 81; and in 1968, on more than 115.[5])

The halcyon days of the Western labor aristocracy had been but briefly interrupted. That that interruption was ended at the expense of renewed and deepened colonial slavery was, at the time – and even now – of little concern to comfortable Western workers.

But the price that was to be exacted from Marxism for its miscalculations in this area was to be high, indeed.

8. Social Democracy and the Scandinavian Myth

Lenin's analysis of imperialist parasitism, brought home to the working class in the main imperialist countries, might jolt some of them free from their cushioned lethargy. Certainly, it could supply meaningful context for vast numbers of the subjugated. So, Social Democracy has an incentive to prevent this news at any cost from leaking out. The illusion of "democracy" in the West must be kept alive, replenished from any available source, with special and frequent reference to the blessings which accrue from it to so many of its faithful followers.

From Social Democracy's viewpoint, no better instance of such blessing exists in the entire moldering imperialist world than Scandinavia. If America, Britain, France, Germany or Japan have unfortunate flaws, like brutality toward colonial subjects, they can be redeemed by the shining example in the north of Europe: these countries own no colonies; they boast large Social Democratic parties, sharing substantially in the parliamentary game. They appear to form a precious exception, invokable to "prove" the lack of need for revolution by workers anywhere.

Thirty years after Marxist predictions of revolutionization of Western workers, the existence of Scandinavia and the Social Democratic myths about it allow a self-avowed Asian spokesman of European Social Democracy still to speak about the wonders of "democracy" in the West.

Dr. Wong Lin Ken, a representative of "Malaysian Socialism," did in fact eugolise European Social Democracy as successor to Marx. In particular, he said:

> "Another false prophecy of Marx is that the proletariat will increase its misery. Instead, the standard of living of the working class in Western European countries and the United States has improved since the days when Marx wrote . . ."[1]

(Note the implied equation between Marx's "proletariat" and "the working class in Western European countries and the United States," an equation to which the text will return later.)

The author continues:

> "Furthermore, the improvements of the standards of living of a working class have owed nothing to the exploitation of colonies. Thus, the workers in Sweden, Denmark and Switzerland, which own no colonies, have always enjoyed higher standards of living than those in France and Britain, the two great colonial powers in Europe. Nor have the living standards of workers in France, Britain and the United States declined after they had liquidated their colonies."[2]

First, in passing, for an Asian to hold up as worthy of imitation on his own continent the Western working class and its standards while in the same breath denying that such standards "owed" anything "to the exploitation of colonies" constitutes, in the face of colonial conditions, a feat of daring unequaled outside the exploits of modern spacemen.

Second, also in passing, Dr. Wong's bland inclusion of the United States as having "liquidated its colonies" may prove amusing to students of the colonial scene. It would probably be less so to Madison Avenue, which laboriously fashions Uncle Sam's "non-colonialist" image.

The main point here, however, is Dr. Wong's ecstatics about the Scandinavian countries. He claims that:

> "The high standards of living of workers in these advanced industrial countries are largely the result of the work of the social democratic parties, working in conjunction with the trade union movements."[3]

What is suggested is a well-known myth two-fold in nature: that high living standards are a Social Democratic "achievement", peacefully attained by collaborating with "understanding" or "intelligent" monopolists; second, the fable entitled "Scandinavian socialism".

But do not facts attest the truth of the idyll? Considering Sweden as not only typical, but the best of the cited lot, does it not boast the highest wage level in Europe and a national income about five times higher than that of, say, Portugal? Don't Swedish workers enjoy the largest fringe benefits of any in Europe? Certainly, there is no blinking the Swedish municipal elections of September, 1962, when Social Democrats for the first time actually culled a majority of votes cast: 50.6%, against 47.8% in the 1960 contests[4] (a majority they have since lost, however: Sweden's Social Democratic Party lost 109 seats, or 8.2%, at municipal elections in September 1966, because of "the Government's tough economic policy.")[5]

Isn't all this precisely what Dr. Wong was talking about?

The acid test of real socialism is expropriation from former owners of the social means of production, leading to a new type of State designed politically to eliminate the ex-ruling class. This is NOT the same as "nationalisation", although the existence of a sizeable "state sector" in any economy is often cited as alleged proof of "socialism".

By this test, Scandinavia cannot qualify as socialist. Even the false test, of a large state sector, does nothing for Sweden's claim to socialism: more than 90% of the national economy of Sweden is in private hands. The government shares in producing water power and in running the railways! Of 50 major industrial enterprises in Sweden in 1960, only nine (18%) were state-owned.[4]

Another "argument" frequently invoked to prove Sweden socialist is the alleged existence of a large cooperative sector of its economy. But in fact, cooperatives play a relatively minor role there. In 1959, Swedish cooperatives operated 7,439 stores and boasted 1,117,222 members.[6] Total population that year, by government estimate was 7,434,000: cooperative members comprised slightly more than 15%. Now, during the same year, in "free enterprise" U.S., some 31,941,000 people belong to cooperatives, out of 177 million population. So, in the champion of champions of capitalism, more than 18% of the inhabitants were in cooperatives. By this criterion, the U.S. would be "more socialist" than Sweden.

The truth is that, if Sweden is anything, it is a showcase of world free enterprise.

Well, then, counter Social Democrats, at least Scandinavia illustrates "enlightened capitalism". That is why Social Democracy has obtained so much for "its" workers from Sweden's ruling class. How about this?

First, a seldom-mentioned fact: that, over the epoch of imperialism, Sweden's ruling classes were virtually uninvolved in Europe's major wars. Investment capital, therefore, had the advantage (to be enjoyed after World War II, in turn, by defeated Japanese capitalism) of being used in Sweden, at least for some time after the war, primarily to expand the national industry.

Second, Sweden's economy is one where monopolies hold all the key positions, a sure test offered by Lenin as to whether or not a capitalist economy has advanced to its "highest" stage. What is more, Sweden's gigantic monopolies are closely allied with foreign capital, mostly British, American and West German. The same tendency to obliterate boundaries exhibited by Western imperialism as a whole operates in Sweden, which is, thereby, an integral part of Western European imperialism.

Third, Swedish economy is heavily dependent on external markets: 20% of her gross national product (GNP) depends on foreign trade.[4] Her best customer is Western Europe, which absorbs 70% of that trade, or 14% of GNP.[4] Sixty per cent of her entire industrial output is exported, including 90% of her iron ore, almost all her engineering goods, and 80% of her cellulose, a product in which only Canada exceeds her.[4] Within this export trade, certain high quality Swedish machine goods enjoy a monopoly of external markets,[4] a condition invariably resulting in super-prices, one channel of super profits especially employed by monopolies.

The usual export of capital began after World War I.[5] A good portion of it goes to South Africa.

Military expenditures are usually the indispensable accompaniment of metropolitan capitalism's advancing parasitic foreign activities. Sweden's truculent bid within the recent past to be included in the European "nuclear club" showed that munitions manufacturable only in countries with affluent bourgeoisies are definitely now within this country's capabilities. Her army consists of 600,000 regulars and a home guard of 100,000—a ratio near 10% of population.[6] The air force is fourth largest in the world, following only the U.S., Britain and the USSR.[6] Along 700 miles of coastline, artillery is dug in to atom-bomb-proof rock shelters, while similar airplane hangars and civilian shelters for 2,000,000 have been built.[7]

In his laudings of Scandinavian Social Democracy, Dr. Wong Lin Ken conveniently omitted reference to foreign investment or any equivalent, spot-lighting territorial possession as the main, if not sole, content of colonialism.

Dr. Wong simply "overlooked" Lenin's proof that territorial possession is not the sole criterion of colonialism. Financial acquisition, he said, is also a form of it, one moreover now rapidly becoming dominant in the West. Lenin said:

> "Finance capital is such a great, it may be said, such a decisive force in all economic and in all international relations, that it is capable of subjecting, and actually does subject to itself even states enjoying the fullest political independence."[8]

Today's England, and most of Western Europe, bear Lenin witness!

So, assuming Sweden mirrors the real Scandinavia, it has a ruling class which was spared the economic drain of the World Wars; a monopoly capital not only NOT pressed for outlets for its surplus capital but, on the contrary, actually enjoying a double source of super-profits: from the usual capital export and from monopoly of the lucrative Western European market for major Swedish machine products. (Of course, these are added to the advanced technological level of Swedish industry in our day, which plays a large derivative role in its present affluence.)

If this picture is accurate, one would, by our definition of Social Democracy, (See Chapter 2) expect a large labour aristocracy of relatively great affluence. And, because Sweden owns no outright colonies (so that not only are the subjugated far away; even the colonies themselves are "invisible"), one would also look for a mass Social Democratic party.

Workers form the vast majority of Sweden's population. Industry absorbs 41% of total labor force; agriculture, 20%, proving the advanced nature of its industrialization.[4] As noted, these workers enjoy the highest wages in Europe (and, at one-third of wages, also Europe's highest taxes). Of the labour force, 300, 000 are on relief, 4.4% of population.[4] Forty-five per cent (45%) of Swedish workers are unionised.[9] (Capitalism in any form must have its "labour reservoir". Sweden is no exception.)

Thus, Sweden has produced a labour aristocracy embracing a majority of population, and forming a leading component of the Western European labour aristocracy. The goodly "size of their earnings" and their affluent "mode of life" express themselves in "an entire outlook" favourable to Social Democracy.

The success of Sweden's mass Social Democratic party is the result, not the cause of Swedish labour's well-being, despite the absence of territorial colonies, but based in large part on foreign economic activities. The Sweden which "owns not a single colony" nevertheless lucratively super-exploits colonial subjects in South Africa and elsewhere, including Western Europe's machinery market.

Far from an exception in capitalism, Sweden turns out as a rather tidy text-book example, complete with "poverty minority", juvenile delinquency, large suicide rate, a "crisis in morals", all advancing merrily to the usual "Hearts and Flowers" trilling about "pure democracy".

Testimony to this effect is now coming out of Scandinavia itself. A number of groups have sprung up in the countries of that area, all nominally repudiating the "revisionist" world outlook. They do not all agree with one another. In Sweden, one such group issues an organ called THE SPARK. In Denmark, another group thinking along the lines set forth in these pages – was attacked by THE SPARK for its position on the conditions of Scandinavian workers. Under the heading, "Does Denmark (and Sweden) Take Part in This Plunder?" the Danish group replied as follows:

> "THE SPARK is extremely indignant that we allow ourselves to be of opinion that there is a connection between the economic situation of Danish working class

and the share of Danish capitalism in the super-profits from the colonial and neo-colonial plunder – and especially THE SPARK is very angry that sensible Swedes exist, who are saying the same thing about Sweden.

"THE SPARK flatly rejects this horrible accusation against Swedish monopoly capital. Swedish capitalism, in the opinion of THE SPARK, has made itself guilty only of exploiting the Swedish workers so heavily that more and more of them are the happy owners of motor cars or summer houses, cameras, deep-freezers, television sets and electric toy trains. No one is allowed to say about Swedish monopolist capital that it has exploited the colonial and semi-colonial peoples.

"As 'proof' THE SPARK presents a number of statistical surveys of how many productive enterprises Swedish monopoly capital is owning in other countries, and where these enterprises are situated. Triumphantly, the result is reached that only about 20 per cent of that kind of enterprises are situated in the oppressed countries in Asia, Africa and Latin America. It is further noted that by far the majority of these enterprises have been built up after World War II, and that the money for the investments has been exported from Sweden with the sanction of the National Bank.

"And where, then, has the money come from? Well, when it has been exported via the National Bank from Sweden, it is clear that it has been stolen out of the pockets of the workers of Sweden.

"Seldom have you heard nonsense the like of this! According to THE SPARK, some way or another Swedish monopoly capital has suddenly emerged from nothing. As far as can be seen from the explanation of THE SPARK it has no connection with the past. It is there - just like that.

"How did capitalism arise in Sweden? How did industrialization take place in Sweden? We do not intend to go into details, but we should not be much mistaken if Swedish capitalism, just as was the case in Denmark, to a very high degree was based on loans from the big capitalist powers – England, Germany. And where did these big capitalist countries get the money to finance these loans? We know that from Marx, from Engels, from Lenin. From the colonies!

"We know that the development of Danish capitalist industry is very closely connected with the long-standing Danish monopoly concerning fine agricultural products (based on import of cheap raw materials from Asia and Latin America) to the English market, where profits from the colonies had created a public with money to buy them.

"What about Swedish export of iron ore to the rapidly growing German industry at the time around 1900? Is there any connection between the strong demand of German industry for Swedish ore and the the exploitation taking place in the German colonies in Africa, which – among other things – meant the total disappearance of whole African tribes? (Does not West German capitalism deal in neocolonial exploitation today, and does it not still buy Swedish iron ore?)

"We think THE SPARK should examine these problems – instead of operating with a Swedish monopoly capital anno 1968 as if it had no previous history, and as if it was all alone in the capitalist world.

> "Since, in passing, THE SPARK expressly states that exploitation is above all taking place in production enterprises, we just want to remind the readers of the fact that during the years after the Korean war a sharp fall set in in the export prices of the oppressed countries to our part of the world and a still sharper increase in the prices which they had to pay for their imports from our countries – also the imports from Denmark and Sweden. So maybe Swedish monopoly capital has also made a little money through the many trade (sale) enterprises which has been set up in the whole wide world since World War II. And maybe this growing difference in export and import prices has also had a certain importance for the increasing real wages of the Swedish workers?"[10]

Disposing of the Swedish legend, as dear to Social Democratic hearts as to the ruling class Social Democracy serves, is more than a mere intellectual exercise. In the context of general Marxist failure to appreciate the decisiveness of imperialist parasitism, this legend bears directly on the slough into which the Western Left has fallen: faced with Social Democratic gloating over Scandinavia's economic success and its implied applicability to the entire capitalist system, Marxists in the metropolitan world – already half-digested into postwar material affluence – seriously botched the job of countering such propaganda. Did Social Democracy claim Sweden the "glorious exception that proves the rule"? Then these Marxists felt duty bound to deny all. Instead of pin-pointing the form of Scandinavian parasitism within the imperialist economy and relating it to the general phenomenon, they point to 300,000 Swedish workers on relief, to high taxes paid by Scandinavian workers[4] and imply that these – not capital – export-based high wages and their resultant political expression in successful mass Social Democracy – were Sweden's currently significant features.

Furthermore, the Scandinavian myth is an indispensable back ground against which to view Palme Dutt (and others) accenting worsening workers' conditions under European Fascism. Echoed by Eastern European Marxists, Dutt and his cohorts, from the depths of the crisis, answered Social Democratic boasts about Scandinavia with predictions of an imminent end to the whole system. Postwar difficulties and ensuing upheavals in the capitalist world involving even the labor aristocracy of the time gulled Marxists into trying to make of such undeniably worsened conditions the only clue to the future. They refused to consider Scandinavia. And so they failed to see over the edges of depression conditions to the relationship between where such conditions lead and the presence or absence of super-exploitable colonial populations. With dog-like persistence, they ignored Lenin's admonition on the significance of imperialist parasitism which held a ruling class solution.

Not very long ago as history unwinds, an interesting example in the Congo provided a peek into future. During Patrice Lumumba's rise, Belgium's monopolists feared the real loss of their colony when "independence" was granted in January 1960. Although their fears were soon proven premature, their answer was an austerity program inside Belgium, a logical attempt to transfer to Belgian workers the increased exploitation aimed at recouping anticipated colonial losses. By June 1960, that program had evoked "chaos" in Belgium; and in December 1960, the declaration of a general strike brought the entire Belgian working class onto the streets. Horrified at the revolutionary potential looming in such a situation, Uncle Sam hastily intervened through his creature Mobutu in the Congo. Patrice Lumumba, murdered January 17, 1961, paid with his young life for that intervention. But his murder at least temporarily solved Belgium's – and America's – immediate worry about revolution at home, by ensuring that the loss of the Congo would be in name only. Before the end of January 1961, the general strike in Belgium was over.

Labor Aristocracy

The case of Scandinavia reveals that the more remote or hidden parasitism is (either by the distance of the subjugated and/or in the apparent absence of colonies themselves), the greater the concessions imperialism can make to "its" workers at home. Continued "democracy" in the West proves parasitism's nonstop growth as long as imperialism exists – a growth which, even as it intensifies the system's inner contradictions, still allows it to totter on.

But, at least partly because Marxists offered no valid answer to Social Democratic claims about Scandinavia, the Western labor aristocracy continued unhindered in its political support for colonialism, either via growing overt racism, as in the U.S. and South Africa; or by pursuing Social Democracy's will-o'-the-wisp where it leads: to uncovering covert racism, as in England.

Meanwhile, colonial casualties mounted in the struggle for liberation. The Western Left's myth that "the working class in the main capitalist countries" is, at this point in history, a battalion of liberation did not help such casualties. Although that Left often predicted a pending change in Western working class adherence to its colonially-derived bribes, the very opposite is what happened – the world labor aristocracy shows a growing attachment to them! The objective result of the cited Marxist position has been paralysis of that Left's ability to make realistic estimates of existing conditions. Yet, only facing facts can make Marxism work in the West once again, as it did for the scientist Lenin up to the mid-20s.

But how can facts be faced when obscured by the attitudes of men with the authority of Georgi Dimitroff, Palme Dutt and Palmiro Togliatti? At the time when they were writing, their every word was taken as gospel – when History certainly called for an entirely different attitude. Lack of criticism developed into a huge weed in the Western Marxist garden, and soon was to over run and choke the ideological soil of the Western Left.

Section B

Imperialist Parasitism in Today's World

Labor Aristocracy

9. Monopoly and "Capital Export"

Although half a century has gone by since Lenin wrote of "The Parasitism and Decay of Capitalism,"[1] his words still apply. But today, they operate in a new context: socialism exists on one-third of the earth; anti-colonial liberation is in world wide upsurge; and inside the socialist world, an ideological split today mirrors its own colonial and neo-colonial base. (Since these words were first written, the fraction of the earth occupied by real socialism has shrunk considerably, with a consequent effect on the vigor of colonial liberation struggles.)

In the pages that follow, modern figures will be applied to some of Lenin's theses on imperialist parasitism. They are generally related only to the US, accepting it as the typical top imperialist power of our time.

Lenin cited the system's trend toward monopoly as the general source of its parasitism. How has monopoly fared in the world's greatest power?

A quite "respectable" spokesman of a portion of the US Left has noted - as background for a discourse on ethics — that

> "only about 35 per cent of the total volume of business in America is individually owned, 92 per cent of our manufacturing (being) done by corporations."[2]

And what is the condition of those corporations?

Comparing net profits of the 500 largest industrial corporations in the US in 1958 and 1959, the picture that emerges is this: 1958 $9,582 million , 1959, $11,987 million.[3]

Among these 500, the net profits of the 100 largest in those same years were: 1958. $6,674 million, 1959, $8.221 million.[3]

Total corporate profits after taxes for those years (in billions of dollars this time) were: 1958. $18.8 billion, 1959, $24.5 billion.[3]

Fewer and fewer corporations garner more and more of total national profits. Monopoly as a major feature of imperialism is still increasing. So, the general base of parasitism continues to broaden.

Monopoly parasitism finds decisive expression in the economy, Lenin had added, through the growing preponderance of income from capital export over that from trade. In his day, he had documented the truth of his assertion.[4] How about today?

One writer has declared:

> "For the United States for the present period . . . for large corporations the export of capital has not only become extremely important, but decisively MORE important than the export of commodities."[5]

There is a very sound reason for such a condition, as an economics teacher in the New York School of Social Research pointed out:

> " . . . the volume of accumulated capital abroad controlled by United States business has been increasing at a faster rate than exports . . . (because) capital . . . reproduces itself . . . the annual flow of capital invested abroad is therefore additive."[6]

Documentation of the escalation from year to year of U. S. foreign investment is done by the US publication Survey of Current Business. One of its issues has noted, for instance, that exports of US merchandise excluding military grants-in-aid, with 1957-1959 at 100, in 1964 amounted to $1.7 billion.[7] The same source showed a net foreign investment in the same year of $6.3 billion.[8]

These figures represent a trend over time. According to one previously cited author, the years 1950 to 1961 in the US witnessed the following changes:

> ". . . the dollar value of the gross national product increased 83%, of private consumption 74%, of private domestic investment 39%, of non-military spending by all governments (Local, State and Federal) 141%, of non-military merchandise exports 82%. Meanwhile, military spending increased 244% and the value of US corporate investments abroad 203%."[9]

Not unexpectedly, the effect at home is the growing influence of profits from overseas economic activity. Before-tax profits on direct foreign investments rose from $1,769 million in 1950 to $3,546 million in 1960, increasing during that decade as a share in profits from all sources from 7.8% to 15.6%.[5] By 1965, the comparable figure was $3,610 million, or almost 22% of total.[6]

In January 1965, to curb balance-of-payments deficits, the US government instituted a "voluntary" program of "restraining" overseas investment. Result? "Farcical", sneered one "economist and analyst of the imperialist nature of the new economics of capitalism." He backed his sneer:

> "During the first year of 'restraint' investment (overseas) jumped to $3.3 billion from $2.4 billion the year before. And 1966 promises to go even higher."[10]

What, meantime, has been happening to capital export? Consider the following table: [12]

Table I

NET OUTFLOW, U.S. CAPITAL, PRIVATE AND GOVERNMENT
(In millions of Dollars)

1950	1955	1956	1957	1958	1959	1960	1961	1962	1963	1964
1,421	1,521	3,619	4,133	3,815	2,728	5,079	5,663	5,953	6,527	6,636

In about twenty years following World War II. at the same time that the share of profits on capital exports as a percentage of total were being doubled, the net outflow of US capital more than likely quadrupled.

Statistics, in a word, appear to confirm that "capital export' still plays, today as it did yesterday, a growing role in imperialism's economy.

To let matters rest there, however, would be to oversimplify. For example, the term "capital export" need not be taken literally in today's international financial maneuverings:

Discussing "Absorption of the Surplus" produced by the workings of the world's most advanced monopoly economy, US imperialism, the late Economics Professor from Stanford University (California) Paul A. Baran and the co-editor of the independent socialist magazine MONTHLY REVIEW in New York Paul M. Sweezy studied "Capitalists' Consumption and Investment", including foreign investments. They make the following points relative to modern monopoly capitalism as exemplified in the US:

1. Capital export as such has dropped in importance in late years:

"... except possibly for brief periods of abnormally high capital exports from the advanced countries, foreign investment must be looked upon as a method of pumping surplus out of underdeveloped areas, not as a channel through which surplus is directed into them."[13]

2. Today, the US shows a net inflow of surplus capital of growing size:

> "In 1963, United States corporations (nearly all giants) had foreign direct investments amounting to $40.6 billion. But a large proportion of this – probably the majority – was acquired without any outflow of capital from the United States . . . Even in cases where substantial sums of capital were exported, subsequent expansion commonly takes place through plowing back of profits; and the return flow of interest and dividends (not to mention remittances disguised in the form of payment for services and the like) soon repays the original investment many times over – and still continues to pour capital into the coffers of the parent corporation in the United States. It is not surprising therefore that while capital does flow out of the country every year, the return flow of investment income is invariably much larger."[14]

The writers supply a table comparing capital export with direct investment income between the years 1950 and 1963 to reinforce their point. It shows that

> "during this period American corporations were able to take in as income $12 billion more than they sent out as capital, while at the same time expanding their foreign holdings (through reinvesting profits earned abroad, borrowing from foreign banks and investors, etc.) by $28.8 billion."[15]

What, then, of Lenin's dictum on the role of "capital export" in aggravating imperialist parasitism?

First, Baran and Sweezy specifically qualify their interest in foreign investment as only concerned with

> "an outlet for investment-seeking surplus generated in the corporate sector of the monopoly capitalist economy."

Lenin, however, had focused on the fact that

> "capital exports yield an income..." (See quotation, Page 66, above.)

His concern was with capital exports' effects in extracting superprofits from the labour of "overseas" subjects, especially in producing non-working sections among the people of the exploiting countries. The export of capital in this sense, Lenin thought,

> "puts the seal of parasitism on the whole country that lives by exploiting the labour of several overseas countries and colonies." (Finally, Lenin cited as consequence that "the world has become divided into a handful of usurer slates and a vast majority of debtor states." (See quote, page 45 above.)

In a word, Lenin's emphasis was on parasitism in monopoly economies: it was the income on capital export which made a country parasitic. Baran and Sweezy's findings for the modern monopoly economy corroborate and reinforce Lenin: they find that economy to be attracting such income in ever-growing amounts, regardless of what new forms the influx may assume. They concluded that

> "foreign investment, far from being an outlet for domestically generated surplus, is a most efficient device for transferring surplus generated abroad to the investing country."[16]

So has Lenin's discovery escalated into our time. All forms of imperialist parasitism are ways of exploiting "the labour of several overseas countries and colonies". The results have made the US today the world's greatest "usurer" nation.

10. Inter Effect of Monopoly on Imperialist Parasitism

There is more to the growing importance of "overseas" income than is contained in absolute figures of quantitative growth. Qualitative inter effects of still-waxing monopoly on the importance of the overseas portion of metropolitan income imply even greater parasitism.

For instance, one means of pooh-poohing the real value of foreign activities to the home front is to note that total US exports are less than 5%, while foreign investments do not reach 10%, of Gross National Product. How can such small GNP percentages be "decisive" to an economy?

The question contains two false premises: a) that GNP is a "thing in itself equitable to national economy; and b) that because among total activities in an economy given ones are statistically few, therefore their importance is also small.

a) GNP is undoubtedly a convenience enabling large amounts of finance from different sources to be moved about en bloc statistically. But it can also confuse discussion of economic concepts. Besides actual material values, it includes government expenditures (salaries, personal and professional services, trade, and activities of banks, real estate and insurance outfits). Exports, however, are mainly commodities – real values –. from farms, factories and mines; and foreign investments come mainly from huge manufacturing firms.[1]

b) As to the activities of the monopoly sector in US Economy, percentage is meaningless until related to the size of control. In fact, the controlling power of US monopoly activities makes these activities more, rather than less, significant .

The first significance lies in the small number of actual firms involved, as an American monopolist has testified:

> "In the United States today . . . 135 corporations own 45 percent of the industrial assets. THESE are the companies to watch. Here lies managerial power."[2]

Furthermore, increasing monopolization involves far more significant increases than those of size. For example:

1. Overseas profits are always under-stated, due to cosseting legislation surrounding them at home. One effect has been that

> ". . . virtually no US income taxes are paid by US corporations on their foreign investment income."[3]

At the same time, actual profits on corporate foreign investments could be even double those reported, while

> "the real value of direct (US) corporate investment overseas may well be on the order not of 19 billion dollars but of 50 billion or more."[4]

By late 1966, the reported value of direct US Foreign investment had increased to that 50 billion estimated in 1956:

> "The book value of this investment has increased from $19 billion in 1955 to well over $50 billion today."[5]

If the $19 billion reported in the earlier year had suggested an actual investment of $50 billion (and assuming that the proportion between the two remained steady over the decade - it is far more likely that it increased), then today's actual direct US foreign investments must be at least$ 131 billion!

2. All discussions of overseas profits in US government and other similar sources take no account of considerable income from a) exploiting patent and copyright agreements; b) non-commodity producing industries like investment and commercial banking, stock market speculations, transportation, insurance, etc.; and c) portfolio investments.[4]

3. It is easy to forget that

> "it is MONOPOLISTIC industry which dominates the flow of investments and that such monopolistic businesses characteristically gear their investment policies to the 'sure thing', where good profits and safety of investment are reliably ensured."[1]

4. Though commodity exports are decreasing in importance relative to foreign investments, relative to total commodity production they have surpassed domestic out put by much more than has yet been conceded.

For instance, when merchandise exports are compared to total domestic output, there is double counting, in that semi-finished products manufactured domestically are counted domestically and then, shipped to foreign subsidiaries, are counted again in the finished foreign product. Furthermore, data of the two categories are not strictly comparable: foreign output is listed as value-of-shipment, while domestic goods appear in a value-added category.[1]

When all similar discrepancies are weeded out, the result is that merchandise exports come to

> "a conservative estimate of approximately two fifths the domestic output of farms, factories and mines.[2]

Forty percent (measured against "domestic output", to be sure) is eight times the usually-contended five percent which merchandise exports are said to be of GNP.

5. Domestic firms producing merchandise in their own factories abroad enjoy other advantages, such as the ability to mobilize foreign capital for their own operations. Taking all such advantages into account, production resulting from US investment inside foreign countries – 4 1/2 times larger in 1950 than imports into these countries from the US – rose by 1964 to 5 1/2 times larger.[1]

6. Considering manufacturing industries alone, the following facts on the role of the foreign market emerge:

a) Total export sales rising faster than domestic sales:

"... when the economy as a whole was experiencing a slowing down in the rate of growth, foreign markets were an important source of expansion. For example, in manufacturing industries during the past ten years domestic sales increased by 50%, while foreign sales by United States-owned factories increased over 110%."[6]

b) An increasing relative importance for the foreign component in plant and equipment expenditures, which

"for United States subsidiaries abroad were a little over 8% of such expenditures of domestic firms in 1957 (whereas) last year (1965) this had risen to 17%."[7]

Ever-increasing armaments and military spending to buttress monopoly and safeguard the system have assumed enormous importance among aspects of growing parasitism in today's imperialist world. In the US in 1957, about 50% of the profits of industrial corporations came from foreign investments and armaments, with "the largest contributing factor" (as compared to armaments) being foreign investment.[8]

(Actually, such a distinction, if valid then, has long since become meaningless: imperialism requires military expenditures to safe guard foreign investments.)

Military expenditures form a larger and larger portion of total foreign investments, _as has been documented. Military expenditures, in fact, have the following current features connected with their role in imperialist economies:

1. "National security and business interests" are inseparable :

> "... the size of the 'free' world and the degree of its 'security' define the geographic boundaries where capital is relatively free to invest and trade."[9]

2. It is misleading to relate military spending to GNP. What is important is the

> "underlying strategic relationships that determine the direction and degree of movement of the economic aggregate."[10]

3. The bases and "far-flung military activities" as well as the multifarious expenditures that follow in their wake bring numerous advantages to the "business community" of metropolitan countries. They a) protect existing and possible raw material sources; b) safeguard foreign investments and markets; c) guard commercial sea and air lanes; d) ensure that US firms get "a competitive edge" in "spheres of influence;" e) through military and foreign "aid", create new foreign customers and new opportunities for investment overseas; and f) run interference on the world market for America's "junior

partners" among the industrialized nations where US capital is becoming an ever-more-important factor.[10]

4. None of these factors, however, provide a proper under standing of

> "the stake business has in the size and nature of military expenditures as a well-spring of new orders and profits."[10]

5. In this context, the main significance of military expenditures is their "exceptionally large impact on the capital goods industries".[10]

Some of the reasons:

a) Capital goods industries – especially those producing non-residential goods – are basic to the mechanics of the business cycle: consumer expenditures, which always drop during a crisis, never, like expenditures on investment goods, reach a practical zero.

b) In 1958, "the latest year for which government did a complete input-output analysis for the US economy", of all industries producing non-residential investment goods, only one – farm machinery and equipment – obtained less than 20% of its business from the field of "the combined export and military demand" (the latter represented by US government purchases). Ordnance and aircraft obtained almost all (88.4% and 92.8% respectively) from this source. The general range of such support was from 20-50%.

c) Furthermore, this 20-50% support from military purchases and exports

> "probably accounts for the major share of the profits,
> and in not a few firms, perhaps as much as 80 to 100
> per cent"

because of the existence of a break-even point, below which corporations do not meet their costs of productions, but after which profits generally soar.[10]

6. Finally, the military goods market a) supplies long-term contracts; such contracts usually b) carry guarantees that minimize and often eliminate any risks in building additional plant and equipment; and c) pay for related research and development activities.[10]

7. Not only do military expenditures as such make modern imperialist economies more parasitic: they reinforce and augment non-military parasitism.

8. Furthermore, military outlays themselves become increasingly parasitic internally:

> " ... there has been a sharp shift in the character of
> goods and services purchased by military outlays. A
> much larger proportion goes for research and
> development, engineering, supervision, and
> maintenance; a much smaller proportion for the kind
> of mass-produced military hardware (artillery, tanks,
> planes, trucks, jeeps, ships) that played the decisive
> role in two world wars. This . . . means that a given
> amount of military spending employs far fewer
> persons today than it used to. In these circumstances,
> even very large increases in military spending, while
> enormously profitable to the big corporations, may
> have relatively little effect on investment and
> employment." [11]

9. The "arms economy", looked to as "stabiliser" for the capitalist economy, fails expectations for the following reasons:[12]

a) Arms production "proliferates inexorably through the system", causing a competitive arms race.

b) "Anarchy remains very nearly absolute internationally."

c) The "space race" cannot overcome the defects of the arms race because "any country opting for high employment and stability through productive investments or even unproductive 'hole filling' public works is bound to suffer in world competition."

d) The system is composed of elements "both interdependent and independent of each other, held together by mutual compulsion", even under an arms economy.

e) The arms economy, once adopted, becomes necessary and permeates the society's entire economic fabric.

f) It becomes a convenient and effective means for US imperialism in particular, the world's most complete arms economy, to gobble up rivals.

g) It cannot prevent recessions inside the system.

h) Arms spending and the employment it at first induces fall after a time.

i) Its alleged benefits in technological advance, and the skills associated with it, are not transferable generally to the civilian economy.

11. Monopoly's Parasitic Methods of Expansion

Lenin had also traced parasitism to the continued swelling of the numbers of "coupon clippers" in metropolitan areas. Dividend payments at least measure the extent of this development as, for instance, in the United States:

Table 2[1]

TRENDS IN U.S. DIVIDEND PAYMENTS[*]
(In Billions of Dollars)

1939	1945	1957	1958	1959	1960	1961	1962	1963	1964	1965
3.8	4.7	12.6	12.4	13.7	14.4	15.0	15.9	15.8	17.2	18.9

Moreover, Lenin also saw parasitism in the fact that imperialism is "an immense accumulation of money capital in a few countries". That his statement is still valid is again illustrated by the American example:

Table 3[2]

AMERICAN CORPORATIONS WORTH ONE BILLION DOLLARS OR MORE

YEAR	NO. OF SUCH CORPORATIONS	THEIR TOTAL CORPORATE ASSETS (Billions of Dollars)	TOTAL, ALL U. S. CORPORATE ASSETS	% TOP CORPORATE ASSETS TO TOTAL
1941	31	66.5	341	19.5
1953	66	174.3	616	28.3
% INCREASE	106	162	81	

The number of billion-dollar corporations, their total assets, and total US corporate assets all grow. But assets of top corporations increase at double the rate for all.

To show that this "immense accumulation of money capital" is still confined to a few countries,

> "The traditional principle (is) that the possibility of (internal accumulation) is a function of the size of income per head in a given economy."[3]

On this basis, the following are some average per capita incomes:

> a) 1840-1850, in US, Canada, Britain, France and Germany: $150-$300, with an average growth rate during that decade of 2.5%.

> b) 1949 (a century later) in "a number of developing countries:" $25-$50. The U. N. statistics cited in this case offer no growth rate.[3]

The next table furnishes corroborating evidence :

Table 4[4]

INTERNATIONAL AVERAGE PER CAPITA INCOME

	1950	1960	% GROWTH
United States	$1,000	$2,500	250.0
Asia + Africa + Latin America	100	150	50.0
No. time U.S. figure exceeds that of underdeveloped areas	10	17	70.0

These figures gauge the rate at which imperialism continues accumulating money capital.

A more recent study along similar lines shows that advanced capitalist countries, in the 12 years from 1953 through 1964, experienced an average change in the index of their per capita gross domestic product of +44.1 points, whereas "third world" countries increased only 21.7 points in the same interval (at constant prices).[5]

America's increased economic dependence on foreign investments and attendant military spending, dealt with as an aspect of imperialist parasitism in the previous Chapter, is sometimes challenged – for instance, as has been noted, by declaring that such dependence involves only a small segment of American business. Monopoly makes nonsense of such statements:

> "In manufacturing industries, 5 corporations own over 15% of total net capital assets (as of 1962). The 100 largest corporations own 55% of total net capital assets . . . and it is precisely among the giant corporations that we find the main centers of foreign and military economic operations."[6]

Among the 50 largest US industrial concerns, 37 – heavily involved in international economic and military activities – account for more than 90% of the top 50's assets.

As for foreign investment itself,

> "only 45 firms account for almost three-fifths of all . . . 80% of all such investment is held by 163 firms."[6]

To imagine that such intense concentration is purely a national US phenomenon is to lose sight of parasitism as the binding factor of imperialism's world economy. Precisely the creation of financial-industrial Gargantuas reduces the "few countries" of Lenin's day to a single one: despite challenges from rival powers, the United States since 1945 has, directly or indirectly, thus far been virtually dictating policy even in a large segment of the once-socialist world.

The mechanisms whereby the US financial oligopoly takes over hegemony are not all new. For instance, one of the earliest was found in vast interlocking directorates, a phenomenon already investigated by Lenin. Today their power and extent have enormously escalated under American domination as a result of World War II.

Testimony to their truly international character – in at least one area of the world in our day – has been offered, eloquently but ironically, by an English Social Democratic M.P.:

> ".. the huge mineral Empire in Africa, stretching from the copper belt of Zambia to the mineral wealth of Katanga, to the diamonds and railways of Angola, to the diamonds of South-West Africa . . . to the gold and diamonds and uranium of the Republic of South Africa . . . is literally . . . one great monopoly...

> ". . . the Société Générale de Belgique, a monarch in Belgian finance and industry . . . is linked with the Union Minifcre of Katanga and the British-owned Tanganyika Concessions.

> " 'Tanks', as the British company is . . . called in the City of London, is interlocked with the Benguela Railway in Angola and the Angola-American Corporation of South Africa.

> "The Corporation, in turn, is linked with the British South Africa Company which has just been deprived of

> its royalties in Zambia, and the De Beers Consolidated
> Mines of South Africa.
>
> "There are many other shared directorships and
> investments."[7]

Another, more modern, device was probed not long ago in TIME magazine, which revealed the following facts:

> "Western Europe is gripped by a growing . . . fear that
> it is falling victim to American economic conquest. And
> that conquest, so the lament goes, is spearheaded by
> American technology. Armed with technological
> prowess that European firms cannot match, giant US
> corporations are winning control over crucial
> industries."[8]

So great a fear, in fact, has been generated in Europe about this take-over that

> "it was on the agenda of NATO's ministerial meeting
> last month (December 1966). The Common Market will
> devote a special session to it in February. British Prime
> Minister Harold Wilson and former West German
> Chancellor Ludwig Erhard took it up in their last talks
> with Lyndon Johnson."[8]

Furthermore, in "the significant international balance-of-patent payments", the United States has better than "a 5 to 1 margin":

> "At last count, the US paid $45 million a year for
> European patents, but collected $251 million for US
> Patents."[8]

As causes of such a potentially "trouble-making" gap, the following factors operate:

1. Europe has plenty of scientific brain-power. But it "flounders" in related uses thereof: a) "translating its laboratory discoveries into sophisticated hardware"; b) "organizing and marketing its achievements".

> "... what Europe faces is not a technology gap but a management and money gap."[8]

2. Europe's outlets are too small: no European country has a market larger than one-sixth that of the US because Europe's companies are "still chopped up into national units", not even the Common Market can overcome the effects of "disparate systems of laws and taxation".

3. Europe "is too stingy about research and development".

> "The US spends about ten times more per capita on R & D and four times as much altogether as Europe ($23.3 billion last year)."[8]

4. Because of its "vast capital and huge home market", US business is able to risk huge fortunes on launching "promising ventures":

> "RCA gambled $130 million on color television before it began to pay off."[8]

But Europe lacks risk capital.

5. Managerial skills are lacking in Europe, according to Italian physicist Massino Bernardini, who said that

> "Here we have brilliant individuals and almost never brilliant organizations."[8]

He blamed the condition on the European practice of picking top managers and directors "not for ambition, skill or diligence, but for their social qualifications."

6. Snobbery tends to cut out many who could become technicians and inventors: a) traditional contempt for manual labor left over from feudal Europe; b) a European contempt for engineers, leading to a "brain-drain" in this category from Europe to the US

7. Education is not designed to get the most out of population potentialities in the technological field: in Europe, "first-rate education still reaches only a handful of elite", because a) Europeans "stream" their young from the age of about ten onward; a chosen few continue to "superb" education; the remainder go to work or to trade schools; b) Europe has no way to utilize "second cut" students, nor to give a chance to "slow starters"; c) European professors run academic departments or institutes "with Napoleonic power and life-time tenure".

8. Tariff walls to protect local industry no longer help Europe: American investment in local industry surmounts that hurdle completely. The article thinks Europe should consider erasing its geographical and political boundaries, unifying its currencies, and – in general – getting rid of the "nation-state concept". Short of that,

> "the only course for the US seems to be to help narrow the gap in what limited ways it can, but keep up the competitive heat."[8]

This well-documented survey points up the rapid infiltration of US monopoly into controlling sectors of European economies, and highlights the truth in an observation by a modern authority who says that the

> "extension of domestic monopolistic trends . . . provide(s) the opportunity to accumulate wealth needed for extensive foreign investment as well as the impetus for such investment."[9]

The overall result has been

> "the transformation of many of the giants of United States business into a new form of multinational organization."[10]

One such US concern boasted of its macromania in an official organ of the huge American construction monopolies:

> "Caterpillar is recognized as one of the leading equipment manufacturers of the world. It has manufacturing plants in 10 countries - including plants of affiliates in India and Japan – and two additional plants are currently under construction. It works with 260 independent dealerships which, in turn, operate 816 sales and service outlets. And these are backed up with nine parts warehouses and 14 depots scattered around the globe. Last year, Caterpillar sales totaled $1.5 billion of which $628 million came from sales to customers outside the United States."[11]

Of course, such a development has its dangers as well:

> "The technology gap has become a sensitive issue in world politics, with anti-American overtones."[8]

The effect of parasitism, then, has been to "internationalize" imperialism's economic base, creating a world bourgeoisie, a world economy – and a world proletariat – all, at the same time, rent by inner contradictions. (An internationalized bourgeoisie, incidentally, could be expected to super-exploit colonial subjects on a non-boundary basis, and to treat its own international economy (the West) more and more as its integral playground.)

For quite a period, such internationalization proceeded blindly. When Marx was writing, Britain had become – through the working out of inexorable economic laws – the richest, most developed of capitalist countries in a system then in its competitive heyday. Its bourgeoisie could make expert use of national jingoism as it began its penetration of others' "spheres of influence". That is why England was the model on which Marx based his Capital.

Today, however, on "its" two-thirds of the globe, imperialism's habit of ignoring national boundaries throughout its increasingly integrated (albeit increasingly conflict-ridden) economy is well advanced. International monopolies, more and more often merged with governments (yet formally "outside and above" them), move heaven and earth by guile and by force to win world supremacy. In this phase of capitalism – its monopoly or imperialist stage – the United States has attained the same comparative position as England in the 19th Century[12], heading the pack – more rapacious, more "powerful," more riddled with inner stresses, and more moribund than any of its rivals.

From the bourgeois world's first "champion of liberty", Uncle Sam has metamorphosed into a monied monster: the napalm nightmare is the direct descendant of the "democratic" dream.

12. Mechanisms of Monopolist Hegemony

Today, then, "internationalization" of imperialism boils down to the leading role of American monopoly finance capital. In such hegemony, the question of control is crucial.

For example, "direct investments" as defined by the US Department of Commerce, are "branch establishments in which United States firms own 25% or more of voting stock."[1]

Control itself is exercised by the pattern of investments, a fact most aptly illustrated by "economic relations with the underdeveloped countries," where

> "In Latin America, Asia and Africa, the majority of the investment is the extractive industries."[2]

However, other aspects of the pattern of investments are also revealing. In the previous Chapter, American monopoly use of patents and licenses was scrutinized in detail. Yet, when it is asked, "How far has the take-over progressed?" the answer seems a bit confusing:

> "By the end of this year, direct US business investment in European companies will amount to about $ 20 billion, which falls a long way short of hegemony. In no European country do US- owned firms account for more than about 5% of total business."[3]

But if less than the 20th part of European business is in US hands, why all the fuss?

> "What upsets Europeans is that the American activity is concentrated in a few high-technology industries which powerfully shape today's economic life (such as oil, autos, chemicals) or promise to remold tomorrow's global

environments (aerospace, electronics, computers). The oil industry is 40% US-owned in Britain and Germany. US-owned or controlled companies account for a third of European auto sales, 35% of the British tire market, 40% of France's tractors and farm machines, 75% of its electrical and statistical machines, 90% of its synthetic rubber."[3]

This pattern ensures the ability to control additionally:

1. Sources of raw materials for industries like steel, aluminum and especially oil:

> "The oil industry has from its outset been dominated by the most powerful banking interests, the Rockefellers, Morgans, Rothschilds, because of the spiraling profits it provides. Today, even with the larger royalties the oil combines have been obliged to pay producing countries, their profits are still mounting prodigiously.

> "Oil trust reserves run into billions. Much has been used in investments abroad, American far and away exceeding all others."[4]

2. Through such control,

> "... these foreign supplies are not merely an avenue of great profits, but are the insurance policy on the monopolistic position at home."[4]

3. Markets.

4. Prices.

5. By ensuring metropolitan control in such a manner, monopolies effectively eliminate competition, especially but not solely among emerging nations.

6. Overseas economic activities, with the spreading controls they evoke, further increase the power of the few metropolitan monopolies by

a) Their involvement in foreign aid: it engenders among the recipients ever-growing debts which flow through international financial centers owned or controlled by "foreign investors, their business associates, and their government agencies".

b) Financial tribute in the form of expatriated profits:

"In the underdeveloped regions almost three times as much money was taken out as was put in ... Besides ... Investors were able to increase the value of assets owned in these regions manifold …

"In Latin America, Asia and Africa, between 1950 and 1965, US businesses owned investments that rose from $5.8 billion to $15.0 billion."[5]

c) International control of financial resources:

"For practical purposes, some of the key European countries are financial servants of the dominant (American) banking monopolistic groups, the Morgans and the Rockefellers. . . Belgium. . . a financial colony of American investment capital. . . American financial capital, of course, had a field day in Germany during the post-war occupation . . . Italian banks . . . Japan, Canada, Australia and New Zealand . . . financial dependence upon America. . .

> Europe's subservience to American financial monopoly, a monopoly expressed in the strategic and political alliances that bind European capitalism to American capitalism."[6]

Control of raw materials sources has become so crucial to the continued existence of imperialism that the subject invariably evokes controversy. For example, one theory subscribed to in some Left circles holds that the modern era has created synthetic substitutes for so many primary materials that the big powers no longer depend so greatly on imports to sustain their industries.

Strangely enough, such a hypothesis is indispensable to the view of "under-development" of those espousing it. Consider for instance an analysis of under-development which appeared in an Accra newspaper during the Nkrumah regime:

> "The principal purveyors of raw materials are the economically under-developed, nations. Most of them have won political independence, but remain part of the capitalist economic system."[7]

Nothing apparently controversial here!

However, the article goes on to note that

> "the position in most (newly-independent nations) is characterized by limited natural resources, exploited moreover by foreign monopoly concerns, a one-sided economic structure and woefully low living standards."[7]

Whether natural resources in such places are really limited or not geophysical surveys on the spot have begun to call into question. But far more important is exploitation by foreign monopolies, just one in a series of characteristics of such areas. Or are the "one-sided economic structure" and "woefully low living standards" causally related to it?

On the foregoing base, the following additional points build up a picture of "under-developed" nations as equal partners (albeit poor cousins) in the imperialist system:

1. Over-production of raw materials:

> "For several years now there has been an over-production of raw materials. Since 1956, prices have fallen steadily or have remained at a very low level."

2. 1963 witnessed an alleged economic decline in Western Europe and Japan ("the principal buyers of raw materials and food stuffs.")

3. A raw materials crisis has caused emerging countries an alleged chronic trade crisis and foreign exchange shortages, forcing them to restrict imports of essential goods.

4. Nevertheless, in 1963 "for the first time in seven years", raw material and food prices went up six per cent in the first half of the year. This had the effect of giving these countries "more foreign exchange revenue and a somewhat better foreign trade outlook. It can safely be said that the raw materials crisis has passed its lowest point."

5. "But will this lead to a fundamental improvement for developing countries?"

6. ". . . the problems facing the under-developed nations are so complex and formidable that last year's greater influx of foreign exchange cannot seriously improve their position. "

First, "complex and formidable" in what way? Second, WHY can no improvement be expected from this "greater influx of foreign exchange" in emerging nations? Third, what about monopoly price-fixing (often with political motivation) as the source of falling prices or of "over-production"? Why was imperialist control of world markets not mentioned nor related to the economic decline among the "principal buyers of raw materials" as cause of the "raw materials crisis"?

Item by item, this discussion of "under-development", typical of revisionist Left circles, simply ignores imperialist parasitism.

Yet the fact is that imperialist dependence on colonial raw materials has been growing – and documented: while improved technology in the West has reduced raw materials consumption per unit manufactured, the system as a whole has greatly stepped up its total consumption of these very imports.[8]

This is true especially for mineral products, which are closely related to modern heavy industry in "the six major imperialist . . . powers – the United States, Britain, France, West Germany, Italy, and Japan".[8] In the nine years between 1953 and 1962, their consumption of aluminum rose 73%; copper, 48%; zinc, lead, 26%; and tin, 23%. In' only five years, 1957-1962, petroleum consumption in the same countries increased by 34%.[8]

Moreover, such increases occurred amidst augmented annual output "at home" of these same products. E.g., US oil production internally between 1940 and 1962 rose from 1,355 million barrels to 2,676 million; while, from exporting 8 million barrels in 1940, the US position changed by 1962 to one whereby she had to import 409 million. For iron ore: the US supplied 97% of its own needs in 1940; but only 68% in 1962. The story for other powers is similar.

A US government Commission in 1952 issued a report which dramatically confirmed this greater dependence by advanced industrial countries on outside sources for raw materials:

> ". . . at the turn of the century, the US produced on the whole some 15 percent more of these raw materials ("other than food and gold") than was domestically consumed; this surplus had by 1950 turned into a deficit, with US industry consuming 10 percent more than domestic production; extending the trends to 1975 showed that by then the over all deficit of raw materials for industry will be about 20 percent."[9]

And where did their imports come from? In 1962 alone, these same six key powers bought more than 240 million tons of petroleum from Asia, Africa and Latin America. In that year, the United States alone "raked in profits of $1,477 million from oil investments" in those continents.

With imperialism, then, depending not less but more than ever on imported raw materials, underlining its continuing need for colonialism, the intensest rivalries arise within the system. These do not, however, always prevent the rivals from reaching "friendly agreement" as part of their struggles for control.

One eminent authority noted how such agreements operate:

> "American and European companies connected with world's most powerful banking and financial institutions are . . . entering upon major projects designed to exploit new sources of primary products . . . In the main . . . confining themselves to the production of materials in their basic or secondary stages."[10]

Here is one good reason why Africa and other colonial areas failed to develop industrially: raw materials they should have been able to use for such a purpose were constantly being exported to metropolitan centers, a trend which

> "has gained tremendous momentum in recent years, following the invention and introduction of new processes and techniques that have quickened the output of both ferrous and non-ferrous metal industries in Europe and America."[10]

In particular,

> "Before the last war most of the Western world's iron and steel output was based upon local raw materials. The postwar years, particularly since 1956, have seen an opposite trend. Something like a quarter of the raw materials (90 million tons out of 400 million) used in the world's metallurgical industries have been imported."[11]

While methods of control create an international bourgeoisie through ensuring the hegemony of one of its sections, hegemony in turn rends the unity by intensifying inner contradictions. An example is the European Common Market. A great deal has been written about it in Marxist publications proving that, while several national capitalisms do come together, they only appear to coalesce: inner rivalries among them become aggravated in "association" with one another.

Former Ghana President Kwame Nkrumah called the Common Market "collective imperialism" and described it as

> "the dumping ground of international investment dominated by the giant American banking concerns and their British satellites."[12]

Finally, a lucid and rather simple corollary follows on the "complex and formidable problems of under-developed nations":

> "As a matter of fact, the Asian, African and Latin American countries are capable of building up their own industries by relying on their industrious people and their

rich resources. On the other hand, the imperialist countries will find it impossible to get on without the raw materials from Asia, Africa and Latin America."[13]

The very development of technology inside imperialist citadels has broken down such remaining self-sufficiency as they once could boast, and has hastened internationalization (while at the same time, as stated before in these pages many times, intensifying internal conflict).

In a word, in this epoch, the imperialist ruling class has escalated, along with its system, into a more-and-more international phenomenon through the development of huge, worldwide, boundary-scorning consortia which tend to control natural resources, world finance, the supply of labor power, etc.

At the same time, this very internationalization intensifies inner rivalries among national centers throughout the imperialist world. And, while increasing internationalization prepares the economic groundwork for world socialism, increasing inner contradictions perform the same service in another way: by objectively weakening the whole system.

13. Imperialist Parasitism and Economic Analysis on the Left

By now, it should be plain how well Lenin's summary of imperialist parasitism' has held up over the years.

Capitalism remains

> "a world system of colonial oppression and of the financial strangulation of the overwhelming majority of the population of the world by a handful of 'advanced' countries." (See Chapter 3, pages 45-47 for full quote.)

Today, it still finds underlying economic sustenance from modern forms of activities replacing "capital export," expressed in "overseas" financial activities, chief of which is "unequal exchange", emanating from metropolitan centers, yielding, in the form of enormous super-profits, an income still superior to that from trade.

Despite the clarity and unequivocal nature of Lenin's ideas, many Marxists have consistently fallen short of understanding the imperialist economy. Forgetting parasitism, they insist to the present on dissecting the "advanced" or Western portion alone. (For a refreshing exception, see Professor Andre Gunder Frank, "The Development of Underdevelopment", MONTHLY REVIEW, September 1966.)

A classic example, reprinted in Accra[1], offered a study of "the chief characteristics of the process of leap-like cycles: boom crisis-recovery" by which "the capitalist economy develops". Covering the year 1963, it reached the conclusion that:

". . . no capitalist country has regained the high rate (of development) of previous years.

"An analysis of general trends suggests that this year, 1964, will bring further deceleration."

Far from proving this point, the article really, if back-handedly, showed imperialist economies continuing to develop. It "merely" missed the reason why.

It revealed: capitalism's "leap-like cycles" going merrily on ward, even if their rate may be uneven in time and place; in imperialist nations in 1963: (a) consumer demand increasing (meaning that Western workers had more money to spend on goods than in 1962, though not as much more as in 1962 over 1961); (b) government investment increased; (c) low levels of private investment were not due to lack of funds, because profits were higher than ever; (d) any sags in the economy were bolstered by producing more cars, expanding credit buying, and increasing state military spending; (e) these increases took place despite four million chronically unemployed and $30-40 million worth of idle plant capacity; (f) exports increased, offsetting lags in engineering, ship-building and steel, with a further increase predicted for 1964; and (g) a tax cut went into effect, though naturally its main benefit went to corporations. (Such measures are perhaps becoming harder to institute; but not, while colonial labour power reservoirs remain, impossible.)

"Increased consumer demand" was "explained" by saying (a) that the rate of increase was less in 1963 than in 1962; and that consumer demand "can hardly be expected" to rise again; (b) "consumer spending continued to grow both in 1962 and 1963, the result of certain rises in wages won by dint of hard struggle". (Undoubtedly wage struggles were a factor; but not all wage struggles result in wage rises, as any worker knows. What was missing: documentation!

From such partial analyses, predictions fall flat, like the perennial prognostication of capitalism's "imminent collapse" which has been emanating from the US Left since the 30s.

Socialist publications like MONTHLY REVIEW still risk specific predictions:

> "... not that the war in Southeast Asia will soon end but that its continued escalation is surely leading American capitalism into a period of frightful crises and catastrophes..."[2]

Obviously, any system rent by enormous and insoluble contradictions must collapse eventually; this is not questioned. The Vietnamese example, furthermore, undoubtedly brings such an eventuality closer. But what will happen when such "frightful crises and catastrophes" strike? It is important to know because that period is actually under way as these words are written: France is convulsed; new violence is spreading through the US , England, Spain, Italy, Germany – throughout the capitalist world. Is the system, at last, about to collapse?

Marxists in many places are implying – and saying – as much. But facts in these pages suggest a possibly different outcome: stepped-up super-exploitation of subjugated peoples – that built-in mechanism by which the system, as in Lenin's day, is able to weather even "frightful crises and catastrophes". This ability is reinforced by the ideological vacuum in Western proletarian politics. And military coups in Africa, Indonesia and elsewhere, were preparing precisely against anticipated "frightful crises and catastrophes."

Unless there is a noticeable change in the parasitic aspect of Western life, what may be expected is for "upheavals" to continue, followed by noticeable deterioration in the conditions of the "overseas" population. The French example shows that the false Left is entrenched and well able to ensure that "its" clients are not made to bear the brunt of a deteriorating system – as yet.

For that reason, the collapse of the system need not, unfortunately, be expected at this time. Facts in this text witness the continued well-being of millions and millions of real human beings living in the capitalist economy. (See especially Section C of this text on the labor aristocracy.) Pretending facts are anything but what they are does not solve a situation in the least. In particular, equating exploitation with poverty constitutes only a partial explanation; and, in this case, part of something is worse than nothing.

Of course, those who keep predicting imminent collapse maintain that they are basing themselves on Lenin. For example, dealing with "the ideological currents of revisionism", one such forecaster had in April 1908 included under "political economy" its theories about crises and about cartels and trusts: that "crises had now become rarer and of less force", and that cartels and trusts would "probably enable capitalism to do away with them altogether" by "organizing" production internationally.

With scorn, Lenin replied:

> "The forms, the sequence, the picture of the particular crises changed, but crises remain an inevitable component of the capitalist system. While uniting production, the cartels and trusts at the same time . . . aggravated the anarchy of production, the insecurity of existence of the proletariat and the oppression of capital, thus intensifying class antagonisms to an unprecedented

> degree. That capitalism is moving toward collapse . . . has been made very clear, and on a very large scale, precisely by the new giant trusts."[3]

But the Lenin who spoke these words also wrote at length about parasitism. That is the context in which his above remarks are to be viewed, and always with the facts of each epoch clearly before the mind's eye.

Lenin always spoke of capitalism as an international system, and others have since described it as a hierarchy with one or a few metropoles at its peak, unable to exist without colonies in turn completely dependent on the center. In between are "various and varying degrees of super ordination".

Karl Marx, too, had been aware of this condition, as witness his picture of the world division of labor between industrialized centers and agricultural hinterlands, and of colonial robbery as the source of primitive accumulation.

But Marx did not live to finish his own work. And, according to some authorities, in what he had set down until his death he did not stress colonial robbery sufficiently. This allegation gave rise to

> "what appears to be a widespread impression that Marx considered the international character of the capitalist system to be of secondary significance. This could not be said of Lenin, of course."[4]

Nonetheless, when Lenin was writing and

> "even today, there are many Marxists who seem to think of capitalism as merely a collection of national capitalisms instead of seeing that the international character of

imperialism has always had a decisive effect on the nature and functioning of the national units which compose it."[4]

In the previous pages, we have attempted to counter the former views by showing that, as long as the internal workings of the industrialized portions of imperialism are studied in isolation; as long as "under-developed" nations are treated as independent "poor cousins" of the same sort; as long as figures do not show how metropolitan economic success continues at the expense of "the world's under-developed", just so long will Western prosperity appear as a "virtue" of international imperialism instead of its main "vice"; just so long will Social Democracy be able to "take credit" for the phenomenon; and just so long will the Left continue to "talk it away" with false predictions and unintelligible editorial comment attached to "analyses".

Articles like the one we have analyzed above[1] support Social Democratic and bourgeois economists' boasts about "their" system. Such thinking explains why Marxists so far have been unable to develop among the Western masses any countervailing ideology.

Just how big is the value of all the resources drained from subjugated soils? How much super-profit is wrung from Asian, African and Latin American sweat, blood and tears? What is the overall size of metropolitan monopoly returns on its modern financial activities "abroad"? What role, these days, does "foreign aid" play in bolstering super-profits? How much wages are not paid because of super-exploitation? How can world prosperity be achieved without super-exploitation?

These and similar questions, answered by Marxists, would fully expose before all peoples not only how parasitic the system is, but how that parasitism works; and what, therefore, can be done to end a system that parasitism sustains.

In such answers, Western workers would have available a comprehensible key to the way out of their coming predicament. Meanwhile, they will continue to follow "their" ruling class and its agents — and colonial misery will continue to deepen.

The political significance of a documented approach is this: that, in the absence of documentation a large segment of the Left can 'write off' colonial liberation as "national bourgeois revolution", of little account to the world revolutionary movement. For that reason, such a segment of the Left can continue to insist that "leadership" for the world revolution is to come from "the working class in the main capitalist countries". Social Democrats have been saying that since 1914 and before.

Naturally, today's events are evoking new suggestions of possible "US financial failure" in the foreseeable future. But before these are accepted, it is instructive to glance, for instance, at the relation between US short-term obligations to foreigners, its gold reserve, and its longer-term foreign investment. Only quite recently, the picture that emerged was presented thus:

> "Here are the latest figures as reported in the SURVEY OF CURRENT BUSINESS of September 1966 (Table 14). They relate to 1965. 'Short-term assets and US Government obligations' held by foreigners (... Dollar holdings) amounted to $32.5 billion. At the same time the United States gold stock was $13, 8 billion, or only 42 percent of dollar claims which could be presented for payment on short notice. It is this gap which is usually pointed to with alarm by those who fear for the safety of the dollar.

> "However, the picture looks rather different if we add that United States long-term private foreign investments amounted to $70.8 billion and United States government credits and claims on foreigners to $25.1 billion. If we

add up the assets (gold + private long-term investments + government credits and claims = $109.7 billion) and subtract the short-term liabilities ($32.5 billion), we see that the United States 'bank' had a safety margin of $77.2 billion, which amounts to no less than 238 percent of the foreign dollar holdings."[5]

This "safety margin" – the "flower" of the system's parasitism and its conditional insurance of continued life despite History's death sentence – is hardly ever mentioned on the Left, although it is a "magic cushion" which protects a tottering economy on the buoyancy of colonial misery. Here in brutal nakedness is the source of the "recovery" aspect of imperialism's "leap-like cycles."

To Lenin's statement that crises can never be eliminated under capitalism, we can add that the same is true of imperialism. Metropoles are seen to suffer more and more frequent "recessions," but those who watch such areas of the imperialist economy alone miss the fact that systematic crises are absorbed internationally through constantly deteriorating conditions in the "hinterlands." (This statement is not denying subsidiary factors and/or methods which may be, and have been, used to stimulate "recovery." I do, however, believe that any or all of them are traceable (given the facts) directly or indirectly to primary super-exploitation.) Imperialism can hold out exactly as long as it has "under-developed" peoples to super-exploit, whatever the form of that activity in our epoch or in the future.

14. Class Collaboration and Fascism

The post-World War II absorption of economic shock by the hinterlands has perhaps been obscured by the role of Fascism in the 30s as the first ruling class "solution" to the general crisis of its system.

In that development, the inner content of class collaboration between the imperialist bourgeoisie and "its" labor aristocracy represented by Social Democracy became clear: when Social Democracy helped Fascism to power, the resulting unholy wedlock concentratedly expressed the growing supremacy of parasitism as the engine of a rotting world economic system.

That engine exploded noisily in the faces of its makers, forcing into being the broad if temporary World War II United Front led by the bourgeoisies of the "great democracies" under American domination. Only in such a way were its creators finally able to achieve Fascism's complete military defeat in 1945.

What, however, has become of Fascism since that time?

As defined by Georgi Dimitroff at the Sixth World Congress of the Comintern in 1928, Fascism Is the

> "open terrorist dictatorship of the most rabid, most chauvinist and most imperialist sections of finance capital."[1]

Dimitroff had been concerned with national finance capitalisms and their national dictatorships. Italy, Germany, Austria and others had provided horrible living examples.

Today, however, his definition might suggest that Fascism is not in power anywhere in the West. Nowhere, there, are visible anything like its Nazi and Italian forms, its scope, nor any like intensity.

Has Fascism, then, become "more acceptable"? Or has it ceased to exist? If not, where and what is it?

During the days when the Allies' 1945 military victory was still in the future, it was not at all clear where the coming victory would lead. Today, however, many trends of that time take on new meaning once imperialism is viewed internationally.

Inside the US, until campaigning for the 1964 elections began, there had for a fairly long period been no necessity to police the people because the majority had usually more or less policed themselves. The Pentagon-White House dictatorship had found that it could achieve "satisfactory" results merely by intimidating the small revolutionary sector of the American community, and its periphery.

During the 1964 election campaign itself, however, a tocsin cry from the Left had hysterically prophesied that, in the outlandish figure of Barry Morris Goldwater, an imminent danger of Fascist take-over was threatening internally. His antics, perfect counterpoint to such ululations, had decoyed one of the largest mass votes in American history into the lap of the reigning elite so ably represented by Lyndon Baines Johnson of racist Texas. In 1968, the "Left" refrained from such discredited tactics. Richard Nixon was "elected".

Was the US Left in 1964 or 1968 correct? Do elections really relate to the danger of Fascism inside the US? Only in parts of the South, like Mississippi, does there appear to be open, recognizeable Fascism.

Although the usual rabid reactionaries in Congress have been periodically sniffing at the anti-Vietnam war movement and at anti-draft and Black Power exponents, their internal assault on "democracy" has not yet attained Nazis proportions. More and more frequently, their victims are "expendable" minority blacks and a few white "recalcitrants".

But Vietnamese resistance continued to snowball up to 1968. In its wake, anti-Establishment activities inside the US also mounted. In the stunned aftermath of the 1968 Tet offensive, US top brass began intensive preparations for open terrorist methods "at home". But international Social Democracy succeeded in forcing the Paris "talks." The end result is yet to come.

Outside the US, from 1945 till now. Fascist dictatorship has clearly been operating on the modern scene: in Spain, in Portugal, in South Korea, South Vietnam, Indonesia, Congo Kinshasa, Brazil.

But can any of these dictatorships truly be described as Mississippi Fascism, Portuguese Fascism, Korean, Vietnamese, Congolese, Indonesian, Brazilian? Only in a limited and formal sense.

Surely it is obvious wherever American finance capital has swallowed colonial "bracers" – territorial or economic – that, even though local puppets make the motions, dictatorship itself is exercised under guidance from Washington by an international ruling class. American – representing world – capitalism's "open terroristic dictatorship" has escalated from Wall Street into colonial hinterlands. There was more than a grain of truth to Ghana's ex-President Kwame Nkrumah's epithet, "Fascist imperialism", used in the Fall of 1964 to describe the most important section of world finance capital.[2] It highlights the historic connection between Fascism and colonialism.

Early manifestations of that connection became visible through terrorism in the West:

When Marxists in 1935 had said – as had Lenin in 1916 – that Social Democracy was "the principal bulwark of the "bourgeoisie" they were not echoing enough of Lenin's thought. By overlooking the decisive nature of imperialist parasitism, they missed the main purpose for which Social Democracy practices class collaboration: if it does act to prevent revolution "at home", that is a by-product of its real function of maintaining the flow of super-profits. These must derive first and foremost from colonies; but, failing that, from whatever source is available.

Because through the 30s metropolitan workers had become temporarily militant under the impact of the great depression, Social Democracy appealed to them from behind a Marxian facade. But that facade became dangerous in countries, like Germany and Italy, which had happened to be deprived of colonies; workers there began taking Marx seriously. In those places, super-profits from the usual sources to keep the ruling classes in power had been cut off; now they had to come from a substantial section of the internal working class. When those workers understandably showed reluctance, Social Democracy quite logically gunned them down; quite logically, it aided Fascism to power.

The simultaneous use of Marxian demagogy in victor nations and of brutality in the vanquished is not at all inconsistent or mutually exclusive: if revolution threatens "at home", or if a country has no colonial subjects whose labour power, super-exploited, can cushion the metropolis from economic shock, then Social Democracy has no choice but to turn its cannibalism, the "labour" parasitism of imperialism, inward.

As soon as renewed super-profits from these activities, or from creating new political and/or economic colonies, enable the bourgeoisie through Social Democracy to buy off enough of the local proletariat, it is no longer urgent – in fact, downright embarrassing – to mention Karl Marx again "at home." So, in 1959, a number of European members of the Second International, including West Germany, deliberately eliminated all references to the author of The Communist Manifesto from their constitutions and other literature, and removed from their programs any mention of socialism. European Social Democracy could now re-emerge into "harmonious" class collaboration: West German "labour lieutenants" soon began to mingle at managerial levels with the "captains" of industry, advising or forcing their own members into concessions on elementary trade union conditions.[3] They do so, of course, "in labour's interests".

Today, the connection between Fascism and colonialism is more concealed, because imperialism has learned to protect its own rear: even Germany and Japan, the defeated enemy of two short decades ago, are being permitted subrosa but substantial access to colonial outlets for their surplus investment capital. (Specific examples and elaboration of the point will be found in Chapter 5, above)

But the connection, nonetheless, remains – and tightens. Imperialism must deal with any upheavals, "at home" or "abroad," if it can. And so far, in one way or another, all major powers have been able to renew and/or retain that stream of superprofits on which their system depends: they still completely control the world market – and prices. In turn, they have been able to continue to "their own" workers their "rewards" which put off the need to turn inward their "open terrorist dictatorship" as used in the 30s.

Social Democratic use of brutality as class collaboration is accepted by "its own" workers to prevent revolution only when that revolution is colonial. This is proven by the record of Social

Democratic governments in office. (See Chapters 7 and 8 above.) And as long as there are SUCH revolutions to prevent, Social Democracy had, and has, no worries about any "at home." For at least that long, the labor aristocracy continues its time-honoured support for "liberal" candidates who can carry on colonialist or neo-colonialist policies with a smile behind the whip.

At this point, the tie between colonialism and Social Democracy comes into play, revealing parasitism as currently the decisive factor within the imperialist system.

The fact that so many colonial or semi-colonial peoples after World War II had begun trying to opt out as sources of super profits constituted the latest and by far most serious threat to continued operation of the whole imperialist system. The specific example of Vietnam reveals the frenzy with which US "Fascist imperialism" therefore defends its life. (It also, of course, shows the growing strength of popular forces.)

Because the mounting struggle for colonial liberation has thus become the focal point of world struggle, NEW forms of Social Democracy had to be found. Now it must act in colonies, but remain based on the metropolis. The "solution" was simple, and best expressed in this: Marxist verbiage, now de trop "at home", was packed up and moved. Social Democracy busily launched various "national socialisms" for colonial consumption. In so doing, it was merely trying to herd colonial peoples into its own service? (Here is why today the only mass manifestations of Social Democracy per se occur in industrialized areas where colonial subjects are still far away (e.g. Sweden): Marxian verbiage in Social Democratic hands "at home" might be dangerous, even in trying to delude the "unruly." To deal with them, imperialism uses other demagogues.)

But because material conditions in colonial territories provide no mass base for such "local socialisms," (All "local socialisms" will be shown to be exported European Social Democracy. Naturally, in order to be introduced at all, even exported European Social Democracy must – and does – find local exponents. Who these are and what their identity means will be explained in Chapters 16 and 17 on "Imperialist Bribery".) Arab, Asian, African and other such types were soon to splinter even further into Malaysian, Malagasy, Neo-Destourian and others.

Yet, they are not to be lightly laughed off: their effect on liberation movements in such places has been serious. European Social Democracy has achieved historically transient successes – at least a pause, a momentary change in direction, even political chaos for a time – in Asia, the Arab world, Africa and so on. And these continue to crop up.

Maybe some defeats are inevitable. But surely – not all!

Accompanying Social Democracy's shift of Marxist demagogy into subjugated areas, anti-communism became more and more prominent in the West, invariably in association with colossal military build-ups traceable to "capitalist hostility to the existence of rival world socialist system:"

> "Capitalist governments do not, in general, trade with each other. Most trade in the capitalist world is carried on by private enterprises, mainly by large corporations. What these corporations are interested in is not trade as such but profits: the reason they and the governments they control are opposed to the spread of socialism is not that it necessarily reduces their chances of importing or exporting (though of course it may), but that it does

necessarily reduce their opportunities to profit from doing business with and in the newly socialized area."3

The fear of real communism today, though concentrated on colonial areas because of their prospective loss since World War II, is still expressed in the West by stark naked anti-Communism.

Thus, Social Democracy's transfer of its revolutionary jargon to colonial places and its anti-communism "at home" must be seen as expressions of a single process to which there are two faces. (A more detailed discussion of anti-communism as related to Racism and Social Democracy is found in Chapter 38, below.)

By participating in that process, Social Democracy once again uncovers its own continued link with modern Fascism of which the hallmark is always anti-communism. Time has altered the form, but not the content, of the historical inter-relations between Fascism and colonialism, Social Democracy and colonialism; and, thus, between Fascism and Social Democracy today.

Labor Aristocracy

Section C

The Western Left and Social Democracy

Labor Aristocracy

15. Imperialist Parasitism and the Western Working Classes

Perhaps the most significant and deep-going – and also little investigated – of the aspects of imperialist parasitism described by Lenin has been that one whereby, out of super-profits, capitalism bribes "the labour leaders and upper stratum" of Western workers "in a thousand different ways, direct and indirect, overt and covert."

This activity, manifesting itself in a variety of forms, has an extremely serious effect on the working class because

> "those strata of the working class who are being BRIBED out of imperialist super-profits and converted into WATCH-DOGS of capitalism, into CORRUPTORS of the labour movement . . . are ALIEN to the proletariat as a class . . . Are the servants, the agents, the conduits of the influence of the bourgeoisie . . . of whom the labour movement must RID itself if it does not want to remain a BOURGEOIS LABOUR MOVEMENT."[1]

At the time when Lenin wrote these words, he was able to describe those "servants . . . of the bourgeoisie" as "a tiny minority" of the working class in industrialized nations. The year was 1916. Since then, the parasitism which gave rise to such "servants" did not die out or shrink. On the contrary, we have seen how it expanded as the imperialist system decayed.

Moreover, this "working-class aspect" of parasitism has specific material bases which can be investigated in detail to ascertain whether "the labour movement" did, in fact, "RID itself of those WATCHDOGS of capitalism," as Lenin urged; or if it has, instead, remained a "BOURGEOIS LABOUR MOVEMENT."

It is not, as we shall see, without significance that the Western Left has never made this investigation, but has contented itself with mouthing Lenin's 1916 phrases.

What material bases, then, did Lenin offer as means of examining the bribed sections of the metropolitan working class?

One of them is suggested by the following of his words:

> "the percentage of productively total population is declining."2

Lenin proved this assertion for his time. Is it still true? A sampling of nine basic industries in the U.S., comparing 1950 and 1960, can be tabulated:

Table 5[3]

RELATIONSHIP OF
PRODUCTIVELY EMPLOYED U. S. POPULATION TO TOTAL
(In Thousands)

INDUSTRY	Number Employed 1950	Number Employed 1960
Mining	532*	519
Industrial Chemicals, Organic & Inorganic	226	278
Petroleum Products	66*	67
Primary Metals	1,036	957
Metal Products	323	337
Non-Electrical Machinery	1,043	1,137
Electrical Machinery	670	865
Transport Equipment	1,036	1,160
Industrial Instruments	35	36
TOTALS	4,967	5,356
Total Population	150,697	178,464
PERCENTAGE	3.3	3.0

*1959 figures

These figures clearly confirm Lenin's point. Yet they furnish only one small glimpse of this aspect of the effects of imperialist parasitism on the working class. There are others.

For example, one study of the U.S. economy, scrutinizing "The Sales Effort", and its non-productive role in the capitalist system as a whole, shows that

> "From being a relatively unimportant feature of the system, (the sales effort) has advanced to the status of one of its decisive nerve centers. In its impact on the economy, it is outranked only by militarism."[4]

Furthermore, the system's successful campaign to create new demands as stimulus to a flagging economy not only increases the economy's number of "drones," but invades production itself. For instance, in the automotive industry, "costs of production" are inflated by non-essential expenses arising from the need to change models, create premature or planned obsolescence, etc., with the significant result that

> "by far the greater part of the sales effort is carried out not by obviously unproductive workers such as salesmen and advertising copy writers but by seemingly productive workers: tool and die makers, draftsmen, mechanics, assembly line workers."[5]

Another cause of the increase in percentage of non-productive workers to total is found in the inroads of automation on large basic industry:

> "At General Electric, less than half of the total employees are now on regular hourly wage scales (i. e., in direct production - H.W.E.). Thus, the blue-collar worker is falling more and more out of style. The white-collar worker . . . is the man of the moment."[6]

Similar considerations apply to the American working class as a whole.

But what IS "the American working class"? How large a sector of population is it?

In Marxists terms, there is a double answer: (a) the "industrial proletariat," or value-producers, off whose labour the entire U.S. society lives in part; and (b) the broader "working class" comprising both the industrial proletariat and all others who, while not producing values, have nothing to sell but their labour - power. Category (b) encompasses sales personnel, clerical workers, private household workers, and so on, who constitute that "non-productive sector" which increases as a percentage of total population. The working class must also include unemployed, who have labour power to sell but cannot sell it.

In our count, we have also included the armed forces because, class-wise, they are overwhelmingly working people, with Afro-Americans composing a segment disproportionately larger then their ratio to total population. While, objectively, the armed forces are the very backbone of the bourgeois – i.e., oppressive – state, nonetheless, the working-class background of the individuals who compose them does come into play at crucial times, as evidenced in the current war by the desertion of the "South Vietnamese" soldiers to the "Vietcong." Moreover, soldiers are far from the only category to whom the ruling class pays wages to do jobs that harm the working class by sustaining the hostile state. Sheriffs, police, prison wardens are among others.

In defining a class, the sole criterion is relationship to the means of production. Ideology and/or size of income seriously affect a class; but they can NOT define it.

Some people say, "A man making £50,000 a year can't be a member of the working class." In the first place, such people are – in their type – numerically insignificant. But the point of their existence is the fact that there are a few such individuals to illumine the meaning and irony of imperialist parasitism.

Social Democrats, especially, try to use "size of income" defining classes: after a worker's income passes a certain arbitrary (but elastic) level, he is said to have entered "the middle class."

The scholar C. Wright Mills provides an excellent example of such an approach:

> "Class situation' in its simplest objective sense has to do with amount and source of income …

> "In terms of property, the white collar people are NOT 'in between Capital and Labor'; they are exactly in the same property-class positions as the wage workers. They have no direct financial tie to the means of production, no prime claim upon the proceeds from property. Like factory workers – and day laborers, for that matter – they work for those who do own such means of livelihood.

> "Yet if bookkeepers and coal miners, insurance agents and farm laborers, doctors in a clinic and crane operators in an open pit have this condition in common, certainly their class situations are not the same. To understand their class positions, we must go beyond the common source of income and consider as well the amount of income."[7]

Such ideas can arise only from the prevalent loose, indeed often emotional, misusage of Marx's scientific category "class". This leads precisely to the structure in the following type of distortions in the U.S. Class structure in the following table:

Table 6[8]

THE MIDDLE CLASSES	% 1870	% 1940
Old Middle Class	<u>85</u>	<u>44</u>
Farmers	62	23
Businessmen	21	19
Free Professionals	2	2
New Middle Class	<u>15</u>	<u>56</u>
Managers	2	6
Salaried Professionals	4	14
Sales People	7	14
Office Workers	2	22

Elsewhere, Mills himself throws more light on the subject of his own "middle class" categories: "Free practitioners", he tells us – that is, people working for themselves – were in 1940 about 1% of total labour force and a fairly constant 2% of (what Mills dubs) the "middle class". Over the last 60 years, salaried professionals expanded from 1% to 6% of total labour force; from 4% to 14% of the "middle class". Even in 1870, only about 35% of all professionals were "free." By 1940, this had decreased to 16%, within a context where 31% of all professional people were school teachers. Among independent practitioners, the greatest proportion – 80 - 90% – is among physicians, surgeons, osteopaths and dentist. Among pharmacists, only 46% are in the "independent" category; among nurses, only 8%.[8a]

So, for Social Democracy, liberals and the bourgeoisie, the middle class does not, as Marx claimed and as life bears out, constantly shrink; it expands. For them, instead of more and more people being driven out of the middle, and even upper, classes into the working class, the reverse is happening. How convenient!

For, by such an approach, the significance of imperialist parasitism vanishes: that incomes of sizes actually found in imperialist citadels can exist among people classifiable as "working class" constitutes precisely Lenin's point. Nothing better expresses the development of a major inner contradiction in the international working class – one that must be dealt with (it cannot be solved under imperialism) before revolutionaries in industrialized areas can clear a path forward. (We shall show that their class situation for productive and non-productive workers IS the same, but what income level alters is their "mode of life" and – especially their "entire outlook." (See Chapter 20, Below.))

Thoughts along similar lines were expressed by Guyana's People's Progressive Party writer, Ranji Chandisingh:

> "Widely current in bourgeois sociology is the theory that the main classes in capitalist society – the capitalist class (bourgeoisie) and the working class (proletariat) – are . . . being swallowed up by the so-called middle class . . .

> "According to the fashionable bourgeois theoreticians, the working class are those who are unskilled, manual workers, with low standards of education and culture . . . So . . . highly skilled workers, technologically trained workers, are no longer members of the working class!

> "We are indeed witnessing a scientific and technological revolution, and this calls forth qualitative changes in the working class . . . . as the scientific and technological revolution proceeds, the unskilled, manual worker is being superseded by the highly skilled, technologically advanced worker . . . proportional changes are taking place between different categories of workers – e.g., as between productive industry and the service sectors, and between different branches of industry itself."[9]

Ignoring terminology, the same information is conveyed in the following table drawn up, again, by American sociologist C. Wright Mills:

Table 7[10]

THE U.S. LABOR FORCE	% 1870	% 1940
Old Middle Class	33	20
New Middle Class	6	25
Wage-Workers	61	55
	100	100

The "old middle class" is the only middle class by Marxist definition; it, in truth, is shrinking. But the "new middle class" has to be added to wage-workers in order to retain scientific categories. And when this is done, what it reveals is that the working class as a whole continues to expand, but its composition alters.

What all this boils down to, Mills himself ironically but succinctly summed up: that

> "fewer men turn out more things in less time. In the middle of the nineteenth century . . . some 17.6 billion horse power hours were expended in American industry, only 6% by mechanical energy; by the middle of the twentieth century, 410.4 billion horsepower hours will be expended, 94% by mechanical energy . . . Technology has thus narrowed the stratum of workers needed in the production process . . . Workers composing the new lower class are predominantly semi-skilled; their proportion in the urban wage-worker stratum has risen from 31% in 1910 to 41% in 1940."[11]

It is within such boundaries that our own Table 8 — which follows — has been compiled. Sources for the figures, together with exact categories of workers included in each major classification, will be found in the 1966 U.S. Statistical Abstract. We have included as working class all who hire out either their brain or their brawn for wages or salaries. Although no method of identifying or separating such categories was found, if it had been possible we would have removed from our table any person earning more than 25% of his income from any form of ownership of the social means of production.(As noted in Chapter 12, above, the United States

Table 8[*]

THE WORKING CLASSES IN THE UNITED STATES

O C C U P A T I O N	1950	1960
	(In Thousands)	
Craftsmen, foremen and kindred workers	8,205	9,241
Operatives and kindred workers	11,150	12,143
Service workers (cooks)	272	326
·Farm laborers and foremen	2,533	1,560
Laborers, except farm and mine	3,644	3,408
A. U.S. PROLETARIAT (Value-Producers)	25,804	26,678
Professional, technical and kindred workers	4,412	6,680
Officials & inspectors, state & local admin.	113	136
Clerical and kindred workers	7,132	9,617
Sales workers	3,606	4,236
Private household workers, living in or out	1,492	1,825
Service workers (except private household)	4,986	6,265
Occupations not reported	1,370	3,453
B. LABOR-POWER SELLERS NOT PRODUCING VALUES	23,111	32,212
C. = A + B: CIVILIAN WORKING CLASS WITH JOBS	48,915	58,890
D. OFFICIAL NUMBER OF UNEMPLOYED	3,351	3,931
E. NUMBER IN ARMED FORCES	1,650	2,514
F. = C + D: CIVILIAN WORKING CLASS	52,266	62,821
G. = E + F: TOTAL U.S. WORKING CLASS	53,916	65,335
H. Total "U.S. Civilian Labor Force"	63,099	70,612
I. Total "U.S. Labor Force"	64,749	73,126
J. U.S. Non-Institutional Popul'n over 14 yrs. old	110,929	125,368

Department of Commerce considers a "U.S. enterprise" one in which U.S. funds constitute 25% or more of the investment. That is why we have used 25% as the break-even point for participation in the ruling class.) This, however, would have been because his relationship of the means of production had changed, not because of the size of income paid to him.

It will be noted that category H, U.S.-Designated "Total Civilian Labour Force", differs from our category, "Civilian Working Class", F, by 10,833,000 in 1950 and by 7,791,000 in 1960. Without accounting for this difference numerically, we can still point to a number of its sources.

First, there is the difference between the Marxist definition of a "worker" and that of the U. S. for an "employed person":

> "Employed persons include those who did any work for pay or profit during the week, worked without pay for 15 hours or more in a family enterprise (farm or business), or did not work or look for work but had a job or business, from which they were temporarily absent during the week."[12]

It was to eliminate those working for profit or owning a business that such "employed persons" appearing in H. were removed from category F.

Second, the U.S. definition of "an unemployed person" accounts for more of the noted difference:

> "Unemployed persons comprise those who did not work at all during the week but were looking for work or were on lay-off from a job."[13]

This definition enables statistician apologists for the status quo to keep official unemployment figures low:

"Between 1960 and 1963, there took place a one percent decline in the labour force participation rate, which means that some 1.3 million workers dropped out of the labour force in addition to the normal losses through death and retirement."[14]

Between 1950 and 1960, this decline was slower: only 65%.[15] Nevertheless, it accounted for some 815,000 drop-outs of the type cited. These were people not "looking for work"; therefore, in official U.S. statistics, they were not "unemployed".

A third source of discrepancies lies in the fact that the U.S. adopted new definitions of employment and unemployment in January 1957, thereby affecting earlier figures. Some statistics in the source material had been revised by the compilers, but not all.

The rest can be traced to normal population changes.

In order to examine more fully the meaning of Table 8, another was compiled showing trends; the abbreviation "W.C." stands, of course, for "Working Class". The figures in G. were used as the totals, measuring percentages of the other categories A, B, C, and F (which are the same as those in Table 8). Item J is the "total non-institutional U.S. population 14 years of age or over" in the years studied. [16]

Table 9

TRENDS IN THE U. S. WORKING CLASS

Table 8 Category	1950			1960			CHANGE		
	Thousands	% to Total Popul.	W.C.	Thousands	% to Total Popul.	W.C.	Thousands	% to Total Popul.	W.C.
A.	25,804	23.3	47.9	26,678	21.3	40.9	+ 874	− 2.0	− 7.0
B.	23,111	20.8	42.9	32,212	25.7	49.3	+ 9,101	+ 4.9	+ 6.4
C.	48,915	44.1	90.7	58,890	47.0	90.1	+ 9,975	+ 2.0	− 0.6
F.	52,266	47.1	97.0	62,821	50.1	96.1	+ 10,555	+ 3.0	− 0.9
G.	53,916	48.6	100.0	65,335	52.1	100.0	+ 11,419	+ 3.5	
J.	110,929			125,368			+ 14,439	+13.0	

While absolute numbers of value-producers and other segments of the American working class all rose between 1950 and 1960 (due mainly to the large rise in total population), the percentage of value-producers shrank (which generalizes the findings of Table 5 on Page 144, above). By 1966, incidentally, this percentage had been still further reduced:

> "only 15% of the U.S. Population . . . produce all the food and goods that the whole nation could reasonably need."[17]

(This ignores any difference between the source of the quotation and ourselves as to who constitute "producers".)

The above Table 9 also shows a shrinking percentage relationship to total population of "Civilian Working Class with Jobs" (C) and of "Total Civilian Working Class" (F). This is due to first, arise in numbers of unemployed; and second, drop-outs from the labor market.

According to Marxists, two effects of the decay of the capitalist system are: the more rapid pace at which the non-productive sector of the working class increases compared to the increase in the productive sector; and the overall increase in the size of the working class itself. Tables 8 and 9 bear these out conclusively.

The American working class comprises at least two-thirds of total population. Now (a) the percentage of poor families is greater among the working class than among total population;[18] and (b) poor families tend to be larger than average.[18] Therefore, it seems fairly safe to conclude that the American working class as a whole now includes three of every four Americans.

This, then, is the proportion in the world's richest country of population of which one speaks in saying "the working class". We have not as yet even considered the size of their earnings or their ideology, although this will be done shortly. At that time, the significance of the real material conditions among this overwhelming majority of the American people will become clear.

16. The Anatomy of Imperialist Bribery

The increase in working class size, with its accompanying change of composition in a non-productive direction, is part of the process which creates a labor aristocracy.

If the latter is, as Lenin said, that portion of the working class which is bribed by a share in super-profits, then it includes not only labor leaders, but all workers who are given an extra material stake in the status quo. Labor leaders are the articulate and usually conscious spokesmen for alleged labor interests in the world's metropolitan areas. The spread of these interests is very wide, indeed.

Now, if the labor aristocracy is that sector of a revolutionary class which is being bribed, should not revolutionaries be obligated to follow its development? And wouldn't a valuable first step be to study the nature of bribery itself as applied to the modern industrial proletariat?

1. What is bribery? .

Webster defines "Bribery" as "the practice of giving or taking a bribe". The word "Bribe", derives from an Old French word meaning "a lump of bread, scraps, leavings." This noun, in turn, springs from a root verb meaning "to beg". The extended dictionary meaning of the word is:

> "A gift or favor given or promised in order to influence the judgment or conduct of a person in a position of trust."

Noah Webster, of course, was no political oracle. But these meanings do throw a pertinent side-light on imperialist bribery:

it need not involve anything tangible, either in purpose or result; a favor or promise that warps only the judgment of the recipient adequately fulfills the function.

Chapters to come will disclose that a significant section of the U. S. working class enjoys a number of luxuries. As luxuries, they qualify as tangible bribery. Nor is their extent bounded by the money available for working class spending: Consumer credit bears visible fruit; and, beyond that, there is entertainment, education, medical care (with all its faults), etc., all enjoyed by growing numbers of Americans, at least two-thirds of whom are workers by hand or brain. (See Table 8 above.) To this must by added the abnormally cheap staples, such as tea, coffee, sugar, tobacco and others, made possible by paying raw-materials-producing countries far below value for their commodities.

In such ways, a majority of U.S. workers and their families enjoy material values to which other workers in the world only aspire. And those aspirations, motivating people largely ignorant of the source of such values, still obscure the path leading to revolution.

2 . Relationship of imperialist bribery to wages and profits.

Lenin had already more than hinted at the source of imperialist bribery in saying that "out of such enormous SUPER-PROFITS . . . the capitalists of the 'advanced' countries are bribing (the labor leaders and the upper strata of the proletariat) . . ." (See Chapter 3 above.)

Consider, however, the following:

> "Unions most certainly do play an important role in
> the determination of money wages, and the workers
> in more strongly organized industries generally do

> better for themselves than workers in less strongly organized branches of the economy. This does not mean, however, that the working class as a whole is in a position to encroach on surplus ... (Here a footnote informs that unions 'do not in fact have any decisive influence over the class distribution of income (which) is determined by a combination of forces in which ... the corporations play a far more important role than ... the unions.') The reason is that under monopoly capitalism employers can and do pass on higher labor costs in the form of higher prices ...
>
> "And whether or not it is common practice to use wage increases as a pretext to increase profit margins, monopolistic corporations unquestionably have the power to prevent wage increases from lowering them."[1]

(See Table 24 and quotation from NEWSWEEK: inflation was eating away, up to 1965 at any rate, only half of U.S. Wage gains.) The authors seem to be saying that, under monopoly capitalism in its advanced U.S. form, the ruling class is able, by maintaining artificially high prices in commodities, to recoup profit losses due to wage increases.

This idea bears looking into.

Consider, for example, the original position of Karl Marx in discussing competitive capitalism, on the relationship between profits and wages:

> " ... I shall use the word PROFIT for the whole amount of the surplus value extracted by the capitalist without any regard to the division of that surplus value between different parties, and in using the words RATE OF

PROFIT, I shall always measure profits by the value of the capital advanced in wages . . .

"Since the capitalist and workers have only to divide this limited value, that is, the value measured by the total labor of the working man, the more the one gets the less will the other get, and vice versa. . . . If the wages change, profits will change in an opposite direction. If wages fall, profits will rise; and if wages rise, profits will fall... A general rise of wages would ... result in a fall of profits, but not affect the values."2

Elsewhere, Marx put this thought as follows:

"What, then, is the general law which determines the rise and fall of wages and profit in their reciprocal relation?

"They stand in inverse ratio to each other. Capital's share, profit, rises in the same proportion as labor's share, wages, falls, and vice versa. Profits rise to the extent that wages fall; it falls to the extent that wages rise."3

In a word, under competitive capitalism, "the working class as a whole" most definitely IS in a position to encroach on profits, according to Marx. The quotation under consideration (about unions) at least implies that monopoly capitalism as far advanced as the U.S. variety has surmounted Marx's law of the inseparability of wages and profits is concerned.

Is Marx's fundamental law, his Law of Value, then, obsolete? Or are there loopholes in the quotation we are studying?

A second glance at that quotation shows up one glaring anomaly at once: although the words "working class as a whole" are used, what was clearly being referred to was the "whole" working class of the U.S. only. Is this, in the era of world-wide monopoly, meaningful? Lenin gave more than a hint that it was not. And the authors of these words themselves have stressed that capitalism has always been an international system (and any system includes all its component parts):

> "From its earliest beginnings in the Middle Ages, capitalism has always been an international system . . . a hierarchical system with one or more leading metropolises at the top, completely dependent on colonies at the bottom. . . . These features are of crucial importance to the functioning of both the system as a whole and its individual components, though this is a fact the importance of which bourgeois economists have consistently ignored or denied and even Marxists have often under estimated.[4]

In this light, the real "working class as a whole" is not the "whole" working class vis-a-vis the U.S. alone, not even when only the American economy is being discussed .

Therefore, the meaning of monopoly price fixing and its relation to the conditions of "the working class as a whole" must be sought elsewhere.

Again, Karl Marx provided an answer:

> "If the price of a commodity rises considerably because of inadequate supply or disproportionate increase of the demand, the price of some other commodity must necessarily have fallen proportionately, for the price of a commodity only expresses in money the ratio in which other commodities are given in exchange for it ...

> "THE REAL PRICE OF A COMMODITY, IT IS TRUE, IS ALWAYS ABOVE OR BELOW ITS COST

OF PRODUCTION; BUT RISE AND FALL RECIPROCALLY BALANCE EACH OTHER, so that within a certain period of time, taking the ebb and flow of the industry together, commodities are exchanged for one another in accordance with their cost of production, their prices, therefore, being determined by their cost of production."[5]

If monopolies really, via fixed prices, take back from the recipients whatever "their" workers force them to disgorge in wage rises, those workers' conditions would never improve. But the whole world can see, and statistics confirm, that the conditions of American workers, and of those in the West generally, have improved. Although the gains may not have been as large as publicized, they have been real. Workers' understanding of this fact is testified to by their migration into metropolitan centers.

At the same time, monopoly profits have continued to soar. Are the monopolists, therefore, getting something for nothing? Science has long since proved that, in all the universe, there is no such phenomenon.

Not long ago, a then-candidate for a PhD at London School of Economics, David Horowitz (author of The Free World Colossus), reviewed the book from which the quotation under discussion derives. He wrote that

> "The question that presents itself at this point is . . . whether there are any limits to the controlled inflation under which the monopolistic corporations can maximize their profits while maintaining the alliance with organized labor on which so much depends. Such limits do exist but they arise from a factor which is neglected by Baran and Sweezy in their analysis of the rising surplus, namely, INTERNATIONAL competition. For here, PRICE

competition still plays an important role and sets a real barrier to creeping inflation as a harmonizing social mechanism, even in the case of the most powerful of international competitors like the United States."[6]

That is, American monopolies operate in an integral international system. Corporations, then – even during capitalism's non-competitive stage – do not have the power Baran and Sweezy attributed to them to prevent wage increases at home from lowering their profits. Yet, as we have noted, their profits have not been lowered. The explanation lies in the fact that Marx's law of the interdependence of profits and wages, and of prices and values, holds for the system of which American corporations are one component. Fixed prices translate themselves into profits, which in turn represent values obtained from somewhere. Marx (above) showed that all profits are limited by wages – somewhere. Lenin had explained that Western super-wages, wherever they exist, derive "out of super-profits."

If, then, the under-priced values supplying monopolies' steady profits are not in the metropolis, they must reside in the remainder of the integral international system:

In 1959, U.S. Negro per capita annual income was $1,162. So, the 18. 9 million black Americans of that year[6a] would have had a total annual income of $21,281 million. Total U.S. population was 177.1 million. Each enjoyed an annual average $2,166, or total U.S. aggregate income of $383.6 billion.

Of the 177.1 million Americans, 158.2 were white and/or non-Negro (black people were, therefore, 92.1% of non-whites[6b]). So, then, in 1959, each non-Negro American (i.e., all other non-whites plus the whites) had an average annual income of about $2,291. (This, of course, is low compared to "pure white" income: it includes the depressed wages of more than a million and a half people who were both non-white and non-Negro.)

The national difference between Negro and non-Negro income was $1,165 per head. For 18.9 million Afro-Americans, this amounted to $22,019 millions that should have been in black pockets, but was not.

> "Today, the absolute amount of which America's black people are deprived in this way has risen still further: The Government figures that if all Negroes could be brought up to the average white American's level of affluence, employment and education, the U.S. economy's output would climb by $27 billion a year, equal to 4% of the gross national product."[7]

Did all this difference go to white workers?

If the $22,019 million which Afro-Americans lost in 1959 was distributed among whites in the same basis as other income, then 5.0% of all U.S. families that year would have picked up 19.9% of it.[7a] On this basis, the upper crust took a cut for itself of some $4.38 billion, redistributing only the remainder as white wages or other income. With the working class at least two-thirds of population, something over $11.7 billion (unweighted, therefore probably too high) may be suggested as the maximum amount given to U.S. white workers. To the $4.38 billion clear profit for the ruling class must be added an unknown amount in super-rents and super-interest charged to Afro-Americans.

But these profits were "obtained over and above those … squeeze(d) from the workers in their 'own' country" by American rulers and so are really superprofits. The Afro-American community stands revealed as an internal quasi-colony. (Because so many statistics are available, Afro-America can − with qualifications to be noted later − exemplify the general colonial phenomenon of which it is an important part. Also, later discussion of these qualifications will explain the use here and hereafter of the term "quasi-colony" in referring to Afro-America.)

Capitalists in the ruling country, then, share their super-profits with "their own" workers. On a world scale, the major effect of this sharing is a redistribution of wages among "the working class as a whole" which creates – and expresses a contradiction between exploited and super-exploited. Since Lenin's time, that contradiction has grown large enough temporarily to obscure the central contradiction in the metropolis between workers and bosses (which naturally is the purpose of the enormous sums thus sacrificed –I nvested, really – by the ruling class).

The example of Afro-America is useful in another way: White workers are receiving a substantial portion of extra – i.e. super -wages which actually belong to – because the values they represent were created by and "meant" to produce the labor-power of –their Afro-American class brothers. Yet, those white workers do not own the means of production on which black workers produce such values. That is why such values, realized in super-wages, constitute bribes which amount to a peculiar participation in super-exploitation. Until removed, such super-exploitation acts as a "difficulty" temporarily outweighing the "principal aspect of the contradiction."[8]

We have now tracked down, without yet discussing collection methods, a tangible portion of imperialism's bribery of "its" own workers. From here, it is only a step to deduce that, if the U.S. working class is only an important metropolitan sector of the collective world working class (including Afro-America) then the differences in wages and conditions between metropolitan centers and the vast colonial hinterland (different parts of a single integral system) represent a further sharing of super-profits via a redistribution of international wages much more drastic than that in the U.S., but always favoring the metropolitan worker.

The resulting flood of tangible bribes buries under its tawdry glitter the (much smaller) exploitation of the labor aristocracy itself which, with automated speed, helps colossally to enrich "its own" exploiters. That is the significance of bribery for Marxists: it must orient their concentration in the making of revolution on the prior destruction of super-exploitation.

While workers are bribed out of a single component of super profits, the take accruing to the ruling class from such sharing is far more numerous and often imponderable.

Although all super-profits ultimately reduce to super-exploitation of colonial labor power, they do not all appear in that direct form. They include exorbitant interest (on loans, on aid, etc.) charged by metropolitan powers to emerging governments or ex-colonies (such governments squeezing even larger amounts right back out of local labor power). There are also: loot from licensing patents, processes and trade marks; the incredible salaries of foreign experts, some of whom are so expert that they can't get jobs at home; the physical removal of incalculable quantities of natural wealth from colonial areas; the effect of the price scissors on the monopoly-controlled international market; non-equivalent exchange; and so on.

As for imponderable benefits of super-exploitation to the ruling class: imagining for a moment that, without any other change in the overall set-up, such a thing were possible, what if American wages were not differentiated by color? Figures showed, above, that "non-black" income in 1959 averaged about $2,291 per head, compared to the national average including Afro-Americans of $2,166. Even at a mere $125 a head, this amounts to some $21,138 million, suggesting a depression of all wages because of employer-created color divisions in the working class. How much higher, then, would all income go if not weighed down by this divisive component? This unfigurable sum, which the ruling class at present need pay nobody (and which under a socialist order would be available for the benefit of all) is pocketed in its entirety by the ruling class. Measurable or not, here are super-profits squeezed from the entire home working class including the labor aristocracy.

Another imponderable: for the capitalist class, the credit system annually draws immense sums of interest. How much of this would Wall Street lose if all workers could pay cash? In any case, how much is gravy due to extra or luxury spending out of super-wages?

Still other imponderables are hidden in prices, rents, educational costs saved by inferior education for black children, unused industrial capacity (which, of course, is also a loss) etc. And how much does the international ruling class get as cut from the incalculable sum pouring into the metropolis from greatly depressed colonial wages? That figure must be positively staggering!

Thus, the by-no-means-puny share of affluence which the ruling class gives out of super-profits in varying proportions to different segments of "its own" workers may be thought of as a cost to that ruling class in extracting its other, much more enormous, super-profits from colonies. The relative quiet of its own labor force thereby purchased on the whole and usually permits it to expand its economy without undue interference or interruption from class struggle at home. This is said in the face of the massive upheavals in France in May 1968: it will be interesting to see whether the system can weather the current struggles wracking it in various metropolitan spots. Its margin of safety may have been reduced. Yet, the continued existence of the colonial labor-power reservoir clearly suggests that it will. It may never be the same; it will have tottered another step toward its doom. But — it will still be there, continuing its parasitic life as long as it can super-exploit; and colonial suffering will continue increasing.

So, the primary result of bribery in the imperialist economic system is the formation, as Lenin noted, of labor aristocracies in "a handful of very rich countries".

In Lenin's day, his thesis was simply represented by the facts. But as imperialism decays and its network of parasitism spreads, those facts necessarily become more complex — in the ever integral system. The writers of the above quotation take into account this increasing systemic complexity:

> "The hierarchy of nations which make up the capitalist system is characterized by a complex set of exploitative relations. Those at the top exploit in varying degrees all the lower layers, and similarly those at any given level exploit those below them ... At the same time, each unit at a given level strives to be the sole exploiter of as large a number as possible of units beneath it. Thus we have a network of antagonistic relations pitting exploiters against exploited and rival exploiters against each other."[9]

These ideas are in turn supported from another source dealing specifically with Latin America but having universal applicability:

> "... metropolis-satellite relations are not limited to the imperial or international level but penetrate and structure the very economic, political and social life of the ... colonies ... Just as the colonial and national capital and its export sector become the satellite of the ... Metropoles of the world economic system, this satellite immediately becomes a colonial and then a national metropolis with respect to the productive sectors and populations of the interior. Furthermore, the provincial capitals, which thus are themselves satellites of the national metropolis —and through the latter of the world metropolis — are in turn provincial centers around which their own local satellites

orbit. Thus, a whole chain of constellations of metropoles and satellites relates all parts of the whole system from its metropolitan center in Europe or the United States to the farthest outpost in the . . . Countryside.

"When we examine this metropolis-satellite structure, we find that each of the satellites . . . serves as an instrument to suck capital or economic surplus out of its own satellites and to channel part of this surplus to the world metropolis of which all are satellites."[10]

Imperialist bribery, while originating from the metropolis and benefiting mainly the metropolis, includes – in the system's darkening twilight – a graduated process that is interpenetrating and ubiquitous. Yet, its role in thus far enabling the system's rulers, in most un-Canute-like style, to hold back the tide of revolution, could be undermined – thus hastening Liberation's time table – by documenting and exposing it. This, the present text attempts.

17. The Source of Imperialist Bribery

Table 3 (page 106) compares US wage levels with those of Asia, Africa and Latin America: even when colonial wages rise absolutely, they continue to fall relatively to wages in imperialist centers.

Table 27 (page 213) shows that, in South Africa (that imperialist world in miniature), the black worker is paid only 4.6% of the "white" rate.

The size of this gap and the continual relative fall of colonial wages, taken together, indicate one specific result of imperialist parasitism: the richer the metropoles become, the poorer colonial peoples.

Imperialist bribery is not limited to wages. Wages gaps are merely one portion of a whole mode of life, which parasitism – as a single process – permits to metropolitan labor while enforcing in reverse on colonial labor.

Guinea's President Sekou Touré has quoted, for income, food production, world trade and purchasing power, the ranking of the US as against colonial areas. His comparative figures, taken from "an international review," are as follows:

> "1. Immediately after the war, the average per capita income in the USA, was $1,000 per annum, while in the underdeveloped countries of Asia, Africa and Latin America it was $100. Fifteen years later the annual average per capita income in the United States was $2,500, and in the underdeveloped countries barely $150. Thus, while in the most developed part of the world the average income was ten times larger than that of the underdeveloped countries, which represent the vast majority of the world territory and population, this difference has now risen to seventeen times. (Table 3 was simply a tabulation of this

Section. It is repeated in words here for the sake of continuity.)

"2. Since the war, the world average per capita production of food has increased by 13 per cent. But in Africa, the production per capita has fallen by two per cent, in Latin America it has increased by two per cent, in Asia by 12 per cent, and in the developed Western Europe by 21 per cent.

"3. Immediately after the second world war the underdeveloped countries' participation in world trade exchange was 38 per cent. However, by 1953, its share was reduced to 36 per cent, in 1959 to 31 per cent, and in 1961 to 29 per cent.

"4. In the course of the last ten years alone, the prices of industrial goods in international trade have increased by 24 per cent, while the prices of raw materials have fallen by five per cent. In other words, the underdeveloped countries exporting raw materials were, towards the end of the fifties, purchasing one-third less industrial goods for a determined quantity of raw materials, as compared with ten years earlier."[1]

The practical, human, outcome illustrated in vital statistics from the two areas is one important consequence of such lop-sided conditions.

Table 10, below, concretizes this consequence. (Because of the poor availability of statistics covering "black" Africa by itself, it can deal solely with Average Years of Life Expectancy and with Infant Mortality Rates; and with South Africa vis-a-vis the United States.)

Table 10[z]

COMPARATIVE INTERNATIONAL VITAL STATISTICS

A R E A	Years Life Expectancy at Birth		INFANT MORTALITY RATES			
	MALE	FEMALE	1948	1955	1959	1961
South African Whites	67[x]	72[x]	36.0	29.8	28.7	27.6
" " Asians	n.a.	n.a.	77.1	63.1	62.1	43.3
" " Coloreds	n.a.	n.a.	133.2	134.5	120.6	126.8
" " Blacks	37[x]	42[x]	n.a.	n.a.	n.a.	200-300[x]
UNITED STATES	67.1[a]	73.5[a]	32.0	26.4	26.4	25.3

[x]Source: Accra EVENING NEWS, June 8, 1963.   [a]1957 figures   n.a.= not available

These figures illustrate a first point about imperialist bribery: that for the system, as a whole, the CENTRAL, ancestral BRIBERY is the one which elevates metropolitan living standards so far above those of colonial hinterlands. What is more, the resulting difference between conditions of peoples in metropolitan as compared to colonial localities is a qualitative one, as will be shown later.

The figures for Asians and Coloreds show that, while such effects are at their maximum between metropoles and colonial hinterlands, there are also graded effects of the same type within colonial lands, and inside imperialist countries as well. (This point is in line with the theme of the quotations from Baran and Sweezy and from Professor Andre Gunder Frank, Note 9 and 10, Chapter 16.)

This encompasses a second point about imperialist bribery, the missing of which has caused, among the Western Left and the Eastern European socialist world, serious judgmental errors about world revolutionary tactics.

To investigate how both these points operate and interact, a start can be made by comparing wages and mode of life inside the US for Afro-Americans as against their white brethren.

If "disposable income" is the amount of money roughly needed to run an economy for a year, the 1963 figure for the US was $420 billion. At that time, Afro-Americans constituted 10.8% of total US population. Hence, had income been distributed on the basis of population, Afro-Americans should have accounted for $45 billion. Actually, however, the figure was $23.5 billion. The remaining $21.5 billion was redistributed among white people of all classes in such a way that income for Negroes averaged only 52% of those for whites.[3] A later figure – 1966 – shows a Negro income of 55.4% that of whites.[4]

The following table compares the vital statistics resulting from the above wage discrimination within the US between white and non-white people. (In 1959, Negroes were 92.1% of all US Non

Table 11[6]

U.S. VITAL STATISTICS, NEGRO AND WHITE

YEAR	LIFE EXPECTANCY AT BIRTH IN YEARS				INFANT MORTALITY RATE[o]	
	WHITE		NON-WHITE			
	MALE	FEMALE	MALE	FEMALE	WHITE	NON-WHITE
1949–51	66.3	72.0	58.9	62.7	26.8	44.5
1955	67.3	73.6	61.2	65.9	23.6	42.8
1959	67.3	73.9	60.9	66.2	23.2	44.0
1959–61	67.6	74.1	61.5	66.6	22.4	40.7
1964	67.7	74.6	61.1	67.2	21.6	41.1

[o]Number of deaths of infants under one year per 1,000 live births

whites.[5] Therefore, this table serves adequately in grading US "Negro vs. white" statistics.)

The years studied were chosen so that this table would be as nearly as possible specifically comparable with Tables 10 and 12. The figures in Table 11, here, show a definite, measurable difference between the vital statistics of Negroes and whites in the leading imperialist country. The significance of this comparison between a metropolitan center and its own, internal quasi-colony will soon become apparent.

Where Afro-Americans fit into the world exploitative hierarchy is clarified in Tables 12a and 12b, which (combining information in Tables 10 and 11) compare vital statistics for South African and American non-whites, revealing a qualitative difference between the conditions of metropolitan and hinterland non-whites.

Tables 12a and 12b show quite clearly the dual position of the US Negro vis-a-vis imperialist bribery. In 1948, their infants were surviving better than those of South African Asians who, by 1961, had however caught up with them (indicating how the exploitative

Table 12a

COMPARATIVE VITAL STATISTICS
SOUTH AFRICAN AND AMERICAN NON-WHITES

YEAR	SOUTH AFRICAN LIFE EXPECTANCY AT BIRTH IN YEARS				U.S. NEGRO LIFE EXPECTANCY AT BIRTH IN YEARS	
	WHITES		BLACKS			
	MALE	FEMALE	MALE	FEMALE	MALE	FEMALE
1948					58.9	62.7
1955					61.2	65.9
1959					60.9	66.2
1961	67[x]	72[x]	37[x]	42[x]	61.5	66.6
1962					61.5	66.8

[x]Source: Accra EVENING NEWS, June 8, 1963. Valid date for figures not given but context made 1961 or 1962 likely.

inner hierarchy of imperialist economy changes as the system decays). The South African blacks infant mortality rate in 1961 or thereabouts was about five times that of local Asians, and also of US Negroes; almost ten times that of South African whites, and about double that of South African coloreds, who themselves suffered three times as much as a South African Asian or a US Negro.

Table 12b

COMPARATIVE VITAL STATISTICS
SOUTH AFRICAN AND AMERICAN NON-WHITES

YEAR	INFANT MORTALITY RATE (Deaths of Infants under 1 year per 1,000 live births)				
	SOUTH AFRICA				U.S.A.
	ASIANS	COLOREDS	BLACKS	WHITES	NEGROES
1948	77.1	133.2		36.0	44.5
1955	63.1	134.5		29.8	42.8
1959	62.1	120.6		28.7	44.0
1961	43.3	126.8	200-300[x]	27.6	40.7
1962					41.4

[x]Source: Accra EVENING NEWS, June 8, 1963. Valid date for figures not given but context made 1961 or 1962 likely.

As for life expectancy, by 1961, the US Negro male had reached on the average a position commensurate with, lagging only slightly behind, that of South African whites who live, on a world scale, second in conditions only to US whites. But South African blacks in 1961 had only one-half to two-thirds the life expectancy of US Negroes or South African whites. All these figures have political consequences to be studied later.

Tables 10, 11 and 12 taken together lead to the conclusion that (a) the US white population enjoys a specific, sizeable, life-and-death benefit from US rulers' super-exploitation of an internal quasi-colony – as measured originally by a specific income differential; and (b) all the US population, who thereby include Afro-

Americans, together enjoy from such super-exploitation enormous monetary and condition advantages over peoples in colonies.

The improvement in South African Asians' vital statistics shown in Tables 10 and 12, above, taken with Afro-American statistics (Tables 11 and 12), further suggests the attainment of a fairly high level of living standards for Asians in South Africa and for Afro-Americans, each as a group. Certainly, it would appear from such figures that a significant section of the internal US quasi-colony is being added bit by bit to an American elite.

Is this the whole story? Or is there in such figures a trap, which – unqualified – may be warping the truth about imperialist bribery?

These questions, as well as their answers, have been suggested – and lucidly covered – by a recent examination of the economic history of American Negroes,[7] which shows that the truth underlying statistical improvements for oppressed areas is, in reality, inseparably connected with imperialism's hierarchical nature.

In his Chapter on imperialist parasitism, cited earlier, Lenin had observed that

> "The export of capital, one of the most essential economic bases of imperialism . . . sets the seal of parasitism on the whole country that lives by exploiting the labor of several overseas countries and colonies."

(See Chapter 3, page 45 above). Since Afro-Americans reside in the world's most advanced "country that lives by exploiting the labor of several overseas countries and colonies", one would – other considerations aside – expect them to participate in that citadel's parasitism. But how could that be possible, since it has already been shown that they are super-exploited by the US ruling class?

The authors of the cited examination of Negro economic history note – and quote US authorities who agree – that most of the real improvements in wages and conditions which have been gained by the majority of Afro-Americans have been due almost solely to their great urbanization since 1910. For, say these writers,

> "The move from countryside to city has on the average unquestionably meant a higher standard of living."[8]

In addition, they offer figures showing how massive a component of Afro-American life has been affected:

> ". . . in the half century between 1910 and 1960 . . . the 3-to-1 rural-urban ratio (among Afro-Americans) of 1910 has been almost exactly reversed: today three quarters of the Negro population are city dwellers."[9]

Urbanization results from industrialization. And this, in turn, is mainly the fruit of continued super-profits. So, the reason benefits have reached a significant number of Afro-Americans, despite their own quasi-colonial status, is (as these authors put it) because the standard of living that accompanies industrialization has created a world-wide condition whereby

> "the bottom of the urban-industrial ladder is higher than the top of the ... agricultural ladder."[10]

Of course, out of this fact, US propaganda would like to present a blissful idyll enveloping its most oppressed. So, one such medium has reported specifically that

> "nine out of ten Negro families (today) own one or more television sets, two-thirds have automatic dishwashers, and more than half own cars."[4]

These "blessings" - according to this source - stem from the fact that:

> "The proportion of poor families among Negroes fell from 52.2% in 1959 to 43.1 in 1964, while that among whites declined from 20.7% to 17.1%."[4]

Also, this report notes, while Negro income was still only $3,971 per family compared to $7,170 for whites per annum (55.4%), it had risen 24% since 1960 while white rates went up "only" 14%.[4]

The implied claim is that Negroes as a whole are catching up with whites, with statistics to support the notion.

However, according to the authors we have been quoting[7], the fact is that once urbanization has taken place, the masses of Negroes experience a real worsening of living conditions: unemployment grows; ghettoization strengthens – even though overall statistics imply a general rising situation.

These authors quote US government authorities to support their position. What is more, even the above "US Propaganda medium" is, in the end, forced to confirm it:

> "Practically all of the gains (made by US Negroes) have been made by the growing Negro middle class, which still constitutes a minority of the Negro population. That is the heart of the problem for it leaves behind the lower-income, semi-literate Negroes, notably the families that are below the Government's $3,000-a-year poverty line. This class contains 60% of all the nation's Negro youths. … While the income of the middle-class Negro rises, that of the great mass of Negroes is actually declining. During the 1960s, median family income for Negroes has dropped from $3,897 to $3,803 in Los Angeles' Watts, from $4,346 to $3,729 in Cleveland's Hough District…

> "The number of Negroes on public-welfare rolls is increasing, and one-third of the nation's spending for public aid, education and housing (or an estimated $3.5 billion in all) goes to Negroes, who constitute only 11% of the US population.[4]

What the mass improvement among Black Americans resulting from urbanization might be said to represent, then, is a benefit to Afro-Americans as a whole accruing to them as dwellers in a metropolis out of general overseas super-exploitation by the US ruling class.

Throughout the imperialist system, urbanization is part of a continuous process of polarization. The fully-documented point made by our study of Negro economic history is that, for American Negroes – and, presumably, for ALL colonial areas – the main weight of statistical improvement shown in governmental surveys over the years goes to "the black (i.e., colonial) bourgeoisie".[7] That is, per se, all figures from such areas actually deceive to a lesser or greater degree because, as averages, they hide the distribution of those improved living standards for significant numbers of people which are a feature of imperialist bribery. Whereas metropolitan polarization produces a labor aristocracy at first tiny, but growing to substantial proportions as systemic parasitism waxes, the same process "overseas" produces a colonial elite, or "bourgeoisie". The former buffers for the ruling class against revolt both "at home" and in "overseas countries and colonies"; but, in colonies (i.e., in the lower echelons of the international imperialist economy), it is, with very few exceptions, the local "bourgeoisie" which plays this same role.

So, improvements in vital and other statistics really illumine qualitative differences in the forms and nature of imperialist bribery as it descends the international exploitative hierarchical ladder.

Now, according to the theses in this text, the type of polarization occurring in colonial areas due to imperialist bribery should have been predictable. For, if the metropolitan labor This will be elaborated in detail later. aristocracy really has its conditions improved at the expense of super-exploited peoples, then the latter, in fulfilling their "function" inside the system, must experience ever-worsening conditions.

Yet, it is frequently said that 30, 60, 12, 20 – unnumbered – millions of metropolitan workers are "living in poverty". So they are – by metropolitan standards, as well as in the light of how "developed" their economy allegedly is. On the other hand, Lenin had declared, as has now been noted more than once in these pages, that super-exploitation , "coupon clipping", foreign investments, capital export, etc. – "sets the seal of parasitism on the whole country" that lives in such a manner. How do "metropolitan poor" fit into this description?

First of all, those out of work in the world's "cities" are kept alive: in the US, there is "unemployment compensation"; in U.K., National Assistance (the dole); etc. However "inadequate" these hand-outs, nothing like them exists in colonial areas. Furthermore, in amounts per week, they sometimes approach monthly wages for employed colonial workers (i.e., California's $42.57 per week compared to a Ghanaian's 47.28 Cedis per month).

Finally, for those who reach the end of their unemployment compensation; for those chronically unemployed – as well as for employed, for rich and for poor – in metropolitan areas there are inexpensive staples available to everyone in the West which go so far toward creating the beneficial overall metropolitan standard of living; because of Western control of the world market, prices paid for raw materials and food staples are enormously below the values of such commodities. But, as has been shown, where prices and values do not accord with one another, the lag is made up on other commodities; in this case (a) by the high prices of manufactured goods sold to raw materials-producing areas; (b) by the high prices of processed food sold back to points of origin; and (c) by the inordinately low wages paid to colonial workers.

In such ways, imperialist bribery creates a material contradiction in "the working class as a whole" between the metropolitan and colonial sectors. Within colonial countries and within imperialist citadels themselves, ever-growing and complicated sub-contradictions result.

Thus, inside "improving" general statistics come about worsening conditions for the world's masses "overseas," i. e. in colonies. Despite (even there) some increment to a small group (slower to rise, and rising less, than that of the American Black) from urbanization; and, despite growing imperialist bribery of a new colonial "bourgeoisie", it is mass misery, their ten-fold super-exploitation, which supplies the "metropolitan factor" to the living standard of the Afro-American in that portion of his role where he acts as part of the West.

At the same time, if Afro-Americans also constitute a super-exploited internal reservoir for the US ruling class (bringing additional benefits to the white American labor aristocracy), then – below that international "sea" on which general Afro-American conditions "float", along with those of the rest of the metropolis where they live – conditions of Afro-America's masses must also be expected, as the system decays, to worsen, while their "bourgeoisie" improves both its size and its lot.

But both effects – in the metropolis and in colonies – show up in statistics as "overall improvement". As Lenin's words indicate, only one of the pictures is faithfully painted by figures covering these two areas. Here is a possible source of that fable which, in certain quarters of the world Left, persists in equating the sufferings of metropolitan and colonial masses.

If now, the tables of vital statistics (see Tables 10, 11, and 12, pages 171-173 above) are again consulted, it will become evident that the reason for showing them, though admittedly they offer only the roughest idea of reality, is not sentimental: they will be shown to support certain political conclusions, provided their meaning is clear.

Such clarity, hopefully, can now be found at the point made by Baran and Sweezy about price-fixing in metropoles. (See quote pages 157-158 above.) If deductions in this Chapter are correct, then (taking the international viewpoint) although monopoly does not have the power these authors postulate to prevent profit margins from being infringed on "at home", they do in actuality not only sustain but even increase (however imponderably) those profit margins when they grant super-wages to "their own" workers.

But this is so only because metropolitan workers are bribed into massive political acquiescence toward the status quo when their labor-power is purchased at such high prices, at least part of the "over-payment" being contained, as mentioned, in abnormally under-valued prices for food and other staples in industrialized areas.

But part of metropolitan super-wages represent values created by colonial workers both "at home" (where applicable) and abroad. This part contains a goodly portion of the true cost of producing colonial labor-power, which is thus bought at a price well below its value – and is nourished on necessaries paid for above their values.

As Marx has pointed out:

> "A quick succession of unhealthy and short-lived generations will keep the labor market as well supplied as a series of vigorous and long-lived generations."

So, in today's "Age of Escalation", Marx's law governing the price of labor-power[12] still applies:

> ". . . with labor, its MARKET PRICE will, in the long run, adapt itself to its VALUE; that, therefore, despite all the ups and downs, and do what he may, the working man will, on an average, only receive the value of his labor, which resolves into the value of his labouring power, which is determined by the value of the necessaries required for its maintenance and reproduction, which value of necessaries finally is regulated by the quantity of labor wanted to produce them."[12]

For the phrase, "in the long run", the expression, "over the system" could now be substituted of added, as the above discussion makes plain. Marx's law is valid only for "the working class as a whole"; and on this — system-wide — basis, the profits-wages tug-of-war between ruling and exploited classes is fought out: Hence, Marx's "on an average" works itself out, among the real human beings concerned, through the two balancing factors just set forth: (a) the indefinitely prolonged "high living" in metropoles, directly at the expense, equally indefinitely prolonged, of (b) the misery and subhuman living standards of colonial areas. (The phrase "indefinitely prolonged" should be interpreted to be co-extensive only with the existence of the imperialist system.)

Here is how the Western labor aristocracy is enchained in imperialism's parasitism, losing sight thereby of its own condition as an exploited class in the world's "cities". Not only does that labor aristocracy not oppose robbery of its colonial class brothers; it actively supports, and grimly acts to preserve, such robbery whenever colonial revolt seems to threaten it, as we shall see.

In such actions, what is revealed is those "ties of blood" which connect metropolitan labor aristocracies inseparably, for as long as imperialism lasts, to its colonial class brothers.

These realities were only partly visible when Marx was writing. It remained for Lenin to illumine them. And, because contradictions of this type are insoluble under imperialism, which aggravates them instead, only the complete destruction of colonialism (and so, of imperialism) can eliminate THIS kind of "blood tie". But the exposure of the contradictions underlying such ties is a major ideological pre-condition for the necessary "elimination". No class analysis of imperialist society which ignores or conceals them can lead to successful revolution "in the West", and History bears this witness.

All these situations, of course, contribute as end-product of bribery to the enormous practical, so-far-never-fully-measured material benefit of imperialist ruling circles, central beneficiaries of the whole parasitic set-up.

Today, international living standard differentials are usually huge, and widespread – yet, accepted as "part of life". This acceptance is abetted by certain earlier explanations of the differentials themselves, traceable to an original text by Karl Marx:

> "Besides this mere physical element, the value of labor is in every country determined by a TRADITIONAL STANDARD OF LIFE . . . the satisfaction of certain wants springing from the social conditions in which people are placed and reared up. The English standard of life may be reduced to the Irish standard ... the average wages in different agricultural districts of England still

> nowadays differ more or less according to the more or less favorable circumstances under which the districts have emerged from the state of serfdom.

> "This historical or social element, entering into the value of labor, may be expanded, or contracted, or altogether extinguished, so that nothing remains but the PHYSICAL LIMIT."[12]

Today, hindsight suggests that this "historical" factor affecting the price of labor power, these "more or less favorable circumstances under which the districts have emerged from serfdom", may be the expressed accumulation of the profits of black slavery and, later, of super-wages in a metropolis under hierarchical conditions like those described by Baran and Sweezy or Professor Andre Gunder Frank, (see Notes 4, 9, and 10, Chapter 16) and the resultant development of a mode of life which eventually engenders an expanding labor aristocracy.

For, if different countries or "districts" tend to develop "a traditional factor" which influences the socially necessary price paid for labor-power there, why does this factor operate in such a way as forever to raise metropolitan, while forever causing colonial wages to fall? What sort of "tradition" is that, if not one the ruling classes have developed for their own self-preservation?

The examples of US Afros and of South Africa, given above, offer refutation of such a factor: both black and white labor in both places live in the same territory and, in the US at any rate, are employed in most cases by the same bosses.

These facts vividly imply that ALL "traditional" factors in wages, resulting in significantly disproportionate living standards as between countries and/or "districts", merely embody that siphoning off of super-profits which turns so many workers in "usurer" nations into parasitic elements of a world working class. As a matter of fact, the same conclusion seems to be suggested in the second paragraph of Marx's own quotation above. And even if Marx's subject is something else rooted in the very foundations of the system, a "birth mark", as it were, it still remains true that this idea as it has been accepted is used to "justify" the unequal standards of living which have developed historically for those in different parts of the imperialist system.

It is precisely to prevent an outcome whereby "the English standard of life may be reduced to the Irish standard", that the labor aristocracy and its economic spokesmen – the trade unions – together with its political mouth-piece – the Social Democratic or "Labour" Parties – are struggling so "valiantly" on all colonial continents among those who have attained, or seem about to attain, independence, interfering in their affairs to the point even of financing and manning the counter-revolution (Guatemala and Guyana).

HERE, THEN, IS THE REAL SOURCE OF IMPERIALIST BRIBERY. TO SAY THAT IT COMES OUT OF SUPER PROFITS IS FAR TOO ANTISEPTIC: THE BEDROCK ORIGIN OF IMPERIALIST BRIBERY IS THE CONTINUING, EVER-WORSENING MISERY OF COLONIAL PEOPLES.

18. The Modern Labor Aristocracy: Definition and Size

Marxists readily and universally accepted Lenin's description of the labor aristocracy as "the labor lieutenants of the capitalist, class inside the working class movement". Their activities left no alternative.

Yet, when studying that "aristocracy" in specific cases, all the European Marxists – from Palmiro Togliatti of Italy, through Georgi Dimitroff of Bulgaria, to Palme Dutt of India and England remembered only part of the full story Lenin told.

That story started, so to speak, with the following point:

> "Engels publicly, in . . . his preface to the second (1892) edition of his CONDITION OF THE WORKING CLASS IN ENGLAND . . . speaks of the 'aristocracy of the working class,' of a 'privileged minority of the workers' as distinct from the 'broad masses of the workers'. 'A small, privileged sheltered minority' of the working class, he says, alone enjoyed 'lasting benefits' from the privileged position of England in 1848-1868, whereas 'the broad masses at best enjoyed only a short lived improvement.'"[1]

About two decades later, Palme Dutt was declaring that

> "capitalist world monopoly gives the bourgeoisie superior resources and the possibility to create a privileged sector of a minority of workers.[2]

Thirty years later yet, the very same author was still saying:

"Lenin, in his analysis of the corrupting influence of imperialism in the Western labor movement, always distinguished between the upper strata and leadership of the labor movement, who were thus corrupted, and the masses. He never included in this analysis of imperialist corruption the Western working class as a whole."[3]

Of course not. Lenin wrote before 1924, when, even in the West, the corrupt section of the Western working class WAS still a minority.

In any case, other words of Lenin's had made it apparent that his quotation from Engels, above, about the "privileged minority" among the workers in industrialized nations was not necessarily intended as a hard-and-fast sole pronunciamento on the subject. For example:

> "The capitalists ARE ABLE to spare a part (and no small part, at that!) of these super-profits to bribe THEIR workers, to create something like an alliance . . . between the workers of the given nation and their capitalists AGAINST the other countries . . .

> "Formerly, the working class of ONE country could be bribed and corrupted for decades. At the present time this is improbable, perhaps even impossible. On the other hand, however, EVERY imperialist 'Great' Power can and does bribe SMALLER (compared with England in 1848-1868) strata of the 'labor aristocracy'. Formerly, a 'BOURGEOIS LABOR PARTY', to use Engels' remarkably profound expression, could be formed only in one country, because that country alone enjoyed a monopoly, and enjoyed it for a long period. Now the 'BOURGEOIS LABOR PARTY' IS INEVITABLE and typical for ALL imperialist countries."[4]

Labor Aristocracy

Lenin also said, to be sure, that

> "We cannot – nor can anybody else – calculate exactly what portion of the proletariat is following and will follow the social-chauvinists and opportunists. This will only be revealed by the struggle, it will be definitely decided only by the socialist revolution."5

Of course, this remains true today. What will be sought here is an order of magnitude: is the labor aristocracy in the West still a minority or not? The answer to this question carries after itself serious political consequences, so it must be fully and honestly faced.

Yet, precisely this became the point upon which alone all Marxists agreed: that the labor aristocracy, the bribed in metropolitan areas, constitute a minority of workers in capitalist countries forever and a day . On this basis, and without ever thereafter applying Lenin's criteria of the labor aristocracy to changing or changed conditions, Marxists in the 30s made their analyses and ensuing predictions about the future of Social Democracy and hence, inevitably, of capitalism itself. They foretold "an end to the international split in the working class".

What kind of split? Lenin placed it into context in this way:

> "The Roman proletarian lived at the expense of society. Modern society lives at the expense of the modern proletarian. Marx particularly emphasized this profound observation of Sismondi. Imperialism changes the situation somewhat. A privileged upper stratum of the proletariat in the imperialistic states lives partly at the expense of the hundreds of millions of uncivilized people."5 .

Elsewhere, he added

the culture of the advanced countries has been, and still is, the result of their being able to live at the expense of a thousand million oppressed people . . . the capitalists of these countries obtain a great deal more in this way than they could obtain as profits by plundering the workers in their own countries."6

It was this split to which an "end" was foretold by Marxist prognosticators of the 1930s. Yet Lenin himself had specifically and emphatically denied the possibility of mending such a split for the duration of capitalism.7 History has backed Lenin, rather than these Western Marxists for good reason: today, the world labor aristocracy has escalated on the flood tide of gigantic super-profits until, speaking formally, it has become a majority of the working class in the USA , and a significantly growing minority elsewhere in the West.

WHO, then, makes up this "privileged stratum'" of the proletariat?

On this: Lenin had the following to say:

> "This stratum of bourgeoisified workers, or the 'labor aristocracy', who are quite philistine in their mode of life, in the size of their earnings and in their entire out look, is the principal SOCIAL (not military) PROP OF THE BOURGEOISIE. For they are the real AGENTS OF THE BOURGEOISIE IN THE WORKING CLASS MOVEMENT, the labor lieutenants of the capitalist class, real channels of reformism and chauvinism."8

These remarks he had elaborated (See Chapter 3, Page 45) thus:

> "The upper stratum furnishes the bulk of the membership of cooperatives , of trade unions , of sporting clubs , and of numerous religious sects . To this level is adapted the

> electoral system which is sufficiently restricted to exclude the lower stratum of the proletariat proper."[9]

With these words, Lenin had provided a complete guide to examining the labor aristocracy, formally, anywhere in any epoch.

So, if now his criteria are applied, they should reveal the present condition of that labor aristocracy which, elsewhere, Lenin characterized as "now typical for ALL imperialist countries." (First quotation, Page 189, above.) This text will attempt such application, but mainly to the USA counting it as the chief world imperialist power and decisive monopoly center of our day, which should manifest all phenomena in their most advanced forms.

During this investigation, furthermore, the important thing is that wages are not only criterion of a labor aristocracy. As shown above, Lenin put first its mode of life, adding to that and to wages its "entire outlook." But all these boundaries must be explored before conclusions may be drawn.

Specific clues to the size of the labor aristocracy lie in Lenin's various detailed criteria: the electorate; memberships in specific organizations, the nature of which he elucidated. These will be applied first.

<u>Table 13</u>[10]

THE U.S. ELECTORATE

YEAR	POPULATION OF VOTING AGE	NUMBER VOTING	%
1920	54,512,000	26,748,000	49.1
1940	80,092,000	49,891,000	62.3
1960	108,122,000	68,836,000	63.7

A. The US electorate, including the portion excluded:

Although the number of people voting and the population of voting age both rose with time, the percentage of one to the other proves that the numerical rise in number voting is not only an absolute but a relative one. If the labor aristocracy is, as Lenin held, found in the electorate, then this table suggests a continual, though lately slowing, increase in the size of the US labor aristocracy as decay rots the imperialist system which US rulers head.

What about those excluded from the US Electoral system?

It is a well-known and now hotly-contested point of struggle that, in the US South, only a minority vote. Not only are five million Negroes disfranchised, so are six million poor whites.

The following table illustrates the context surrounding this fact:

While Southern states furnished 31.4% of the US Electorate, they contained 47.2% of the disfranchised. Put another way: while 36.3% of all US population of voting age did not vote in the 1960 elections, the comparable figure for the US South was 54.6% (74.6% in Mississippi).

Table 14[11]

U.S. PRESIDENTIAL ELECTIONS OF 1960

A R E A	POPULATION OF VOTING AGE	NUMBER VOTING	%
United States	108,122,000	68,836,000	63.7
Southern States	33,995,000	15,423,000	45.4
Mississippi only	1,171,000	298,000	25.4

<u>Table 15</u>[12]

AVERAGE PER CAPITA ANNUAL INCOME BY AREA (1959)

A R E A	INCOME (Dollars)	POPULATION AFFECTED
United States	2,166	177,100,000
Southern States	1,663	54,300,000
Mississippi only	1,162	2,162,000
Negroes, all U.S.	1,126	18,900,000
Negroes, South	798	11,700,000

Do these disfranchised comprise, as Lenin claimed, "the lower stratum of the proletariat proper"? The following table suggests the answer:

Tables 13 and 14 together show that the US Electorate contains a substantial majority of US citizens over 21 years of age (of whom, it will be recalled, between two-thirds and three-fourths are workers (See Tables 8 and 9); while Table 15 adds the information that, of those excluded from the US electorate, the vast proportionate majority are in the poorest sections of population. Whether or not such "poor" are in "the proletariat" will be discussed further later.

Here it can be said that there is at very least a large over-lapping of the two. Quite significantly, today, the excluded "lower stratum of the proletariat proper" constitutes, by any criterion, a minority of total US Population.

Table 16[13]

UNION MEMBERS AS PERCENT OF U.S. POPULATION

E V E N T	YEAR	NO. UNION MEMBERS	TOTAL U.S. WORKING POPULATION	% TOTAL WORKING ORGANIZED
Afl merges with CIO	1955	15,000,000	65,848,000	23.7
In March	1961	12,500,000	71,011,000	17.6
September	1966*	13,500,000*	75,000,000*	17.9

*Source: NEWSWEEK, Sept. 26, 1966: "The New Militancy of Labor"

B. Memberships in organizations:

Trade Unions:

The generally lower percentage and numbers through 1966 of total working population in unions indicates loss of militancy by the labor aristocracy as imperialism decays. (See Chapter 21 below). The .3% increase of organized in the 5 1/2 years between March 1961 and September 1966 was due in large part (40% of it) to the entrance into unions of about 600,000 government employees:[14] the labor aristocracy rises particularly in the non-productive working-class sectors.

In what might have been a commentary on the above table, Lenin had said:

"In the nineteenth century . . . Marx and Engels did not . . . forget first, that the trade union organizations directly embraced a MINORITY OF THE PROLETARIAT. In England then and in Germany now, not more than one-fifth of the proletariat was organized. It cannot be seriously believed that it is possible to organize the majority of the proletariat under capitalism."[15]

(Today, of the "labor force", in Sweden 45%; and in Britain, 40%, are organized.[17])

Cooperatives:

The following figures for 1959 encompass credit unions, voluntary group health plans, housing cooperatives, farmer retail supply, electric power and rural telephone consumers' co-ops: 24,382,000 members. Farm marketing and supply co-ops: 7,559,000. Total cooperative members comprising mainly working people in the US in 1959: 31,941,000. [16]

Sporting Clubs:

Complete information on this subject was not immediately available. However, the following table shows trends in the memberships of five sports in the US — by no means the most popular in the land. The table does not help much in gauging the specific size of the overall labor aristocracy. What it does

Table 17[18]

MEMBERSHIPS OF FIVE U.S. SPORTS CLUBS

1950–1965

TEAM, CLUB MEMBERS	1950		1955		1960		1965	
	1,000's	%	1,000's	%	1,000's	%	1,000's	%
AMATEUR SOFTBALL[x]	3,195	2.12	3,303	2.02	3,450	1.93	5,308	2.77
TENPIN BOWLING	1,937	1.28	2,511	1.55	5,538	3.10	8,010	4.17
DUCKPIN PLAYERS[*]	172	.12	279	.17	372	.21	485	.25
GOLFERS	3,215	2.13	3,500	2.15	4,400	2.48	7,750	4.04
BOAT MOTORS IN USE	2,811	1.86	4,210	2.53	5,800	3.26	6,643	3.47
TOTALS, ABOVE SPORTS	11,330	7.54	13,803	8.42	19,560	10.98	28,196	14.70
U.S. POPULATION	150,790		162,967		178,153		191,874	

[x]Number teams multiplied by 9, plus number of youth participants (this would be low, as no allowance is made for understudies on the team).
[*]Number teams multiplied by 6. Also low for same reason.

indicate, however, is that during the years 1950 to 1965 in the US the trend in sports club memberships, said by Lenin to reflect a labor aristocracy, was upward, both numerically and percentage-wise.

Except for golf, the sports selected have a high working-class composition among participants; and even golf is making inroads among them since 1960, aided by factory – or Company – sponsored golf clubs, and the like.

Religious Sects:

a) In 1957, when total US population was 165,270,000, of the 119,333,000 persons over 14 years of age, all but 5,844,000 listed themselves as belonging to one of the three major US religions (Protestants, Catholics or Jews), including sub-sects, especially among Protestants.[19]

b) Of 314,345 churches reporting (said to include practically all US churches), only 17,407 claimed memberships of less than 55,000. That is, of 112,227,000 persons reporting themselves church members in those years, only 2,529,000 (2.76%) belonged to a church with less than 55,000 members.[20]

c) By 1964, a well-known US magazine was noting

"a 2% increase over the previous year in church membership, compared with an overall population increase of 1.5%. [21]

d) Historically, church membership figures offer the following picture:

Table 18[22]

HISTORICAL TREND OF U. S. CHURCH MEMBERSHIP
AS PERCENTAGE OF TOTAL POPULATION
(In Thousands)

YEAR	CHURCH MEMBERSHIP	TOTAL U.S. POPULATION	%
1926	54,576	117,399	46.6
1940	64,502	131,954	48.9
1950	86,830	151,234	57.5
1959	112,227	176,511	63.6
1964	123,307[*]	192,120[x]	64.4

[*] TIME Magazine, January 14, 1966.
[x] Survey of Current Business, Dec. 1965;
Page S-12; July 1, 1964, figure

19. The Modern Labor Aristocracy: More of Its Size

If wages and wages alone were the criterion of a labor aristocracy, then today – more than 50 years after Lenin wrote his quoted words, with super-profits pyramided to unheard-of pinnacles – it could still be said that "only a minority" – though no longer "tiny" – of Western workers are bribed.

Table 19 has been compiled from information covering 156 different industrial categories in non-agricultural enterprises counted by the US government. Included along with trade and finance are service and government workers.

This table shows that in 1960 $100 per week or more was earned by 21.8% of all production workers and non-supervisory employees in US non-agricultural industry in 47 of the total 156 examined by the US In 1950, workers in those same industries had been 23.8% of total, though the categories with the highest pay rates shifted with time.

The underscored industries (15 in all) comprise some 5,962 thousand workers who, in 1960, made $115 per week or more, for a yearly total of $6,000, assuming each worked the full year. These workers were 49.3% of all those in the 47 industries shown in Table 19, or 10.8% of the total number of workers in the 156 industries in the US information from which this table is taken.

The minimum $6,000 per annum earned by this 10.8% was roughly equal to the amount calculated by various respectable government or bourgeois agencies in the US in 1959 as "modest but adequate" for a family of four. Therefore, it approximates the minimum socially necessary cost of production for average US labor power. Or, put another way, in order to qualify for this minimum category, a worker lucky enough to work the year's full 50 weeks with two of paid vacation would have to earn about $115 per week. And wage-wise, only about 10.8% of US production workers appeared, as late as 1960, to do so.

This has undoubtedly been the basis on which Western Marxists have kept insisting that "only a tiny minority" of metropolitan workers are bribed. But if, now, a study is made of historical trends in consumption, income distribution and the effects of militarism on the working class, it will become clearer why wages constitute only one portion of US living conditions. The fact is that after 1950,

Table 19[1]

TOP WAGE EARNERS AMONG U. S. WORKERS
(Production Workers and Non-Supervisory Employees)[*]
(In Thousands)

INDUSTRY	1950		1960	
	NUMBER EMPLOYED IN INDUSTRY	AVERAGE WEEKLY EARNINGS (Dollars)	NUMBER EMPLOYED IN INDUSTRY	AVERAGE WEEKLY EARNINGS (Dollars)
Metal Mining[a]	97	65.58	92	111.49
Bituminous Coal Mining[a]	368	70.35	159	117.72
Petroleum & Natural Gas Production	254	73.69	288	114.49
Non-Building Construction	448[c]	73.46	553[c]	120.18
Building Construction	1,885[c]	73.73	2,219[c]	119.64
Ordnance & Accessories	30	64.79	150	107.71
Pulp, Paper, Paperboard Mills	246	65.06	275	105.03
Newspapers	280	80.00	330	111.43
Periodicals	58	74.18	64	116.43
Commercial Printing	190	72.34	231	105.72
Lithography	52	73.04	69	108.63
Miscellaneous Publishing	68[x]	109.05[x]	68	117.73
Industrial Chemicals (Inorganic)	73	67.89	105	115.37
Industrial Chemicals (Organic)	229	65.69	341	110.54
Soap, Cleaning, Polishing Products	51[x]	85.07[x]	53	111.64
Paints, Pigments, Fillers	69	64.80	77	100.86
Petroleum Refining	185	77.93	182	122.51
Coke, Coal Products	47[x]	86.31[x]	47	105.93
Tires & Inner Tubes	107	72.48	103	116.42
Flat Glass	33[x]	114.38[x]	32	127.66
Cement, Hydraulic	40	60.13	41	102.87
Blast Furnaces, Rolling Mills	611	67.46	569	116.66
Non-Ferrous Metals, Primary Smelting	48	63.71	57	109.23
Same: Rolling, Drawing, Alloying	104	66.75	113	110.03
Same: Foundries	77	67.65	62	101.30
Miscellaneous Primary Metal	147[x]	97.10[x]	150	111.48
Tin Cans, Tinware	57	60.90	60	114.54
Fabricated Structural Metal Products	211	63.29	289	100.12
Metal Stamping, Coating, Engraving	192	64.22	238	105.88
Engines, Turbine	66	69.43	102	112.19
Agricultural Machinery & Tractors	180	64.60	148	102.48
Construction & Mining Machinery	100	65.97	125	100.95

Metal-Working Machinery	198	71.54	256	116.75
Special-Industry Machinery	168	65.74	176	101.40
General Industrial Machinery	185	66.33	228	102.16
Office & Store Machinery	92	66.95	140	104.34
Motor Vehicles & MV Equipment	825	73.25	781	114.65
Aircraft & Parts	282	68.39	653	110.16
Ship-, Boat-Building & Repairing	85	63.28	140	105.57
Railroad Equipment	60	66.33	57	108.29
Laboratory, Scientific, etc., Equipment	64[x]	88.99[x]	66	114.68
Photographic Apparatus	53	65.59	67	107.83
Class I Railroads (Transportation)	1,221	64.14	781	108.42
Telegraph[b][a]	44	64.14	37	100.73
Gas & Electric Utilities	526	66.60	579	110.43
Motion Picture Production	248[x]	93.78[x]	187	115.05
T O T A L S	10,654[o]	64.80[*][do]	11,540[o]	108.00[do]
TOTAL, all such workers, U.S.	44,738[o]		52,898[o]	
% Top Earners to Total Industry	23.8		21.8	

[*]Only industries where weekly earnings in 1960 average $100 or more. [d]Average
[o]Total in Industry [a]1960 data not strictly comparable to 1950 [x]1959 figures
[b]Excludes messengers [c]Actual construction workers only [*]1950 figures only
[e]Production workers only

in the wake of World War II, affluence in the West grew with
noticeable speed.

Consider first minimum income distribution.

Table 20[2]

U.S. MINIMUM INCOME DISTRIBUTION

MINIMUM MEAN FAMILY ANNUAL INCOME (Dollars)	% OF U.S. FAMILIES	
	1961	1964
6,000	47	50
15,000	6[x]	7
26,368[a]	27,368[a]	28,482[a]
2,000[*]	16	12

[x]Represents 3.7 million families.
[*]Maximum
[a]Top 5% by income rank of families,
who garnered 20% of national income,
made this average amount per annum.

This table shows that, wage-wise, in the 1961 almost half (47%) of the American people could be said to have been able to meet the socially necessary cost of producing their labor-power. Table 19 suggested that only 10.8% of actual industrial producers were among this 47%. It will be recalled that no attempt was made earlier to ascertain how many individuals among total population each producer represents (Table 8, Page 151). Rather, we accepted 75% of total population as an operational figure covering the category "working class", including both producers and non-producing labor-power sellers and their families not otherwise counted. If we continue here with the 75% estimate, then the above table means that about 35% of the American people were meeting the minimum costs of production, labor-power-wise.

In any case, the figures from 1964 strongly suggest that for the US people – as well as for the wage workers whom they include – wage-measured affluence increases with time.

The next table attempts to trace affluence historically, and to compare it to corporate profits as well as to Gross National Product.

Table 21[3]

TRENDS AND COMPARISONS IN U. S. FAMILY AFFLUENCE

YEAR	(1) % U.S. FAMILIES w/INCOME $6,000 OR MORE	(2) PER CAPITA (in Dollars) DISPOSABLE PERSONAL INCOME	(3) U.S. PERSONAL CONSUMPTION EXPENDITURES	(4) G.N.P.	(5) CORPORATE "TAKE" AFTER TAXES (Millions/Dollars) PROFITS	(6) DIVIDENDS
1940	11.9[a]	555	544	762	5,000[x]	3,800[x]
1950	18.7	1,346	1,286	1,876	19,000[*]	9,000[*]
1959	42.9	1,904	1,772	2,722	23,800	13,400
1964	49.6[c]	2,267[b]	1,937[b]	3,272[b]	57,400	19,800
% CHANGE	+37.7	+ 310	+ 256	+ 339	+ 1,048	+ 421

[a] 1944   [x] 1939   [*] 1951   [b] Includes Alaska, Hawaii   [c] 1962

The increase in US Corporate "Take" (Columns 5 and 6) supplemented by the material in Chapter 17, above, shows that not only does the "take" itself rise yearly, but an ever-increasing portion of it comes out of "overseas" economic activity. The per capita figures (Columns 2, 3 and 4) show that disposable (i.e., spendable) personal income, personal consumption expenditures, and gross national product all increased substantially in the period under observation. Of course, the largest of these increases was in GNP That is what the system exists to accomplish, just as its goal is also expressed in the leaping advances of Columns 5 and 6.

At the same time – as Columns 1 and 2 taken together suggest – a growing percentage of US people (who are at least two-thirds working class) continue to consume ever-rising absolute amounts each year, based on thus-far-rising income. The following table attempts to relate these findings specifically to labor itself:

Table 22[4]

RELATION OF CONSUMER SPENDING TO SIZE AND REMUNERATION OF LABOR

YEAR	PERSONAL CONSUMPTION EXPENDITURE (Billions/Dollars)	TOTAL U. S. CIVILIAN LABOR FORCE (Thousands)	TOTAL U.S. WAGES AND SALARIES (Billions/Dollars)
1957	285.2	65,011	238.5
1963	373.8	75,712	311.2
1968[x]	541.1	78,874	469.0

[x]Third Quarter figures

This table says that wages and salaries, as well as personal consumption expenditure, increased faster than the size of the civilian labor force. This at least suggests that labor was getting a bigger share in both. (Personal consumption expenditure includes "durable goods, non durable goods and services." Wages and salaries cover the same persons as total civilian labor force; but, since this includes a good many who work for profit, some ruling class personal spelling must thereby be included in Table 22. The point being made, however, is relative, nor absolute.)

Another way of showing that conclusions from Table 21 may validly be applied to the working class consists in comparing per capita meat consumption with income distribution, meat consumption being an accepted yardstick of high living standards. This yardstick has the advantage of being far less amenable to the arguments about "improvements distribution" discussed in the previous Chapter: the ruling class is numerically too small to warp these averages in the same way it distorts wages figures from colonial areas.

Table 23[5]

U.S. PER CAPITA MEAT CONSUMPTION AND INCOME DISTRIBUTION

YEAR	APPARENT CIVILIAN PER CAPITA MEAT CONSUMPTION (Lbs)	% OF U.S. POPULATION WITH MINIMUM MEAN FAMILY ANNUAL INCOME		
		$ 6,000	$15,000	$ 2,000
1930	129.0	1.8[o]	1.1[d]	89.2[o]
1940	142.4	5.8	1.6[a]	45.3
1947	145.2[+]	10.2[x]	2.5[a]	34.5
1955	162.8	24.4	1.2	25.3
1960	160.8	38.4	3.2	20.2
1963	169.4	52.6	5.4	10.6
1964	174.5	55.6	6.3	9.5
1965	166.7	58.3	.7.6	9.1

[+]Top   [o]1935-36   [a]Over $10,000   [x]$6,000-$10,000
[+]1945

From this table, it is plain that not only did a growing percentage of US families enjoy better mean family incomes with each passing year, but that these incomes represented real material advances, despite inflation and monopoly price fixing. The most spectacular advances occurred after 1940 (i. e., after World War II), when undisputed hegemony was established by the American ruling class over the international imperialist scene.

The above data also confirm that, wage-wise, the US labor aristocracy prior to World War II, was a very small minority of both US population and of US workers, while poverty then was fairly widespread in that country.

From their entry into World War II until the present, the US economic rulers kept their economy on a war footing. This fact throws new light on a remark by English economist J. A. Hobson, (Quoted by Lenin in his discussion of imperialist parasitism. Chapter 18, Note No. 9) to the effect that in many towns and industrialized countries "important trades" depend on "government employment or contracts."

This dependency Lenin cited as another indication of imperialism's growing parasitism. Today, that same condition, and its effect on the US people and working class, have advanced immeasurably. Today, in the US, there are states like California (one of the biggest) where

> "the defense industry is the major producer of revenue . . . and thousands of people are employed by it. The University itself obtains a large portion of its revenue for research from Defense foundations and the San Francisco Bay is surrounded with military installations — air bases, army bases, armament stockpiles, the embarcation point for many on their way to Vietnam, and one of the points from which supplies are shipped to Vietnam."[6]

Here is suggested the type of government contract upon which, today, the most highly-paid section of the US working class depends. Nothing more vividly illustrates the monstrous growth of imperialist parasitism than its ever expanding military spending which, in one form or another, now comprises the overwhelming bulk of government contracts.[7]

In an appeal to the American people to oppose US Aggression in Vietnam, the British sage, Lord Bertrand Russell, drew the following picture of US war expenditures:

> "When the US began its war against the Vietnamese, after having paid for all of the French war against the same people, the US Defense Department owned property valued at $160 billion. This value has since doubled. The US Defense Department is the world's largest organization, owning 32 million acres in the US and millions more in foreign countries.

> "By now, more than 75 cents out of every hundred are spent on present wars and preparation for future wars. Billions of dollars are placed in the pockets of the US military, thereby giving the Pentagon economic power affecting every facet of American life.

> "Military assets in the US are three times as great as the combined assets of US Steel, Metropolitan Life Insurance, American Telephone & Telegraph, General Motors and Standard Oil.

> "The Defense Department employs three times the number of people working in all these great world corporations. The billions of dollars in military contracts are provided by the Pentagon and fulfilled by large industry. By 1960, $21 billion were spent on military goods. Of this colossal sum, $7 1/2 billion were divided amongst ten corporations and five corporations received nearly $1 billion each . . .

"The subcontracts (the Pentagon) award to smaller industries and war contractors involve every American city, and thus affect the jobs of millions of people. Four million work for the Defense Department. Its payroll is $12 billion, twice that of the US Automobile industry. A further 4 million work directly in arms industries. In many cities, military production accounts for as much as 80% of all manufacturing jobs. Over 50% of the gross national product of the US is devoted to military spending."[8]

Here, in all its nakedness, stands the incubus currently sucking the world's economic and physical blood: such monumental parasitism is unequaled in history. Russell's eight million workers in industries or categories connected with direct military spending comprise about one in seven of all those with jobs in the civilian working class of 1960. (See Table 8.)

What is more, the military factor today has become the clue to all current imperialist motivations: for, militarism is this system's "defense" against socialism, which it still hopes eventually to conquer.[7]

20. The Mode of Life of the US Working Class

It will be recalled that Lenin placed first among his general criteria of a labor aristocracy its mode of life.

In the previous chapter, personal consumption was cursorily examined. Income – and nutrition-wise, we showed that from the mid-40s onward increasing numbers of lower income US People moved upward in their mode of life. But this presented only part of the picture.

Another salient feature of the American mode of life is its gargantuan credit system. The following table shows both the size of credit cumulatively extended to the American people and the direction of its motion:

<u>Table 24</u>[1]

<u>TRENDS IN TOTAL U.S. CONSUMER CREDIT</u>
(Installment and Non-Installment)
(In Millions of Dollars)

YEAR	INSTALLMENT	NON-INSTALLMENT[*]	TOTAL
1940	5,514	2,824	8,338
1950	14,703	6,768	21,471
1959	39,852	12,267	52,119
1964	60,548	17,894	78,442
1968[x]	82,940	21,382	104,322

[*]Credit cards, charge accounts, etc. [x]Sept.

In 1959, and again in 1964, the size of the stock of outstanding credit accruing over the years to the account of the American people was 12. 2% of the size of G.N.P. Credit is being extended to the people of the US far more rapidly than they are repaying. Such an accumulating consumer credit debt permits a significant number of lower-paid workers to enjoy – in the form of real TV's, refrigerators, cars and other attributes of affluence – the material fruits of colonial super-exploitation. So, in this way, credit extends the boundaries of the labor aristocracy.

Nevertheless, this enormous consumer debt is the source of considerable "weeping" by certain Leftists who bemoan the "fate" of the "poor" American people who have taken it on. These "tears" are justified insofar as the imperialist system has become an anachronism. But meantime – debt or no debt – the fact is that, for those who inhabit imperialist citadels, goods actually used form an indispensable portion of the modern labor aristocracy's mode of life. Their enjoyment of such values constitutes a substantial part – above and beyond wages – of the real content of imperialist bribery. An idea of how far-reaching this enjoyment of real physical values actually is can be formed from the following facts about American life in 1960:[2]

> — California, with a population of 15.7 million, had 7.8 million registered automobiles on its roads. Of total US families, 77% owned cars; and of US auto owners, 61% bought theirs on credit, to the tune of some $513 million of outstanding debt in that category in 1960 alone – an amount equal to about 20% of total wages and salaries disbursed the year before.

> — Driving through California countryside, it is not unusual to see outside tumble-down shacks the latest model expensive automobiles. This is how the credit system extends the enjoyment of real values beyond wage boundaries. And a

specific slang term for this condition has sprung up: such people are described as "car poor," used adjectivally.

— On weekends, it is difficult to negotiate California's 143,598 miles of superior highways because of the crush of such cars, a significant number of which trail small boats behind. A total of more than six million outboard motors were in use in the US and some 300,000 boats were sold to consumers.

— The following table lists a few luxuries enjoyed by substantial sections of US population:

Table 25[3]

ELECTRICAL APPLIANCE AND CAR OWNERSHIP
(1967)

A P P L I A N C E	% OF TOTAL U.S. HOMES OWNING
Home Freezers	25.7
Clothes Driers	30.5
Electric Blankets	38.7
Electric Shavers	44.9[o]
Electric Sewing Machines	46.2[o]
Phonographs	49.2[o]
Electric Skillets	50.3
Electric Coffeemakers	76.0
Electric Mixers	76.0
Automobiles	79.0[x]
Steam Irons	81.2
Electric Toasters	86.3
Electric Washing Machines	88.2
Electric (or Gas) Stove	96.2[o]
TV Sets	97.8
Electric Refrigerators	99.6

[x]Percentage of families owning. [o]1963

— Of all occupied housing units in the US in 1960, 61.9% were owner-occupied (64.4% among whites; 38.8% among Afro-Americans).

—The increased standard of living that comes from urbanization includes a substantial increase in suburbanization. Between 1950 and 1960, the population living in what the Bureau of Census calls "Standard Metropolitan Areas" went up some 36.8 million, or about 50%.[4]

Other indications of superior living among significant portions of the American people are shown in Table 26a and 26b.

One development on the American scene lately appeared to threaten the US labor aristocracy's growing affluence: the automation of industry.

This "revolution in technology" has been responsible for displacing huge numbers of unskilled and semi-skilled workers. In this way, it has been largely responsible for a rate of Afro-American unemployment double that of whites. It has also swollen the trend already inherent in the system toward increasing the number of non-productive workers as percentage of total population.

This problem has been the subject of much discussion in the larger US weekly magazines, one of which recorded that "organized labor as a whole has hardly begun to face up to the problem – and the opportunity – of automation".[6] Labor's fear of advancing automation, this source said, was one cause of its recent boldness in making demands of various types.

And with reason: the article noted that automation "blunts the strike weapon", explaining that when an industry is "overwhelmingly automated", a few "unorganized and supervisory types" can easily keep equipment running despite picket lines. This really happened during the 1964 strike by the Communications Workers Union

Table 26a[5]

TRENDS IN RETAIL SALES
Especially in Appliances and Luxury Goods
(In Millions of Dollars)

YEAR	TOTAL RETAIL SALES [x]	HOUSEHOLD APPLIANCES TV & RADIOS	TOTAL APPAREL SALES	EATING & DRINKING PLACES	LIQUOR STORES
1957	200,002	3,983	12,277	14,787	4,212
1958	200,353	3,688	12,559	14,792	4,439
1959	215,413	4,053	13,266	15,601	4,729
1960	219,529	3,835	13,677	16,083	4,880
1961	218,811	3,816	13,730	16,403	4,904
1962	235,351	3,817	14,338	17,305	5,401
1963	246,435	4,147	14,460	18,071	5,659
1964	261,630	4,199	15,282	19,577	6,011
1965	283,950	4,223	15,752	21,423	6,305
1966	303,672	4,905	17,276	23,431	6,758
% NET CHANGE	+51.8	+24.9	+40.8	+58.5	+60.5

[x]On concerns operating 11 or more stores or organizations

against California's General Telephone Company: after 100 days, the union was forced to abandon the strike "without winning a single significant benefit."

Nonetheless, ways are already being found by which the "upper stratum" of labor can foist consequences off its own back: when automation's tendency to unemployment falls heaviest on Afro-American backs. Some workers displaced by automation started to join a new union organizing workers in government, slum tenants and unemployed.

In addition, new labor gains in a number of fields have been traced to automation, as one of two main recent sources:

"Automation and the successful elimination of much union featherbedding have so reduced costs that some

Table 26b[5]

TRENDS IN RETAIL SALES
Especially in Appliances and Luxury Goods
(In Millions of Dollars)

| YEAR | S P E C I F I C   A P P L I A N C E S | | | | | | | | | |
| | AIR CONDI-TIONERS | | CONSUMER ELECTRONICS | | DISH WASHERS | | FOOD WASTE DISPOSERS | | HOME FREEZERS | |
	NUMBER	AMOUNT	NUMBER	AMOUNT	NUMBER	AMOUNT	NUMBER	AMOUNT	NUMBER	AMOUNT
1957	1,276[a]	383[a]	18,013	n.a.	295[a]	90[a]	520[a]	60[a]	1,100[a]	440[a]
1958	n.a.	n.a.	n.a.	n.a.	n.a.	n.a.	n.a.	n.a.	n.a.	n.a.
1959	1,660	447	n.a.	n.a.	547	140	789	63	1,205	397
1960	1,580	439	21,426	2,266	555	142	760	61	1,045	308
1961	n.a.	n.a.	n.a.	n.a.	n.a.	n.a.	n.a.	n.a.	n.a.	n.a.
1962	1,580	411	24,057	2,407	720	174	890	67	1,070	284
1963	1,965	492	23,390	2,447	880	212	1,090	80	1,090	278
1964	n.a.	n.a.	n.a.	n.a.	n.a.	n.a.	n.a.	n.a.	n.a.	n.a.
1965	2,945	624	34,955	3,915	1,260	276	1,360	82	1,160	271
1966	3,553	742	37,822	4,773	1,511	327	1,438	86	1,096	255
% NET CHANGE	+178.5	+93.8	+110.0	+110.1	+412.0	+253.0	+176.5	+43.4	–	–46.3

[*] In units of 1,000   [a] 1955 figures   n.a. = not available

Tables 26a and 26b outline the American "mode of life." The appliances selected mark at least the beginnings of luxury living in the U.S. labor force. For further interpretation, Table 22, Page   , may be consulted. It shows increases between 1957 and 1966 of 89.5% in consumer spending; of 96.7% (nearly double) in wages and salaries; and of 21.3% in size of civilian labor force. By October 1968, retail sales had reached a rate of $330,782 millions, or an increase of 65.6% since 1957.[6]

industries have already been able to grant substantial wage increases without damaging their profits. "8

The other source which in the long run will originate in automation to bring labor "enormous benefits" is contained in "the increased productivity and profits" made possible. This was illustrated for the Communications Workers referred to in the case of the lost California strike. This union had already made such gains

"because automation has helped the industry to expand its services about 170%" out of which "the union, even though fewer plug-pullers and pole-climbers are required, has also increased its membership."[7]

The trend in labor gains that ensues is

"to reduce the time men work through longer vacations, sabaticals, earlier retirement, etc. Such benefits constituted nearly half of last fortnights steel settlement."[7]

But perhaps such rising affluence is ephemeral? Is not every wage rise under monopoly capitalism redeemed by the ruling class through price rises, not to mention other forms of inflation?

The following table shows that wages and salaries rise more rapidly than the purchasing power of the dollar falls off:

The import of this table in effect corroborates the report which said that

"inflation . . . at an annual rate of 3.5% is eating up nearly half of the workers' yearly wage gains."[7]

Compared with "profits that have nearly doubled" since 1961,[6] such wage gains illustrate how the system apportions its "benefits" by class.

<u>Table 27</u>[9]

WAGES AND PURCHASING POWER

| YEAR | WAGES & SALARIES | | PURCHASING POWER | |
	MILLIONS OF DOLLARS	% NET CHANGE	OF THE DOLLAR CONSUMER PRICES 1957-59 = $1.00	% NET CHANGE
1940	49,818		2.048	
1950	146,391	+ 194[x]	1.194	-41.7[x]
1959	258,206[*]	+76.3[x]	.985	-17.5[x]
1964	332,151	+31.0[x]	.925	- 6.1[x]
1966	392,300	+18.1[x]	.884	- 4.6[x]
1967	423,400	+ 8.0[x]	.860	- 2.8[x]
1968	469,000[o]	+10.7[x]	.818[+]	- 5.1[x]

[*] July 1965 <u>Survey of Current Business,</u> Page 12.
[x] Changes shown are from <u>previous</u> figures.
[o] Third Quarter   [+] September 1968

None of what has been said herein is intended to "refute" or deny that there are and will continue to be "poverty pockets" in the US Though they have been for some years now a minority manifestation of internal conditions there, their very existence is grossly anomalous, and not objectively "socially necessary." The American poor, harbingers though they be of the future, are concurrently a phenomenon adequately described by saying that

> "the basis of the law of accumulation is the reserve army, whose function in the system is to enable the capitalist class to maintain its control over the labor force, to prevent wages from eating into profits, and in this way choking off the surplus."[10]

The "poor", though not necessarily all unemployed, inhabit a similar economic level of existence.

Furthermore, material in these pages is not to be taken as denying that imperialist contradictions, expressed in such phenomena as the Vietnam war, will not inevitably produce losses for the metropolitan labor elite sooner or later. Indeed, they have begun greatly to shake the entire imperialist economy. But this has not yet become crucial or decisive: between August 1965 and the same month in 1966, real wages dropped from $87.15 to $86.22.[11] But this net decrease of 93% amounts to 1.1%. In the light of Table 27, real net gains are not yet substantially affected. That they will be affected is likely. Indeed, the VIETNAM COURIER of Hanoi soon reported a new slide:

> "According to unofficial statistics, the real wages of industrial workers in New York in September 1966 dropped by 5.4 per cent . . . compared with the corresponding period in 1965."[12]

Though a local phenomenon, this may be indicative. What remains to be seen is whether this drop "takes" and grows, or whether it is one of the "downs" among the system's "ups and downs" which will disappear only with the system itself.

In any case, the major US unions, representing the labor aristocracy, are now attempting to see that any real losses are paid for by others than their members. The tables we have been developing suggest that so far, unions usually get pretty much what they are after. The "ups and downs" of the system are "solved" at the expense of colonial people, a point still being developed.

From the above material, the following conclusions related to the size of the US labor aristocracy seem reasonable:

> 1. Wage-wise, the affluence of the American working class has increased with time so that, from an insignificant minority, its topmost layer (of highly paid workers) has grown to a significant minority (nearly 11%) both in absolute size and in the influence of its mode of life on the rest of labor.

2. The American mode of life embraces a still-growing number, of workers in ways defined as making them a labor aristocracy:

a) The enormous US consumer credit system not only furnishes an indispensable part of the real values enjoyed by Americans, working class in their majority; it also extends the boundaries of the US labor aristocracy to include a significant portion of lower-paid workers. This is illustrated in Table 25 by the almost universal ownership of automobiles, TV sets and refrigerators.

b) Trade unions and cooperatives encompass the wages aspect of the labor aristocracy. Since upper-bracket wages affect a minority of US workers, these organizations embrace, correspondingly, a minority of the US working class.

c) The electorate and church and sports club memberships reflect the "outlook" of a labor aristocracy: "status", "prestige", etc. – which influences all but the tiniest minority of US population and the working class. (See Chapter 21, below).This is so whether or not their "outlook" is matched by money wages; in the majority of case, it is not.

These conclusions are all compatible with the ever-growing parasitism of decaying imperialism, and should therefore also have been predictable.

Now, based on American monopoly capital's leading role in the world imperialist system, all of this, of course, has referred to the US working class only. It is, however, instructive and politically important to note that American trends are being followed now in Western Europe:

"While US employers have reason to complain about soaring labor costs, the fact is that wages have been rising much faster in other major nations, notably those of

Western Europe. Between the 1958 start of the Common Market and 1965, US workers' pretax wages went up 4%. During that seven-year period, pretax wages jumped 25% in Italy, 29% in France, 40% in Denmark, 41% in The Netherlands, and 53% in West Germany.

"To be sure, European workers, having started lower, still have a lot of catching up to do. The average American factory hand collects $108 a week before taxes. By contrast, the British auto worker last year had a pretax income of $63 a week, the German $55, the French $43. But income figures are only part of the equation. When living costs, government services, and the many immeasurable fringe benefits are added in, the balance – while still favoring the American worker – is distinctly lopsided. The fringes, for instance, account for 20% to 25% of the US worker's earning, but up to 55% of the European's."[13]

These figures show that a majority concept is at least becoming a real possibility for the labor aristocracy throughout the West.

The Western labor aristocracy, including that of the US, is and will remain a minority of world labor. This is said despite the fact that in the sense of its "entire outlook", and – even if a bit less so – of its "Western" mode of life, it already is a majority of the Western working class.

President Sekou Toure had by December 1962 already suggested a similar conclusion, adding his version of where the majority of the world proletariat was to be found. According to him, within the total world imperialist economy. Western workers by and large constituted a world labor aristocracy while the colonial peoples furnished the "world proletariat", that phenomenon which Lenin called "the lower stratum of the proletariat proper."

21. The Entire Outlook of the Modern Labor Aristocracy "At Home"

Among his general criteria for a labor aristocracy, Lenin had included their "entire outlook". And how could it be other wise? Had Lenin not warned that "capital export" – together with the enormous stream of super-profits it pours back into industrialized nations – "sets the seal of parasitism on the whole country which lives" by thus "exploiting the labor of several overseas countries and colonies"? Did he add, "except for labor"? He did not.

How accurately he had assessed the truth is revealed by exploring the outlook specifically of American labor:

1. American political support for the ruling class and its policies;

2. The state of American working-class militancy, as expressed in its attitude toward events at home and abroad; and

3. Labor lieutenants in the working-class movement and their effect on working-class attitudes.

1. Political support for American ruling class policies.

Except for short periods of revolt – and certainly without break since 1950 – the overwhelming majority of the American people have throughout their history with a regularity and lack of dissent almost uniform played the bourgeois game of parliamentarism, including all but a fraction of a working class which has been estimated, above, at a minimum of 66% of population.

Whenever dissatisfied with conditions, they have found ready to hand an admirable safety valve: "the Party not in power." National popular malaise has invariably abated as the U.S. electorate (and not only there!) has oscillated pendulum-like between the two heads of a single major political party. Developed by an astute ruling class which divides the spoils of office at periodic intervals, and emerging under a number of historically generic names, this political vehicle in the U.S. today is called by its owners alternately "Democratic" and "Republican".

November 1966 was a case in point: despite rising inflation, growing casualties in the Vietnam war, and innumerable annoying consequences of the latter, a sizeable number of "Democratic" officials were merely replaced by "Republicans": the same foreign policies will thereby continue, while labor and its aristocracy's spokesmen wring concessions from the alternating "in's." Nor is this diagnosis altered by the "election" in 1968 of "Republican" Richard Nixon to the Presidential chair.

One thing is sure: rich returns on overseas economic activities, including some extremely lucrative ones newly come by in South Vietnam, will – as long as they continue, guarantee the repetition of such political oscillation.

Table 28 traces the history of American popular political support for the status quo, starting at a point only twelve years after the betrayal of Reconstruction in the Hayes election of 1876:

Out of 20 reported elections, in only seven did the total independent vote pass the million mark; in only two, approach (and in only one of these, surpass) the five-million level; in only three did popular dissension reach 10%, the last of these having been in 1924; and all three occurred prior to the Great Depression.

A most enlightening explanation has been offered by sociologist C. Wright Mills in his documented study of the U.S. Labor force cited earlier. On American politics, he comments:

> "No U.S. political leader with following (with the possible exception of Debs with his 900,000 votes in 1912) has

<u>Table 28</u>[1]

<u>POLITICAL DISSENSION AMONG THE AMERICAN ELECTORATE</u>
(1888 through 1964)

YEAR[oo]	TOTAL POPULAR VOTE (In 1,000's)	TOTAL INDEPENDENT[a] PARTIES (In 1,000's)	%
1888	11,383	297	2.6
1892	12,061	1,323	11.0
1896	13,907	312	2.2
1900	13,968	393	2.8
1904	13,521	810	6.0
1908	14,884	797	5.3
1912	15,037	5,254	35.0
1916	18,531	869	4.7
1920	26,748	1,475	6.3
1924	29,086	4,983	17.3
1928	36,812	404	1.1
1932	39,732	1,163	2.9
1936	45,643	1,215	2.7
1940	49,891	262	.5
1944	47,969	347	.7
1948	48,681	2,615	5.4
1952	61,303	149	-[*]
1956	62,015	402	-[*]
1960	68,836	502	-[*]
1964	70,645	336	-
TOTALS	700,663	23,908	3.4

[a]Includes: Socialist and Socialist Labor;
Populist (1892); Progressive (1912, 1924);
States Rights and Independent Progressive
(1948); Prohibition; Communists.
[oo]20th Century figures are grouped by years
between wars.
[*]Less than 0.1%

ventured even to discuss seriously the overturning of property relations . . .

". . . Progressive' political movements have . . . been technologically reactionary, in the literal sense; they have been carried on by those who were defending small property by waging war against the large concentrations of property. Breaks in the major parties have been breaks caused by conflicting tendencies among old middle class politicians. By 1912, for example, when Theodore Roosevelt broke away from the Republican Party with his Bull Moose campaign, he was on the one hand fighting those who wanted to give absolutely free rein to monopolies, and on the other restraining the nomination of LaFollette as a Republican candidate. As Matthew Josephson has shown, the small men 'who feared and hated monopolies', who wished 'to make secure the small property holder's way of life' . . . gave and received support from LaFollette; it was primarily for such little men that twelve years later, in 1924, the largest third-party vote in the history of the United States was cast."[2]

2. The state of American working-class militancy.

It is customary among the Western Left, and uncritically echoed by most of the socialist world, to talk at length about "the growing militancy of the working class", or of "the proletariat in the main capitalist countries" in general.

For instance,

"The part played in the revolutionary movement by strikes against capitalist exploitation has latterly grown substantially . . . particularly . . . in the industrially developed countries. While the number involved in the whole of the capitalist world more than doubled between 1958 and 1963 (rising from around 25,000,000 to 58,000,000), that in the industrially developed countries increased more than three times over (from 13,500,000 to 43,000,000) . . . .

"Strikes often go together with meetings and demonstrations, economic demands with political – strikers demand nationalization of private firms and monopolies, and participation in the management of nationalized enterprises, protest against reactionary bills and military provocations take action in defence of peace...

"The rise of the strike movement in the industrially developed countries testifies to the growing organizational level and determination of the proletariat in its class struggle against the bourgeoisie, to the growing solidarity of the workers in the struggle against capitalist oppression and for social progress, democracy and peace."[3]

(What ever happened to "socialism"?) Documentation in this article included the USA, and Japan, with a short paragraph mentioning Britain, Belgium, Finland and Greece as "other developed capitalist countries" of the same sort (Greece, at least, is a semi-colonial country).

Another example of this position emerged elsewhere:

"In the capitalist countries, the strike struggle is expanding on an unparalleled mass scale, the political nature is more prominent, and the unity of action of the working people is being consolidated. . . . The surging struggle of the working class whose political consciousness is enhancing is giving a severe blow to the aggression and war policy of U.S. imperialism, the chieftain of international reaction."[4]

Notice carefully that even when statistics were used, the claims of political content of strikes, or of the various alleged demands put forth generally by workers "in the industrially developed countries" in their strikes are NOT DOCUMENTED. In the U.S. at least no such general claim can be documented because no supporting facts exist. In any case, we shall soon discuss how much, and exactly what, meaning it would have if such claims could be "proven."

What has been the record of the American working class as regards militancy at home, or of the West in general? Have strike struggles really been "expanding on an unparalleled mass scale"? Has "the political nature (been) enhancing" or becoming "more prominent"? And has any such struggle of the Western working class as yet given "a severe blow to the aggression and war policy of American imperialism"?

The events of May 1968 in France have been avidly seized upon by most of the Western Left to "prove" once again that all these questions have an affirmative reply. When the dust had settled over French soil, it was still being raised elsewhere all over the "revolutionary" Western Left with sighs of "if only . . ." France's "almost revolution" is measured by the old customary criterion offered for decades by Western Left economists: the "size of the strike struggle." Let us, therefore, meet them first on their own grounds.

What are the facts about the U.S. strike struggle? And their meaning?

Do the continuing strikes in industrially developed countries really indicate increased militancy among the working class?

Strike struggles in the USA

It is not enough to count the number of strikers or strikes in order to estimate even the size of the strike struggle, let alone "working-class militancy." Numerical assessments of this type must be related to the size of the labor force.

The following table attempts this:

Table 29[5]

TRENDS IN U.S. WORK STOPPAGES
(In Thousands)

YEAR	(A) CIVILIAN RESIDENT POPULATION	(1) TOTAL U. S. CIVILIAN LABOR FORCE	(8) % OF (1)/(A)	(2) NUMBER OF STRIKERS	(3) NUMBER/ MAN-DAYS LOST	(4) % OF (3)/(1)	(5) % OF (2)/(1)
1945	128,112	52,820	41.2	3,467	38,025	72.0	6.7
1950	150,790	59,748	39.6	2,410	38,800	66.6	4.0
1960	178,153	64,267	36.1	1,320	19,100	29.7	2.1
1961	181,207	65,516	36.2	1,450	16,100	24.9	2.2
1962	183,796	71,854	38.2	1,230	18,600	25.9	1.7
1963	186,667	72,975	38.2	941	16,300	22.0	1.3
1964	189,372	76,971	40.5	1,640	22,900	29.7	2.1
1965	191,874	75,635	34.4	1,550	23,300	30.9	2.0
1966	193,780	75,770	25.6	1,900	25,400	33.5	2.5

Between 1950 and 1960, something happened which cut the percentage of man-days lost to total labor force drastically. Could it have been the Korean war? It is interesting, though perhaps not particularly pertinent here, that the labor force, which increasing numerically, has fallen steadily as related to the total civilian resident population. What is important here is that the ratio of strikers to total labor force has not risen notably since 1960. Even the slow upward creep since 1964 has not taken it much over half way back to its 1950 level. Again, the ratio of man-days lost to total labor force by 1966 had reached half the 1950 value.

Another factor which might assess "militancy" would be the composition of the strikers. In three separate issues, two Big Business weeklies recorded developments in the American labor movement, citing "a new restless mood",[6] and "a riptide of new militancy . . . flooding this placid landscape in a sea of revolt".[7]

These periodicals listed a number of actual strikes: pilots on Pan-American World Airways; two big Manhattan department stores; a construction firm at Cape Kennedy; towboat owners in Pittsburgh; and three machine-tool plants in Detroit." Other strikes were reported "threatened " ; New York newspaper workers; the Transport Workers Union in Philadelphia.[6] Moreover, even where strikes were not on,

> "Unions are making stiff demands in the rubber, aero space, aluminum, shipping and textile industries, all of which must renew labor contracts in the coming months."[6]

In corroboration of these claims, the following were offered:

— A noticeable "toughening" of the "customarily docile" International Union of Electrical Workers, demanding a "10% plus package increase."[7]

— A victory of striking fruit pickers in California, being followed by the National Farm Workers Association with a strike of vegetable growers in the Rio Grande Valley of Texas.[7]

— Two-thirds of the firemen in Atlanta, Georgia, out on a strike "that is probably the most important shut-down of public safety employees since the abortive Boston police strike of 1919."

— The AFL-CIO's Industrial Union Department (IUD) "in cooperation with Rev. Martin Luther King," "successfully organizing a 'labor union' of slum tenants in Chicago," with the "sole purpose . . . to bargain for contracts with landlords", and reportedly had actually won contracts covering 4,500 tenants with a commitment by some landlords to supply hot and cold running water for tubs and sinks "at all times."[7] (The IUD expected "a full 15% of (slum tenants) to become ... members".)

— "Even more indicative of labor's renaissance has been the fresh efforts of big unions to sign up the vast pool of unorganized workers at the bottom of the economic ladder: farm workers, day laborers, and even the unemployed".[7]

— The AFL-CIO "parent organization" officially announcing that "its unions would ignore the President's 3.2% wage guideline in collective bargaining". (As a result, the August 1965 strike of airline machinists won a 5%-plus wage hike.)[7] Walter Reuther had won 4.8% from the auto industry the previous fall.[6]

—Public service workers striking or threatening to: social workers in Los Angeles; nurses in San Francisco; firemen in Kansas City, Mo.; also, in Atlanta, Georgia; teachers in Michigan; garbage collectors in Dayton, Ohio; and "a group of New York hospital doctors."[7]

— A new union drive, about to get under way for "organization of vast numbers of new members". Such a drive was claimed to be already on. From 12.9 million members in 1964, the AFL-CIO was said now to have "spurted 5% to a present level of 13.5 million." (See Table 16, page 156, above) A good 40% of this growth, it was testified, had

> "its fastest growing frontier among public employees
> . . . The number of union members in state, local and
> Federal employment has soared from 915,000 in 1956
> to an estimated 1.5 million today."[7]

While one of these two sources presented this increase in union membership for the first time in a decade – and other factors – as an indication of "Labor's Increased Militancy,"[7] the facts, as well as certain other considerations, make such an interpretation doubtful.

Militancy and the American Working Class.

First of all, despite the vague way in which the information is presented by these articles, a table can be compiled of the unions probably involved in all the actual strikes reported. This table cannot, with the information available, be definitive or statistically exact. It simply suggests an order of magnitude in the "new upheaval" for the number and type of workers involved.

The total number striking or threatening to strike, as summarized by this table, was less than one and a quarter millions (1,153 thousands). Eight different cities were named; and eight out of 50

Table 30[6, 7]

"LABOR'S INCREASED MILITANCY"[o]

CATEGORY OF WORKER INVOLVED	TOTAL NAT'L MEMBER- SHIPS 1964 (1,000's)	AREA INVOLVED	ESTIMATED NUMBER INVOLVED[+] (Less Than)
Airline Pilots	n.l.	Pan-World Airways Line	1,000
Retail Clerks	428	2 Dept. Stores, Manhattan	2,000
Tool and Die Makers	n.l.	Detroit, Mich.	600
Towboat Owners	n.l.	Pittsburgh, Pa.	1,000
National Farm Workers Association	n.l.		
Fruit Pickers		California	
Vegetable Growers		Rio Grande Valley, Texas	25,000
Firemen	80[x]	Atlanta, GA (500, actual)	1,000
Public Service Workers[xx]	139	L.A., S.F., K.C., Atlanta,	
Teachers	100	Dayton, O., N.Y.C.	
		State of Michigan	5,000

[o]"National and international unions reporting 100,000 members of more," all "with headquarters in the U.S., sometimes contain a sizeable membership in Canada: in 1964, there were 1,135 thousand Canadian members included as AFL-CIO members in the U.S. under this definition.[8]

[+]Estimates of numbers of workers involved in the actual strikes were based in part on the union's size nationally, simply guessing at what proportion would be involved in the locality concerned.

[x]World Almanac, 1960; Page 49; International Union of firefighters

[xx]AFGE, including Cape Kennedy (American Federation of Government Employees)

n.l. = not listed: either less than 100,000 members; or, not unionized by 1964.

stated (16%). The total estimated number of union members involved was 40,600, admittedly quite "iffy".

Even if the numbers of strikers estimated are low, it is clear that only a small percentage of total U.S. membership in unions is taking part in this alleged "upsurge" of American labor. The percentage of strikers to population is very small, indeed. This would be so even if all the national unions concerned had gone on strike as a whole, which they clearly did not. All instances cited were sharply localized.

Slum tenants would add greatly to this number if they could be included. Only 4,500 were actually mentioned. Also, presumably among them some union memberships might be duplicated. Anyhow, all the article said was that the IUD "expects a full 15%" to join a projected union. The single area involved was Chicago, Illinois.

Among those estimated as striking in the above table, the majority (31,600) were in basic trades: airline pilots, tool and die makers, transport workers and farm workers. The "industrial proletariat" wants more – inside the system – and is still able to get it.

In these articles, the largest single number dealt with the advance in union membership cited, of which 40% accounted for a single bloc: government employees. These have always been notoriously under-paid; maybe some of them are already those displaced by automation from former highly-paid jobs. The effects of the prolonged war in Vietnam, accompanied by zooming corporation profits which the richest unions make the basis for their demands, are seen here. What these workers are after is "their share" of the increasing national swag, which one of the reports put into context via a chart, showing corporate profits doubled since 1961.

Naturally, it is inevitable for lower-paid workers to want more. What concerns us, however, is this: does that constitute working class militancy? So far, we have been examining the claims of those who say it does without discussing the merits of their claims.

However, such an examination is in order. And for those who so vehemently insist that the workers' economic struggle is equitable with class struggle, a recent discussion out of Copenhagen, Denmark, is of great interest.

In 1879, to a request from Bernstein for "an article on the struggle of the English working class", Friedrich Engels wrote:

> "For a number of years past the English working class movement has been hopelessly describing a narrow circle of strikes for higher wages and shorter hours, not, however as an expedient or means of propaganda and organisation, but as the ultimate aim . . . One can speak here of a labor movement only in so far as strikes take place here which, whether they are won or not, do not get the movement one step further."[9]

The Danish source comments:

> "Two things here are decisive:

> "First: Economic strikes – for higher wages, shorter hours – MAY be of importance, if they are being used as an expedient or a means of propaganda and organization. That is not what (the revisionists) have in mind . . . They want to lead the economic struggle, hoping that then the workers are going to listen to them when they talk politics.

> "Second: Whether the kind of strikes of which Engels is talking are won or lost, they do not get the movement one step further. Seen from a political point of view – from a revolutionary point of view they are utterly trivial. That is to say: these economic struggles are not a part of the class struggle."[10]

Not surprisingly, Lenin had also had a word to say on this subject:

> "We are all agreed that our task is that of the organization of the proletarian class struggle. But what is this class struggle? When the workers of a single factory or of a single branch of industry engage in struggle against their employer or employers, is this class struggle? No, this is only a weak embryo of it."[11]

Again, comment from the Danes:

> ". . . Under certain circumstances the economic struggle – the 'weak embryo' – develops into class struggle, which is to say that the struggle CHANGES ITS CHARACTER. But this does not happen automatically. First of all the 'weak embryo' seen in the historic perspective – an embryo in the history of the proletariat from its birth as an exploited class to the day on which it seizes power from the bourgeoisie . . . a struggle . . . is class struggle only when the object . . . is power in society."[12]

But Lenin had had more to say about this vital matter:

> "Only when the individual worker realizes that he is a member of the entire working class, only when he recognizes the fact that his petty day-to-day struggle against individual employers and individual government officials is a struggle against the entire bourgeoisie and the entire government does his struggle become a class struggle. 'Every class struggle is a political struggle.' These famous words of Marx are not to be understood to mean that the struggle of the workers against employers must ALWAYS be a political struggle. They must be understood to mean that the struggle of the workers against the capitalists BECOMES a political struggle INSOFAR AS it becomes a CLASS struggle."[13]

To this, the Danish writers add:

"Struggle for higher wages, shorter working hours, longer holidays, better working conditions, etc., can NEVER in itself become a political struggle, a class struggle. In 'What is to be Done?' Lenin unequivocally asserted that it is the purest of nonsense to try to 'lend the economic struggle itself a political character'. On the other hand the economic struggle may – under certain circumstances – be raised to the level of a political struggle."[14]

The meaning of these last words is left to Lenin to clarify:

". . . to conduct all propaganda and agitation from the viewpoint of revolution as opposed to reforms, systematically explaining this opposition to the masses theoretically and practically, at every step of parliamentary, trade union, co-operative work, etc. Under no circumstances to refrain (save in special cases as an exception) from utilizing the parliamentary system and the 'liberties' of bourgeois democracy; not to reject reforms but to regard them ONLY as a by-product of the revolutionary class struggle of the proletariat ."[15]

And now, the Danish protagonists warn:

"The last words – to regard reforms only as a by-product of the revolutionary class struggle – should not be under stood to mean that all reforms, which are actually carried out on demand from the workers, must be regarded as such by-products of the revolutionary class struggle. (This would lead to a conclusion: . . . We have had a great number of reforms – this proves that we have had many revolutionary class struggles.) Lenin's words must be understood to mean that communists should never make the struggle for reforms – higher wages, shorter working hours, etc. – THEIR object. These things are the spontaneous objects of the working class in the struggle against the bourgeoisie – they are never the objects of the communists, of conscious revolutionaries. If and when the working class will spontaneously start a struggle for objects of that kind, it is the task of communists – whenever possible –- to RAISE this spontaneous struggle to a struggle for another object, the object of class struggle. In so doing, they must – as pointed out by Lenin in the above quotation – explain to the masses that revolution and reforms are two diametrically opposed things. Reforms are concessions from the ruling class which maintains its rule. Revolution means to take power from the ruling class."[16]

For decades, the "working class in the main capitalist countries" has been carrying on struggles for economic goals. The end result, revolution-wise, it seems to us, can only suggest a fervent "Amen" to the above discussion. This discussion, and its context alone, forms the background in which it is permissible to study and evaluate the role of work stoppages in relation to the "militancy" of any labor movement anywhere in the world.

It is with this thought in mind that we continue that discussion:

WHEN did even the work stoppages believed to indicate "militancy" fall off; and WHY?

Table 29 shows that in the U.S. – the KEY imperialist country, where activities now influence all others – work stoppages fell off again sharply between 1950 and 1960: As has been suggested already, in between those dates was the Korean War. When the profits it "stimulated" began rolling in and labor's purely economic demands were satisfied by hiked wages, the "revolutionary strike struggles" likewise fell off. They rose, but only slightly, during 1964 and 1965: the prolonged war in Vietnam was dragging and not going well for the aggressors. Thus, during two periods when – if ever – the political stance of American workers was put sharply to the test, they failed to rise to the occasion.

But even if "lower echelons" of U.S. workers now enter the fray and demand their proper share in affluence – never mind how derived – even to a point of intensity equivalent to or greater than that achieved in France in May 1968, it will still not be necessary- or correct – to hail any "revolutionary class struggle" by American workers. For they will still be FAR from challenging capitalist rule; it will be the sheerest self-delusion to read into aggressive behavior on behalf of purely economic demands the "revolutionization" of the American working class.

What is crucial is not numbers per se; it is not behavior per se. It is the GOALS pursued; the purposes; the aims. Very small numbers of workers were really involved in distinctly localized actions in the above examples. Yet the Big Business magazines were claiming these actions as "increased militancy", despite their own unlimited nation-wide facilities for collecting all necessary statistics: if more examples had been available, they would have known. We can be sure they did not miss any such activity going on. And the "revolutionary" character of such periodicals is well known.

What, then, was the purpose of their hullaballoo?

Their motive peeps through the welter of reasons they advance for the alleged "militant upsurge" by American labor: All three articles agreed that "the healthy U.S. economy is itself responsible for much of the ferment."[6]

A composite list of specifically what they meant thereby included:

a) The "long U.S. economic boom"[7] ("an unprecedented 50 months"[6]).

b) A drop in unemployment [7] ("in March . . . 4.5%, the lowest in seven years."[6]).

c) The short supply of skilled labor with "buyers clamoring for their goods".[7]

d) "The spectacular rise in corporate profits".[7]

e) "The fact that inflation . . . at the annual rate of 3.5% is eating up nearly half the workers' yearly wage gains".[7]

f) "A new industrial revolution in automation".[6]

It was recorded that

> "Union members have worked full time and even overtime for the past three years; most have money in the bank, many are weary, and some would actually welcome a strike imposed vacation."[6]

In a word, two big U.S. business weeklies raised a hue and cry about new militancy only in order to bring out what they call the "health" of the U.S. economy. But their claim that the workers are determined to obtain their share of the swag is borne out: though numerically few were involved in these strikes, their GOALS were PURELY ECONOMIC, and they included some already-well-paid crafts.

The truth of their estimate is further borne out in a discussion of "tokenism" as a means for draining off "Negro" militancy:

> ". . . it is of the essence of tokenism that not many should be (affected by the results of the given struggle). But this does not deprive the phenomenon of its importance. The mere existence of the possibility of moving up and out can have a profound psychological impact . . .

> "... even those who have no stake in the system and have no hope of ever acquiring one may become reconciled to it if they come to believe there is a chance that their children, or perhaps their children's children, may be able to rise out of their own degraded conditions."17

In this quotation is summarised the debilitating effect of illusions that die hard among large segments of anti-colonial liberation.

Strike struggles in the USA, at very least, to this day do not embody working class militancy in the sense of class solidarity, or in the sense of any struggle for power or challenge to the system.

How else should be interpreted the protracted "negotiations" practiced by gentlemen "labor leaders" like George Meany of the AFL-CIO and gentlemen industrial aristocrats like the officials of U.S. Steel and other international giant U.S. corporations? It is assumed that the distinction is understood between subjective awareness of the need for socialism and objective reality: since the existing system can never satisfy the demand for full "non-poverty" (of which existing capacity and technology is quite capable) among America's internal colonial subjects and oppressed minorities like Mexicans and Puerto Ricans, any fight for such "non-poverty" will not inevitably lead to the eventual destruction of imperialism and to socialism EVEN in the U.S., but ONLY if there are real revolutionaries on the scene capable of raising such a fight for "non-poverty" to the level of a struggle for actual power. This, in turn, depends on the factual experience of those involved: as long as their demands can be carved out of the existing system, Marx taught that they would NEVER seek to change it ... and they are "right", while the Leftist "wish-dreamers" have deserted them.

Not only will such economic struggles not be the preliminary cause of any challenge to the system even eventually; they are also not at the moment any kind of decisive factor.

What such struggles express is the size and shape of working class illusions about the system which emanate from and are deliberately fostered by Social Democratic and other bourgeois ideological fountainheads. And these illusions can persist – can BE nourished and fostered – because of the ever-swelling super profits squeezed from "overseas" colonial labor. What these struggles are is a form of what Lenin called "economism" within the labor movement. Economism has been defined thus:

> "... economism is the limitation of perspective to immediate economic issues, with the role of trade union organization seen as simply the pursuit of those economic gains, but always within the bounds of a capitalist society ... The main symptom is the illusion that the constant pursuit of better wages .and conditions will eventually lead to a more equitable order of society, coupled with the belief that the aim of organizing is to participate in the present system and thereby assist its gradual conversion."[18]

Just to keep the record straight, let us add one inseparable thought:

> ". . . those not employed in industry . . . find it difficult to appreciate this situation. As a consequence they tend to underestimate the importance of this aspect of working-class struggle."[18]

(See Pages 28, above, for boundaries of what may or may not qualify as "working-class struggle".)

The author of the definition of economism, above, declares that the "limitations" (i.e., "of perspective to immediate economic issues") cause a "tendency to see economic struggle as as end in itself'. He added one thought with the main content of which we heartily concur:

"To recognize economism and the reasons for its influence is to take the first step towards its elimination. Unless it is eliminated, the working-class movement, in spite of all efforts, will be restricted to reformist activity within the framework of a system designed to maintain the dictatorship of the capitalist ruling caste.[18]

The truth of these statements is strikingly proven by the record of "working-class militancy" regarding the struggles for their own liberation by colonial workers "abroad", which the next Chapter will examine.

22. The Labor Aristocracy's Entire Outlook "Abroad"

If such, then, is the record "at home" of American labor militancy, what of its attitude toward the anti-colonial liberation struggle involving its "class brothers" in colonies?

Because both Britain and France have had "labor" or "socialist" governments "in power", a brief glance at their records will be included in this analysis to supplement examination of the US labor movement.

In their relationships with colonial struggles, honorable exceptions to the contrary notwithstanding, workers in the capitalist countries by and large have an unbroken history of active opposition .

Such is not, however, the picture painted by the Western Left or that of Eastern Europe. For instance:

> "The contributions made by the French working people to the liberation of Algeria, and the resolute stand taken by the British working class in support of Egypt at the time of the Anglo-French-Israeli aggression, and other similar instances, are well known."[1]

This expresses the official stance of the Western Left from the beginning. But how does it square with reality?

At the start of Algeria's independence struggle (November 1954) (and in one or two cases toward the end of it), the French Communist Party organized and supported activities directed against France's role. Unfortunately, though, this was not typical of its doings during most of the war years.

First, at the time, the French Government itself, so assiduous in militarily opposing Algerian independence, was headed by Social Democratic Guy Mollet, representing the French labor aristocracy. As the war progressed, early Left expressions of opposition died away and there were only the smallest protests.

Here is the testimony of a famous French radical, never a Communist, but never anti-Communist, accepted and sought after by Eastern European socialist government like the Soviet Union:

> "The Communists either organized or supported these demonstrations (against the war in Algeria). After the friendly reception given to Mollet and Pineau during their visit to Moscow in June, the Communists became less vociferous, however. Sartre wanted the Peace Movement to condemn the war in Algeria. A Soviet delegate of some importance who happened to be passing through Paris, told him that such a motion would be inopportune; he himself wanted a motion passed declaring that the Movement was opposed only to wars of aggression: the French in this case were not aggressors. We thought that the USSR was holding back because it was afraid the Mahgreb would become part of the American zone of influence. Also the Communist Party feared it would be cutting itself off from the masses if it appeared to be less nationalistic than the other parties. Officially it expressed its opposition to the government; but it no longer urged all those who could to defy it.

> "It made no effort to combat the racism of the French workers, who considered the 400,000 North Africans settled in France as both intruders doing them out of jobs and as a subproletariat worthy only of contempt . . . What is certain is that by June (1955) all resistance to the war had ceased . . . the entire population of the country — workers, employees, farmers and professional people,

civilians and soldiers – were caught up in a great tide of chauvinism and racism . . .

". . . provided it was properly costumed for them, the people of France were prepared to accept this war with a light heart . . . I was not at all upset when the ultras demonstrated . . . They were just ultras. What did appall me was to see the vast majority of the French people turn chauvinist and to realize the depth of their racist attitude . . . I was even more stupefied and saddened when I learned with what docility the young soldiers sent to Algeria became accomplices in the methods of pacification."[2]

Other testimony has since appeared, to the same effect:

"In September, 1945, the French, with British help, seized the city of Saigon in complete violation of Allied orders for the British for Indochina", began this source, and continued:

"Two days later, the French Communist Party organization in Saigon submitted a paper to their Vietnamese counterparts on behalf of the French and Russian parties. The paper warned Vietnamese Communists not to do anything which would hurt Soviet foreign policy in Europe. They were asked to wait for the results of the October, 1945, election in France, in which the French Communists expected to make gains ...

"Yet it was the French Communist party which later sat on its hands as the first war appropriations for Vietnam were voted. They were members of the government which appointed and supported the ultra-colonialist Admiral d'Argenlieu, which permitted the failure of the Fontainebleau conference and the attack on Haiphong and which refused to negotiate with Ho Chi Minh after December, 1946."3

The British workers seemed, in any significant numbers, to have exhausted their militancy in support for any cause outside their own borders in 1920 or so, when one tiny group of London dockers refused to load arms to be used against the infant Soviet Revolution in Russia, one of the mentioned "honorable exceptions" to the general Western record of international relations.

In general, in every case up to and including the dispatch not so long ago of Royal Scottish troops to strike-break against Swaziland miners, the British section of the world labor aristocracy either, under Labour Governments, actually directed police violence against colonial workers, or supported Tories who did.

Testimony to this attitude, at least insofar as it affected Africa, exists from the British Left itself. Writing after the 1964 electoral victory for "Labour", one Englishman said:

> ". . . it is unlikely that the African people have forgotten how they were treated in the (Labour Government) years of 1945-1951. For despite the Labour Party's claims, the fact is that . . . this was a period in which there took place some of the most ferocious attacks on the national movement and on the growing working class and trade union organizations that Africa, in all its stormy history, has yet witnessed."4

These remarks were part of an "appeal" to the new Labour Government under Harold Wilson to "take warning" and, so to speak, "be nice to Africa". Less than a year later, Wilson's course had been laid bare. It was summarized by another well-known British "Communist":

"From the outset the strategy of the Wilson Labour Government was geared to the most zealous upholding of the interests of British imperialism; the military alliance with the United States; the continuance of the commitments of NATO, SEATO, and the cold war; the maintenance of Britain's military world power, and especially the most loudly proclaimed strategy of maintaining Britain's military strength 'East of Suez', that is, in the Middle Eastern Gulf area and in South-East Asia, with the continued maintenance of the bases of Aden and Singapore."[5]

A proper understanding of Social Democracy would have made this record less of a shock. But then – we have yet to show that the British and other Western "Communists" are the "neo-Social Democrats". Of this, more later.

As to the attitude of US unions toward the colonial movement, it may be judged, for example, by their approach to the boycott of South African products.

In San Francisco, the International Longshoremen's and Warehousemen's Union (ILWU) under the leadership of Red labeled, Australian-born Harry Bridges, stood out like a sore thumb when its members actually held up the unloading of South African cargoes for 24 whole hours on at least two occasions in the recent past. In one case – that of the Dutch ship Raki in December 1962 – the ILWU was respecting picket lines already set up by local Afro-American organizations, primarily the NAACP. An arbitrator ruled in this particular case that the longshoremen must "ignore the picket line and honor their contract". But such contracts are with billionaire shipping magnates whose class bloats itself out of South African investments. To breach the contract would be an act of great rebellion.

American workers are not about to desert legalism and jeopardize their cushy jobs just because some far-off "blacks" think they should be "helped".

Yet no wonder the ILWU was considered bold: on the East Coast, the ILWU's counterpart, the National Maritime Union, under red-baiting Joe Curran, also struck a few times, refusing to load or unload cargoes – from Cuba to the USSR!

American workers sense that the source of their present well-being and socialism do not mix.

Added to this record is an additional fact: when metropolitan Communist Parties (mainly in Britain and France) formed "brother Parties" in colonies, it is a matter of record that they made the "new" Parties sections of the "home" Party, subject to "home" leadership. Beginning in 1956, however, African Marxists began a tough – till now only partially successful – battle to break free..

Labor and radicals in all Western countries (but again, especially Britain and the US) have an infamous record vis-a-vis colonial workers in that of the at-first-British-dominated, and after 1959 for a time AFL-CIO-run International Confederation of Free Trade Unions (ICFTU). The latter's activities in Africa have been bitingly described by African trade unionists:

> "The ICFTU's principal objective in Africa was to capture control of the African trade unions for Western ruling circles and monopolies, who will in turn use them in extracting colonial super-profits from Africa."[6]

ICFTU's history in Africa and in Latin America and Asia, as well, supplemented by the records in those areas of individual US and British unions and union leaders, fully substantiates this charge.

British Guiana furnished a most blatant example of the Western labor aristocracy itself deliberately destroying a colonial revolution. (For a discussion of this situation in detail, see Chapter 41.) Huge intervention into this colonial country by unions, their federated bodies and, of course, other outright US Agencies, governmental or not, eventually achieved the result desired by imperialism. Such intervention could have gone on failing, as it had at first, had the interventionists not been able finally to involve substantial numbers of Guyanese people, whose revolutionary experience had not prepared them for trade unions in the role of betrayer.

Thus, when a colony had clearly demonstrated its desire for, and intention of, attaining independence, it was direct representatives of the US labor aristocracy who administered to that colonial revolution the coup de grâce, thereby completing larger, official US Intervention.

These activities, of course, were directed solely by union leaders. Yet in unions of the home countries involved – Britain and the US – there has as yet been no sign of any significant opposition to leaders executing such policies. Some old men have been replaced at top rungs of the union hierarchy by younger, and allegedly more aggressive ones, pledged to go after bigger shares of advancing profits. That is, such changes, aside from being minor, foreshadow no change in union policy. Rightly so, for these "leaders", old OR new, "bring home the bacon" for their members. And for non-members, too: unorganized industry in the US, in order to continue competing on the labor market, follows the pattern set by the unions.

So, FACTS show that, especially since 1950, the Western proletariat, including a large portion of lower-paid workers and notably in the US, have consistently supported colonialism because they have the not-unjustified feeling that they have a big stake in the status quo, exactly (as noted below) "as long as they support capitalism."

Progressives inside the West but independent of the organized Left, have observed this phenomenon as well,

> "If one assumes the permanence of monopoly capitalism, with its proved incapacity to make rational use for peaceful and humane ends of its enormous productive potential, one must decide whether one prefers the mass unemployment and hopelessness characteristic of the Great Depression or the relative job security and material well-being provided by the huge military budgets of the 1940's and 1950's. Since most Americans, workers included, still do assume without question the permanence of the system, it is only natural that they should prefer the situation which is personally and privately more advantageous."[7]

To workers in colonial countries, the facts of Western labor attitudes toward colonial struggles are no big news. For instance, an American Left poet, Marc Schleiffer, reported some conversations he had overheard while living in Cuba. One was between Che Guevara, the Latin American revolutionary martyr then still in Cuba, and an Italian Communist novelist, Italo Calvino. It went, in part, like this:

> "CALVINO: The European working class isn't interested in this talk about sacrifice. Or in this association of socialism with sacrifice and voluntary work. They are interested in cars and TV and higher wages. They support the Party because it leads the fight for higher wages. And they have a right to want this.
>
> "EL CHE: I'm very happy for the European working class with their higher wages. But don't forget who is

paying for those wages. We are – millions of exploited workers and peasants in Latin America, Africa and Asia."[8]

Africans, too, having been direct victims of Western labor attitudes, report their own awareness of the facts via a crucial question:

> ". . . why should the representatives of the oppressed workers of Western Europe and the USA, be hostile to the anti colonial stand of the African workers and on the contrary rather assist the monopolies in their domination of Africa?"[9]

Bitterly, they answer their own query:

> "Western workers today enjoy a very high standard of living (TV, cars., etc.). This high standard . . . has been obtained primarily at the expense of the grinding exploitation and bloody repression of the workers in Africa, Latin America and Asia – where Western ruling circles . . . have drawn the colossal profits which enable them to make wage concessions to 'their own' workers. In other words, the Western workers have an economic stake in imperialism and neo-colonialism, as long as they support capitalism."[10]

What is more, since it works both ways, this "economic stake" has been carefully nurtured in American and foreign working class minds by all official, including trade union, propaganda.

3. Labor lieutenants in the working class and their ideological influence.

What is being discussed here, of course, is really the extensive class collaboration practiced by "labor leaders and the upper stratum of the labor aristocracy" in the United States which, despite having the world's largest and most affluent labor aristocracy, never produced a mass Social Democratic party. (See Chapter 25 below.)

Despite some temporary, depression-fostered periods of real militancy, the last of which in the early 30s really gave the US bourgeoisie a bad scare, by and large the organized US Labor movement – representing the labor aristocracy – have either in "theory" and/or in practice found that class collaboration usually pays its practitioners and advocates off.

So, certainly, testified a well-known US periodical:

> ". . . to an unprecedented degree, labor and management are forced to work together. In this sense, Labor Secretary Willard Wirtz is fond of quoting Lewis Carroll's Hunting of the Snark:

> "But the valley grew narrow and narrower still,

> "And the evening got darker and colder

> "Till (merely from nervousness, not from good will)

> "They marched along shoulder to shoulder.'

> "What is keeping them marching along together . . . Is above all a common share in America's vast affluence."[11]

And there is always a "labor lieutenant" handy to say "Amen" to Big Business sentiments, like some comic-relief Greek chorus:

> ". . . nobody doubts that management's and labor's business are in fact the nation's business. Says AFL-CIO President George Meany, without apologies to industry's late 'Engine Charlie' Wilson: "What is good for America is good for the AFL-CIO."[11]

Big business adds its "pat on the head", pontificating:

"It is more than that: it IS capitalism. Its relations with management remain adverse to a degree; but the action is that of cogwheels moving in opposite directions to operate the whole free enterprise machine."[11]

There have been practical proofs of this contention which can not be wished away. Two of them that sharply illustrate it are as follows:

1. In the USA., so-called "labor leaders" have parlayed union treasuries worth millions of dollars into Big Business investments in basic industry like mining and shipping, and into insurance, banking, housing, department stores, etc. Union leaderships have melted into the capitalist class itself on one side of their "union activities".

2. In Western Germany, trade union "leaders" now participate as captains – or, is it as "lieutenants"? – of state enterprises and have been aiding big German capital – resurrected from military defeat by US assistance – against specific demands of "their own " workers.

Where Marxists have fallen short of the ideological needs of this situation has been in failing to demonstrate with facts and figures to exactly what degree working-class relations with management are "adverse". It is not fringe poverty that demonstrates this point; it is Karl Marx's "growing social gulf, which makes the labor aristocracy's benefits into "peanuts" on the "home" front. Marxists have made their comparisons on the wrong end of the scale, using a magnifying glass and a set line of patter. This has left the field wide open to "the enemy", as the Big Business mouthpiece we have been quoting concluded:

"Some labor leaders expect to develop new forms of cooperation with management . . . (because of a) common stake in a country that gives the worker a better

> life than he has known since the wheels of the industrial
> revolution first started to turn."[11]

The record confirms this mealy-mouthed assertion as one of the major facts of US labor life, always allowing for "poverty pockets". It determines the real political orientation of the US working class. But here, again, it is that the honorable exceptions crop up, only to be turned against the working class through the use that has been made of them.

For, by discussing them outside their context, the Western Left, echoed by its Eastern European counterparts, has tallied and used them for unjustifiable conclusions about the political level and direction of the Western proletariat.

It is true that these honorable exceptions (obviously) represent the correct manner in which a proletariat ought to act in order to qualify for the role which eventually will be its own. But real Marxists, as scientists, have to use FACTS as the only feasible stepping stone to what ought to be. They cannot WISH it into existence on the strength of mendacious repetition of half-baked truths.

The full truth is that until today, exceptions aside, American labor in its majority still does see its future in varied forms of class collaboration as a means of increasing its share in American prosperity, which Lenin proved comprised ever-growing corporate super-profits from overseas economic activities.

When class-conscious ruling-class organs analyze a sensitive spot in the decaying corpse of their economy, they can usually be relied on to produce a fairly accurate estimate of reality. It is not necessary to contradict truth merely because it has been uttered by the enemy. That is to underestimate one's opponent, a dangerous game.

In the Western Left, the expression of such thoughts is strictly proscribed. Rather, in the face of Lenin's criteria and relevant statistics to apply to them, it became fashionable in the US Left during the 30s (and to this day) to concentrate on the poverty aspects of the American economy, saying or implying that they are currently the decisive ones. (See discussion, Chapter 17, above.)

Nor has such an approach been confined to Communists. For instance, Lord Bertrand Russell broadcast to American troops in Vietnam, saying inter alia that "66 million Americans live in poverty".[12]

Figures in Chapters 17 through 20, above, show that 20% of Americans (working class in their majority) existing below the American poverty line, while in 1959 over 50% of US people lived less than "modestly but adequately" by American standards, 16% living very poorly.

In his State of the Union Message to Congress in January 1967, President Johnson admitted to no less than 23 million Americans (i.e., more than 12% of population) who must live "on social security payments", which, he also confessed, are below "subsistence level".

Thus, inside US borders, figures show a significant segment of relative – and even some absolute – poverty. Moreover, as imperialism continues to decay, this segment, narrowing numerically, nonetheless grows to a point where even the Great Liberal, Lyndon Johnson, is forced to produce an "anti-Poverty Program". Up to now, however, that program is a very small proportion of already-existing Federal assistance, and is an excuse for buying off developing militants among the American poor, besides providing good jobs to create ex-militants among the Afro-American people. Very little is done to implement the program – and this is at least in part because poverty in the US is as yet far from decisive.

From November 1964 through December 31, 1966 (excluding rural loans, adult basic education, "Vista" and small business loans), the US Federal Government allotted in its "War on Poverty" Programs to 2,200,326 people, $2,245,989,000.[13] That this was for show and not required by the situation is shown by the fact that, in 1965 alone, the US Federal Government, out of its total $15.34 billions of aid to State and Local government and to Individuals, allotted the following funds:

	Dollars (1,000's)
Unemployment insurance	515,649
Anti-Poverty funds (1965 only)	324,804
Food distribution	681,935
Public Assistance	3,088,955
	4,531,343 [14]

Without the "Anti-Poverty funds" for 1965, the figure is $4,206,539 thousands, about 4.3% of total wages and salaries disbursed in that year.[15] That is, 36.4% of all Federal funds to Local, State Government and Individuals (excepting rural loans, adult basic education, Vista and small business loans) was already going to people in need of it. But the "Anti-Poverty" funds were a measly 7.2% of the total amount of Federal aid to the "poverty" segments of the American people.

Still, rather than face this reality – so as to deal with it – the pundits of the Western Left have refused to be dislodged from their "poverty" position. The reason they cling to it may be attributable to words written at one time by Karl Marx, and now mechanically adhered to:

"As capital grows, the mass of wage labor grows ...

"A noticeable increase in wages presupposes a rapid growth of productive capital. The rapid growth of productive capital brings about an equally rapid growth of wealth, luxury, social wants, social enjoyments. Thus, although the enjoyments of the workers have risen, the social satisfaction that they give has fallen in comparison with the increased enjoyments of the capitalist, which are inaccessible to the worker, in comparison with the state of development of society in general."[16]

The truth in these words has yet to be made visible to the working class the Marxists must lead. First, the Marxist "poverty approach" falls on deaf ears because of "bribe" conditions. But in addition, very few real people actually SEE how capitalists live. On the other hand, especially in this era of increasingly easy travel, thousands of colonial subjects HAVE seen how ordinary US and British people live. They have compared this "mode of life" with their own, and consequently aspire to "an American standard of living" – without the slightest notion of how that standard got where it is. In turn, even greater numbers of Western workers, probably the majority of them Americans, have traveled to colonial areas and to socialist countries and made the same comparison in reverse, thereby reinforcing their support for their own status quo.

Anybody who has ever lived in colonial areas (or, according to testimony from increasing numbers of witnesses, in Eastern European socialist countries) knows that "the American Way of Life" holds a tremendous attraction for workers all over the world; from Western Europe to Eastern, from there to Africa, including unbelievable numbers of Africans and people of African descent everywhere – where ever one looks, ordinary people regard Hollywood's popular version of this "American Way of Life" as their most cherished dream.

No amount of croaking can wipe out the statistics of Western – especially American – affluence. What has been lacking is a proper explanation for them by the Left. Yet that explanation, simple and clear, has been staring the world in the face ever since 1916 when Lenin first analyzed imperialist parasitism.

23. The Modern Labor Aristocracy: Summary and Conclusions

Thus far, the text has covered the following points:

1. Imperialism is able, to this day, as its parasitism grows, to bribe an ever-increasing labor aristocracy "at home" at the expense of super-exploited populations in colonies, who constitute the globe's over whelming majority.

2. Imperialist bribery includes not only super wages, but the mode of life of metropolitan labor. The bribery itself constantly expands in amount, affecting not only metropolitan workers in imperialism's more "advanced" stages but to a far lesser though significant degree, reaching certain colonial and/or semi-colonial peoples like US Negroes, industrial workers in colonial urban areas, and the like.

3. Wage-wise:

a) In 1960, workers constituted at least 66% of US Adult population outside institutions.

b) Solely in terms of money and purchasing power, less than 50% meet the cost of production of their labor-power.

c) As bribery expands, US poverty shrinks: 7.6% of all American families earned $15,000 or more in 1965 (Table 23, Page 202). With a total for that year of 47.7 million families in the US,[1] this means that 3 2/3 million families were in this wage bracket. The total estimated number of persons in these 3 2/3 million families earning more than $15,000 per annum would have been about 13.4 million. (The number of primary families, i.e., "heads of households and all other persons in it related to the head"[7], was in 1965

47.7 million.[8] Total Civilian Resident Population in that year was 193.815 million.[9] If from this is subtracted the total number of primary individuals (persons forming a household by themselves[7]), the result is 184,284 individuals in all the primary families. Dividing the latter by 47.7 million shows an estimated 3.86 persons per primary family on the average.) This compares with 4.7 million in 1960.[2]

d) The "upper stratum of the labor aristocracy" is represented by the trade unions and cooperatives. The stratum itself, which is all white, includes more than 10% of production workers or "proletarians".

4. The mode of life of US workers extends the labor aristocracy beyond the high-wage limits, especially via the credit system, which brings real values to significant numbers of lower-paid workers (Tables 21 & 25, Pages 200 & 208) which they could not enjoy on their current wages alone. The outer boundaries delineated by this factor are found in the electoral system, which embraces at least two-thirds of US Population (Table 8).

5. The entire outlook of the US worker is one of

(a) open class collaboration and

(b) support for colonialism.

Table 28 shows that overall less than 5% of US population have, in the traditional channels furnished for that possible purpose, rejected this entire outlook. The top evidence of dissent by this means came in 1912, when 35% of the electorate (i. e., of the elite) voted for a candidate from an assertedly independent party. US working people generally, and significant segments of the working people of the West as a whole, ARE a WORLD labor aristocracy today.

6. In size, the "upper stratum" of the labor aristocracy shrinks numerically in proportion to the growing size of the working class; more and more, the said "upper stratum" comes from the increasing outer, or non-value-producing, ranks of the working class (Tables 5, 6 & 7).

7. The labor aristocracy of the West, typified and led by that in the US, is, by Lenin's own criteria, no longer a minority in the industrialized countries themselves. That feature it retains today on a world scale only.

8. An expression of the increase of bribery and the size of the labor aristocracy is the improvement as time goes by of US vital statistics and the spread of "good living", seen also in the percentage drop of "poor" families.

9. These vital statistics highlight metropolitan working class bribery by suggesting that, in its majority, the American working class is paid above the socially necessary cost of producing its labor-power.

10. The source of imperialist bribery is the super-exploitation of colonial labor-power by international monopoly capital headed by that of the US. This bribery is effected when colonial wages, appropriated as super-profits, and thus removed from super-exploited people, are redistributed in part as super-wages heavily favoring the workers in "advanced" nations. From such transactions, the imperialists appear to extract an additional cut for themselves. The existence and continued growth of super-profits are indispensable to maintaining such a redistribution of international wages, which process in turn ensures the continued existence of the system.

11. The political significance of such facts shows up in part in the progress or lack of same in anti-colonial liberation struggles. In this context, the following erroneous ideas generated in the

Western Left and among Eastern European leaderships have concomitant significance:

a) The labor aristocracy is still a minority inside metropolitan areas, so that imperialist bribery affects only a few in the West.

b) The poverty aspects of imperialism inside metropolitan areas are said to be decisive now.

c) These poverty aspects are said to be engendering increased militancy among Western workers, whose "revolutionary struggle" is credited with "shaking imperialism". This struggle, now typified by the May 1968 events in France, is interpreted as "opposition to imperialism".

From all these erroneous postulates, certain consequences flow. Some of the most important of these are:

A. Since both colonial and Western workers are "poor", and since both allegedly struggle with equally increasing militancy against imperialism, therefore the problems of both and their paths to solutions are declared "the same". (The same thought is sometimes expressed another way: since workers in the capitalist countries and those in colonies are exploited by "the same boss", therefore they allegedly have "the same problems.") What is forgotten in such an "equation" is that workers in capitalist countries are exploited; those in colonies, super-exploited "above and beyond" exploitation in metropoles.

B. If problems and solutions are, indeed, "the same" for both these segments of world labor, it follows that Western labor – being in large measure Karl Marx's "industrial proletariat" – must lead the world revolution. Even Liberation, therefore, is to be subordinated to this "leadership".

Are metropolitan workers and those in colonies really "the same"? This question is not new. Long ago, Lenin had posed it:

> "Is the ACTUAL condition of the workers in the oppressing and in the oppressed nations the same from the viewpoint of the national question?

> "No, it is not the same.

> "ECONOMICALLY, the difference is that sections of the working class in the oppressing countries receive crumbs from the SUPER-PROFITS the bourgeoisie of the oppressing nations obtains by always doubly exploiting the workers of the oppressed nations . . .

> "POLITICALLY, the difference is that the workers of the oppressing nations occupy a PRIVILEGED position in many spheres of political life compared with the workers of the oppressed nations.

> "IDEOLOGICALLY, or spiritually, the difference is that the workers of the oppressing nations are taught, at school and in life, disdain and contempt for the workers of the oppressed nations . . .

> "Thus, ALL ALONG THE LINE, there are differences in objective reality, i.e., 'dualism', in the objective world that is independent of the will and consciousness of individuals . . .

> "In REAL LIFE the International is composed of workers DIVIDED into oppressing and oppressed nations. If its action is to be MONISTIC, its propaganda must NOT be the same for both."[3]

Who, then, says that such workers are "the same"?

Consider the following:

> "Under imperialist domination, the position of the working class in the capitalist countries is the same as that of the oppressed peoples."[4]

Or this:

> ". . . much as we are horrified at Verwoerds' Apartheid policy in South Africa, we should be under no illusion — Apartheid is an extreme case of something very much widely distributed in the world as it is today . . . (that has) existed as long as the exploitation of man by man . . .

> "In fact, whether at home or on a world scale, since the exploiters are always a minority, the doctrine of 'superiority' — 'class superiority' at home, 'racial superiority' abroad — is an essential aspect of all exploiters' ideology."[5]

That there are elements of apartheid in all imperialist society is just a truism. This statement goes beyond that into the realm of fantasy. First, super-exploitation, the material base of apartheid, has not existed "as long as the-exploitation of man by man", but is the specific attribute of imperialism alone. Second, super-exploitation is not simply "an extreme case" of the ordinary variety. It is qualitatively different from "exploitation at home". True, steam is "only" a particular case of water. But in practice, the qualitative difference, which comes out in using water, is quite clear to the man who is scalded.

So, in the case of the qualitative difference between Western and colonial workers expressed as apartheid in South Africa: what has yet to be faced is that "class superiority" always predominates "at home", while "racial superiority" is always directed "abroad" , even when it occurs nominally "at home" as in the US (or against "the wogs" in Britain, etc.).

That this difference is one of kind rather than of degree is proven by the vital statistics resulting from the extraction of super-profits, made possible by the extreme separation of workers by skin color.

Such statistics alone (Table 10, Page 171) clearly raise the question: can black Africans, of every 1,000 of whose babies two to three hundred die before their first birthdays, be "the same" as South African or US whites, whose infants die at a rate almost ten times less? Can South African blacks who die at 37 be "the same" as the metropolitan white who lives to surpass the Biblical "three score and ten"?

Look at it this way: all workers in the imperialist system are "in the same boat." But there is a distinct "division of labor" between various groups among them. There are those who sit at the captain's table, on deck in the sun, occasionally permitted to try steering the boat under the captain's vigilant eye; but others are confined to the hold, in the bilges, never allowed on deck except to serve meals and wipe boots – doing all the dirty work. Not only are their wages vastly' different, but the concrete results of such differences – in life expectancy, poor health, etc. – accentuate the basic division until a qualitative difference develops in the way of life of the two groups, resulting in practice that – although they do indeed travel in "the same boat" – they can no longer communicate with one another. In fact, the condition of those in the hold has become the indispensable price for the well-being of those on deck, as long as they travel together in this vessel.

If, in this light, those "on deck" really are "the same" as those "in the hold", why have Marxists never been able to wean the former from the captain's influence, despite specific, concentrated and capable efforts to this end (in the era ending with the mid-30s)? Quite obviously, those who live somewhat like the captain will never agree to "help" those in the bilges so long as (a) they are convinced that their lives, their course and their future are safe in the captain's hands; and (b) that the captain requires this way of life to include them in his circle. What those in the bilges know – but to which sailors on deck will never listen when told by "the lowly" (who are the only ones who really know it to tell) – is that the whole boat is leaking like a sieve. Yet, as long as those in the hold are forced to man the pumps, the old hulk will stay afloat far longer than its condition warrants – and the sailors on deck perceive no cause for alarm.

Of course, if it is insisted that "the proletariat in the main capitalist countries" must LEAD the world – including colonial – revolution, then iron logic requires "proof" that workers in both situations have "the same problems" and "the same interests".

Yet, by placing such thoughts on paper, one is accused rather loudly of espousing, rather than reporting, them: "You are disrupting anti-imperialist unity", claim the critics. "By bringing in arguments irrelevant to the main struggle, you are causing disunity."

Exactly how a fact-based argument which puts into question the main tactical line of the moment can be "irrelevant" to the "main struggle" is a mystery which only these fairy-tale tellers can clear up – if they would. Furthermore, in any case it is not the reporter but imperialism which long ago created the real gulf between the world labor aristocracy and colonial peoples, a gulf based on the demonstrable material reality that the former enjoys a well-being achieved under present circumstances, directly or indirectly, at the expense of the latter.

For this reason, allies for Liberation in metropolitan countries AT PRESENT must come from elsewhere than from the labor aristocracy. And in fact, today (1968), a real US Left is arising, with its vanguard in the most exploited, the Black Freedom Fighters who are already in some cases consciously aligning themselves with the world's freedom movements. This US Left has white allies, but they ARE NOT – and at present CANNOT be – in the unions.

Consider where the New Left in the US is headed:

> ". . . the Vietnamese revolutionaries . . . offer a clear and positive . . . vision of something better than the misery and oppression to which they had grown accustomed.

> "A not too dissimilar vision is sweeping the oppressed and colonized black communities of this country . . . .

> "But to have goals . . . is not enough. The Vietnamese, through the Lao Dong (Communist) Party in the North and the NLF (in the South) have managed to create effective disciplined organizations which can achieve . . . the popular demands. Movement people in this country have rightly been turned off by . . . parties which degenerated into dictatorships and were the vanguard of nothing. Yet, and . . . especially . . . in the black movement, an increasing need is felt for disciplined organizations which can be effective in struggle . . . Black militants frequently speak of the need for such disciplined cadre organizations . . . if serious struggles are to be waged."[6]

In a word, advanced metropolitan militants have begun to act upon their experience of the kind of facts set forth thus far in this text. By relying on the world's freedom struggle as focal point, they are opening a vital "Second Front" in the heart of reaction's fortress. (The "First Front", thus far, has been mainly in Vietnam.)

Here is the point of reporting the facts of metropolitan life: to hasten the REAL revolutionization of those sectors of that society who do not draw their main sustenance out of super-exploitation but are, in varying degrees, super-exploited themselves. All talk of the present "revolutionary" nature of the world's industrial proletariat has the objective effect, willy-nilly, of preventing such real political development in metropoles, whether the talkers are conscious of this or not.

24. Effect on Western Marxists of Wrong Estimate of Labor Aristocracy

Marxists in the West have never balked at admitting colonialism's immense rewards for "their" ruling class. They concede, since Lenin said so, that the system may benefit a few Western workers. But the more statistics show those "few" growing in number, the less these Marxists care even to mention the labor aristocracy – even to this moment when basic proletarians are acting, in metropolitan areas like England, in a most unproletarian manner.

But it is self-contradictory and harmful to "the correct handling of contradictions among the people" to nod vigorous assent that imperialism does squeeze colonial peoples, yet – by refusing to face facts – to deny the most important consequences:

Under the tutelage of Social Democracy and racism, Western workers have, because on the whole it has treated so many of them so well, been helping to prop up a system which cannot survive real colonial freedom. With an infallible instinct for their own presently-dominant class interests (See quotations from Lenin, Pages 143 and 188, above) which Social Democracy and/or racism expresses, the labor aristocracy senses that, within "its" system, colonial peoples could – if such an achievement were possible, which it is not – achieve freedom worthy of the name only at the expense of metropolitan living standards. In fact, those colonial people who have attained real freedom have done so only because they left the system.

How have Marxists living amidst this labor aristocracy reacted to such irrefutable logic? From their well-appointed studios they have poured forth a veritable Niagara of articles and books promulgating their main proposition on colonialism: that, under super-profit nurtured system, it is conceivable for colonial peoples to be "given" their freedom without infringing on, if not actually bolstering, living standards in the "home" countries. Thereby, they objectively deny that sometimes a contradiction can develop where none grew before; that under some conditions a good thing can turn into a bad thing. And thereby, too, they have passed up the chance fully to illumine the parasitic workings of a system which divides to rule and turns people blind to their own deeper interests. And this failure constitutes political defection, for it has permitted Western workers to pursue purely economic goals in a spirit even more inimical to that revolutionary brotherhood which Lenin dubbed "proletarian internationalism." (See Reference Note 14, Chapter 1, above.)

As they watch their TV's or drive their cars, (See Table 25 above.) the majority of Western workers smile cynically at what they regard as quaint fancies; and, passively or actively, they contradict them when the chips are down – while the influence of real Marxism in their midst has plunged to an unprecedented low.

Under the tutelage of Social Democracy and racism, Western workers have learned no real truths about socialism. They have vaguely assumed, when they think about it at all, that socialism would somehow destroy their own present good conditions, perhaps because they have heard that its "aim" is to rectify visible economic inequalities throughout the world by enforcing a "leveling" which, for them, would mean a big come-down virtually to the "poverty" line.

But how have Marxists resident in the world's rich cities countered these lies by the "labor lieutenants"? First, always foremost, by assuring the well fed labor aristocracy that it needs socialism because "it is not living well".

By thus correlating exploitation solely with poverty, such Marxists have for decades left the ideological arena open for Social

Democracy to spread its lies about the source of the system's benefits to Western workers. Lenin's characterization and analysis of parasitism as the chief feature of the whole system is ignored and forgotten, a sin for which the Marxists in the West are quite deservedly paying heavily, at least in lack of influence.

When this "poverty approach" fails, metropolitan Marxists switch to extolling an infant system (long screened by kept publicity media from public view "at home") beset by real and potential military intervention, economic encirclement, and historically-conditioned low levels of internal accumulation – operating, moreover, according to moral standards currently incomprehensible to the vast majority in the venal West.

Yet both these types of propaganda misfire even worse than before nowadays because the most venerated of socialist parties, with the original assistance, benediction and accompaniment of most of its Western followers, has lost its way: all Revisionism's crimes are committed in the name of "socialism".

So, when Western workers take their annual paid vacations, some of which in the U.S. are now 13 weeks long, they can only compare imperialist-falsified "new worlds" with their own – well-established system's gifts to them of material well-being; and they smile, unmoved. Seeing the resulting rejection of their own tenets, certain Marxists thereupon bow low and murmur placatingly: "As YOU say, dear Sirs."

Under the tutelage of Social Democracy and racism, Western workers have been assured that imperialism – by its absorption of the many territories and peoples still economically ingestible – is "really" evolving quite peacefully into socialism without need for class, or any other, struggle. It is, Western labor has been taught, due solely to collaborating with "benevolent" of "intelligent' imperialists that their high living standards have been achieved or can be maintained. Communist union leaders in industrialized countries play "snap the whip" in the Social Democratic line, and wind up panting, with the majority of union members, after purely economic goals.

As far as they themselves are concerned, Western workers at the bench know full well how the boss gets rich every day. In the fact of their exploitation, therefore, exists the material basis out of which to link their own needs with those of the class brothers "overseas". But this can NOT be done with an economic approach; it is a political matter.

Yet, when for the first time in more than a century there is a political strike in a Western country, it happens in England with Social Democracy in the saddle, in support of a virulent form of racism! This speaks volumes about the real position of Western Marxists in the world proletariat. It reveals, in Communist union "leaders" and their mentors, a singular blankness toward the integral nature of the system of which they and their members form only a single part.

But how has the labor aristocracy's Marxist section countered these fantasies? Monotonously, it joins the chorus that most colonies have now – because "imperialism sees the hand-writing on the wall" – been "given" what Western labor is assured is their "freedom." Or, failing that, when "freedom" is "scheduled," it pretends this is due to the "support" of the "revolutionary working class in the main capitalist countries." Such Marxists prate of the "far-seeing section of U.S. ruling circles," and solemnly egg the labor aristocracy into therefore supporting imperialism's rapacious political candidates in its lucrative parliamentary game. And, with their "peaceful co-existence" between "the witch" and "Hansel and Gretel" all dressed up as "new theory," they bore the world by trotting out the political skeletons of Bernstein and Kautsky.

Yet, this "non-violent" or "flexible" approach has been tried in Guatemala, Brazil, British Guiana, Congo Kinshasa, Ghana, Indonesia, and elsewhere. Events around the world today have surely made it obvious that wherever capitalism exists, it pays not the slightest heed to the sycophantic slobberings of its own agents, making short work of all who try to alter even by a hair's breadth its own precipitate decline.

No wonder that, at last, the Western worker – abandoned by real Marxism-Leninism "at home" – finds he can heed "the Marxists" after all: they have now started using words he has been hearing before. They have become "respectable", even though to attain this shining goal they have had to forfeit leadership to senior Social Democracy. After all, that old tart has performed the the same antics longer, more skillfully and with far bigger (electoral) "success." So, colonial babies continue to die in their millions before their first birthdays roll around.

The way to counteract existing lies is not by inventing new ones; nor is it by agreeing with the old ones but "proving" they mean something else. This procedure by "Marxian economists" has led its proponents into objectively reinforcing apologists for a rotten Status Quo, either by the manifest failure of "conclusions" drawn from poverty in the West, or by creating the illusion that the system itself can be "improved" by making a totally parasitic set-up less parasitic – with the assistance, if not under the leadership, of the top parasites themselves!

Though the world's Marxists say: "In the capitalist countries, the basic contradiction (See Chapter Reference Note 10, Chapter 1) is between the imperialist ruling class and the proletariat",[4] mechanical minds refuse to admit that a basic contradiction may become obscured by a subsidiary one, which for many reasons becomes temporarily its principal aspect. For them, if a situation has a main conflict, therefore no other can enter the picture, let alone play a major role in it.

According to some Marxists writing today, agreement by the kind of "Marxists" being discussed above on this point may constitute the seat of their troubles: "Let us . . . stress the fact that of course the history of all hither-to existing society is the history of class struggle, but class struggle is NOT the final motive force behind development, the contradiction between classes is NOT the fundamental contradiction in class society.

"Mao Tse-tung writes in 'On Contradiction':

"When Marx and Engels applied the law of contradiction in things to the study of the socio-historical process, they discovered the contradiction between the productive forces and the relations of production, they discovered the contradiction between the exploiting and exploited classes and also the resultant contradiction between the economic base and its superstructure (politics, ideology, etc.), and they discovered how these contradictions inevitably lead to different kinds of social revolution in different kinds of class society. When Marx applied this law to the study of the economic structure of capitalist society, he discovered that the basic contradiction of this society is the contradiction between the social character of production and the private character of ownership. This contradiction manifests itself in the contradiction between the organized character of production in the individual enterprises and the anarchic character of production in society as a whole. In terms of class relations, it manifests itself in the contradiction between the bourgeoisie and the proletariat.

"The contradiction between bourgeoisie and proletariat – the two basic classes in capitalist society – is the class expression of that very contradiction which is defining capitalist society, the contradiction between social production – big industry, division of labor - and private ownership of the means of production, private seizure of products. The struggle between bourgeoisie and proletariat, therefore, is a result of capitalist society itself, and in the final analysis it depends on the more or less predominant balance between the relations of production and the productive forces in capitalist society, how sharp the class struggle is."[2]

"Marxist" daydreams – built on refusal to face unpleasant or unforeseen developments – about how the decaying system could be made to "work better" are wasted time and effort. They make a mockery of any claim by such dreamers to being "revolutionary." The same time and effort might have gone into using existing facts, interpreting them in ways consistent with what every Western worker knows, the only "hook" on which truth may be hung to gain his respect. In such ways, it might have been possible to explain how the system really works, and to have produced proof that precisely in abolishing imperialist parasitism lies the secret of true, feasible economic democracy; lies the KEY to socialism. For, under that system, the astronomical drain of society's resources that a parasitic economy now sucks for private gain from the inexhaustible well-spring of man's labor-power could be turned into wealth for all (even colonial peoples) within a historically relatively short period – with poverty for none.

Marx had shown how to do this when he had said:

"Profit can only increase rapidly if the price of labor, if relative wages, decrease just as rapidly . . . "To say that the worker has an interest in the rapid growth of capital is

> only to say that the more rapidly the worker increases the wealth of others, the richer will be the crumbs that fall to him, the greater is the number of workers that can be employed and called into existence, the more can the mass slaves dependent on capital be increased ...
>
> "If capital is growing rapidly, wages may rise; the profit of capital rises incomparably more rapidly. The material position of the worker has improved, but at the cost of his social position. The social gulf that divides him from the capitalist has widened."[3]

Marxists in the West have interpreted this profound analysis on a "national" basis in a system which, if it ever did, no longer has much national meaning. They have cried "poverty" at home, while ignoring the international character of the "widening social gulf". They have closed their eyes to metropolitan parasitism.

What Western workers must be made, sooner or later, to see is this: as long as imperialism can fall back upon colonies (in name or fact), it has in the super-exploitation of colonial peoples, including those enjoying political independence, the magic cushion against its own inner contradictions which was defined earlier, and set at a recent $77.2 billion in the US. (See Page 130, above.) By grinding "overseas" subjects down still more, the ensuing super-profits streaming to metropolitan capitals keep the "home" workers quiet chewing on the latest bone tossed to them form the fatted calf. This magic cushion thus far not only has protected imperialism's industrial centers from the total effects of its growing inner contradictions; it has also shielded the world labor aristocracy from having to share very greatly the burdens of advancing economic chaos resulting therefrom.

Even though eventually the system must crash because of the historical development of such contradictions, the size of colonial casualties that are currently being paid, and would still have to be paid, for unnecessary postponement of the inevitable indicts the alleged "friends" of colonial liberation as long as they persist in their course.

Men's minds are conditioned by their material environment. The ugly truth is that the super-profits on which imperialism continues to rely to escape from its multiplying difficulties will dry up only after colonial liberation has been economically successful on a large enough portion of the globe to affect this source of imperialism's artificially prolonged life in some massive way. After that, the Western labor aristocracy will be forced to see with its own eyes that (a) colonial peoples can manage very well in general without them; (b) can organize societies specifically superior to those of the West in material comfort, education and culture; and (c) can teach them, "the proud whites", lessons, despite having for so long been depicted by imperialism as "inferior" .

At their present level of understanding, any real Western support for liberation could come ONLY as the result of lofty moral standards. But a people living partially off stolen wealth are unlikely to build up high ideals. Nor can such ideals be instilled by continuing to pat the labor aristocracy on the head, repeating endlessly how "nicely" it is behaving toward its "class brothers" overseas. It already owns a grossly over-inflated class ego, which is virtually worthless to the liberation struggle. Before the labor aristocracy "in the main capitalist countries" can qualify for the exalted role assigned to it by Social Democracy, racism and revisionism, it is going to have to come down off its high horse, starting specifically with its obligations to its "overseas" class brothers whom it has, for its own betterment, for so long cynically allowed to be done out of so much of their wages, and whose agonies it has watched with that "objectivity" and lack of "unseemly" emotion so prized by the imperialist murderers and their apologists and extollers.

Furthermore, as the crisis in the imperialist system, focused on Vietnam, deepens, events themselves are going to force struggle upon these workers. It is very urgent, therefore, that it be entered upon with the greatest possible clarity.

Although struggle itself is usually pointed to as the guarantee of ideological clarity, events prove this to be by no means an automatic consequence.

The corollary to this is equally plain: that liberation CAN – and perhaps MAY HAVE TO at first – be won by colonial people with or without assistance from Western labor. For, the fight for colonial liberation is a fight for life. This has been proved wherever Liberation has adhered to the sound doctrine of self-reliance, notably in Korea, Vietnam and China.

At one time during imperialism's history, perhaps there was no alternative; but today, colonial suffering is an anachronism. All those infants who die when science and a decent life could save them; all those millions whose lives are cut off in mid-span, are casualties of today's class war just as much as their brothers whose life-blood spills visibly in Vietnamese, Congolese, Venezuelan or other "limited war" soil.

The progress of liberation demands above all that facts be faced at the earliest possible moment in order to expose colonial misery and death as the basic major source under imperialism of Western affluence, with socialism as the ONLY CURE for such misery.

And colonial territories are so rich in resources, they play such a key role in the trade of the West, while their peoples form such an overwhelming majority of world population, that with practical unity among themselves, they have a firm material base from which their victory can and will be archived.

In this general context, facts expressed in these pages, though recording its objective absence, constitute no call to spurn Western labor assistance, when available, for liberation. Nor does facing the truth about the size, living standards, and inevitable resulting political consequences of the Western labor aristocracy involve "maligning" the "proletariat" of imperialist citadels.

WHAT IS AT ISSUE IS THE ABILITY EVER REALLY TO REACH ANY DECISIVE SECTION OF THAT PROLETARIAT FOR REAL SUPPORT TO LIBERATION AND SOCIALISM IN TIME TO AFFECT MATERIALLY THE NUMBER OF CASUALTIES THAT LIBERATION'S ARMY IS HAVING TO PAY FOR ITS INEVITABLE TRIUMPH.

What is at stake is not the success of liberation, but its price. In the opening of his famous memorial to Dr. Norman Bethune, that noble and true representative of the "Western proletariat" who was a middle-class professional, Mao Tse-tung of China said:

> "Leninism teaches that the world revolution can only succeed if the proletariat of the capitalist countries supports the struggle for liberation of the colonial and semi-colonial peoples and if the proletariat of the colonies and semi-colonies supports that of the proletariat of the capitalist countries."[4]

Do these words not contradict all that has just been said? Do they not specifically say that without the support of the Western proletariat, colonial liberation must fail?

No, they do not. What they say is that, in such a case, "the world revolution" will fail.

But Lenin had gone even further. He it was who said:

> "The social revolution cannot be the united action of the proletarians of ALL countries for the simple reason that

> most of the countries and the majority of the world's population have not even reached, or have only just reached, the capitalist stage of development ...

> "ONLY the advanced countries of Western Europe and North America are ripe for socialism ...

> "Socialism will be achieved by the united action of the proletarians, not of all, but of a minority of countries, those that have reached the ADVANCED capitalist stage of development."[5]

Based mechanically on this statement, apparently, the Eastern European socialists and the Western Left and its followers are still claiming that, in OUR time when many new developments have occurred since Lenin wrote these words, the world revolution is still to be LED by the "working class in (precisely) these advanced capitalist countries".

But modern events are giving a new and broader interpretation to such words. Referring to the MATERIAL BASE, what Lenin said was true, then and today. The question is: WHICH countries fit the WHOLE picture? Are colonies not really at the most "advanced capitalist stage of development?" Note: he did NOT say, at the most "advanced stage of capitalist development". So, in the context of the system's "advanced" parasitism, History appears to have elevated the colonies.

One thing is certain in any case: this quotation does bring out the enormous significance, as one major "new development" since Lenin's day, of the attainment of majority numerical status by the labor aristocracy in the United States.(See Table 8 above.)

Actually, other words by this same Lenin bring out Chairman Mao's above meaning perhaps a bit more clearly:

> "The social revolution cannot come about otherwise than in the form of an epoch in which are combined civil war by the proletariat against the bourgeoisie in the advanced countries and a WHOLE SERIES of democratic revolutionary movements, including the national-liberation movement, in the underdeveloped, backward and oppressed nations."[6]

Lenin made clear in a later portion of the same article that he was speaking specifically about the objective economic maturity of the more highly developed countries. The advance of the Afro-American Freedom struggle in the U.S. onto a revolutionary path, which has begun, would seem to suggest that such an epoch as Lenin described may now be coming into being. The "WHOLE SERIES" of events he portended may soon be in progress. Will it occur alone? Or will it be "combined" with "civil war" in the West?

The world revolution, or Lenin's "social revolution", can only mean the extension of socialism over all the earth. Even after the success of colonial liberation, that world revolution will therefore not be complete: there will still be "the West".

Today's struggle, it has been said, contends for the minds of men. In liberated China – an ex-colonial area – for the first time in history that struggle has entered the arena of culture in a practical mass way. Chinese Marxists, led by Chairman Mao, have already concluded that true revolutionaries cannot operate only politically and economically. They have the inescapable duty of participating in the cultural lists. There, their first task is "to sweep away monsters of all kinds".

COLONIALISM IS CURRENTLY THE WORLD'S FOREMOST SUCH "MONSTER".

Since the Western labor aristocracy is – as demonstrated – the present repository and active cherisher of this (and corollary) monsters – ideological left-overs of a dying world – it remains for the anti-colonial liberation movement to lead the way to the realization of man's loftiest aspirations. And, we have suggested, so matters will stand until colonial liberation has advanced far enough to force Western proletarians to face their exploiters "at home". The unstoppable total victory of liberation will be the first great full international leap along this noble road.

For then at last, in their bloody final battle with rapacious imperialism, the Western working classes, from whose eyes the ensuing bitter battles will rip the festering ideological blinders, will at last realize that liberation for colonial peoples is in their own real, long-run interests. The resulting struggle they mount to finish the world revolution in their own habitat will constitute an unbreakable support for colonial liberation.

In that last tremendous conflict, but very likely not much before, the Western labor aristocracy will destroy its own position as "the principal social ... prop of the bourgeoisie", whose supply of bribes the colonial liberation movement will virtually have eliminated. Nor can there be the slightest doubt that, when the Western proletariat does start its own final revolution, its colonial class brothers, being greatly advanced over Western workers by their conditions and struggles, will most assuredly give them every support.

Then the last window into Western minds will finally have been opened to let in the light of socialism, with its promise of self-salvation for the world's peoples. The Norman Bethunes will cease to be prophetic exceptions and, multiplying in the struggle, will become representative of the new Western worker.

25. Relationship Between Western and Colonial Workers

Before that final revolutionary moment of which we have just been speaking arrives, however, solutions are needed for certain problems involving the relationships between Western and colonial workers. The problems have existed for a long time; solutions – still only on paper!

In his 1928 analysis of Social Democracy, Italy's Togliatti, in a search for such solutions, reached some conclusions which have not stood the test of time. The considerations which influenced him stemmed from some then-small theoretical aberrations.

One of these involved, precisely, the nature of the relationships between Western and colonial workers. The other was rooted in his consequent answer to a key question of the colonial revolutionary movement: WHO IS TO LEAD IT?

Togliatti had noted that

> "... the process of unmasking the socialist agents of imperialism before the masses is not yet completed. There are masses which must still be reached in order . . . to make them understand that the struggle against Social Democracy is part of the struggle against the bourgeoisie and imperialism. These masses exist today not only in the capitalist countries but also in the colonies."[1]

Togliatti's description of the task was prophetic: the influence of Social Democracy – specifically EUROPEAN Social Democracy – in the colonies has, for imperialism's benefit, done considerable damage to liberation. And there truly are "masses" in the colonies who are still gaining experience in distinguishing their friends from their foes.

But Togliatti's approach to the relationship which should exist between workers in colonies and those "at home" – though perhaps prophetic – was not quite so commendable. Those "at home", he implied, must "make" the "others" understand. (See page 321, below.)

These germs of a Social Democratic attitude by Ercoli toward colonial masses simply sprouted to become the entire position on "colonial masses" of most Western Communist Parties and of the socialist ideologues of Eastern Europe. As a result, far from winning over such colonial masses, Western Marxists and Eastern Europe have instead themselves fallen into the Social Democratic trap.

A typical example of the growth of this position of late exists in one of a short series of policy statements for the 1964 elections by the British Communist Party, dealing "with certain immediate problems" rather, so they claim, than with tactical or long-range British Communist programmatic points.

A. British Communist attitude toward imperialism.

> "The Tory, Liberal and Labour Parties still strive to maintain the outdated system of imperialism. This policy distorts the British economy and hampers the expansion of our industries and social services."[2]

To "distort" means either to "twist out of regular shape", literally or figuratively; or to "wrest from the true meaning; pervert". What is being said, then, by Englishmen calling themselves Marxist, is that imperialism is causing the British capitalist economy to deviate from its true nature. By implication, colonialism is simply an "aberration" of British capitalism, rather than its essence. If it could be removed (painlessly, of course), a more "regular" British economy, full of "our" expanding industries, would supposedly emerge, without need for any fundamental alteration in the system.

This is in no way distinguishable from the Social Democratic position on imperialism which Lenin castigated half a century ago, when he took on Karl Kautsky, the Bid Man of that era's revisionism :

> "... we definitely come into conflict with K. Kautsky ...who defines imperialism as a POLICY which is 'preferred' by finance capital . . ."3

Lenin's definition of imperialism, on the other hand, proved conclusively that, FAR from "perverting" capitalist economy, colonialism fulfills it. In the same speech, Lenin emphatically insisted that

> "The distinguishing feature of imperialism is the domination ... of finance capital, the striving to annex ... ALL KINDS of countries."3

B. The British Communist Party and socialism.

It is significant that this British Communist "short policy statement" about colonialism does not ONCE use the word "socialism" . In this, the metropolitan Party would appear to lag behind even the colonial nationalist parties, which in a number of cases started forth to gain, or to govern, their newly independent countries with "socialism" inscribed on their banners.

C. The cause of colonial poverty.

Speaking of colonial peoples, the British statement says that "the cause of their poverty is robbery — robbery by the big imperialist firms in whose interests the colonial system was established."[3]

How delicate! Is it the system of imperialism, or only the system's "big firms", which commits colonial robbery? What of the immense benefit not just to "big firms", but to whole Western peoples? What role is played by Syrian, Lebanese and Asian traders who wax fat in Africa? What of the hordes of individuals – often totally incompetent – sent by governments and international organizations as "technicians" to colonies at enormous salaries such as they could never drag down "at home"?

Furthermore, if something "was established", so too, it can presumably be "dismantled", inferentially at the whim of the same "big imperialist firms" – if "someone" could only "persuade" them to do so. Obviously, British Communists see that the local Social Democrats are no longer so adept at such persuasion and are offering themselves for the chore.

Colonialism constitutes the legs on which imperialism walks. Were legs "established" to serve the activity of walking, which, then, might conceivably be accomplished in some other way?

D. Relations between Metropoles and Ex-colonies.

Between ruling country and ex-colony, the British statement declares,

"In place of the old relations of exploitation and robbery, new relations of mutual benefit could be established."[3]

Such "mutual benefit" is envisioned by these British Communists thus:

— "Long-term credits on easy terms from Britain... To reconstruct their economies, to build their industries, and to develop their agriculture.

— "They need . . . a whole range of machinery and engineering products which British industry is well-suited to provide. Orders for such commodities could help to wipe out unemployment in many hard-hit areas of Britain and at the same time help the new states in Asia and Africa to build up their economies …

— "The economic development of these states would … Make possible a continued flow of goods from Britain — and in return we could receive the numerous items, including foodstuffs, raw materials, processed goods, and certain lines of manufactures which these countries would be turning out.

— "More equitable prices too could be granted to the new states for their raw materials and this would help them place bigger orders here for the goods they require."[3]

(By what, incidentally, those "areas of Britain" were so "hard-hit" is politely passed over, as is the question of WHY British industry is "well-suited to provide" that "whole range of machinery and engineering products" which self-styled Marxists now propose to continue supplying to "ex" colonies.)

Involved in this set of proposals is not a mere academic "definition", but the question of whether or not Marxists accept or reject colonialism itself, which evoked and deliberately maintains this type of metropolitan-colony relationship.

Outlining its version of "new" relations of "mutual benefit", this "Communist" document repeats over and over that England, the metropolitan area, will supply "engineering goods" to "former" colonies in return for "foodstuffs, raw materials, processed goods" (i.e., raw materials in a "secondary" condition) and certain lines of manufacture" common to colonial areas (i.e., assembled manufactures using metropolitan parts and processes). So what is "new"? This is the same old horse-rider relationship of OLD colonialism: "on easy terms" means "at lower interest rates than before . . ." Interest is a form of profit; extraction of profit is exploitation. So British "Communists" blandly announce their intention to continue exploiting the colonies and using them to solve "home" problems.

In this "policy statement" one sees why Africans – and other colonial and ex-colonial peoples – more and more seriously object to accepting advice, let alone "leadership", from outside their own ranks. Quite plainly, too many of their "advisers" – whatever their noble intentions – have for too long had a great material stake in colonial subjugation. As far as colonial peoples themselves can see, these "advisers" have as yet shown no practical inclination to renounce that stake.

26. Early Marxist Illusions About International Working-Class Relations

What this British Communist Party policy statement on colonialism proves is that Marxists have not been exempt from Social Democratic influence. On the contrary, with their compatriots, they have shared in the spoils. In saying so, no moral judgment is intended; merely a statement of FACT regarding a position of which the origins can be found in Tolgiatti's speech of 1928, which can now be seen as an incomplete exposition of colonialism, especially around the question: WHO IS TO LEAD THE REVOLUTION IN THE COLONIES?

Winding up this long speech, Togliatti quoted "the most important point in the resolution" of the Social Democrats at Brussels in 1928:

> "The Labour and Socialist International calls upon all its affiliated parties to get into touch with the independence movement of the oppressed peoples in order to support them . . . and to assist in the development of the political and trade union labor movement in these countries, influencing them in the spirit of democracy and socialism."[1]

Togliatti wondered whether this call imposed any threat to Communists:

> "Are we really today faced with the danger of reformism in the colonies?"[1]

He answered himself:

> "If it is true that the basis for the development of reformism in the ranks of the working class is to be found

in the fact that the bourgeoisie, by enjoying special profits and especially surplus profits from the colonies, is in a position to corrupt a section of the working class, we must also state that there are in the colonies very special conditions which favor the formation of a labor aristocracy and its liaison with colonial imperialism. This phenomenon may perhaps offer an even greater danger in the colonies, than the reformist movement which is developing in the ruling countries."[1]

What facts did he summon to support his contention? He declared:

"First of all, and in the first stages of development in general, the labor movement is much more inclined to subject itself to the influence of another class than in its more advanced stages. Consequently it is necessary to take into consideration the particular character of the labor movement in the colonies and the fact that the colonial proletariat is still bound up with certain strata of the petty-bourgeoisie and that it includes a vast number of gradations among which the imperialist bourgeoisie finds sections which it can corrupt and make tools for its domination.

"Reformism, then, exists in the colonies as well as in the advanced capitalist countries as the result of an influence which is exercised upon the proletariat by another class. In all colonial countries in recent times we may observe this tendency to the formation of a reformist movement. It works side by side with the tendency of the colonial petty-bourgeoisie to desert the camp of the revolution at a given moment and to ally itself with the imperialists. I do not wish to go into details, but the problem exists and we must deal with it …

"Now we must thoroughly understand that it is in the colonies themselves that we must struggle against reformism."[1]

To illustrate where Togliatti's position eventually led, an example is now offered:

"The growth of the national liberation movement is facilitated by the revolutionary struggle of the working class in the main capitalist countries, a struggle which. weakens the position of imperialism at home, thus hindering monopoly capital from exercising its colonial policy in the crude form of the past."[2]

Possibly anticipating disagreement, the authors warn anyone wishing to deserve the title "revolutionary" to accept this position on pain of

"taking the leadership of the world revolutionary movement out of the hands of the working class (of the main capitalist countries – H. E.) and its offspring, the socialist world system . . . leaving it in the hands of the national bourgeoisie which in most countries heads the liberation movement."[2]

The first thing to be noted from the above remarks is this: it is clearly implied that modern imperialist policy toward colonies, often called "neo-colonialism" because it no longer works "in the crude form of the past", therefore constitutes an improvement for colonial peoples. But, in fact, today such peoples are discovering – and being vindicated by statistics in many respects – on the price scissors, growth of repatriated profits, non-equivalent exchange, the results of foreign "aid", and the like – that neo-colonialism is costing the masses of colonial peoples more than ever before. As has already been suggested, it merely elevates a tiny new elite composed mostly of comprador exploiters to a relative affluence that shows up as "improved statistics" in certain "international studies". (See Chapter 17, page 169, above.) For the vast colonial masses, material and cultural conditions continue to WORSEN under neo-colonialism – because colonial labor power is the source of super profits, as before.

Of course, the authors of the cited quotation have not here claimed that the "revolutionary struggle of the working class" in capitalist countries has SO FAR "weakened . . . imperialism at home" as to make it give up its colonial policy altogether. But even what is said – that neo-colonialism is imperialism's response to "struggle at home" – amounts to crediting the Western labor aristocracy with such hard-won success as the national liberation movement has managed thus far at high cost to wrest from brutal imperialism – often in the face of guns sent against it by "Labour" or "Socialist" government.

To see how this modern position logically grew out of earlier ones, we consider now one by one the point raised by Togliatti in his 1928 speech quoted at the beginning of this Chapter:

1. ". . . the bourgeoisie, by enjoying special profits and especially surplus profits from the colonies, is in a position to corrupt a section of the working class."

Lenin had expressed the same thought in his Imperialism – with the exception that the only "section of the working class" to which he referred was that in imperialist countries. But Togliatti uses Lenin's concept in order to point at the colonial working class. This is a significant difference, as we shall see.

DOES the bourgeoisie corrupt a section of the colonial working class? If so, which section?

In Africa, it has not always been necessary to bribe the working class. At first, the imperialists extracted super-profits from their colonies by sheer unmitigated brutality and terrorism against all sections of the African working class (which always fought back).

When it became apparent, especially after World War II, that

(a) the recent anti-fascist victory would make such unrelieved brutality internationally embarrassing at a too-potentially revolutionary historical moment, and

(b) that it was in any case having the opposite effect from the one intended – a change took place.

A small number of African workers in slightly "advanced" jobs or positions, such as mine foremen or office head clerks, suddenly found themselves raised from salaries in the environs of £5 to £7 a month to £30 or £40, with their "titles" changed: they became "advisers" to the white boss. This was not without effect. This small number of African workers did become bosses' tools.

In the late 40s, the British and other imperialists gave up their obviously futile struggle against the formation of African unions. Unable to fend off the inevitable, they installed these same "advisers" as the core of new "legal" unions (or other organizations), many times in leadership positions. In Ghana, for example, these trade union leaders were the ones who – with glorified civil servants and professionals, the colonial petty-bourgeoisie – helped form the United Gold Coast Convention. When the latter evolved into the Convention People's Party, however, it did so without these workers and officials, many of whom stayed with the UGCC.

Thus, a tiny fraction of super-wages stolen from the African working class did return to an even tinier fraction of it as bribes which created this small nucleus of a labor aristocracy "in the colonies". (See Chapter 17, page 169 above.) This nucleus did, as Togliatti said, ally itself with the petty-bourgeoisie.

2. "There are in the colonies very special conditions which favor the formation of a labor aristocracy and its liaison with colonial imperialism."

That there are in the colonies "very special conditions" goes without saying. BUT – do they "favor the formation of a labor aristocracy" or "its liaison with colonial imperialism"?

What ARE these "very special conditions"? Do they not consist of a central super-exploitation affecting the entire colonial population? Does this in turn not give that entire population a common incentive against "liaison with colonial imperialism"? At imperialism's own initiative, such a common incentive was even carefully (although unintentionally) planted when colonialism used a visible trait common to the majority of Africans – black skin color: the varied forms of colonial discrimination, from brutal to subtle, affected to one degree or another everyone whose skin color fit the ticket.

(Of course, there are still class differences despite such "solidarity factors". But are they at this time more "favorable" to the formation of a labor aristocracy than imperialism itself is to the formation of a new colonial elite? Which is the main contradiction in colonies: the one between the colony and the metropolis; or, the one inside the colony itself between the new elite, many of them of the petty-bourgeoisie, and colonial workers? This is the point at issue here: until the success of the national-democratic revolution, the internal contradictions in colonies must be subordinate to that of the colony virtually as a whole against metropolitan imperialism.)

Second, Lenin had noted that the labor aristocracy in the super exploiting areas are the beneficiaries of super-profits extracted from colonies. The few Africans bribed by imperialism are no "aristocracy" by imperialist standards, as a glance at wage levels immediately discloses.

In the mid-50s, according to one authority,

> "It takes an African worker usually a year to earn as much as an average worker in Britain earns in a month."[3]

If that African worker is a bit more than mid-way up in this writer's "one shilling a day up to under five shillings a day" as the average African wage, he earns about £5 a month. If the African "labor aristocrat" makes £30, his wage is six times that of the African laborer. But the average British worker who makes twelve times as much as the African laborer thereby makes twice as much as the African "aristocrat". And that British worker is still a long way from the standards of the highly paid crafts that make up the cream of the cream of Western labor Elites. For example, an American building construction worker in 1950 earned £114 ($320) per month, or twice as much as the British worker; in 1960, the American made more then £185 ($520);[4] that is, four to six times that of the few African labor elite.

In a word, the most favorable circumstances in colonies did NOT tend to create a local aristocracy. Furthermore, the bribed in colonies actually are a small comprador elite; not, by and large or in as yet politically significant numbers, colonial workers. (See page 170, above).

What colonial conditions, rather, helped spawn was the expansion of the WESTERN labor aristocracy. This is a crucial distinction.

3. "This phenomenon may perhaps offer an even greater danger in the colonies than the reformist movement which is developing in the ruling countries."

To find out if this is so, history must be consulted about the results of bribing these few African workers. What was the reaction of colonial peoples to them? Are African sell-out artists blessed with a mass following which militantly pursues "reformism"?

First, when the Convention People's Party was formed in Ghana, and representatives of Ghana's tiny "labor aristocracy" remained with the UGCC, together with what there was of a colonial bourgeoisie and petty-bourgeoisie, where did the popular masses go?

History records that they supported the CPP, NOT the "labor aristocracy". The same, by and large, is true of other African countries which pursued a progressive or socialist-oriented course. This African "labor aristocracy" was either swept aside into the backwashes of history, or – as in Ghana – it loudly "supported" liberation.

Second, after 1949, in metropolitan countries, the bourgeoisie's "labor lieutenants" gathered in the ICFTU aimed at directing the colonial labor movement. This was entirely in line with Social Democracy's cited function of ensuring in the interests of super-wages the continued flow of super profits from colonies to industrial areas.

At first, the ICFTU tried to keep the colonial labor movement "non-political." But by the late 50s and early 60s, the colonial labor movement itself had thoroughly frustrated this aim. As a result, in 1959, a series of "shake-ups" began inside the ICFTU during which the U.S. AFL-CIO first captured control of the Executive Board (Brussels, December 1959) and then, thwarted by the ousted but much-concerned British T.U.C. in their exercise of this control, split away from the ICFTU to set up the African-American Labor Center in New York.

How did Africans react to these representatives of the world's real labor aristocracy? Was the ICFTU, under their surveillance, making progress on that continent? Or were they being dislodged from one position after another? Did they not, in fact, stand in real danger of being swept off African soil altogether? And do not these facts tend to explain in some measure imperialism's military interventions, and use of local military puppets, in the mid-60s in so many African countries where – quite significantly, as in Ghana – the ICFTU is brought back to dominate the local trade union scene?

It is wrong to say that the formation of even a small and relatively poor "labor aristocracy" in colonies is a "greater danger" than the reformist movement in the ruling countries. A greater danger to what? Togliatti was obviously discussing the colonial liberation movement. Was the colonial "labor aristocracy" then a "greater danger" to colonial liberation than "reformism" in the ruling countries? To say this can only indicate failure to understand what "reformism in the ruling countries" was really about – which is just what we are saying actually happened.

4. "It is necessary to take into consideration the particular character of the labor movement in the colonies and the fact that the colonial proletariat is still bound up with certain strata of the petty bourgeoisie, and that it contains a vast number of gradations."

The "particular character of the labor movement in the colonies" does NOT rest primarily either on its ties with any other class nor on "the vast number of gradations" in it. Both features are consequences of the colonial labor movement's character, not its essence.

The particular character of African labor is that it is super-exploited in all gradations, along with the petty bourgeoisie to whom it has ties. Even its "bourgeoisie", if such a designation is even proper, cannot exist alone, but must abjectly tie itself to outside imperialism.

Thus, universal super-exploitation of African people gives them primarily a basis for cohesion rather than for separation into sections. That is why some Africans who did link up with imperialism were forced when the chips were down to turn, at least for the moment, against imperialism and to side with liberation, or be swept away.

The significant thing about the colonial labor movement is not that it is "still bound up with certain strata of the petty bourgeoisie". Whether true or not, the significant thing about it is its super-exploitation by overseas imperialism.

5. "Reformism, then, exists in the colonies as well as in the advanced capitalist countries as a result of an influence which is exercised upon the proletariat by another class."

Since the subject involved in this quotation is extensive, it is discussed separately in the next Chapters.

27. "Reformism" at Home and Abroad

There is a distinct difference between efforts from the metropolitan center to set up "reformist" movements in colonies in the image of Social Democracy "at home", and the growth of such a phenomenon from colonial ranks.

A number of such specific attempts have been made by European Social Democracy. All have failed: there has been no case of any mass Social Democratic party ever having been formed in a colony, nor can there be, due to the material conditions in colonies and the "function" of the colonial working class as the reservoir of super-profits.

Nevertheless, Western Social Democracy constitutes a specific and growing danger to colonial liberation movements because it has refined the old techniques of bribery as well as because the material conditions for its success continue to escalate with the decay of the system.

Therefore, insofar as "reformism" in colonies is concerned, it would be instructive to examine some actual efforts to spread European Social Democracy in these territories. In addition, there will be discussion of a possibly related phenomenon: the fact that certain highly developed industrialized nations with large, affluent labor aristocracies have never produced mass Social Democratic parties.

Western Social Democracy has made two specific attempts to build mass parties in their own image. The first was in GREECE, as the following statement notes:

> "One of the weaknesses of the Greek bourgeoisie and
> its foreign patrons is that no party of any significance of

the Social Democratic type has been able to take root in Greece, although not a few attempts have been made in this direction. (Much effort is being exerted now to create such a party artificially with the aid of the Socialist International and with the strong support of German Social Democracy.)"[1]

The second such attempt was in CANADA:

"There is as yet no real and workable understanding between the working class of French Canada and the working class of English-speaking Canada . . . The part played by the leadership of the New Democratic Party (the Social Democratic Party in Canada . . .) has been to flinch from full support for French Canadian national rights . . . the New Democratic Party, for this and other reasons, has little appeal among the French Canadian masses. Their efforts to form a mass N.D.P. in French Canada have failed largely because they have failed to become the champions of French Canadian national freedom. The N.D.P. leadership is tinged with Anglo-Canadian chauvinism and even those among them who sense the historic nature of the French Canadian movement refrain from drawing the full conclusion for fear of having to combat the ingrained chauvinism of their followers."[2]

Recognising the labor aristocracies of industrialized countries as the material base of Social Democracy would have made both these failures predictable: representatives of labor aristocracies cannot easily persuade the very workers out of whose super-exploitation metropolitan well-being in significant part derives to acquiesce in their own even greater super-exploitation.

There is, however, one country which in part has colonial features where a mass Social Democratic party does exist: JAPAN. Is this an exception to examples like those of Greece and Canada, just cited?

The salient feature of the Japanese Socialist party seems to be that it is split into a Right and Left wing. Why? Has there been some particular circumstance setting Japan off from other colonial or semi-colonial areas?

First of all, an authority on Latin America, engaged in showing that "under-development" was really a "growth" which accompanied metropolitan "development", both having constituted the single ingestion of the whole system, asked the following question:

> "Why, one may ask, was resource-poor but unsatellized Japan able to industrialize so quickly at the end of the century while resource-rich Latin American countries and Russia were not able to do so . . . after the same forty years of development efforts?. . . Japan was not satellized either during the Tokugawa or the Meiji period and therefore did not have its development structurally limited as did the countries which were so satellized."[3]

After the Meiji period, however, the island WAS "satellized", and Japan thereby entered its DUAL position in the WORLD imperialist economic system: First, vis-a-vis ASIA, Japan was for better than half a century (and is again, with U.S. assistance) an imperialist power. Its ruling class has reached an advanced stage of development as an industrial capitalism interlocked with banking capital in the classical imperialist pattern of monopoly with its aggressive search for and attainment of colonial areas. Its expansion on the Asian mainland brought in super profits which created, among sections of the large Japanese proletariat, a labor aristocracy which definitely benefited from the proceeds of super-exploitation by Japanese finance capital in Korea, China and other Asian areas. These colonies were distant: the super-exploited did not live in the "home" labor aristocracy's midst. Under such conditions, as we shall see, a mass Social Democratic Party usually develops.

On the other hand, vis-a-vis the UNITED STATES, Japan has been and remains in a semi-dependent position, with American monopoly capital playing an ever more dominant role in the Japanese economy. As an extremely valuable study of this question revealed:

> "All measures taken by the U.S. imperialists in Japan after the war were, in the last analysis, for the . . . Establishment of U.S. domination over Japan . . . Japanese monopoly capital is subordinated to the United States in capital, raw material, technology and market. Ninety per cent of foreign capital introduced into Japan is from the United States. The amount of U.S. investments in Japan is rapidly increasing. A direct tie-up subordinating Japanese monopolies to U.S. monopolies is taking place. The enterprises jointly run by U.S. and Japanese capital numbered more than 200 as of the end of 1963."[4]

These figures suggest an economic position in which the Japanese population including a goodly portion of its labor aristocracy is to a certain degree super-exploited by American monopoly capital in a manner bringing to mind later developments in Western Europe. Such circumstances usually make the development of a mass Social Democratic Party unlikely.

Thus the Japanese economy is caught in a world dichotomy which the split in its Socialist Party expresses: the Right Wing, which is openly Social Democratic in the European sense, represents the Japanese labor aristocracy, collaborating with Japanese ruling circles in their colonialist role. The Left Wing, on the other hand, expresses the drive of the Japanese nation, led by the militant and ideologically-advanced section of its Communist Party, for national independence; i.e. , to shake off the increasingly heavy yoke of U.S. Imperialism.

For other colonial areas, the case of INDIA'S Social Democrats may be taken as typical. During 1965, an American research fellow in India under a grant from the United States-India Comparative Education Exchange Program, showed that such Indian Social Democracy as exists has never been able to get off the ground; and even that was in definite danger of complete extinction, This would be a logical development of the well-known, intense "satellization" of India, leading to unmitigated super-exploitation of India's hungry masses. Some pertinent quotations on the subject follow:

> "India claims to be a socialist country, and has been committed to a 'socialist pattern of society' for a number of years. Yet; at the present time, the Indian Left Wing is in the process of total collapse . . . not limited to the democratic socialist organizations which have suffered a number of ruptures in the past year; the collapse extends to the Communist Party, which has split along Sino-Soviet lines, and is virtually paralyzed . . .

> "The two main (Congress Left) groups have been the Praja Socialist Party (PSP) and the Socialist Party. Until recently, the Praja Socialists, who are social democrats in the European tradition, were the largest socialist party in the parliament and one of the most important of the opposition groups in India . . .

> "Although the socialist movement has never been a mass movement (in India), it did have substantial support among intellectuals and in urban areas . . . 'The future of the Communist movement in India is not much more hopeful than that of the socialists. There are at present in India two separate Communist Parties . . . The right-wing Communist Party, led by veteran Bombay trade unionist, S. A. Dange . . . receives strong ideological and financial support from the Soviet Union …

> "The Left Communists, however, have maintained a surprising degree of militancy, despite . . . harassment and detention . . .

> "The future for a mass socialist movement has never been bright, and recent events indicate that . . . the movement stands disunited, disillusioned, and virtually leaderless at a crucial period of its development . . . India's commitment to a 'socialist pattern of society' has been seriously compromised.[5]

This "worry-worry" of a recipient of U.S. educational "aid" about Indian Social Democracy's weakening confirms our diagnosis that it is primarily forces in the WEST which spur this movement in colonies and neo-colonies. (Note, above, the fact that Social Democracy never had a mass following in – colonial or neocolonial – India. Our analysis has led us to expect this.) The splits, maneuverings, and loss of prestige for Social Democracy in India further confirm that, as India's material conditions continue worsening under the blight of foreign (now mainly U.S. And Russian) investment, any existing "mass base" for Social Democracy dwindles away. The quotations also support our conclusion that when "local" Social Democrats arise in such areas, what they are doing is mainly the "dirty work" of European Social Democracy: significantly, the largest and most effective Social Democratic party in India, such as it was, was "in the European tradition." And the class base of this European-oriented Social Democracy is pin-pointed as "intellectuals and . . . urban areas", the soil out of which Social Democracy always arises in colonial areas.

The significance of the Dange faction in the Indian Communist Party and its reported reliance on Soviet support and assistance is part of a world-wide phenomenon which is to be dealt with in a separate volume.

This American writer, above, found the mass support among the Indian Communist LEFT amazing enough to comment on several times. However, it is not so amazing; it merely proves that, in colonial areas, only a militant, genuinely revolutionary ideological position can count on mass support. Militancy and Social Democracy are, for very real material reasons discussed in these pages a number of times, mutually exclusive.

In countries like Southern Rhodesia and South Africa on that colonial continent where significant white minorities control the economies and collaborate with international imperialism, no mass Social Democratic parties have developed despite capitalism's spawning of distinct labor aristocracies made up of the white worker minority. Countries like these illustrate the qualitative difference between the. metropolitan-based white labor aristocracy, formed from the spoils of super-exploitation of the most extreme type (based on color), and the tiny African labor pseudo-aristocracy examined earlier: the two exist side by side, so comparison is visible to the naked eye.

Since fuller understanding of this situation is to be obtained from a discussion of U.S. developments, it is to the latter that the next Chapter now turns.

28. "Reformism" and Racism in the United States

The UNITED STATES OF AMERICA has the world's largest and richest labor aristocracy. Yet no mass Social Democratic Party ever took root there as it did in England, Germany, Italy and other Western countries.

Many attempts have been made to explain this phenomenon. None, however, it seems to us, have really taken to heart the following words of Lenin:

> "The difference between a definitely formed (Social Democratic) party ... and, say, a semi-formed incomplete party... is unimportant. The important thing is that the economic desertion of a stratum of the labor aristocracy to the side of the bourgeoisie has matured and become and accomplished fact. This economic fact, this change in relations between classes, will find for itself political form of one kind or another without much 'difficulty'."[1]

These words suggest that the American lack of mass support for Social Democracy as such has its own significance which illumines Social Democracy's foundations. In fact, nowhere is the kind of political form this "change in relations between classes" takes of greater portent than where Social Democracy cannot operate in its own name.

Organized Socialism in the U.S. has had what is often called a "checkered" history. From mid-19th century on, it was a casualty of historical conditions. Waves of immigration from defeated revolutions in Europe, notably Germany in 1830 and 1848, had swept Marxist thought into the New World. Karl Marx himself had written for Horace Greeley's New York DAILY TRIBUNE. Carl Schurz, one of the best-known of these early German immigrants, had participated in Abraham Lincoln's Civil War government, and had later participated in the Reconstruction Era in the South between 1865 and 1876. Other German revolutionaries were active in early U.S. trade unions. Some were responsible for inserting into early craft union constitutions clauses specifying socialism as "the only solution" for American workers. (Such clauses have since been removed in favor of prohibiting the right of "non-Caucasians" – meaning mostly, Afro-Americans – even to work in the given trade, let alone to become members of its union.)

All the same, Social Democracy as such knew no mass success among U.S. workers with their hard-bitten "Anglo-Saxon" traditions and their growing affluence. The high point of socialism in the U.S. came and went with Eugene Debs' almost-a-million (929,000, Chapter 21, Reference Note 1) votes in 1912.

However, after the sell-out of the 1876 elections, its internal market now national in scope, the Northern bourgeoisie had shuddered at possible post-war unity among the exploited. Faced with such a possibility, nascent American imperialism cynically united in what it saw as self-protection with its erstwhile enemy, the conquered Southern plantation oligarchy, and at about the same time began allocating to "its own" (i.e., white) workers an ever-growing share of its profits. This, of-course, was not the only reason that white labor in the more-and-more industrial North saw the new freedmen not as a class but as a threat to their own social position. Certainly official racism played its part in ensuring that, when the Afro-American was sold down the river, the sale was underwritten by all major U.S. Unions. Thus, Afro-Americans were made, then and to this day, to bear the chief burden of whatever suffering American workers do because of imperialist contradictions.

At the same time, white labor's anti-black stance ensured the destruction in the U.S. labor movement of Marxist influence so that U.S. labor grew up in a world minimum of socialist ideas. (The military crisis in Vietnam, stirring at first top revolutionary layers, may have made a dent in this situation. Whether the crisis continues and deepens rests first of all with what happens in Vietnam out of the Paris talks, and also with how much understanding of American realities can be brought home to the small U.S. revolutionary sector.) The current was there; but bourgeois reformism soon caught up with and overwhelmed it. By mid-20th century, there were few avowed Social Democrats. But, of them, Sidney Hillman was an arch-type. (SIDNEY HILLMAN: 1887-1946, b. Lithuania; to U.S. at age 20. From 1915, President, Amalgamated Clothing Workers of America. From 1939, Vice-President, CIO; Chairman Executive Council Textile Workers of America. With William S. Knudsen, from 1941, Co-Director, Office of Production Management (in Roosevelt Administration); from 1942, Head of Labor Division, War Production Board (also Administration). Such men had roots only in surroundings like the New York garment trades, where Middle-European immigrants to whom socialism was not unknown had, as part of American monopoly's policy of keeping its labor market saturated, been enticed to the Land of Opportunity.

These few real Social Democrats did, however, leave their mark on the U.S. scene through the activities of Franklin Delano Roosevelt, who saved American imperialism for the imperialists against almost-insane opposition from some of the beneficiaries themselves.

While a Republican administration had fiddled with time-worn panaceas, the exploited had waxed ever more restive, insisting on improvements in their situation in what American rulers saw as a most ugly and frightening way. Democrat Roosevelt had been swept into the Presidency on a wave of strikes, riots, hunger marches, huge demonstrations in the national capital and other signs of imminent revolution at home. Schooled in rough maxims which had guided their robber barons to power, the U.S. working class had publicly proven that it was not, like its European counterpart, to be bludgeoned into bearing alone the profound consequences of the epochal economic crisis.

It is an open secret that in this situation Social Democrats were invited – at the very historical moment when their German confreres were already shooting down "their own" workers in Berlin streets – to advise Roosevelt. And the genial New York aristocrat accepted their advice that in critical times, if financially possible, a ruling class which hopes to continue to rule must make large but not basic concessions to the angry working class. The Social Democrats stuck around in the New Deal administration until the crisis was safely over.

The final solution came with a providential new war in Europe which opened new investment possibilities for U.S. Monopoly, which quickly acted on the chance.

The substantial gains of American labor in the 40s and 50s of this century can, thus, be traced at least partly to Social Democratic origins. Why, then, did "socialism" fare so poorly in the U.S.A.?

One excellent picture of its inability to get started has been given by the American historian, Philip S. Foner.[2]

Among socialists in the U.S., ideological divisions prevented a united socialist movement, particularly among the numerous German immigrants who, already divided in Germany, had transplanted, their differences onto American soil, at the same time as they acted as "carriers" of Marxist ideology.

However, these rifts of ideas were derivative before they became causative. It may be true to say, as Foner did,

> "Had the labor movement and its allies among the Western farmers continued to exert their influence upon the industrialists and financiers in the Republican Party, as they had done in the years before the Civil War, the

overthrow of progressive governments in the South might never have occurred ."4

But slackening of labor-movement "pressure" on "the industrialists and financiers in the Republican Party" did not arise out of a vacuum without antecedents: The wide-open frontier and a liberal lands policy; waves of cheap immigrant labor to increase splits inside the working class; the aggressiveness and unity binding the capitalist class in the North, all these and more formed economic and political foundations for the thereby-inevitable ideological splits which rent U.S. labor in its formative years. And such splits caused it to reject Marxism, reject the black class ally, and above all else, finally embrace the openly capitalist Democratic Party which, during World War II, was temporarily reduced to slinging certain European Social Democratic lingo about "the peepul", "national unity", and other well-known catch-phrases.

Until the first major crisis in the Vietnamese war early in 1968, these well-fed workers remained faithful to the Democratic Party (early known as "pro-labor"), even after the latter had abandoned its temporary "Left deviation" of before and during World War II years. Now that the Democrats are floundering in their own contradictions, working-class anger in the U.S. has no where to go. In general, and with monotonous regularity, the world's largest and richest labor aristocracy can only swing from one to another of ostensibly two major bourgeois parties, the programs of which began to approach each other after World War I and practically to coincide after World War II.

The U.S. labor aristocracy reached its present affluence through open class collaboration, unadulterated by rationalizations or demagogy about "Marx" or "labor": it swallowed nearly whole the imperialist position that "What's good for General Motors is good for America". This is true in spite of the counter, minority, tradition of real working-class militancy established by the Molly McGuires, the IWW ("Wobblies"), the Haymarket martyrs, and labor heroes like Joe Hill and Big Bill Haywood. Despite temporary influence in certain restricted though recurring American historical periods, their tradition, warped by syndicalism, could never win a majority of American workers because U.S. imperialism, though lacking formal colonies as such, was too "successful".

What accounts for the course of U.S. labor's development? Did something in its working-class conditions differ from those in Europe? Decidedly! Besides the "Wild West", "pioneer traditions" or any of the other usual glib "explanations", there was some thing basic which constituted the main difference: the presence within total metropolitan population of an internal quasi-colony composed of a large number of BLACK subjects.

In Europe, the super-exploited were, till quite recently, conveniently absent, though riches squeezed from their misery were abundantly present. The colonialism which distributes such spoils could be practiced under the polite guise of Social Democracy. As Karl Marx, talking about India, once put it:

> "The profound hypocrisy and inherent barbarism of bourgeois civilization lies unveiled before our eyes, turning from its home, where it assumes respectable forms, to the colonies, where it goes naked."[5]

So, British, French and other European workers could call themselves "non-racist", could support mass Social Democratic organizations, and could thereby consider themselves superior to crude Americans, a superiority often, as we have noted, transplanted with its carriers to the U.S. itself. Yet, the truth is that Europeans were merely not openly racist; because the moment any colony threatens to break free from "their" ruling classes, their actual racism and chauvinism bursts immediately from its hiding-place into the open. (See Chapter 22, page 239, above).

Labor Aristocracy

In England, racism has become blatant and visibly displays itself among workers under the impact of heavy immigration from the West Indies, Africa, Pakistan, etc. British Social Democracy AS SUCH has been forced to change its tactics considerably as confrontation with colonially super-exploited subjects has grown. In such circumstances, the "politeness" of Social Democracy always gives way to open racism. The majority in the Labour Party has now (predictably) more or less abandoned "Social Democracy" to its defeated, often militant but never revolutionary Left, and is becoming (like the U.S. Democrats) indistinguishable from the Republican-like Tories. The first and second Immigration Acts, bids to reduce the causative "alien presence", comprise perfectly logical moves by British Labour in its effort to retain its classical function of serving a metropolitan labor aristocracy. A more recent wave of hysteria against Indians from Kenya further underlined these points, as will all subsequent English developments in this particular area.

But in the United States, because of the slavery of Africans, RACISM was palpably present in the working class from the beginning of its history. Before the Civil War, there had been scattered labor understanding of the need for Emancipation as the prelude to ending wage slavery. But it was only fragmentary:

> "The division in the ranks of the workingmen on the slavery question continued through the controversy on the Wilmot Proviso. The German-American workers, meeting in a national convention when the debate over the proviso was reaching a climax in Congress did not adopt a single resolution on chattel slavery."[6]

Foner also mentioned New England textile workers and "a Philadelphia labor leader" as instances of understanding. But in general, he noted,

"Most (American) workers were not yet ready to join a campaign to abolish slavery, and some were more willing to attack the Abolitionists than the slave owners . . .

"To the fear of splitting the ('pro-labor') Democratic Party was added the fear that emancipation would bring thousands of Negroes to the northern states, increasing the competition for jobs and sending wages and living standards down . . .[7]

". . . to most workers, as to most small farmers, the basic issue (on the eve of the Civil War) was not the extermination of slavery but the prohibition of its spread to new areas . . . [8]

". . . the most representative statement of the position of most northern workers on the slavery question before the Civil War . . . does not call for the abolition of slavery, but neither does it attack the Abolitionists. It emphasizes the point uppermost in the minds of most workers: if slavery were permitted to expand, labor in the North would be reduced to the level of the Negro workers in the South."[9]

Significantly, even advanced labor leaders like William Sylvis frequently were narrowly trade unionist in outlook and Sylvis himself, although he wrote "enthusiastically" about the organization of Negro workers during his trip through the Reconstruction South,[10]

"showed little understanding of the revolutionary changes occurring in the South, and expressed no sympathy for the Reconstruction policies of the Republican Party."[11]

On their side, the Abolitionists – such as Wendell Phillips – were "indifferent to the demands of organized labor", which "did little to overcome the fears of the working class regarding the so-called dangers of Negro emancipation", according to Foner. Actually, such Abolitionists were "particularly hostile to the eight-hour day".[12] Foner added,

> "In fact, they did a good deal to convince many workers that they were concerned only with the welfare of the Negro slaves and considered the problems of free labor insignificant. In the first issue of THE LIBERATOR, William Lloyd Garrison denounced the trade union movement as an organized conspiracy to 'inflame the minds of our working classed against the more opulent' ... Garrison was not alone ... [13]

> "But until the viewpoint of some of the leaders of Abolitionism towards the problem of free labor underwent a change, really cordial relations between them and most wage workers were almost out of the question."[14]

While Foner noted some trade unionists and workingmen who did understand the tie between chattel and wage slavery, and could overlook the irritants produced by Abolitionist sectarianism, he admitted in general that

> "it was too much to expect, however, that most workers would accept so advanced a position in 1848; indeed, the majority of workers did not at any time before the Civil War advocate that 'slavery must be extinguished'."[15]

If this picture changed after the Civil War, it was, except for the briefest of moral flurries, only for the worse. It is quite true, as Foner abundantly set forth, that

> "the degrading and paralyzing effects of chattel slavery were definitely threatening the status of every free worker in the United States . . . Organized labor took up the challenge."[16]

That is, as some white workers displayed moments of understanding, a number of unions took action on the question. For instance, in 1870, the Carpenters and Joiners National Union repealed a resolution formerly passed by the members calling it "inexpedient" to admit Negroes as members. They resolved to invite ALL carpenters and joiners regardless of skin color to join as members.[17] But this was neither typical nor long-lasting:

> "Few trade unions were willing to follow the carpenters and joiners."[18]

More typical was, perhaps, the case of Lewis Douglass, son of world-renowned ex-slave and Republican leader Frederick Douglass. Lewis Douglass had been refused admission to the International Typographers Union, of which the 1869 convention brought the matter up for reversal: the move failed. And,

> "This capitulation set a pattern for other unions in which the Negro workers were not so few in number, and the NATIONAL SLAVERY STANDARD (July 17, 1969) reported that some local unions in New York were inserting the word, WHITE, in all places where the character of the members was described."[19]

The fact is that only Negro workers fully understood the need for black-white unity. For instance, at the 1869 convention of the National Labor Union, where nine of 142 delegates were, for the first time, Negroes, Isaac Myers, delegate from the Colored Caulkers Trade Union Society of Baltimore, delivered "one of the most magnificent addresses ever made by an American trade unionist."[20] He gave "a brilliant analysis of the need for unity"[21], as he spoke of Negro labor's readiness "to offer full cooperation in the common struggle."[22]

Responsibility for what happened thereafter thus rests with U.S. white workers and their unions. Such traditions of solidarity as had been raised by Civil War and post-Civil War fervor (and, as we have seen, they were not decisive) hung on into the 1890s, covering over what was really happening: At that time, A. F. of L. head Samuel Gompers was still replying to questions that Negro workers were to be organized; must not be barred as delegates to city and state A. F. of L. bodies; that where locals barring Negroes existed, "an effort should be made to eliminate such anti-labor barriers".[23] Meanwhile — and here was the hole in the dike — Negroes were organized into separate locals.

Left historian Foner finds it in his heart to apologize for this crucial hypocrisy:

> "... it is significant to note that, at this time, it was only one feature of the approach, emphasis being placed upon the fact that separate locals were to be organized only when no other method could be used to bring Negro workers into the Federation, and that these separate locals were to be temporary only."[24]

He has to admit, however, that

> "in later years ... as the A. F. of L. itself became a Jim Crow organization, separate locals were regarded by the A. F. of L. as the preferred way of permanently organizing Negro workers."[25]

This, he blames on the policy of "organizing by crafts".[26] Yet, Jim-Crow locals were precisely the path to present conditions!

The relation of this policy to the future of working-class unity in the U.S. was absolutely crucial:

> "During the 1880s and early 1890s, Negro labor in Southern cities was important in railroading, shipping and building. Beginning in the late 1890s, the Negro workers in Southern cities were steadily eliminated from skilled jobs."[27]

So, the bosses didn't have to do the real dirty work of dividing the U.S. working class. The growing white labor aristocracy through its trade unions, those craft unions then riding high and embracing (as Lenin said) "only a tiny minority" of the proletariat, performed the chore all too willingly:

> "By refusing to admit Negro members and by preventing union members from working with men who were not in the union, the craft organizations pushed Negro workers out of skilled positions. Where Negro craftsmen were organized in separate Jim-Crow locals, they received little or no assistance from the city central labor bodies, composed of white men drawn from white locals . . . The national unions to which the Jim-Crow locals were affiliated refused to protect their jobs or wage scales. . . .[28]

> "Thus the Negro was steadily driven from the ranks of skilled labor and diverted to menial occupations. . . .[29]

> "That the more backward workers in the South supported this policy is true. But essentially it was part of monopoly's program of complete segregation of workers by which it was able to prevent unity of action and through which it could prevent the wages of white workers from rising much above those of Negroes."[30]

Of course the policy of segregation was "essentially" that of the ruling American monopolies in their own interests. But the role of white labor – i. e., the U.S. labor aristocracy – via its organizations, the trade unions, and as masses of individuals infected with racism, in smoothing the path for this policy was the significant feature of U.S. labor history.

The point is that

> "The A. F. of L. leaders continued to make declarations of the necessity of organizing Negroes, but did very little about their affiliated unions which kept out Negroes, other than blaming the Negro workers themselves. The result was the effective exclusion of the vast majority of Negro workers from the Federation. In 1910-12, most A. F. of L. affiliates had either no Negro members or 'a few'."[31]

In 1911, a study had revealed in the whole state of Pennsylvania

> "Fewer than 200 Negroes 'who boasted skilled union status.' And what was true of Pennsylvania was true for the United States as a whole. 'The net result of all of this,' wrote W.E.B. Du Bois sadly, 'has been to convince the American Negro that his greatest enemy is not the employer who robs him, but his fellow white workingman.'"[32]

All the more so if we consider a notable individual exception to the lack of mass support for outright Social Democracy in the U.S.A. Philip Randolph, head of the a All-Negro Pullman Car Porters.

Does he disprove the rule cited earlier that Social Democracy cannot develop a mass base among the super-exploited? The answer is: he and his union are such an exception exactly as, among super-exploited peoples, the entire Afro-American community is. That is, somewhat analogously to Japanese imperialism, (See previous Chapter.) Afro-America plays a DUAL role in the world imperialist setting (See Chapter 17, Pages 169, above):

On the one hand, it forms a super-exploited internal quasi colony living among its own super-exploiters and the resulting labor aristocracy. This is illustrated by is wages, standing at 55.4% of those for whites.

At the same time, relative to the world hinterland, the Afro-American community belongs to the U.S. labor aristocracy as a whole – the wages of even its lowest categories are considerably better than the average wage in Black Africa; and, for what it is worth, its average family income is close to the British one.

This duality is epitomized in the Pullman Car Porters, which embraces some of the few worker elite among Afro-Americans. Even – or especially? – Jim-Crow locals have been made to pay off for sections of discriminated-against workers! Randolph's adherence to Social Democracy embodies the role of metropolitan Social Democracy in mobilizing colonial Elites behind the policy of the home labor aristocracy. In the rich United States, a small but important number of quasi-colonial workers do form part of the satellite elite – only because of the enormous wealth the metropolitan ruling class could drain from other (i.e.,"overseas") colonies.

An A. Philip Randolph is necessary to a metropolitan labor aristocracy in order to sell its policy to the super-exploited, to keep it "in line" so as to ensure the regular flow "homeward" of superprofits. The fact that Randolph is an exception illustrates the fact that any kind of mass base for Social Democracy can be formed only in special "dual-role" colonial areas like Afro-America or Japan. Such a duality is, in reality, an expression of the subsidiary (metropolitan-colonial) contradiction within the international working class of the imperialist system, plus a factor introducing another subsidiary contradiction among those inside super-exploited nations. In this case, the overwhelmingly majority status of the proletarian element offers the material basis for at least a partial solution of the first of these subordinate contradictions, as we shall see.

The fact is that anachronistic slavery growing on the U.S. historical body more than offset the ruling class lack for some time of external colonies. A "non-colonialist" image of Uncle Sam, in fact, became a fiction particularly convenient soon after 1898, when U.S. capital began penetrating Latin America.

Labor Aristocracy

Popular support in the U.S. jingoism after 1849 – and for "aid" programs today – reveal the true American mass mind. Mass support for the Status Quo comes in the frankest, most ingenious manner: the daring arrogance of self-appointed white "saviors of the 'free' world".

The conclusion vis-a-vis Social Democracy that emerges from American history is this: wherever there is confrontation between a metropolitan labor aristocracy and those super-exploited by "its" ruling class – in more obvious terms, whenever colonial people live directly in the midst of their own super-exploiters – Social Democracy is replaced by open chauvinism which, in THIS situation, becomes the FORM of class collaboration ensuring the continuous influx of super-profits to the metropolis. This phenomenon is most clearly visible when the super-exploited are black, in which case "chauvinism" is expressed as outright COLOR racism. The latter case embraces a large segment of world super-exploited and heavily influences the ideological approach toward the rest.

All this, again, is perfectly logical. When a super-exploited people live amidst an affluence they are not allowed to share, no polite form of repression can contain them, nor gain majority adherence among the affluent. Only "justification" based on brutally-formulated and equally-brutally-enforced national – especially racial – "superiority" suffices. Racism is the mirror image of Social Democracy in this way: Social Democratic class collaboration results in shooting metropolitan workers only in exceptional cases; whereas confrontation-based racism makes "polite" relations, when possible at all, the exceptions.

The target and results are the same in both cases: the super exploited are relieved of as large a portion of their wages as the political situation, the oppressed's degree of militancy, the ruling class' degree of stability, etc., will support.

29. The "Carriers" of Social Democracy in Colonies

What conclusions can be drawn about the section of Togliatti's report just discussed?

First, Social Democracy ("reformism", in his words) is in no way "a greater danger" to the real revolution "in the colonies than ... in the ruling countries".

Second, Greece, Canada and Japan offer valuable examples of how Social Democracy really functions because color prejudice does not obscure the central issue: that colonialism supplies the main nutriment of Social Democracy. Where black people enter the picture, they sharpen and focus this point, because the baldest, most brutal – and most lucrative – form of colonialism is and always has been the super-exploitation of black people. Hence, color prejudice is the ultimate, rawest subjective expression of COLONIALISM. Far from being "a mere-idea in the super-structure", racism determines the DEGREE of super-exploitation, as wage comparisons testify.

Third, comparison makes it plain that racism replaces Social Democracy in cases of mass confrontation between colonial subjects and a labor aristocracy because in such cases it is impossible to hide behind polite phraseology the colonialist content of Social Democracy. Even to attain its own objectives in these situations, Social Democracy as such must depart from the scene.

Thus, Social Democracy acts like a belt conveying from colonies near or far into metropolitan countries super-profits, part of which are transformed into super-wages. Racism is the most efficient form of the colonialist conveyor. The degree of racism varies directly with the darkness of pigmentation among the colonial subjects involved, a material fact embodied in the Afro-American saying:

"The darker the skin, the lower the wage." In this way, racism is clarified as an extremely lucrative imperialist invention which all over the world helps keep the rotten system going today.

Fourth, super-exploitation affects all people in a colony because all are sources of super-profit, though agricultural and industrial workers are the biggest majority. Especially in Africa South of Sahara, actual conditions permit the formation of no significant labor aristocracy; for, by Lenin's definition, the latter is a product of super-exploiting colonies.

Fifth, "reformism" does NOT exist "in the colonies as well as in the advanced countries", in the sense that Togliatti postulated. Those few colonial workers who become bribed have, and can have, no lasting mass influence. So, all attempts to build mass Social Democratic parties among them must come from outside and, in the long run, will fail. Conversely, if ever a mass Social Democratic Party IS found in such an area, it will be a sign that imperialist bribery has penetrated new international levels in a new way.

In the main, so far, not workers but others are the "carriers" of Social Democracy in colonies. At this point, it is instructive to consider them briefly.

It has been noted that urban areas in colonies act as a metropolis of sorts to the agricultural colonial hinterland.[1] From such urban areas, come local spreaders of European Social Democracy in colonies.

From Asia, the text has already offered two examples: Lee Yuan Kew, prime minister of Singapore and a "Big Wheel" in the Second International; and Dr. Wong Lin Ken, a European-trained intellectual spokesman for "Malaysian Socialism".

In recent times, European Social Democracy's most ambitious bid for African consumption has emanated from Kenya under the leadership of a genuine (ex)trade unionist, Tom Mboya, Minister of Economic Planning and Development, and "trade union" darling of the ICFTU's African arm. The "bid" in question[2] was written by one or more Americans – representatives of the world's racist citadel – a fact, as should now be perfectly clear, which is no accident. For, as the "benefits" of imperialism begin penetrating the hinterlands, Social Democracy's real content becomes more and more visible.

Kenya's ambitious ideological Social Democratic potpourri has had a strong and deleterious effect on African national movements. For instance, in Ghana, it was loudly espoused by Kwesi Armah, [3] erstwhile Minister of Trade in Nkrumah's last cabinet, under the undisguised influence of Mboya's "African Socialism". Having, only a few months before the February 1966 military coup, returned to Ghana from several years as his country's High Commissioner in London, Armah almost immediately gathered around himself most of the officials of government and Party who opposed real socialism. For a while, his cabal looked as if it were going to get rid of Nkrumah and his ideas, effectively if not literally for Armah had his Chapter offering the expected "eulogy" – and, in this writer's opinion, would have done so had not the actual coup intervened. In fact, with Armah's swift apparent success, a struggle between the elite factions (if not more) evidently came to a head and was resolved by the coup.

Kwesi Armah and Tom Mboya – the former a government official in a once-"socialist-oriented" country; the latter, first a "labor leader" then a government official in ICFTU-controlled Kenya – represent an African ELITE which, under European Social Democratic influence and guidance, formed fairly recently in the special conditions under which certain African countries achieved political independence after World War II. The significance of these men is that they are NOT (if ever they once were) part of African labor in any sense whatsoever.

Labor Aristocracy

That a new local bourgeoisie turns up in colonies as conveyor belt for European Social Democracy should not be too surprising: in order not to be totally shut out of such key areas, it MUST have some local base.

The international exploitative hierarchy results in this: that in a colony, only a class able to make connections with external imperialism (especially with imperialism's more colonially acceptable labor aristocracy represented by Social Democracy) could hope to benefit from out-going super-profits. Since the source of such super-profits "at home" is colonial labor power, colonial workers can never in any significant numbers constitute such a class. This leaves a possible very few "labor aristocrats" in colonial urban areas, as well as chiefs, comprador "capitalists", "feudal" landlords who use local peasants as "corvée" labor, and – finally – professionals and civil servants. If the system is not overthrown, all these categories may be expected to grow a little in numbers and quite a bit more in wealth.

The post-colonial and neo-colonial African elite forms anew counterpart in colonial areas to the labor aristocracy in the metropoles. In the colony, it, so to speak, "plays the role" of a "colonial labor aristocracy". At the same time, these new and old parasites in turn find outside Social Democracy an excellent crutch when looting their own people.

Whether this elite arises from investing capital stolen (i.e., primitively accumulated) from the public treasury and/or through unlimited and aggressive bribery and corruption in collusion with foreign investment capital; "by arrangement" with foreign capital already in the country; or however, matters not. The point is, the net result in countries where the phenomenon operates, notably in Africa since political independence, has been a new economic mouth sucking at super-exploited colonial labor power. The existence of this elite merely increases the DEGREE of super-exploitation experience by the colonial working masses.

Yet, precisely because the worst enemies of colonial peoples among their own ranks do work openly and arrogantly with agents of outside imperialism, colonial revolutionaries could expose neo colonialism there the more easily in the long run. Without such outside support, colonial peoples would among themselves make short work of such individuals, rolling over them in a wave as they did over the UGCC elite at the time of Ghana's independence. Nor could such a tiny minority halt or even retard that wave. But outside Social Democracy HAS retarded it. That is why its methods and ideas as they function in colonies deserve careful study.

One other point: although the Social Democracy active in colonial areas has been pin-pointed as a foreign export, this does not mean that it could not, for example, be enforced. Social Democracy, though "Western", is – like its masters – adept at devising new and varied methods of fulfilling its role as major bulwark of colonialism and neo-colonialism and, thereby, continuing colonial peoples' mass misery.

To sum up:

> "Reformism and internationalism are incompatible. A reformist party is attached by innumerable strings to the national state. Hence the collapse of the Second International in 1914. In particular, reformism cannot build a bridge between the workers of the advanced countries and the colonies – hence the Second International was practically a white-man's organization."4

This frank statement out of the horse's mouth, so to speak, adequately sums up the real relations between the Western working class and those in colonies, and accurately focuses on the place where racism enters the picture.

From the "other side of the fence" have come expressions of somewhat the same point, as it appears to would-be Social Democratic "mass leaders" in colonies:

"Democratic Socialists in the advanced countries are fortunate in that the relatively comfortable state of their societies makes it possible for them to maintain their tenets of tolerant but progressive society against more totalitarian creeds.

"For us in Asia and even more so in Africa the acute pressure of mass poverty, hunger and despair, and, worse, the obscene and often also ostentatious display of individual wealth in the midst of grinding poverty, is a constant incitement to sudden and violent revolution . . . And if we approach Asian problems of poverty and underdevelopment through the rosy spectacles of the Western European Socialists we are sure to fail."[5]

Here is a ruefully sober appraisal of the basic realities facing those who, like its author, hope by selling the admired foreign bauble to their own peoples, to "do well" out of the sale (and the writer of these sentiments has done well in this way).

30. Who Is to Lead in the Colonies?

The final point in Togliatti's quotation (on page 283 above) which this text has been scrutinizing at length:

> 6. "Now we must thoroughly understand that it is in the colonies themselves that we must struggle against reformism."

These words encompass those who, from their well-cushioned vantage points in blood-sucking metropoles, today airily "decide" the leadership of colonial revolutions without the slightest by-your-leave from colonial peoples themselves. The seeds of this state of affairs were already sprouting in Ercoli's words.

In the course of his speech, he had quoted a Social Democratic resolution from the Second International's Paris Congress in 1900. It instructed that

> "wherever economic conditions render it possible, socialist parties should be formed in the colonies which should maintain contact with those of the ruling countries."[1]

Not only Social Democratic parties (with results in Greece and Canada already noted, (See Chapter 27, page 293 above) but also Communist Parties in Western democracies have followed this advice (certainly, insofar at least as their relationships with Africa are concerned). In countries like Algeria, Morocco, Tunisia, Sudan and Egypt, Communist Parties have been kept under the wing of metropolitan leaderships. (See Chapter 22, page 244 above.)

Only after 1956 when the rising flames of national liberation had begun to sweep even Africa did the Party sections in colonies struggle against this connection, and after considerable difficulty, start to free themselves from the presumably well-meant embrace of their friends. But the scars remain, as was revealed in conversations with African Marxists passing through Accra in the years between 1962 and 1965.

The question raised is this: is there any reason at all, beyond issuing revolutionary instructions to metropolitan revolutionaries when circumstances so dictate, why genuinely socialist parties in ex-colonies (or in colonies) should maintain ANY Contact whatsoever with so-called counterpart parties in a particular metropolis just because the latter happens to operate in former ruling territory? Do not historical circumstances suggest exactly the opposite in the relations between the two areas?

Socialist parties in a colony want not only full independence, including the absolute right to secession, but also to continue uninterruptedly to socialism. The first step on this path is to break completely with the former ruling country. Should this break include all metropolitan parties? Formerly, in the sacred name of "proletarian internationalism", the answer was "No", as Togliatti suggested. Isn't it high time that this term was finally prevented from being used to cover up continued colonial relationships, as set forth in the British Communist Party "short policy statement" analyzed earlier?" (See Chapter 25, page 277 above.)

In former ruling countries, not just the ruling class but entire peoples have enjoyed and still enjoy material benefits, including super-wages but far beyond that, out of so many centuries of imperialist super-exploitation of that self-same colony. Does not real "proletarian internationalism" require that the metropolitan revolutionary make the first move in suggesting a complete break, as a mark of foremost respect for the absolute sovereignty of Subjugated peoples?

At least one anti-colonial leader implies the validity of this approach:

> "It is absurd to suppose that an American laborer can think and act in the same manner as the president of a

great New York bank. It is just as absurd to conceive of the African or the African nations acting in terms that are supposedly universal but actually are only relative, depending on particular historical or social conditions.

"Poor peoples, underdeveloped nations, have needs and demands which are essential to the fulfillment of their hopes and which have nothing in common with those of the highly developed nations and their rich populations….

"Because of their historical past and their present state of underdevelopment, Asians and Africans obviously have more in common with one another than with Europeans…."[2]

In the epoch – now finished – of euphorious belief in concepts like "Positive Non-Alignment" in a bitterly-divided international class society, did not the world Marxists acknowledge the validity of these sentiments when they went along with and encouraged organizations like the Afro-Asian Peoples' Solidarity Organization (AAPSO) (of which only remnants still exist - split - with the active portions under revisionist "leadership")?

An example related to trade unions – the mainstay of Social Democracy in Europe and the West – clearly exposed the meaning of organizational contact between groups in colonial areas and those "at home":

"The African trade unions, on the general level and on the level of each African country, were affiliated to the different trade union headquarters of the metropolitan countries, and by these intermediaries they were scattered throughout the international organization. Trade unions of conflicting tendencies were fundamentally regrouped within the same territory or in a regional federation in unions, at the same time retaining direct ties with the

> metropolitan headquarters. This situation was the double or triple affiliation which prevented the organic unity of Africa as a whole, each trade union being at that time the organic extension of the metropolitan trade union. It is impossible at the same time to refer to the political and economic exigencies of African life and respect the programs and methods of action of the trade union federations of industrialized and developed countries."[3]

Applied to the economies of metropolitan and colonial areas, the organic nature of the world imperialist system (See Chapter 17, page 169 above) is here again implied.

The attitude toward the relationship between socialists in the metropolis and those in colonies foreshadowed by the Paris resolution of Social Democracy (quoted on page 320) is clearly echoed in Togliatti's own instructions concerning revolutionary activities in colonies. A decade and a half later, it was being reflected in the actual Communist approach to "brother" parties in colonial areas.

Speaking of the need to struggle against "reformism" in the colonies, Togliatti said:

> "There we must work to show not only the proletariat of the 'civilized' countries but also the proletariat which is in the process of formation in the colonies, the natives (sic!), the great mass of peasants as well as certain strata of the petty-bourgeoisie, which is the true path which they must follow if they wish to struggle effectively for their liberation."[4]

What essential difference is there between this exhortation and the Paris resolution Togliatti said he was criticizing? Togliatti states openly that "we" are to lead the colonial revolution; the Social Democrats, at least in their Paris resolution, confined themselves to hinting as much. Moreover, such an attitude (see example Chapter 25, page 277 above) has developed into the current policies of Western Communist Parties toward the "colonial future".

In the light of all that has been said up to now in these pages, the conclusion seems inescapable that the struggle over who IS to lead the colonial revolution is one form of the struggle against Social Democracy.

But how did Marxists fall into the same bog with Social Democrats?

Part of the answer is implied in our discussion of the modern labor aristocracy. (Chapters 14 through 22 above). To recapitulate: in imperialist countries (especially the US), material conditions specifically built upon the continued influx of super-profits from colonies not only reinforced and enlarged the already existing labor aristocracy into a majority of Western population, but even "promoted" most metropolitan Communists into the elite. In turn, material conditions naturally evoked an ideological position among the Western labor aristocracy of support for colonialism, source of those indispensable super-profits: first, mass political support for the ruling class expressed by the success in the West of parliamentarism; supplemented, generally, by failure among Western labor as a whole to support liberation – positively, in their coldness to specific Liberation causes; passively, in failure to fight (for example) against imperialist brutality in colonies. (A failure in no way improved, of course, by deliberately-maintained lack of factual data in the major media of Western public information about the specifics of such brutality).

In addition, it must be specified now that, so far, we have presented mainly only a generalized statement of the Western labor aristocracy's relations with the colonial class brothers. What specific form did support for colonialism take?

The aftermath of Social Democracy's presence in the West, especially where it actually formed the government, was always the elimination of any significant militancy among working classes inside imperialism's borders. The Great Depression of the 30s had brought on a temporary increase in militancy over most of the capitalist world – soon countered by the Versailles-evoked improvement in overseas investment for the ruling classes in the "Great Democracies." Once the militarily-renewed financial activity took hold, a rapid rise ensued in material blessings for an ever-growing portion of the so-recently restive working classes in the victorious metropoles. The specter of revolution there receded. The Blue Eagle of the National Recovery Administration became the dove of class peace. (The symbol adopted for display by merchants and others complying with Franklin D. Roosevelt's National Recovery Act. Its message, over and under the familiar US eagle in blue, was: "N.R.A. We do our part.") The labor aristocracy's future seemed endlessly assured ...

But wait! Far off, rumblings become audible. Has the spirit of "revolution at home" been dispelled only to resurrect in Asia, Africa and Latin America? Are "inferior" peoples beginning to "sass back"? Do some rash black leaders dare to proclaim even socialist goals?

National Recovery, so comforting, so indispensable to Western workers, but so sensitive to "intransigence" in colonies, is again threatened!

Since World War II, confrontation between well-off white workers in industrialized countries and dark subjugated peoples – so long commonplace in particular areas like the US, South Africa, etc. – bids fair to become the universal pattern of the system itself. And back of its drama, in the wings of History, lurks the decisive question: WHO IS TO LEAD THE COLONIAL REVOLUTION?

The immediate effect of confrontation, when colonial subjects will no longer stand still to be squeezed dry "as usual" for the benefit of God's countries, is that "politeness" in politics becomes an economic sieve: Racism comes into its own!

Long rampant in specific imperialist areas, RACISM began spreading soon after World War II to become the most common form – in fact, an essentially urgent form – of the Western labor aristocracy's support for colonialism: in the US, existing racism intensified in ghetto after ghetto; in staid old Britain, interrupted first at Nottingham Gate, in by-elections and later on the London docks and in the industrialized Midlands. Even in the lofty atmosphere of "Communist debate" – in the Sino-Soviet conflict – charges of racism began, with good reason, flying back and forth. For racism, now more than ever, is one of imperialism's most devilishly effective mechanisms for coining its greatest super-profits out of black people.

Obviously, in order thoroughly to understand the relationship between Social Democracy and colonialism, the time has come to take a closer look at the anatomy of racism, NOT as a DETOUR but as an integral part of this attempt to delve to the very bottom of Social Democracy.

Labor Aristocracy

Section D:

Social Democracy, Racism and Anti-Communism

31. Racism as the Least Common Denominator of Social Democracy

While anti-Communism has become the general brake against abandoning the imperialist system itself, racist ideology is the specific bridle on colonial revolution and provides the background against which the world labor aristocracy and its friends, whether they know it or not, view all matters colonial. Racist undertones counterpoint the "humanity" beneath the banner of which capitalism originally paraded (making open racism not quite "polite" – a thing to be hidden where possible; deplored, where not).

From the 15th century until 1917, racism grew almost unchallenged. Once the black slave trade was under way, a new "color note" had begun to be heard in official pronunciamentos, and soon dominated colonialism's theme song. Within the shell, after 1917, of anti-Communism, its twanging monotone became, of all imperialism's ideological instruments, the most widespread, most effective "justification" for the Western labor aristocracy's continued receipt, enjoyment and protection of colonially-rooted super-wages.

We have seen how, in industrialized areas, wherever colonial subjects live conveniently at great distances, polite – even liberal – Social Democracy and other "labor"-oriented groups could get along by and large without open racism in serving the labor aristocracy. In general, since all ruling class political and economic activities in such areas are basically inseparable from imperialist parasitism, generalized support for the Status Quo in and of itself "painlessly" supported colonialism. But even this condition was not, could not be, smooth, lasting or uninterrupted: sudden devastating manifestations of the system's real basis (lynchings, race riots, and the accepted clubbing down of colonial subjects) divulged in irrepressible flashes that imperialism's carefully-instilled racism was (and remains) necessary in itself to buttress colonialism, because the latter is inherently and potentially explosive.

Ideologically, such racism has been fostered through a collection of color myths, with anti-black prejudice as their underlying theme. Steeped in such fairy tales, American white workers and those of Africa wherever black people confront a white labor aristocracy in significant numbers could (and, indeed, had to) dispense with Social Democracy. They openly flaunt their racism.

Nowhere is this truth so well-illustrated as in South Africa where two worlds confront each other as politically naked as anywhere under imperialism. It is a matter of record that white workers in South Africa enjoy a standard of living second only to the American. As labor aristocracies, both might be expected to be solidly Social Democratic. Not so. Their stock-in-trade has been an anti-Bantu attitude in the first case; anti-Negro in the second.

The impact on South Africa's white trade unions of employers' increasing use of black labor, including semi-skilled, has been to split them:

1. One faction, represented by the leadership of the Trade Union Council of South Africa (TUCSA), warned that

> "unless the workers stood together ... many were going to be priced out of the labor market. South African industries were converting to advanced mechanization."[1]

The result, of course, was failure to win support of black workers, a failure emphasized by the dissolution of the TUC-affiliated Federation of African Trade Unions of South Africa (FOFATUSA) in January 1966.

2. On the other hand, right-wing workers opposed the TUCSA position. For example, the Amalgamated Engineering Union with 20,000 members, TUCSA's largest single member, disaffiliated from the central body because it disagreed with "TUC's color policy". Here was a faction that would see automation – i.e., would "be priced out of the labor market" – rather than allow black labor to move ahead.

The central concern of both these lily-white unions was to protect their own super-wages; they were at odds on method. But that, precisely, we have seen, is the classical function of Social Democracy in Europe. Here is how that function is fulfilled by racism in confrontation with large numbers of super-exploited.

Unexposed color myths founded on anti-black prejudice have allowed racism to live on in our day even in the socialist world. There, the economically-based historical need of racism was destroyed by revolution, and socialist policy reflects this fact. Yet, left-over imperialist-instilled attitudes linger, weighting socialist people's relations with Africans – and their governments' attitudes toward Africa.

In Asia, centuries under European colonialism left some color mark. There, skin color was only one – not the major – form in which super-exploitation occurred. Racism against Asians could be, and to a degree was, offset by Western-type racialist feelings against black people, deliberately inculcated.

Because color played a lesser part, compared to the West, Social Democracy in Asia to this day retains some usefulness per se there. It can maintain local spokesmen in its own name: the Lee Kuan Yew's; the Drs. Wong Lin Ken.

Latin America is the earliest example of what is now called neo-colonialism. After about a century and a half of political independence, Latin American economies are more highly super-exploited by imperialism than ever. American finance capital operates in alliance with a small, predatory, local comprador elite and a so-called feudal aristocracy. (Actual feudality of such classes has been lucidly challenged in Latin America by Professor Andre Gunder Frank, Visiting Professor of Economics and History at Sir George Williams University in Montreal. See his book, *Capitalism and Underdevelopment in Latin America*, Monthly Review Press.)

Did Social Democracy as such develop any mass base in Latin America? Not to this writer's knowledge. Lack of a labor aristocracy would preclude that.

At the same time, as in Brazil and Cuba, the colonisers introduced large numbers of black people into Latin America. They did not disappear. Color discrimination left its mark on the population, thereby doubly barring Social Democracy per se or en masse.

Social Democracy attained what ideological hold it has in Latin America both late and indirectly – perhaps ironically – through policies objectively Social Democratic but pursued by self-styled Marxist-Leninists. Fairly recently, public differences of opinion have broken out about how to achieve socialism in Latin America. An apparent majority of those claiming to be Marxists have favored a "peaceful" solution along the lines of European Social Democracy and the Soviet position. As might have been deduced from the lack of a labor aristocracy and from the partial black presence, these Marxists never developed mass parties of, say, the Swedish Social Democratic type (though they themselves would never accept the Social Democratic label).

In Europe, Social Democracy espouses class collaboration "in the workers' interests". The fiasco in a country like Brazil occurred because a Social Democratic position served an avowed aim of "genuine independence with a socialist orientation". Doesn't this prove that, regardless of subjective or proclaimed aims, Social Democratic policy can lead only to the support of imperialism?

In Africa, imperialism's most consistent brutality accompanied a super-exploitation founded unequivocally South of Sahara on pure "color justification." Among black people, Social Democracy could not sustain support for its own spokesmen as such; it had to link arms with racism.

When unbroken imperialist brutality, from Tory and Labor alike, lost its effectiveness, demagogy had to be found for Africa. What arose called itself "African Socialism", pretending to be unconnected with anything "non-African." While – under demonstrable foreign imperialist instigation – this "ideology for Africa" had originated in so-called French Africa, today's brand sprouts in neo-colonial Kenya under the "labor" sponsorship of European Social Democracy in alliance with and under the guidance of US Racism. (A fact of more than passing significance, of which discussion must be reserved to a separate study.)

Obviously, Social Democracy's modern involvement with racism in sub-Saharan Africa did not arise full-blown like Minerva from the brow of Jove. What has today become visible is merely the development of a phenomenon implied in and underlying Social Democracy from its inception. It is visible now because anti-colonialism has escalated to a point where black people (the very bottom of the colonial heap) for the first time in history have been in major motion.

Social Democracy's link to racism, especially the latter's anti-black content, by leaving it as naked as the legendary Emperor, strikingly clarifies its real role in other subjugated areas, even "at home".

So, in the decades when Marxism (as espoused by men like Dimitroff, Palme Dutt and Togliatti) was making predictions which happened to involve dark-skinned people, their judgment – like everyone else's – was weighted by their very existence in Western society. In their epoch, the destruction of colonialism had not yet risen (as it has today) to the very first place on History's agenda.

It is not the fault of these men if the overwhelming majority in countries where they fought for justice happened through the agency of Social Democracy more and more to benefit materially out of super-exploitation; it was not their fault if such benefits rose in direct proportion to the darkness of skin pigmentation of the super-exploited. (See Tables 10, 11 and 12, above.)

Neither was it any of their doing that the vast majority of the world's inhabitants in the colonial hinterland happened to wear dark skins.

None of this was "their fault". But all of it constituted a material context from which they, as human beings, could not be isolated. Of course, Marxism-Leninism can be, and some times is, an effective instrument by which individuals can and do overcome a substantial portion of their own prejudices, although they are under the same heavy ideological pressures as others inside a historically-evolved system. But this occurs only if or when specific attention is paid to achieving this particular aim: overcoming racism is NOT and NEVER CAN BE the automatic by-product of studying, espousing. or even practicing Marxism-Leninism. Of course, over coming it must eventually become part of that practice – or Marxism-Leninism will become eroded.

In fighting for socialism, and against super-exploitation, people subjectively overcome and negate a good part of their era's racism in themselves. But it is a general tendency for ideas founded on the material foundations of one age to survive well into the next, specifically retarding the evolution of the new ideology.

It should, therefore, not be too astonishing that Marxist predictions which failed were usually those tied to colonialism and its indispensable racism.

To understand this more fully, the next Chapter will consider the economic realities under imperialism's ideological atmosphere.

32. Racism, Major Tactical Ideological Factor of Imperialism's Superstructure

Racism in these pages is not viewed as "just one idea in imperialism's super-structure"; it is the warp of the fabric of which super-exploitation is the woof (while anti-Communism is a "plastic cover" designed to preserve the entire fabric "forever").

History supports this analogy to the hilt. What is more, Lenin's prophetic warnings about parasitism in the dying system expressed his concern with related underlying economic facts.

Capitalism (it is often forgotten, frequently denied, and rarely admitted) was launched not only out of the brutal expropriation and subsequent inhuman exploitation of English peasants, but, in contrapuntal accompaniment, out of the black slave trade, involving an estimated 100 million Africans, about half of whom, after being kidnapped from their continent, survived to furnish through their literally-owned labor-power the inordinate profits of slavery itself.

The traffic in human beings began in the 15th century in time to help expand industries made possible by completing the already-well-advanced process of creating the English proletariat. By the beginning of the 17th century, that trade was fostering new industries, the growth of which obtained added impetus from intense exploitation of the new proletariat they had called forth at home.

For example, the ship-building industry made possible that portion of primitive accumulation called piracy; it aided and helped carry forward the huge search for a "path to the Indies", success of which flooded the formidable riches of Asia – notably of China and India – into a now-rapidly-burgeoning industrial world at whose head

337

England soon marched; it made possible colonies in a "New World," which for two hundred years siphoned off and absorbed Europe's "trouble-makers" and "surplus" human beings, thus effectively dulling in the West the sharpest edge of that class struggle which Karl Marx was one day to analyze.

So, not only modern civilization itself, but also its major way of life – colonialism – arose in large part upon an originally BLACK BASE, which is the material foundation of the anti-black lies referred to previously.

To try to agree on apportionment of growing empire, Europe's major powers, with the United States already even then discreetly maneuvering in the background, came together in 1885 at the Berlin Conference. Having erected an already-unprecedented prosperity on the sufferings of dark-skinned people, they proceeded to carve up the continent of Africa, with an eye on the future, opening the era of colonialism.

As this historical sequence unfolded, the West grew richer while places like Africa grew poorer. Like that of Asia and Latin America, Africa's material wealth was literally physically removed to bolster Western well-being.

But, in addition, Africa alone was stripped of her HUMAN resources in such a way that their labor power was at the disposal of the rising new METROPOLES. The export of Indian and Chinese labor-power to Latin and North America was but a numerically-pale shadow of the population decimation of Africa as the West's massive free labor-power well-spring.

The robbery of Latin America perpetrated by Spain, Portugal and then England, took place at first side-by-side with the black slave trade. Great Indian civilizations were annihilated and their populations enslaved to coin bullion out of Latin American stolen treasure as well as out of its silver mines. But the labor-power of these slaves ceased to benefit Spain and Portugal when English sea-power – virtually government-supported – made maintenance of Spanish and Portuguese New World colonies impractical. This was at least one reason why these two powers could not compete over the centuries with England, which successfully implanted kidnapped black people into the West Indies and other places in Latin America.

It was this solid labor-power foundation which first allowed England to grab the lion's share of Asia's wealth via the naked robbery of India and the opium trade in China. The "Pilgrim Fathers" from England and their descendants in the northern New World destroyed an indigenous population which stood in their way as they seized "Red Indian" land. But they were never able to make significant use of the labor-power of these people. For the New World to grow, we know, millions of black people had to be imported from across the waters and subsequently made the United States the world's foremost imperialist power.

More recent depopulations in the colonial world (for instance, the floods, droughts, diseases and famines that periodically decimated pre-revolutionary China) have been similarly unproductive – though often, as in Indonesia today, politically "necessary".

Hence, from the removal of both its physical wealth and its best people, including the successful use of black slave-labor-power, it was primarily Africa which first made possible the rise of "Civilization As We Know It". This material fact of history is not taken into account as yet by Marxists anywhere when they consider the problem of the world colonial hinterland. Yet, it influences those problems in a way which has thus far left them unsolved.

For, another major aspect of the modern black slave trade has been that it was financed by and benefited exclusively white men, sometimes employing black agents (the role of such black people who aided this traffic is a separate, subordinate and derivative subject), but having mainly black victims.

Another undeniable material fact is that the colonialism which the slave trade soon made possible also arose, developed and decayed; and liberation therefrom now advances over three-quarters of the earth, along the so-called Color Line between dark and white skinned people.

This Color Line expresses a real condition specifically, carefully and deliberately fostered by imperialism, became absolutely indispensable. Without super-profits, imperialism cannot exist; without continual "justification" of super-profits, especially in the form of racism, imperialism cannot continue extracting them.

That is why, today, the imperialist-spawned Color Line constitutes a MAJOR very REAL aspect of the ideological atmosphere in which the struggle between imperialism and socialism proceeds; and it continues under this condition: that while imperialism does extract super-profits, socialism has not yet proven able to "over take and surpass" imperialism: it does not, it will not, it cannot super-exploit. When it starts trying to, it is no longer socialism.

The strategic contradiction of our era – manifest as the conflict between imperialism and socialism – causes all other ideology to operate within the confines, and by the aid, of anti Communism. But within that context, the major inner contradiction of the system, being expressed as conflict between the imperialist ruling class and the colonial peoples, finds its place in the superstructure via the supremacy of racism as the main ideology of imperialism, the least common denominator of imperialism's inner ideological atmosphere.

The fact that imperialist parasitism generally increases indirect proportion to the darkness of skin pigmentation has reinforced racism, further engraining it in the "ideological atmosphere." And it is Social Democracy which is primarily responsible for fashioning the mental outlook – the ideological atmosphere – of the majority of Western population. This causal sequence explains why the West's racist ideological mask for its underlying colonialism has an inseparable "anti-Red lining", and cannot be separated from Social Democracy in some form.

In order to develop the above points, we turn once again to and re quote Lenin: (From Chapter 3, Pages 45-46, above.)

> "Capitalism has grown into a world system of colonial oppression and of the financial strangulation of the world by a handful of 'advanced' countries…

> "What is the economic base of this world-historical phenomenon?

> "Precisely the parasitism and decay of capitalism which are characteristic of its highest historical stage of development, i. e., Imperialism…

> "Unless the economic roots of this phenomenon are understood and its political and social significance appreciated, not a step can be taken toward the solution of the practical problems of the Communist movement and of the impending social revolution."[1]

In the light of these words, racism is not only ideological; not only subjective; not merely some "portion of the ideological superstructure" of imperialism. Racism also has – and always has had – a material content. Certainly, it is expressed in a mountain of perverted ideology. But its materiality is its basis – and measurable. (Again, refer to Tables 10, 11 and 12.)

Facts of even the most elementary sort prove the imperialist-designed material relationship between the degree of super-exploitation and of skin pigmentation, expressed in the already-quoted well-known Afro-American saying: "The blacker the skin, the lower the wage."

The following table clinches the last point. It exposes the phenomenon in South Africa where, within the borders of a single country, all the major contradictions of the imperialist system as a whole are visibly concentrated.[2]

Table 31[2]

RELATIONSHIP BETWEEN COLOR AND SUPER-EXPLOITATION
(1937-1948)

"COLOR" GROUP	PERCENTAGE EACH RACE CONSTITUTES OF CLASS OF SKILL				WAGES (British Pounds)	% OF EUROPEAN INCOME
	Skilled	Semi-Skilled	Unskilled	Total		
Europeans	83.8	33.8	1.5	35.4	350. 3s.	-
Asians	5.6	11.2	4.5	6.0	91. 5s.	26.1
Coloreds	4.8	20.8	13.2	11.6	51. 4s.	14.7
"Natives"	5.8	34.2	80.8	47.0	16. 2s.	4.6

The enormous differential between Western super-wages and the pittance grudgingly allowed colonial peoples – with Africa at the bottom of the imperialist economic heap generally – at least suggests that Western wages in our era already contain a larger portion of super-values not created by Western workers but accepted by them as a gift out of colonial super-exploitation than of the "original value" of its own labor-power. That is, the "bribe" portion of Western super-wages may now possibly exceed the value of labor power in the "unbribe" portion. What other meaning can be attached to the fact that a black South African earns only 4.6% as much as a white one, even admitting that "other factors" besides the statistical gap itself may operate within the relationship between the two figures?

Today, the modern Western labor aristocracy would appear to have reached a point where, subjectively and within the limits of its understanding at least, it has a bigger stake in maintaining colonialism than in overthrowing the system. And this observation has not yet even taken into account the bigger-still difference between Western and colonial modes of life!

Moreover, this differential measures the materiality of racism, a fact of political significance in all events bearing on Africa or on people of descent from Africa.

This differential also proclaims racism as the major form in which black people have experienced, and still experience, super-exploitation. Furthermore, racism's success in ensuring a limitless stream of super-profits for imperialism depends on the receipt of super-wages by workers "at home". Super-wages – being that part of super profits shared out to "their own" workers by the ruling moguls – gives those same workers their stake in the Status Quo, successfully thus far keeping subordinate the main contradiction "at home" between rulers and ruled.

The result has been admirably expressed in 1935 by the great Afro-American scholar, Dr. W. E. B. Du Bois:

> "In the South the great planters form proportionately a quite small class, but they have, singularly enough, at their command some five million poor whites . . . it would have seemed natural that the poor white would have refused to police the slave. But two considerations led him in the opposite direction. First of all, it gave him work and some authority as overseer, slave-driver and member of the patrol system. But above and beyond this, it fed his vanity because it associated him with the masters. To these Negroes he transferred all the dislike and hatred he had for the whole slave system. The result was the system was held stable and intact by the poor white."[3]

The clue to the poor white's role, of course, was that at all times his wages were maintained a bit above those of the Negro: he got his "crumbs" from the super-profits wrung out of his black class brothers.

Today, the US economy stretches its tentacles into every corner of the earth in one way or another. Even its own internal quasi-colony benefits to a considerable extent out of super-profits derived from Asian, African and Latin American super-exploitation.

After Lenin's time, with imperialism's inevitable decay – colonialism becoming more and more indispensable to imperialism's existence – that universal racism always present in capitalism as its memorial to the economic fecundity of the black slave trade became more highly developed. Therefore, after the usual ideological time lag, such racism is inescapably visible in the present crisis of moribund imperialism wherever colonial peoples challenge the masters.

And because of its universality wherever the "black-white" factor enters the colonial picture, racism in such places, by its tenacious and widespread hold on minds on both sides of the Color Line, over-rides all other ideological concepts used by the international ruling class except – sometimes – anti-Communism. In alliance with the latter, racism has been a brake against the successful overthrow of colonialism. Specifically it warps the world anti-imperialist struggle on both sides of Socialism's borders and on both sides of the Color Line.

To one degree or another, the imperialist system infects all individuals, even men who espouse Marxism-Leninism, with racism. In all white people, however many its myriad forms, racism expresses itself as White Supremacy.

In all black people, it is mirrored in countless shapes as a Colonialist Mentality.

The next Chapter examines particular forms that White Supremacy and the Colonialist Mentality assume, analyzing them and their effects.

33. The Black Stereotype and the Colonialist Mentality

Basically, the material precondition for the ideological developments of White Supremacy and The Colonialist Mentality was the export of capital from metropolitan economies to colonial areas, made possible by the slave trade. The extraction of super-profits resulted in an enormous differential between wages in both areas, translated into qualitatively different living conditions.

Ideological "justification" that was destined to prepare for these conditions was first attempted during the black slave trade. After the 15th century, the entire world outside Africa (though, in the obverse sense, Africa too) in practice swallowed at first slave-trading, then colonialist, lies about black people. These lies permeated ALL the capitalist world; NO territory was exempt.

In Europe, such ideological "justification" first took shape in the sphere of religion: darker peoples were presented as "inferior beings" ordained "by God" as the concern of "superior" whites: "the White Man's Burden".

Religious myths of inferiority associated with skin pigmentation were soon reinforced by "science" and "history" with official backing. The result was a Black Stereotype – a pervasive though entirely fanciful concept of what black people are like.

In Europe and the "New World", it became accepted that black people are all happy, docile, ignorant, obedient, and clown like. They allegedly all hang breathlessly upon the "largesse" of their "betters", grateful for any small favor the latter may deign to bestow. These imaginary creatures all live in dense jungle, surrounded by animals to whom they are so "naturally" close that they can practically converse together. Nor have they any history of their own. Instead, they have merely existed for aeons, until the "Christian" white man appeared. Thereafter, they "developed" under his "civilizing influence", as ordained by the ruling white god. Naturally, no black person is capable of making decisions, even in matters concerning himself alone. That is why the "mission" of "Christians" has been to "liberate" the black "savage" when the "right time" happens along (which always seems to be only after massive revolt by the "docile blacks" is either under way or obviously imminent).

Around these falsehoods, an infinite variety of corollary hypocrisies sprang up. Together, they formed the indispensable context within which landlords and employers in metropolitan areas were able out of segregation and wage discrimination to coin additional super-profits whose amount they deliberately ranked by degree of skin pigmentation.

The resulting practical separation of peoples differing in skin colors has made it both slow and difficult to destroy the myths that nurture it.

Nor was the metropolitan area alone affected. White Supremacy exacted perhaps its most dreadful toll among subjugated peoples in the form of a "mirror image" – the widespread Colonialist Mentality.

The latter's main characteristic among subjugated peoples, especially Africans, is its acceptance in practice over a fairly long historical period of the imperialist-imposed Black Stereotype. When people are thus conditioned to act like a false Stereotype, human dignity is crushed, but in a context wherein such people are torn by terrible, subjective contradictions: hatreds, frustrations, and above all hopelessness and lack of self-faith.

White Supremacy's basic crime in perpetuating the Colonialist Mentality has been the attitude toward work which it developed among subject peoples: Work is always presented as punishment (pupils in mission or government schools are forced to do manual labor for the teacher or head master when they break a school rule – "free" labor for the teacher or head master, of course – but its value here is for its effect on the punished). NOT to have to work is held up as the "ideal" – the purpose for which education should strive. Pupils in Africa are taught to aim above all for some petty "white collar" job, preferably "in government", the object being to have "lesser" members of one's own community subject to one's "authority").

At the same time, the colonial subject is encouraged to expect "something for nothing" (though, naturally, whatever his situation, he never achieves that). Nevertheless, the search for this "something for nothing" leads to a deep-rooted tendency to believe in promises and to wait for them to materialize before taking action. Such expectations, needless to state, are also encouraged among metropolitan workers – but in a different context, both politically and economically, as we shall see at once.

For in colonies, in practice, wherever such attitudes are inculcated, the vast overwhelming majority are forced to perform the most tasteless, monotonous, menial and back-grinding labor for a pittance, the very condition "theoretically" pictured for them as one to be avoided at all costs. Thus, a conflict, insoluble under capitalism, arises at the very source of value, operating to the detriment of colonial peoples.

Few colonial subjects can attain the demoralizing "working ideal" because it exists only among ruling classes. So, the conditions which colonialism has foisted on such peoples are ironically used to "prove" their "inferiority"! Thus, the poisonous blossoms of original rationalization for the black slave trade encumber the current ideological atmosphere with the crippling concepts of a bygone era.

The postulation of "inferiority" among subject peoples implies that the "superior" motherland's prosperity is due to the "efficiency, superiority and knowledge" of its people, machines and Way of Life.

The fact, however, is that – launched from the springboard of the black slave trade – the "technological mastery" boasted of by "Western civilization" which characterizes the epoch of imperialism has been occasioned NOT by its undeniable "efficiency" of which it is Social Democracy's role to brag, but by its unparalleled parasitism expressed in colonies, where "super-wealth" comes from an inexhaustible source of cheap human labor-power.

For example, the WASTE in the West's allegedly efficient economy, which has been dealt with by innumerable Marxist economists, is so tremendous and glaring that one of imperialism's "popular" mouthpieces devoted a major article to it,[1] citing failures in education, the energies wasted in a vast bureaucracy, and useless luxury spending. Still, much of the waste attributed to the US economy – this source claimed – was "really" being plowed back and used in one way or another. But naturally, there was NO mention of idle capacity, decreases in "labor force participation" (i.e., "retirement from the labor market" by millions of jobless), unemployment, and the real, far more basic waste implied in the irrationality of the system.

Far from being able to eulogize "resourcefulness", as such mouthings would have the public believe, such waste testifies to built-in inefficiency, irrationality and parasitism, even according to practical testimony taken "from United Nations sources."[2]

1. In the first six months of 1963, the entire African continent experienced a trade deficit of 70 million dollars. From 1953 to 1963, this deficit averaged one billion dollars a year.

2. Yet, in the first six months of 1964, the continent of Africa, excluding South Africa, had a favorable trade balance of 42 million dollars. Total exports has been $3,671 billion; total imports, $3,529 billion, not including gold, diamonds and other mineral exports of South Africa. Could that country have been counted among the "free nations" of Africa, the increase in favorable trade balance would have been "staggering."

3. In 1965, Britain, to defend her pound sterling against devaluation, borrowed something like $532 million from the World Bank and a consortium of private bankers. In addition, she had a trade deficit of some £800 million. Nobody called this help from foreign sources to a Western power "aid to Britain". Commented the writer:

> "Aid is a new expression coined deliberately by the Western countries in an effort to perpetuate the economic and political inferiority of the developing world.

> "It is far more important for the industrialized countries to give the so-called 'aid' than for the developing countries to receive it."2

Colonial areas can live without manufactured goods from metropolitan areas, the article continues, whereas the latter cannot survive without colonial raw materials. What is more, if the "developed" economies were not able to invest in the "developing" world, they could no longer secure against loss the finances of their "commercial" and savings banks, insurance companies, building societies, trust companies and fiduciary funds"2. The colonial areas can also live without this form of financial "security".

4. If all of Southern Africa were liberated and its resources added to those of the rest of the continent and were used jointly in a socialist way, Africa

"would not only have the sum required for the development of Africa but would be lending the West money.

"In gold alone, the West receive over a thousand million pounds per annum from South Africa only. This does not stay in African banks but goes into Western banks to become part of the economy of the West.

"They therefore are lending us our own money and they call that foreign aid."[2]

The ruling class has marshaled all its forces to ensure continuation of a situation so favorable to itself:

The International Confederation of Free Trade Unions (ICFTU), representing the labor aristocracy in metropolitan areas, has in Africa deliberately nurtured the Colonialist Mentality: for those African unionists who "do as told", there have been cars, mimeograph machines, lush offices, typewriters, salaries high by colonial standards, and above all, "recognition": honors, titles, and the permission to hobnob with "superior" white Western officials.[2]

The French tactic of giving independence to thirteen of her African colonies in 1960 may have been at least partially in response to freedom struggles among those peoples. But it also had the real, observable, effect of "pulling the teeth" of such struggle; of handing the countries so treated over to neo-colonialism (political independence tied to the metropolis by the same if not worse economic strings as before).

Until recently, the international ruling class was able to keep its own racist under-belly from public gaze except in places like the US South or South Africa. But as issues sharpened in places like Watts in Los Angles, USA., in South Africa, Southern Rhodesia, etc., the effectiveness of the ICFTU and other Social Democratic agencies, fell off sharply – up to mid-1965, when a series of military coups in colonial areas began. In a word, imperialism directs its policy into whatever channel seems most likely to ensure that it retains Africa, the world's richest potential source of super-profits for the moribund West.

It is clear, then, that the imperialists not only created the Black Stereotype among white people everywhere, but also inculcated the same White Supremacy "principles" in reverse as a "mirror image" into peoples subjugated under their control. BOTH, to a single purpose: "eternal" super-exploitation of colonies.

Despite anything imperialism can do, however, material conditions in colonies make clashes and conflicts inevitable and irrepressible. The imperialist tactic has been as successful as it has only due "at home" to that stream of super-profits which for so long has enabled the metropolitan ruling classes to wax fat virtually without challenge, simply by giving their "own" working class a substantial share in colonial loot.

Such super-wages and a "mode of life" completely out of reach for, though sought after by, colonial peoples, have acted as a material screen, hiding from the vast majority of those affected by knowledge of it on both sides of the Color Line, the fact that beneath these super-wages are working people, themselves exploited, while imperialist parasitism is the real source of Western well-being.

As the next Chapter will show, failure to discern the "real source" DID NOT AFFECT ONLY POLITICAL ILLITERATES in the West.

34. Western Marxist Underestimation or Repudiation of Color's Role

Western Marxists, by sharing in colonially-derived prosperity, were absorbed into the labor aristocracy. Gradually, their judgement became indistinguishable from Social Democracy's. On issues related to colonialism, far from exposing and fighting against imperialist parasitism, they unwittingly contributed to its "justification" in many of their theoretical postulates. (e.g., Chapter 8, above.) In addition, they accepted in many implied ways, without fully comprehending, the "world outlook" toward Africa and Africans which has "rubbed off on all past and present inhabitants of once-global imperialism; an acceptance which shows itself in regard to the "Color Question" as well.

It is instructive in this regard to read some remarks by a president of the East African Students Union in the Americas:

> "The imported oligarchy who came (to Africa) as settlers and trading adventurers based their exploitation partly on their imported capital but mainly on the ideology of racial superiority – ideology because it is a belief and not a fact.

> "It is indeed true as Jack Woddis states in the opening sentence of his book, 'Africa – The Roots of Revolt,' that

>> "The history of African contact with the West has been a history of robbery – robbery of African manpower, materials and agricultural resources and land."

> "This epitomization may sound pontifical among well-known international militants, BUT THE AFRICAN

STAGE HAS STILL ANOTHER SCREEN – that of color. For a race that has seen slavery, contempt, discrimination, lynching and colonial subjection, all these within living memory, the constant harping on capitalist exploitation is not moving enough."[1]

The typical European Marxist responds to this approach variously. He may equate any mention of the "Color Question" with "overemphasis" on it. He may try to assure the black speaker that his experience is "the same" as that of his "white brothers":

"It is true that the great majority of the black people of the world are oppressed by imperialism – but so are the great majority of white people."[2]

He will undoubtedly berate the black person for his "racialism":

"The notion that 'white racialism' is reactionary while 'black racialism' is progressive and even revolutionary is a complete illusion. All forms of racialism are equally reactionary in that they help the imperialists to 'divide and rule.'"[2]

Then there is always that patronizing appeal to the black man "not to be emotional," good heavens!

"There have indeed been some highly emotional speeches at this Congress, and emotion can play a useful and valuable role in revolutionary struggle. We need to hate our enemies and cherish our friends. But it is necessary first to analyze coolly who are our friends and who are our enemies.

"Without this, one may be so blinded by anger that one strikes out at one's friends and allies and helps one's enemies."[2]

Finally, anyone who even dares call attention to Color as a pervasive FACT of African life can be – and usually is – accused of "attempting to cover up the basic facts of exploitation."

To those who try to point out the damage done to liberation by racism, one stock "Marxist" answer up to now is that "racism is irrelevant" to the anti-imperialist struggle because the troubles of colonial peoples are not caused by white people as such, but by imperialists (who just happen to be mostly white).

Anyone who hints that imperialism itself has made racism relevant to any discussion of, say, anti-imperialist unity, is then charged with advocating racism, of "turning the struggle aside from anti-imperialism", an accusation "justified" by the truism that "only the demise of imperialism can correct racism". It is useless thereafter to note that imperialism's demise in Eastern Europe did NOT automatically lead to the demise of racism; or that imperialism's very demise itself is being unnecessarily postponed by the same racism which that demise "alone" can supposedly destroy.

Moreover, such a reaction is not even theoretically justifiable. In his famous August 8, 1963, statement of support for the Afro-American Freedom Struggle, Chairman Mao Tse-tung of the Communist Party of China remarked that "in the last analysis, all national struggles are a matter of class struggle".

Facts and figures set forth in these pages prove the truth of this remark beyond question. For, today's nationalists globally, by and large, are the colonial peoples still fighting for real freedom despite some kind of political independence in some places for two decades or more.

But if national struggles "are a matter of class struggle"; if the struggles of black people are among national struggles; and if "the color factor" enters into the nationalist struggles of black people (to a degree determined by imperialism over centuries of lies and distortions about black people), then how can discussion of the Color Problem be "irrelevant" to discussion of national problems among "Colored" people – whose freedom struggles today form the heart of anti-imperialism?

Rather, if national struggles really are, in the final analysis, "a matter of class struggle," if racial struggles are a majority special case of national struggles; then the racial point of view is NOT ipso facto either "irrelevant" or even condemnable. It could even be correct to substitute a racial view-point for the class viewpoint temporarily when the latter obscures super-exploitation (e.g., as above, by equating "exploitation" and super exploitation) – with the understanding that racial struggles are or lead to class struggle under correct leadership.

Those who announce "over-emphasis" on Color the moment it is mentioned merely expose their own need to listen and participate in such discussion – the sooner, the better. Anyone thus sententiously ducking behind "capitalist exploitation" to avoid discussion of the "Color Question" is revealed as one who objectively reinforces the present role and status of the Color Problem itself by refusing to let it be aired.

For, no matter how much it may hurt those who objectively want the Status Quo to continue, the COLOR LINE CUTS DEEPER THAN CLASS LINES: it is founded on SUPER-profits, which Lenin specifically noted are "obtained OVER AND ABOVE the profits which capitalists squeeze out of the workers in their 'own' country". And super-profits, we know, are the fruit of parasitism, without which a qualitative upsurge in the class struggle "at home" could no longer be postponed, thus signaling the final doom of the ruling class.

Here is the meaning behind the above-quoted statement by an East African!

There are reasons why, after centuries of imperialism, very few Marxists, especially in the "white world", have as yet seen the need to take, let alone really taking, the specific time and effort for the difficult, delicate but exigent political surgery which alone, either before or after the world revolution itself, can reveal and excise racial prejudices which so successfully all over the West – and elsewhere – today reinforce colonialism.

This has not happened: not because such Marxists are "nasty", but because history has only very recently made such an exercise materially necessary:

1. Only during the past ten years has it finally become possible for such Marxists to meet individually actual black African people in any significant numbers, though while it lasted such contact was usually neither frequent nor, certainly, intimate. Imperialist policy did all it could to prevent actual meeting between real socialists – or (perish forbid) communists – and Africans. So, it was only after 1957 that such meetings could even begin. Significantly, one effect of the recent and continuing military coups in Africa has been again to cut back such contacts with the clear aim of ending it altogether if possible. Only the Russians remain inside most of West Africa, with a few Poles, Czechs or Bulgarians. Most citizens of formerly-colonial-countries-gone-socialist (Korea, China or Vietnam; Cuba; or Albania) have been driven away from Africa. The ruling class, at least, is class conscious and precisely aware of what it is about.

2. The brand of Marxism-Leninism which arose after centuries of colony-fed colonialism, in Europe first and in the West in general, could not but be interlarded with aberrations, of which the main one today is revisionism, a new expression inside the socialist world of Social Democracy in our era. (Revisionism

itself as related to Social Democracy is to be treated in a separate study.)

3. When contact did begin between socialism and Africa – in Europe, where African students finally traveled in significant numbers for education; or, in places in Africa, where Europeans from socialist countries serve as experts – it was assumed on both sides of the Color Line that, because good-will was present, because socialism and socialists theoretically and avowedly oppose racism, therefore the phenomenon itself somehow would or should automatically absent itself from such encounters. Only severe shocks, like those "student incidents" involving Africans in a number of Eastern European socialist countries, disclosed the depth and pervasiveness of the general, imperialist-spawned Black Stereotype and its continued existence under socialism in countries that once were also Western Metropoles. (See next Chapter.)

Actually, only mass contact could make White Supremacy's existence evident and reveal its basis in the Black Stereotype, which deliberately caricatures real black human beings. Finally, "incidents" were needed to prove that this Stereotype is the ideological reason why racism does not automatically evaporate on coming into the presence of Socialism. To illustrate just how deeply the Black Stereotype has become ingrained in even the most advanced socialist lands, let us consider an example:

At a mass rally in Peking on August 8, 1966, celebrating the third anniversary of Chairman Mao's statement of support for the US Negro Freedom Movement, Robert F. Williams, fugitive from the infamous "incident" at Monroe, North Carolina, a decade or so ago, recorded certain facts known to black freedom fighters:

"We have some white Americans with us in our struggle... (but) some so-called socialists, whom we thought to be our comrades and class brothers, have joined the international Ku Klux Klan fraternity for white supremacy and world domination. To our consternation, we have discovered that the bourgeois-oriented power structure of some socialist states, even one with a black and white population, would prefer to preserve a white reactionary anti-communist power structure in racist America."[3]

What was the response to this condemnation of the role being played by "white Marxists" toward black workers actually living in their proximity? Unfortunately – a traditional one: the black man is impliedly admonished for his "sin" in mentioning unpleasant facts.

Sidney Rittenberg, a Southern white American living in China, and then in charge of Radio Peking English broadcasts, said:

"Class conscious American working people know that America's future belongs to them, to people's power, black people's power, and white people's power, against racism, exploitation, oppression, and aggressive war."[3]

So, by implication, Rob Williams, a black leader, is NOT "class conscious." Rittenberg, incidentally, is currently in the lock-up in China, but nobody has as yet repudiated this sententious and patronizing lie of his.

Kuo Mo Jo, high in Communist Party circles in China's active cultural front, repeated from Chairman Mao's 1963 statement supporting Afro-American struggle of three years before, the main point which Chairman Mao omitted from his 1968 statement, with good reason:

> ". . . in the United States it is only the reactionary ruling circles who oppress the Negro people. They in no way represent the workers, farmers, revolutionary intellectuals, and other enlightened persons who comprise the overwhelming majority of the white people."[3]

So Rob Williams, the black leader, impliedly does NOT know his friends from his foes, while Kuo Mo Jo of China feels competent – without the meticulous investigation which always preceded Chairman Mao's pronunciamentos on China – to tell him who they are.

In each of these replies to a black worker, there is also an implied rebuke, based on a false estimate of a situation which he had correctly characterized for their attention. Of course, the sentiments expressed by these non-black communists in Peking are "splendid" – even if they do merely repeat without documentation the attitude of the 30s among leading members of the US Communist Party, which itself by its attitudes and policies drove thousands of Negroes OUT of the Party over some decades.

Of course racists do not represent the working class and progressives, any more than Social Democrats, spokesmen for the labor aristocracy, do. This point is hardly at issue; moreover, as used, it amounts to a lie, because it ADDS itself to a statement about "the working class and progressive" in the US which, however desirable, is just NOT SO.

And hundreds of thousands of Negroes at one time or another involved in the countless recorded and unrecorded race riots in big and little US industrial centers and rural backwoods, like Detroit, Chicago, Los Angeles or anywhere in the benighted South, KNOW; and the families and friends of unnumbered Negroes who have died in unspeakable agony in lynchings and beatings, or suffered in their millions the ignominy of racial harassment and segregation, KNOW that it is NOT "only the reactionary ruling circles" who "oppress" them. They KNOW that basic white workers in those cities, and poor white farmers and workers in the rural South perform the bestialities against them. This approach in Peking is on the same level as the one that sees a colonial army as a "people's army" because the imperialists have no other choice than to people it with "workers." There is a real difference between a condition and a potential.

Afro-Americans understand these things. In a best-selling novel, John Killens, Afro-American author, presented a detailed picture of life among his people in the South. The Youngbloods are a family who represent the militants among Southern Negroes. A visit is paid to this family by an Afro-American teacher from New York who goes to Crossroads, Georgia, to the school for black children. The following conversation takes place:

> "The young school teacher shook his head ... He felt like anything but a know-it-all...
>
> "'We're not exactly alone in this' , he said.
>
> "He cleared his throat.
>
> " 'We have friends all over this country — colored and white.'
>
> "...Thinking out loud...
>
> " 'Where the white friends at?' Joe Youngblood asked.
>
> " 'In the labor unions – the – the white workers – and some of the more educated liberal-minded white people.'

"He read the doubt in both of their faces. Laurie smiled at the teacher, a thin bitter smile.

" 'I sure do hope it's true', she said. 'But I sure don't know where our good white friends hiding. Lord Have Mercy.'

"Joe Youngblood said,

" 'I sure want to see them crackers that's my nackerl-born friends. They must be kinda shame-facey . . . Maybe it's different in New York City, but down here in Georgia the poor white peck is the black man's worstest enemy. Labor Unions – These people down here won't let you get one foot in the door. White workers. Hmph. Anybody'll tell you. It ain't the rich man that lynches the colored down here. It's the poor crackers. If they my friend, they sure got a real funny way of showing it. I sure do wish they would come out of the bushes and make themself known. I be looking for the high sign sure as you born.'"[4]

That "poor white crackers" and "workers in labor unions" are carrying out the policy of "the reactionary ruling circles" is a truism. Does that fact absolve them of their political, bribe based responsibility for participation? Were the German masses implicated in Nazi bestialities? Does it lessen the blood debt to the Afro-American people which "poor white crackers" have been piling up by their deeds over centuries? Don't these same deeds form the inseparable background for the gassings and napalmings carried out by "ordinary American workers" who, as GI's, murder their Vietnamese class brothers?

Rob Williams spoke in biting words of those who, without studying, investigating, documenting, experiencing or understanding the REAL situation, glibly admonish and advise those who already know:

> ". . . there is a mighty tendency, promoted by the sinister American devil himself, to engender more sympathy and fraternalism for the so-called 'good reasonable American' than for the wretched victims of vicious and brutal US imperialism...

> "What is the motive of those who plead for the exemption of liberal Americans whose feigned liberalism merely serves as a cloak and shield around the naked power of savage and racist US imperialism?...

> "The myth of the good reasonable American who is yet to be heard is a ruse perpetrated by the psychological arm of the imperialist forces of tyranny . . .

> "A good man who is silent and inactive in times of great injustice and oppression is no good man at all. He is no ally to freedom and justice, but is a silent partner to tyranny and oppression... Those who are without principle and conviction to declare themselves for the righteous cause of the oppressed must be prepared to suffer the consequences of the gathering storm of violent and turbulent . . . retribution."[5]

Moreover, Williams' feelings have been vindicated in international law – in the particular case of Vietnam:

> "The first that should answer for these inexpiable war crimes are the American leaders who are liable for their policy of intervention and aggression in Vietnam and their barbarous orders to 'escalate' the war.

"Then come the executants – American or non American – who have been acting on their orders and owe the Vietnam people a blood debt.

"The Statute of Nuremberg Court is unequivocal about this matter. According to its Article 8, the fact that the accused has acted in accordance with the orders of his government or his hierarchical superior does not clear him of his responsibility.

". . . according to criminal law in most countries, the real criterion of penal liability has nothing to do with orders. It lies in moral liberty, in the faculty of choosing of the accused."[6]

Ideals of real brotherhood and anti-racialism are really held in the US today only among the vanguard of the black Freedom Movement; a minority of militant students more and more supporting that Movement as they become more deeply involved in preventing themselves from becoming additional victims of criminal US aggression; and a national assortment of honorable individuals, largely professionals. Certainly, this number must grow if the Vietnam situation and its contradictions deepen. Nonetheless, at the moment, and despite the fact that it represents the future, it still constitutes a small minority of Americans.

Expressing such facts usually evokes charges of "slandering the American people", charges too convenient as excuse for not examining the facts.

Facing facts now could help shorten the time needed for the progress that must come eventually, and thus help to decrease growing colonial casualties. Here we have a serious "contradiction among the people". Will closing one's eyes to it ensure that it is solved – or even tackled?

The illustration chosen was deliberate: in Peking, the world's most advanced Marxists now operate. If this is where the best is found, what of the worst? This example is also intended to illustrate that when a black worker states from his own experience facts which are unpleasant, even the most advanced, but non black, Marxist ears still cannot hear him too well.

This is the result of the imperialist-spawned Black Stereotype. It affects not only white people in the Western world, but even socialist relations with Africa and Africans. The mass persistence of old racist myths in socialist locales drags practical consequences in its wake which materially affect the course of revolution – at the very least, on the African continent.

Therefore, the next Chapter will delve concretely into the remnants of racism in once-socialist countries – mainly Eastern Europe, where it is most pronounced.

35. The Black Stereotype and "Student Incidents" in Eastern Europe

Probably the most flamboyant example of racism left over in Eastern Europe was embodied in a series of incidents in which African students in such countries allegedly "rioted", while violence erupted between Black Africans and white socialists.

Of course, anti-Communist stories in the Western press inevitably exaggerated such happenings. Nonetheless, they were only piling their lies over a core of truth. So, it is of primary significance that socialist countries, and their satellite apologists, chose to pretend that such things did not occur. When the facts could no longer be denied, they switched to the canard that none of it was their responsibility. A Czech with whom I was corresponding, and a Rumanian with whom I talked at length in Ghana, both told me in all seriousness that these "student incidents" were traceable solely to "CIA agents". But neither charges of CIA involvement nor exaggeration in the Western press explains why said CIA agents enjoy such success with their antics, or why "incidents" of such scope happen at all in "socialist" lands.

Africans see two implications:

1. The "CIA agent" argument suggests that "Africans are fools", easily manipulated by anyone, regardless of their own interests.

2. The insistence that such "incidents" are exaggerated calls into question whether Africans can have real grievances against a "socialist" country.

But thousands of black Africans witnessed the truth; and many of them, bearing physical evidence of serious mistreatment in "socialist" lands, returned home, where news travels fast even without newspaper coverage. (If Eastern Europe was even then revisionist, it must be remembered that, at the time of the "incidents", everything was not as clear as today, and all the evils were done in the name of socialism. Most Africans were not in a political condition, historically, to make the nice distinction.)

Since these occurrences offer clear-cut examples of left-over racism in action in the socialist world, let us examine as typical those in Bulgaria in mid-1962.

In Ghana, at that time under Nkrumah, the first Bulgarian "incident" received no press coverage whatever. During or directly after it, however, four Ghanaians who had been studying in Sofia returned home with bandaged heads. Within 24 hours, news of this event was known in the most remote corners of the country. That, in fact, was how I myself heard of it.

Six months later, early in February 1963, a more serious occurrence did receive news treatment in Ghana. This time, the trouble had been too widespread, had involved students from too many African countries, to be hushed up, even in Ghana. The Ghanaian press, accordingly, discussed the matter: from February 14 through 18. Thereafter, official silence again fell.

The Bulgarian government issued at least two statements: one was to the United Nations and omitted any mention of Africans with bandaged or swollen heads. It claimed or implied that the whole affair was "CIA-incited" and NOT of serious proportions. The other was offered in Ghana by Peter Ivanov, Second Secretary of the Bulgarian Embassy at Accra. He said that it was

> "slanderous to accuse the Bulgarian people of racial prejudice."

This remark, unfortunate in the face of the large number of Ghanaians who saw their countrymen's bandages and bruises, was printed only in the pro-West DAILY GRAPHIC, then just recently purchased by the Ghana government from the Cecil King newspaper empire of London.

Brief though they were, however, discussions in the Ghanaian press contradicted even the facts officially presented by Bulgaria. Yet, the Ghana government was at the time avowedly pro-socialist – and pro-European socialist, at that. It had permitted discussion during those few days solely to allay the flying rumors.

Where the Bulgarian version mentioned "a demonstration", Accra papers were quite specific that there had been a series. "Slanderous" though it might be to accuse Bulgaria's people of racial prejudice, the Ghanaian TIMES spoke openly and bitterly of

> "the brutal suppression of African students during a non-violent demonstration in Sofia, Bulgarian capital, against a ban by the Bulgarian government on a recently formed All-African Students Union in the Republic."[1]

At least one African view of these incidents was offered by the Accra EVENING NEWS, official organ of the then-ruling Convention People's Party:

> "While the pros and cons of the imbroglio are being sorted out, we wish to condemn in no uncertain terms this flagrant repudiation of socialist principles and unabashed disrespect by so-called socialists for the color of the African which, we are sure, is the underlying psychological factor creating a complex in the minds of those primitive partisans who provoked the demonstrations . . . By indulging in the unedifying orgy of bacchanalian revelry, the Bulgarian Republic has brought disgrace on the whole socialist world."[2]

The most thorough analysis of the Bulgarian "imbroglio" was printed during the last day of press discussion. It was contained in a commentary by H.M. Basner," and its most significant portion dealt with a question very agitating to African's minds: WHY did the Bulgarian government, supposedly socialist, ban the All-African Students' Union? WHY did the students need to form such a body? Said the TIMES writer:

> "If African leaders make the question of African unity the main political motivation, how shall African students from different parts of Africa refrain from putting that unity in to practice when they are gathered for a long time in a foreign country? If the constitution of the Bulgarian people forbids that, the Government of Bulgaria had no business to invite African students."[3]

The typical "answer" of Western Marxists who still insist that "socialists in power" (in European countries, at any rate) can do no (specific) wrong is usually expressed in words like the following:

> "Of course, there have been mistakes. Nobody should be surprised at this. But the peoples of socialist countries will learn from such mistakes. In time, they will come to act differently in some of these cases. Meanwhile it is urgent that such incidents do not get exaggerated as they often are in the capitalist press."[4]

In short: a general lip-service to the "inevitability of mistakes", but a real refusal to consider any specific one.

When I challenged a European Marxist about the last student incident in Sofia, he countered by citing a telegram from a delegation of African students sent from England to Bulgaria to investigate. This telegram declared that the investigators had found "no trace repeat no trace" of prejudice in Bulgaria. (In how many days there?)

At the same time, official socialist policy toward African students themselves was in itself (objectively; not necessarily intentionally) provocative. This policy was at least partially responsible if the Black Stereotype was able to rear its ugly head among so many ordinary citizens in a "socialist" land.

Almost every citizen from such countries to whom I spoke on this topic commented that African students were given allowances by the socialist governments noticeably larger than those for students of the country itself – who might be classmates of said Africans.

Per se, there may be nothing wrong with this. It was a policy based on the theory that, since Africa had been brutally exploited, special allowances must be made for her subjects when far from home. As a matter of fact, special allowances are generally granted ANY foreign student away from home, and not just in socialist countries. Thus, they were actually given to, say, Zambians in Ghana. Yet even these were resented by Ghanaian students because of failure by the government or Party to explain carefully the reasons. The similar socialist policy took too little account of this – and of another reality applicable particularly to Africans: (a) that special allowances for Africans were given in a context where the "color factor" already had conditioned Europeans unconsciously to "expect" Africans to live at a lower scale than themselves; thus, to ordinary resentment was added the COLOR variety; and (b) that most African students – at least, this was so in Ghana – sent to study over seas (whether in socialist or capitalist countries) came from those few colonial families which had benefited from colonialism: those who had been absorbed by the colonial administration to become part of a new elite; civil servants; and professionals (whose arrogance at home played a large part in discrediting the Nkrumah regime which made such broad use of them). Often, these students had, in addition to their allotments from the socialist governments, allowances from their well-to-do families at home. As a result – and many a socialist citizen griped to me specifically about this – a number of such African students had cars and money to impress – and attract – the local girls; many Africans were living ostentatiously above standards possible to socialist students. When such things were done within a context of surviving barbarous prejudices – embodied in the Black Stereotype pervading all white people's minds – the outcome was virtually inevitable.

Yet, the incidents themselves were not nearly as deplorable as their aftermath: Because the West's monopoly press immediately reported, magnified, and "made hay" of these "incidents", it became fashionable among European and Western Marxists to deny all. In this way, a golden opportunity to advance the cause of socialism among brutally colonized black people in Africa went down the historical drain.

Since when did Marxists cease necessary and sharp self-criticism because ("naturally") the bourgeois press picks it up and sneers at it? At a crucial point in history, with Africa by no means settled on a socialist path, such a position, rather than open self-criticism (where so sorely needed), played into the hands of imperialism and neo-colonialism. Moreover, as we shall see, it furthered already serious anti-Communism on the African continent.

36. The Black Stereotype and Eastern European Socialism in Africa

Such, then, is the background of the "student incidents" in Eastern Europe. Their significance went far beyond anything that appeared in the few days of press discussion permitted. For they were only one of innumerable instances I myself witnessed of unconscious racism by Eastern Europeans resident in Ghana.

These, of course, were not vicious, deliberate incitements based on conscious race hatred. They were the results of never before having had personal contact with real Africans, combined in modern socialist – and non-socialist – Europe with the persistent Black Stereotype among people living there.

Just one of many examples: a Russian, in my presence, jokingly told his illiterate steward when the latter had brewed bad coffee, "Oh, Issaku, I will kill you for this". What impinged on the steward? Very familiar threats issuing from someone in a white skin . . . in a situation where the African had no frame of reference for detecting the difference in intention: in this typical instance, he knows only what the words have always meant; in 65 out of 100 cases, he cannot read, so he knows nothing of socialist policy, or "aid without strings" or any of the political differences between imperialism and socialism. He has only the evidence of his senses and his intimate knowledge of the history of his people.

With this sort of personal relationship as background, more knowledgeable Ghanaians had their faith in socialism severely shaken by some of the following errors made by socialist countries:

At the big printing press in Tema put up by technicians from the German Democratic Republic, the statement was made by pro socialist Ghanaians (not as a charge, but as a sorrowful and exasperated commentary at finding their own friends "pulling the rug from under" them) that the only machines in the plant which worked correctly on installation came from West Germany and Britain. Equipment supplied by the GDR allegedly was never complete or would not work right. (In Hungary, in mid-1966, a citizen told my son when he brought this up during a visit there, that none of the European socialist countries were as yet producing quality goods.)

At Kumasi, it took five years to get the shoe factory which Ghana had bought from Czechoslovakia into operation. While this in itself cannot be laid at the Czechs' door, it was stated to me that the Czechs had "pushed too hard" in that – although they had been told that the ground had not yet even been broken for the building that was to protect the machinery from the weather – once they knew the money was available, they sent the machinery to Ghana almost immediately. As a result, that machinery sat out in the weather on the Tema docks for two solid years and took weeks to recondition before it could be used. Furthermore, one knowledgeable Ghanaian claimed that the Czechs made no effort to canvas the Ghanaian market before deciding on shoe styles. He said that they simply transplanted their own type of shoes onto a market previously conditioned to Italian styling. Considering that they were to sell these shoes at the same price as Italian shoes, this man (it was June 1967 at the time) predicted that Ghanaians wouldn't buy them. Perhaps this is a small thing. But it illustrates a mechanical approach based on failure to see any need to take African problems into account.

But most of the gripes I heard centered on the Russians. Having paid for up-to-date equipment, I was told the Ghanaians got mainly 20-year-old material obsolete on arrival even in European socialist countries. This included army equipment, which was an especially sore point. Enormous Russian lorries could sometimes be seen en route to the North, lumbering along a few miles an hour; when I commented on them and wondered why they weren't more used because their size would obviously save trips, the bitter comment was that they got all of six miles to a gallon of petrol – in a country where that fuel sold for close to a dollar per gallon.

Moreover, while Americans, English, Swiss, Italians, West Germans and other Westerners mingled freely and in apparent camaraderie with Ghanaians, the personnel exclusiveness of the Russians was the talk not only of Ghana from one end to the other, but even of socialists from other European countries like Rumania, some of whom privately told me that such "clannishness" was hurting the cause of socialism – and, indeed it was. In Tamale, where they were building what was to have been the largest airfield in Africa, the Russians lived by themselves, went to work in closed vans, returned the same way, and almost never mingled socially with Ghanaians.

Instance after instance of a similar nature I either saw with my own eyes or had cited to me ruefully by Ghanaians who were trying, in Nkrumah's regime, to work toward socialism under heavy if then tacit, opposition from the rising new elite among themselves.

Is it any wonder, then, that the conclusion drawn by such Ghanaians was that European socialists, being white, felt that second-hand merchandise was "good enough for black people." Even if the charge itself were not true, it must be understood that such would be the reaction of honest Ghanaians.

Another side-light on socialist relations with Africa: the big expatriate distributive firms, like Kingsway (United Africa Company, Lever Brothers) and UTC (Union Trading Company, a Swiss firm) utilized the entry of socialist goods into Ghana to buy large quantities of it at low prices. After the first month or so, during which lucky purchasers bought such things at the usual percentage markup and thus considerably below that of Western goods, the prices on them were raised to Western levels. Thus, the big capitalist monopolies found a way to make super-profits out of socialist goods! After the coup, these same stores put prices on socialist goods back to their original levels in "sales" to clean them off their shelves for good. So much for "peaceful economic competition" in Africa!

The overall approach to Africans implied in these typical cases is also reflected in Marxist discussion of African problems. Although the number of such discussions began growing about 1964, only just recently has the Color Question been mentioned – and then, only indirectly and by Africans.

For example, the WORLD MARXIST REVIEW (known in Africa as PROBLEMS OF PEACE, FREEDOM AND SOCIALISM) ran a series reporting an extended conference under its auspices in early 1962 on "Paths of Development for Newly Emergent Countries." In it, not unexpectedly, Africa came in for some mention. Yet, the composition of participants failed to reflect the crucial nature of Africa's struggle in relation to the future of world socialism: out of a total 31 participants listed, only three were Africans – one from South Africa and two from the North. Their talks, moreover, dealt primarily with specific national questions; the continent was "represented" by a Frenchman and an Englishman!

Around the end of 1964 or beginning of 1965, short, purely reportorial items began appearing in this publication from certain "Black" African countries like Nigeria and Cameroon.

The AFRICAN COMMUNIST, official organ of the illegal South African Communist Party, printed two articles dealing with color in several years' copies spot-checked (1962 to 1967 inclusive): in Third Quarter 1966, "Bending the Color Bar", by Z. Nkosi (attitudes of white unions toward black labor in South Africa); and Second Quarter 1967, "Trade Union Apartheid", by R. E. Braverman (divisions in South African trade unions over the attitude toward black labor). Neither of these articles discussed the Color Problem as such; rather they recorded the fact that the existence of deep racial prejudice among white workers (industrial, at that), causes in the South African labor movement divisions among the white workers themselves, and more concentrated exploitation of black workers.

Other ideological symptoms testify to persistent chauvinism in World Marxist ranks. For instance, the colonialists (where politically ousted) left behind – especially South of Sahara – few reliable statistics. In Ghana, for instance, the first industrial census was made during the Nkrumah regime to determine the size of basic industry, the working class, etc. It required two years merely for gathering data. When, a few months before the coup, the contract of the Rumanian assigned by the UN to direct this census ended, he naturally had to leave. With the coup, apparently the census will be forgotten. It will be dubbed one of Nkrumah's "prestige projects". So far as this writer has been able to ascertain, to this day the census has never actually been completed, let alone analysed. Undoubtedly, similar surveys must have been undertaken in other African countries. Most of these were Western-directed, which would result in figures far less capable of use for Marxist analysis. One of these carried out in Nigeria, for instance, was an internationally-notorious flop, resulting in what was claimed to be prodigious over statement of population – 58 million claimed; 40 million actual: a 45% error!

Yet, it is on such surveys that many airy conclusions have been made by "Marxist experts" on Africa. The fact is that, until completion of reliable, "people-directed" surveys on many economic aspects of "emerging" countries, any analyses of– say – Africa's "class composition" or the actual "orientation" of economic development in various countries can at best be "educated guesses", based on UN statistics – or wishes.

For example, any attempt to obtain meaningful vital statistics for South Africa out of the 1962 U.N. Statistical Yearbook – latest available when the writer consulted the Kumasi Public Library in 1966 – was frustrated by the fact that for most categories – life expectancy, etc. – figures were given for whites, colored, Asians and Africans all lumped together, so that the inordinately high levels for South African whites (conveniently) conceals the reality of the vast majority. (See Chapter 17, page 169 above.)

Nonetheless, the lack of statistical data done from below has not thus far hindered European Marxists and socialists from continuing to make definite analyses of Marxist categories like classes and economic orientation. Such people, who include the numerous Russian Africanists and well-known Left authorities like Jack Woddis, Idris Cox, etc. , may well make contributions to the solution of African problems. But when they "act the oracle" at all times, make hard and fast statements for African consumption and implementation (too often on the basis of mechanical application to available "African" statistics of conclusions from European conditions), they do not serve the cause of socialism in Africa. Scientists must contribute to each other's work without regard to geography. What is being objected to here is that the would be contributions under discussion fall short of being scientific because certain real material factors on the African scene are being omitted. Nor is it taken into account that, as a result of their history, Africans are extraordinarily sensitive, notably when white people are involved, to "interference" in anything they are doing, as the figures on the numbers of Communists in Africa suggest. (See Table 32, Chapter 39, above.)

Perhaps the following statement expresses such misgivings:

> "The Nigerian People's Party as the Marxist-Leninist political party of our Nigerian peoples shall help to enrich the international socialist pool BY ITS ORIGINALITY AND STAND AGAINST DOGMATIC AND BLIND

COPYING OF POLICIES AND TACTICS OF THE MARXIST-LENINIST PARTIES OF OTHER COUNTRIES."[1]

When challenged to explain such statements, European Marxists simply repudiate the Party concerned. This may get rid of the problem for such Europeans, but in effect it amounts to arrogating to themselves the decision as to who shall lead, or speak for, Africans.

37. The Black Stereotype and the Soviet Union

Although such was not their purpose, Russian authorities themselves have testified to the causes behind socialist blunders toward Africa and Africans. Chief among these causes is a theoretical ignorance on the subject of Africa which constitutes a perfect screen against seeing – let alone admitting – any error in that sphere.

Consider this:

> "The study of the languages and culture of the peoples of tropical Africa has started comparatively recently in the USSR.

> "Before the October Revolution many outstanding Russian scientists studied the history of ancient Egypt, medieval Ethiopia, and the history of the peoples of North Africa. But the life and culture of the peoples living South of the Sahara were never studied. This could be explained by the fact that the destinies of the people of North and Northeast Africa were always closely connected with the history of Europe and Asia Minor, while the countries lying south of the Sahara developed independently for a long time, being far removed from European culture."[1]

The lack in Russia of any study of the "languages and cultures of the peoples of tropical Africa" – typical of all European countries – was fostered by those in control of the educational and information media of the era, the Western European slave traders in medieval Europe's power centers whose countrymen became colonialists. The particular Russian lack merely marks that country, for a long period, as part - though a johnny-come-lately — of capitalist-imperialist Europe, where such study was systematically suppressed.

An honest explanation of such facts would have had to include the fact that there WAS a "close connection" between Europe and Africa South of Sahara which completely destroyed that area's developing "independently . . . from European culture" (manifested, e.g. by the great, world-renowned University at Timbuktu) – the incredibly profitable black slave trade, to participate in which Russia arrived too late on the capitalist world scene.

The only classical touch omitted from this "explanation" is in suggesting that there could have been development South of Sahara "independently. . . from European culture". Otherwise, the whole thing is a mere sickly echo of the past.

But the "explanation" continues:

> "Until recent times, the history of the African peoples could be studied only by the scientists of those countries who possessed African colonies.[2]

After 50 years of socialism, without a blush or a quotation mark, a Russian professor, dubs misrepresenters of Africa "scientists." Liars about history receive the Soviet accolade. How does this differ from imperialist practice?

A pacifist publication in London, studying racism in Moscow, declared that

> "It seems that most of the racial intolerance comes not from official quarters, but from ordinary people."[3]

Not in the least! It is from "official quarters" that "explanations" like the above come. It is in "official quarters" of Eastern Europe that new "scientists" have arisen to give "socialist" support to old saws about Africa.

And what do these new "scientists" come up with? What have the old "scientists" promulgated regarding these "connections" between Europe and Africa South of Sahara? Exactly what the Russian professor offers:

> ". . . the idea that it was the white race that had created the foundations of African culture."[2]

The new "scientists" don't say so; the old ones did. In a word - quite "scientifically", of course – ALL Europe wallowed for centuries in deliberately fabricated misconceptions about one of the world's great continents, thereby developing everywhere in Europe certain traditional attitudes toward Africans, such as an overall acceptance of their "backwardness" and "helplessness", leading to doubts about African abilities in any field.

A British Communist who prefers not to be named answered my query why Africa was still "represented" in European Marxist discussions about Africa by Frenchmen and Englishmen by describing for me the "difficulties" involved in "trying to develop" African spokesmen. Africans, he complained, produce written work about their own problems which are "full of mixed-up ideas", which of course must be "corrected" at once. "And they thank us", he assured me. The present status of Western Communist Parties and their abysmal stand on Africa leads one to question the concept "mixed-up ideas" when uttered by one of their spokesmen.

There are two significant aspects to the problem of left-over racialism in the Western and Eastern European Left: The first is that, after 50 years of socialism, a Russian "Africanist" is still mouthing the old myths. "Ordinary people" in such countries still express – because they still harbor – race prejudice. And anyone who tries to point out the reality is at once termed "anti-Soviet", thus ensuring NO discussion. So, racism in Eastern Europe and the Western Left may be expected to increase.

Second, every error made by a Russian in Africa or toward Africans anywhere is resented by Africans on a color basis, even when they themselves deplore such a reaction. Many Africans who react that way know that what they are feeling was created by imperialism; but that knowledge does not automatically erase the historically-conditioned response.

Actually, neither of these is very surprising. As yet, all Europeans have lived under imperialism a lot longer than under socialism. Eastern European countries under capitalism had never developed fast enough or early enough to become colonizers. Yet, they lived in the "metropolitan atmosphere" and absorbed it. Till recently, Africa could hardly be of major concern to any socialist nation: after World Wars I and II, first Russia, then the smaller countries of Eastern Europe, had been kept militarily and economically busy protecting the very life of their new social system. Where private ownership in the means of production had been abolished, the need for prejudice in any form went, too; and there official socialist policy at once expressed opposition to racism. But this alone did not and cannot prevent racism itself from (inevitably) persisting in the mass consciousness, because it had been deliberately ingrained there during centuries.

In a word, neither the USSR nor other European socialist countries which arrived at socialism later than Russia, have had time adequately to overcome, or even properly to lay bare, all the misconceptions embodied in unconscious approaches by socialist citizens to Africans – even supposing those nations had been anxious to do so.

On any other subject, socialists readily admit that many misconceptions are left over from the old way of life. Immediate mass education is undertaken. But it was only in 1957 that Ghana's independence, coupled with her orientation for the first time on that continent avowedly in a socialist direction, opened the way from the African side for any extensive interchanges with socialist Europe. Previous to that, none was permitted.

So, for forty years, mass education on this topic, not being urgent, could not be fitted in. Ironically, and perhaps significantly, by then, other "old" ideas had become rampant in the USSR. Did the hold of racism on European minds play any role in this ideological deterioration? (An answer to this question will be sought in a separate study of Revisionism.)

Whether so or not, no mass educational campaign about Africa has yet, to this writer's knowledge, been undertaken anywhere in Eastern Europe. Many Africans and Afro-Americans will tell you that some Europeans – French, Russians, and others – do not "see color". But this turns out in practice simply to mean that living with these Europeans may be preferable, at least at first, to residing among outright racists from or in other metropoles. It certainly did not prevent the Russians, under socialism, from taking an "educational" road vis-a-vis Africa exactly like the West's: they have created a small elite of "African experts" concentrated in their "Afrika Institut", whence floods of expertise, like that quoted above, issue.

The existence and nature of the Black Stereotype in the mass Western mind anywhere has yet to be acknowledged, let alone fought.

The "student incidents" in the USSR, Bulgaria, Czechoslovakia and elsewhere offered a tremendous opportunity to have launched just such an educational program. My own experience was that when such ideas as the existence of a Black Stereotype were brought to the attention of socialist individuals personally, from the countries involved, they not only seemed very objective about it, so that thorough discussion was held, but they appeared most eager to rectify the now-understood position in which they usually acknowledged themselves. One Rumanian whom I came to know fairly well stated after such a conversation: "If only I had known these things before coming to Ghana, I would have done many things differently!"

Politically, however, this point has been left far behind in Eastern Europe by now. The only importance to airing it now is to expose the facts for possible later use.

The attitude of politically advanced Africans is another side to this story which must be understood. Africans from various countries, none of them anti-socialist, made to me in Ghana illuminating comments on the student incidents and other evidences of left-over imperialist prejudices in the socialist world. Many of them had spent time in one of the socialist countries, where they had met other Africans of similar background.

All of them concurred that, generally speaking, socialist Europe was in no way comparable in its racism to the West. Yet, all had experienced specific and repeated individual instances of prejudice from citizens in or from Eastern European socialist countries. They agreed that such instances were all, in and of themselves, trivial and so recognized by their victims. They were damning in their aggregate.

A single illustration, told me by a number of Africans independently of each other, is the following: each claimed to have been asked by some socialist citizen in Eastern Europe whether it was true that "you people live in trees". (Later, Eastern Europeans in Ghana to whom I quoted this recurring remark categorically refused to believe that it could really have been said. But the story had come independently from more than one source, all reliable in other tested ways.)

Trivial though such incidents were, however, their importance lay in a total corrosive effect from piling up over an extended period of time. Certainly, they corroborate the existence in Eastern Europe among people calling themselves socialists, and representing to Africans a land of socialism, of definite, widespread and typical misconceptions about real Africans. All such socialists have in common, for better or for worse, as seen by Africans, a white skin. The major injury suffered by the Africans on account of these petty instances of racism did not stem from the prejudice itself, although that never ceases to hurt. It came from the fact that such errors originated in a socialist source which, in too many cases – especially officially, when the incidents were publicized – refused to admit any error, consequently denying the need for any corrective.

One Ghanaian who had been deeply involved in a well-publicized incident in Eastern Europe told me that, when he tried to explain African grievances to his Eastern European socialist comrades, their reply invariably was: "Oh, Comrade! You think about color too much!" In a word, exactly as in racist history everywhere in the West, anything bad that happens to Africans out of chauvinist mistakes by whites is "the African's fault": he is "too sensitive" about "color"! Any American who ever had contact with the Afro-American community readily recognizes this old saw.

The Black Stereotype was bound to come abruptly to the surface the moment real Africans, conditioned by centuries of imperialist brutalization, ran head-on into Europeans loaded with Western misconceptions about Africa deposited in their part of the world in super-exploitation's wake.

When Social Democratic outfits like the International Confederation of Free Trade Unions send their cohorts to Africa to undermine African progress for the benefit of the Western labor aristocracy – and naturally, therefore, of the imperialist ruling class – they quite easily exploit socialist errors derived from left-over racism, and can hook these mistakes into their virulent anti-liberation activities. Considerable real damage to the African freedom struggle results, especially insofar as the achievement of unity on a continental labor basis is concerned.

But even all this is not yet the total. Africans, only recently emerging from centuries of tight imperialist domination in its most vicious form, have to an extent hard to realize until one is set down in its midst, had their minds filled with various far-reaching anti-Communist lies. It is into THIS context that "student incidents and other socialist errors of racism fall. It is within these boundaries that remnants of the Black Stereotype and the strongly-persisting Colonialist Mentality both operate.

38. Some Disclaimers and a Summary of Racism's Effects Today

Obviously, a detailed Marxist examination of racism, especially its relationship to Social Democracy, is long overdue. But experience since this attempt at it was started shows that it is vital to specify first certain positions which are NOT being espoused:

1. Racism is most blatant when there are differences in skin color. But it is not confined to such cases. Nazism, for example, shows that, even in the absence of color differences, racism can be a major ideological weapon for imperialism: color prejudice is a special case of racism. But while racism can not be equated to color prejudice, clearly it is related to it. Colonialist practice has illuminated this point because colonialism always "justifies" its extraction of super profits from ANY subjugated people by referring to its victims' "inferiority", setting the degree of such alleged "inferiority" in general in direct proportion to differences in skin color. The overwhelming majority of peoples actually subjugated by colonialism did have and still do have pigmentation darker than those prevalent in metropolitan areas. So, under imperialism, racism is indissolubly tied to color of skin.

Furthermore, racism reduces to outright, straightforward color prejudice as its major content when the subjugated are black. Historically, the most basic and brutal super-exploitation has been practiced precisely against black people.

Basically and specifically, racism is the subjective side of colonialism; in particular, of super-exploitation, which latter is its material base. Its ideological content is a mythical "superiority" postulated, in the overwhelming majority of cases, upon the degree of absence of skin pigmentation; and, in the rest, upon some physical – i. e. inborn – claim to speciality.

2. The writer has been accused of claiming that "racism is the major cause of all the strife in the world today". Let us set the record straight: Racism is the major tactical ideological pillar upholding the moribund imperialist system AT THIS TIME in history. Concretely, what does that mean? Is ideology "causative"? Originally, no; as it develops, it moves from the expressive state to an equally – dialectically – causative one. A knowledge of contradictions reveals that racism could not cause "all the strife in the world today"; but it's doing a masterly job of keeping it going. Racism – present not only in conscious agents of the system – and specifically color prejudice, play a major subjective role in most of the strife in "Black" Africa and among people of African descent. Racism is a derivative of imperialism. Imperialism is its father, teacher and husbandman, the real culprit behind colonial misery. But this basic fact is obscured, hidden, buried – and a very potent weapon there by withheld – by the smokescreen, Racism.

Yet, because imperialism is the basic perpetrator of this condition, the World Left has thus far refused to tackle the material force which racism constitutes, especially in that area of anti-colonial liberation involving black people. There are probably endless numbers of people who think that this does not matter. But, being at the bottom of the economic totem pole, black people happen to play a far more crucial role in the immediate outcome of anti-colonial liberation than pervasive racial prejudice on both sides of socialist borders throughout the world has yet been willing to grant.

Recent events on the African continent bolster the contention that the outcome of the African and Afro-American struggles may, after all, be a decisive factor on the world scene today.

3. Analysis of racism and its relation to Social Democracy, plus insistence that racism is present even in advanced progressive quarters such as among Western Marxists and in socialist countries, does not constitute "over-stressing the race question" or "advocating racism", as has already been declared. Stating facts is no more causal than an accurate weather forecast: if people are imagined who for ages had feared thunder and lightning, their motives would be readily apparent if they accused the meteorologist of "over-stressing" or "advocating" thunder storms. And if they imbued such "advocacy" with negative virtues, it still wouldn't change the objective facts.

If you ignore racism, it will NOT go away. If you tackle the problems it creates, you will come to see that they have no solution short of socialism. But if, consequently, you think you can wait until socialism before dealing with such a serious matter, you merely leave the field clear for its unchallenged rampage. WORDS ARE NOT ENOUGH. VERBAL CONDEMNATION IS NOT A SUBSTITUTE FOR ANALYSIS, nor for active proof of understanding. The pervasive Left refusal to face and fight racism as such is, in my opinion, testimony to just how deeply it has penetrated all human beings.

4. Although it has been stated in these pages that anti-colonial liberation is in fact advancing along a front defined by the Color Line, this is not attributable to the existence in itself of differing skin colors. That is, it is not claimed that being born white produces a congenitally color-prejudiced person.

What is being said is that being born white in today's world constitutes a specific material fact in a specific material environment carrying in its train specific and unavoidable ideological consequences which have persisted from a historically-determined past, and which carry therefore certain material consequences predetermining the success of "Color" as a tactic. This is the meaning of the pervasiveness in the entire world today of the Black Stereotype. Its success stems from the fact that the black slave trade, and the colonialism that followed, allowed imperialism to use degrees of pigmentation as its excuse for extracting from the labor of peoples it had subjugated super-profits in direct proportion to the darkness of skin.

When Africans correctly note that certain Russians, Czechs, Poles, etc., "act like white people", they are referring to the facts we have been trying to make clear:

a) that the economic foundation of imperialism is colonialism, without which it will cease to exist; and

b) that ALL white people on this earth lived for a LONG time under imperialism. Since white people, like any others, cannot be abstracted from their material environment, the fact that EVEN people from Eastern European "socialist" lands all too frequently do "act like white people" merely reflects the fact that they are "white people" who, during a long historical period, starting IN EUROPE, lived in metropoles which exported capital, the source of imperialist super-profits, as "justification" of which the ruling class created an artificial and mythical "Master Race".

5. Unfortunately, widespread racial prejudice exists among Marxists, as all black people know who have come into contact with them. But few white people, though they claim to be Marxists ready to face any objective fact, know it or will admit it even when it is pointed out, a symptom of great importance in proving the thesis.

In particular, the many serious "student incidents" in the 60s in Eastern European socialist countries have shown beyond question the persistence of racism and color prejudice into the socialist era. So, in order to forestall the usual refusal in these quarters to discuss the points raised herein, certain false objections must be disposed of:

a) Nobody, including Africans or this author, questions that genuine socialist policy opposes racism. By its nature, real socialism has no need of racism because it has no profit-based economic motive to divide people in order to squeeze super-surplus-value from them.

b) Nobody, including Africans or this author, denies that Africans make mistakes, including serious ones, any one of which, made abroad, could become the immediate spark setting off "incidents". But are their mistakes any worse than those of others? It is the exaggerated, and so usually physical, reaction to African mistakes which is of interest, because it "gives the game away." It ignores the fact that such mistakes, clearly derivative, are so handy for confusing the issue. The ISSUE is the need to face and eradicate left-over White Supremacy among progressives in the West generally and in the post-capitalist world in particular. The latter, especially, constitutes the indispensable precondition for correct future relationships between peoples in former metropolitan areas and those in former colonies, with special emphasis on Africa.

c) One major response of actual Eastern Europeans and of Marxists in the Western Left when their attention is called to such left over race prejudice in their own ranks has been to claim that "all these incidents are set off by the CIA". We have dealt in part with this shibboleth.(See Chapter 35, Page 367, above.) But the implication of the contention itself is that, were it not for the CIA, no such incidents would occur. Objectively speaking, it is quite apparent that CIA agents are NOT either the ONLY or the MAIN cause of these troubles. Activities of the CIA, etc. – as the Bolshevik Party under Lenin clearly proved – can be thwarted by correct policy accompanied by mass understanding of how history is made, and mass participation therein. Such activities can NOT be thwarted by pretending that the prejudices in question do not exist; nor by trying to out-maneuver the CIA.

In the long run, history is made NOT by the maneuvers and cheap intrigues of Hollywood-type political gangsters. It develops out of the world relationship of forces, among which the masses in politically-correct action cannot be defeated. The examples of China, Korea, Vietnam and Cuba stand witness.

With all the foregoing qualifications in mind, a summary of this discussion of racism suggests that:

A. Race prejudice is universal in the world which lived for centuries under capitalism. White people harbor it as "great nation chauvinism", the main subjective expression of which is White Supremacy in myriad forms that, together, constitute a Black Stereotype. Black people reflect it in an attempt to escape racism's results called "Black Nationalism"; more generally, in "The Colonialist Mentality", the negative or mirror image of the metropolitan areas' Black Stereotype.

B. This Stereotype, a pervasive accomplishment of imperialism, left-over even in the socialist world, especially its European part for so long integrated in Western capitalism, today has begun to play a material role in BRAKING the anti-imperialist struggle, of which the current MAJOR material content is anti-colonial liberation.

C. Social Democracy from its inception was basically intent on thwarting precisely this liberation struggle in any of its forms.

D. Because Social Democracy needs and supports colonialism to guarantee high Western living standards through the constant flow of super-profits into the metropoles, and because colonialism has in fact subjugated mainly the earth's darker peoples, Social Democracy unfailingly has RACIST features: at first, hidden; but as imperialism decays, more and more open.

E. In fact, the lowest common denominator of Social Democracy IS racism (subjectively expressed in the Black Stereotype). Conversely, the Black Stereotype has been and remains a material factor evoking mass support for Social Democracy. Its materiality is expressed in wages and living conditions differentials between metropolitan and colonial peoples.

F. The Black Stereotype has played, and still plays, a significant and thus-far-unrecognized role in promoting Social Democracy under specific conditions, as proven by the fact that, when confronted by black people in significant numbers, Social Democracy reduces to outright color racism. Witness recent history in England.

G. The Black Stereotype, and the Colonialist Mentality that complements it, are so deeply imbedded, so unconscious, and so irrational because emotionally based, that they cannot automatically disappear with the appearance of Socialism. They linger on, undetected in their carriers – and will continue to do so until consciously recognized, analyzed and uprooted – because until very recently, there was no material reason for any other course: other material factors, such as defending the very life of Socialism, were more urgent.

H. In the light of this background, it is not racism among Marxists that shocks; rather, it is the continued refusal among white Leftists to FACE it. What is more, exposure of racism's full content and its ways of manifesting itself would be a genuine spur to the struggle against colonialism; it could lay bare the real path to final, economic success for anti-colonial liberation.

Because racism is a disorganizing force which conceals imperialism's basic economic and political truths, this exposition is indispensable – and inseparable from Lenin's admonition to "understand" and "appreciate" the effects of imperialist parasitism. It is by the racist umbilical cord that hundreds of millions of victims on both sides of the Color Line are still bound to the cancer-ridden mother long since doomed, but kept alive by their misguided support, and by their equally-misguided hatred and/or fear of their own natural allies across the Color Line.

As a result, among Marxists in that portion of the capitalist world where the foreign economic activities of metropolitan monopoly capital is crucial to maintaining outmoded imperialism; and, in those sectors of the socialist world where the need for foreign economic activities by "home" capital once dominated (i.e., before socialism) and hence, where racism was ideologically required, there has been a very significant failure properly to estimate the role of anti-colonial liberation as the KEY factor in current world revolution – a failure characteristic of Revisionism.

Revisionism can be proven to be a modern, intra-socialist form of Social Democracy; ipso facto, it must have specific racist elements.

I. Finally, Social Democracy, its racist variant, and its "intra-socialist" form Revisionism, all operate within a shell of virulent, widespread anti-Communism, which both feeds on their misconceptions, and reinforces them.

Because anti-Communism is the major strategic ideological pillar of moribund imperialism today, we cannot leave the subject of racism without at least a cursory look at anti Communism.

39. Anti-Communism and Racism

If racist errors are being made by Eastern European socialists or Western Marxists today, it is nonetheless no secret that racism and color prejudice do not benefit from, nor did they originate in, socialism, but in capitalism, which is founded, and continues to exist, on their fruits.

For the basic fact of today's world is that, objectively, socialism constitutes for the whole colonial world, and for Africa in particular, its main bulwark against, and hope of destroying, imperialism. Of this fundamental truth the desperate international imperialist ruling class is acutely conscious. Its long-run program and all its major actions are directed first and foremost toward foiling colonial revolution, the success of which would destroy imperialism completely. Even though racism may be successful for the time being in frustrating revolution in the colonies themselves; even though it enchains the ideologically-impoverished populations "at home"; nonetheless, as long as a socialist world exists, the permanence of colonies for imperialism's milking can not be assured.

In this light must be seen the role on the revolutionary front of anti-Communism. It forms a context in which the success of racism takes on new and ominous meaning. As previous Chapters have noted, it is simply an unfortunate fact that on the African continent the concept of "Color" is Siamese twin to anti-Communism, providing the springboard from which imperialist ideology rockets onto the African scene. For, in Africa, anti-Communism operates in a milieu where — because of colonialism's history — the vast majority of Africans are deeply conscious of humiliation, degradation, exploitation and deliberate unmitigated violence and brutality, all experienced almost exclusively on a racial — nay, more, a color basis.

Thus, when all is said and done, racism furnishes the fulcrum at which imperialism uses its anti-Communist lever to try to overthrow the socialist countries, reconstitute capitalism on their soil, and thereby not only secure them as restored lucrative colonies, but – so it believes – preserve its existing colonies "for all time." And, perhaps its hopes are not without basis.

The "incidents" and other race-based errors of socialist countries and citizens vis-a-vis colonial countries, especially Africa, occur in a world where anti-Communism has been accepted by millions of its victims. Testimony to this statement comes from Africans themselves:

> "No one should know better than the present-day leaders of our national liberation movements how false and harmful these anti-communist frenzies of the imperialists have been in Africa. They themselves have been the sufferers and victims . . . Yet it is surprising that some of our own national leaders seem not to have fully realized and absorbed the lessons of these so-recent events."[1]

More recent writings by Africans suggest that the "lessons" are still not "absorbed". On the contrary, anti-Communism and its effectiveness have escalated in Africa. For instance, a report about the deteriorating situation in Kenya noted:

> "A furious and reckless anti-communist campaign was . . . launched, master-minded and financed by Western intelligence agencies and aimed in the first place at Odinga and the men around him."[2]

What happened to Odinga has been recorded.

Furthermore, an assessment of "the coups and other events on our continent", noted "certain outstanding facts":

". . . in every case the imperialists and local reactionaries have made full use of the corrosive weapon of anti-Communism. They have taken advantage of lingering prejudices against Communism existing in the minds even of sincere patriots and revolutionaries, or of their opportunist fear to defend the rights of Communists to participate with other anti-imperialist fighters in the vital tasks of national construction and the evolution of policy and concepts . . .

"The weakness and even the absence of organized Marxist parties in Africa has meant that much of the discussion (about policy – H.E.) has been dominated by trends other than and even hostile to Marxism-Leninism."[3]

As early as 1962, this significant "absence of organized Marxist parties in Africa" had been documented. The following table appeared in a publication put out in Czechoslovakia:

Table 32[4]

NUMBER OF COMMUNISTS IN CAPITALIST COUNTRIES
OF ASIA, AFRICA, AND LATIN AMERICA

Third World Area	1939	1957	1960
Asia	over 20,000	over 1,700,000	approx. 2,500,000
Latin America	90,000	200,000	250,000
Africa (approximations)	5,000	20,000	50,000

This table had been printed in order to prove that Communist ideas were penetrating Africa, even though "there are as yet no Communist Parties in most African countries that have recently won their political independence". It is now almost ten years later, and imperialism has managed – thanks in large part to errors by the Communists listed in the table – to reduce drastically these numbers. This is probably good for the quality of the remaining Communists. But it emphasizes the point we are about to make.

For this table is eloquent witness to the effectiveness of linking racism to anti-Communism in the post World War II era: on the Asian continent, where racism is present but not dominant because of the absence of large number of black people, the number of Communists in 1960 was ten times that of any other subjugated area of the world. In Latin America, where black people are present in significant numbers but are not the majority of the oppressed, so that racism is one factor in the ideological atmosphere along with anti-Communism, the number of Communists is signally smaller. But in Africa, where the majority are black, so that racism has been the dominant theme of oppressing ideology, linked with anti-Communism, the number of Communists is negligible (and those who do exist have been tied to metropolitan apron strings).

This absence of Marxist Parties with any significant mass influence, accompanied by a seemingly infinite number of splits and splinters among those who do espouse socialism, is in fact perhaps the most telling result of racism combined with anti-Communism in Africa. (We are, of course, not suggesting this as proof of, but only as support for, our proposition.)

Factors among Africans leading to the temporary success of this combination include some of the following:

1) Among educated Africans, the majority up to now have been mission (meaning "church") educated, and have completed their advanced courses in WESTERN institutions. It is most instructive to listen to such people discussing socialist countries, because what is revealed is the extent to which they accept

anti-Communist lies. This real factor must be taken into account in any attempt by outsiders to establish meaningful relationships with Africans. It can not be wished away. Nor is it confined to the formally educated.

2) One of the bitter heritages of colonialism is that, to this day, the vast majority of Africans are illiterate. Of the minority who have any formal education, most have gone through Middle School (i.e., Junior High), enabling them to hold certain jobs above laborer work, but hardly conducive to wide reading of political analysis. For those who do read, there are floods of WESTERN material freely available and heavily financed by the US while, at the same time, there is very little if any from Marxist-Leninist sources.

This condition was explained by ex-President Kwame Nkrumah of Ghana:

> "Dating from 1961, the US has actively developed a huge ideological plan for invading the so-called Third World, utilizing all its facilities from press and radio to Peace Corps . . . At the centre of its programs lay the demand for an absolute US monopoly in the field of propaganda, as well as for counteracting any independent efforts by developing states in the realm of information . . . the chief executor of US psychological warfare is the United States Information Service Agency (USIA) . . . staffed by some 12, 000 persons to the tune of more than $130 million a year. It has more than 70 editorial staffs working on publications abroad. Of its network comprising 110- radio stations, 60 are outside the US. Programs are broadcast for Africa by American stations in Morocco, Eritrea, Liberia, Crete, and Barcelona, Spain, as well as from off-shore stations on American ships. In Africa alone, the USIA transmits 30 territorial and national radio programs

whose content glorifies the US while attempting to discredit countries with an independent foreign policy.

"The USIA boasts more than 120 branches in about 100 countries, 50 of which are in Africa alone. It has 250 centres in foreign countries, each of which is usually associated with a library. It employs about 200 cinemas and 8, 000 projectors which draw upon nearly 300 film libraries.

"This agency is directed by a central body which operates in the name of the US President, planning and coordinating its activities in close touch with the Pentagon, CIA and other Cold War agencies, including even armed forces intelligence centres.

"In developing countries, the USIA actively tries to prevent expansion of national media of information so as itself to capture the market-place of ideas. It spends huge sums for publication and distribution of about sixty news papers and magazines in Africa, Asia and Latin America.

"The American government backs the USIA through direct pressures on developing nations . . . for instance, many agreements for economic cooperation offered by the US include a demand that Americans be granted preferential rights to disseminate information."[5]

It is small wonder that, under such pressure, even the progressive press and information media of Africa, as illustrated in Nkrumah-led Ghana, presented a picture of "socialism" at best confusing, and at worst, a carbon copy of imperialist-sponsored lies. Most material from the socialist world, while it poured into Ghana in liberal quantity for some period before the military coup, was – at best – "hard reading."

3) Between the USIA, the difficulty of understanding literature from socialist countries, the confused state of national publicity channels, and imperialism's success in preventing Africans from having mass contact with real socialists, only a small minority of Africans had or have the foggiest notion of official socialist policy toward their countries, such as "aid without strings", or formation of societies for friendship with Africa. As noted before, the ONLY way most Africans had of judging socialism was through such few personal contacts as they or their friends happened to make with individual citizens of such countries. That is why little is known by Africans even of actual projects being built on African soil by technicians and other personnel from various socialist lands: they reached only the few workers at or around actual sites, a condition largely due to imperialist-influenced government policy, but partly to socialist underestimation of the tremendous importance of personal relationships. As noted in previous Chapters in addition, on such sites European socialists often acted in such a manner that they gave the wrong impression about socialism as a whole; either, they were too exclusive like the Russians at Tamale; or, they were too imperious and demanding, like those at Bui, both in Ghana.

4) Neo-colonialists have been and remain active, well-financed and very capable all over Africa. In the absence of organized parties of Marxism and the consequent lack of full understanding of class forces, historical laws and some of the more general tenets of Marxism-Leninism among Africans generally, not to mention the lack of actual people-directed investigations of real conditions "on the spot", these reactionaries are able temporarily to influence the course of events against the people's interests. The various attempts to assassinate President Nkrumah which presaged the February 1966 coup illustrated the results of pre-financed neo colonialism. Certainly the many coups and assassinations in Africa between

1964 and 1967 – still continuing: witness, Mali – indicate something less for the moment than victory for anti-colonial revolution there.

In the wake of such a statement, certain questions arise: concerning the general danger, whenever there is no organized Marxist-Leninist party, of just this type of set-back, since without such parties the advanced classes of Africa cannot exercise leadership. Real African Communist parties under African leadership would offer their countries a hard corps of unswerving cadres who could be relied on to carry forward in any crisis. Their dialectical, class analysis of various aspects of the African scene and struggle, sadly lacking up to now, would enrich all Marxist-Leninist theory, African in particular but by no means solely.

These considerations pose another question: WHY have political events occurred precisely as they have in Africa? Why so many assassinations? Why did so many military coups follow one another on the African continent during the three years following 1964 with such apparent ease? Do factors operate in Africa which are not present (or are weaker) in Asia and Latin America?

To this writer, it seems absolutely obvious that the strength of racism in Africa (and wherever black people are subjugated in significant numbers) acts as a brace and buttress to pervasive, world-wide anti-Communism: the latter, in turn, boosts racism; so that the two create an ideological battering ram for imperialism, with specific political consequences:

> A. As early as 1963, this writer was warning that, despite the number of African countries then openly espousing socialism as goal and policy, the future on that continent of socialism was by no means settled. Now, the set-backs to African progressive forces have not yet had time to bear all their bitter fruit, nor are the consequences to the rest of the

liberation camp completely obvious as of this writing. Nonetheless, such negative examples must become foci of new efforts to overcome this twin weapon of imperialist ideology. For, mention of political set-backs is not defeatism; negative lessons are as valuable and necessary as positive ones. Only – one cannot help wondering how many of these negative lessons were really unavoidable.

B. The tacit acceptance of basic socialist policy as anti-racist is a factor favorable to world revolution. But it is NOT an AUTOMATIC GUARANTEE of such an outcome, especially if socialists persist in race-rooted errors when dealing with African countries and individuals.

C. The reservoir of "colonialist mentality" among educated and uneducated Africans – recognized by politically-aware Africans themselves and consciously fought against – is a factor NOT favorable to revolution, but to neo-colonialism.

D. The penchant of white people apparently everywhere on earth at this moment – to deal with "African errors" in physical ways, as in the "student incidents" in socialist countries or in Watts in the U.S., is clear proof of the survival in virulent form everywhere, even in socialist lands, of the centuries-old deliberately-inculcated Black Stereotype spawned by imperialism to "justify" black slavery and the colonialism which grew up on its back. Injuries inflicted on Africans by socialist police and individuals or groups in or from European or other Western countries cannot be silenced out of existence or swept under the political rug. The outcome of anti-colonial revolution will have decisive influence on the fate of world revolution for decades to come. The decision is in the mill NOW – and history, like time and tide, does not wait.

E. Personal observation, plus first-hand accounts from Africans, prove beyond doubt that, among white representatives of socialist countries, the remains of the Black Stereotype expressed in such individual cases of chauvinism on their part as cited earlier, under circumstances of rampant, pervasive, engulfing anti-Communism, contribute at present to discrediting socialism itself on the African continent . This was vividly shown in Ghana right after the first coup in February 1966 when anti Communist feeling was easily whipped up.

Why has the United States taken on its own shoulders the expensive task of "fighting Communism" and "making the world safe for (its) democracy"? Why the United States rather than, say, Germany or Japan? And why has it been so successful with its tactics in Africa up to the present?

To answer these questions, the next Chapter will take a closer look at anti-Communism.

40. Anti-Communism — Major Strategic Ideological Pillar of Imperialism

A central political fact of our epoch is the self-appointed "Savior" role of the U. S. ruling class. Shielding the putrefaction of his own mortal illness behind the blazing lies of anti-Communism, Uncle Sam spreads corruption, destruction and death wherever his agents go. Yet, he does so under the tattered mask of his once-proud "democratic traditions."

It was one thing for a maniac and abject political tool of German monopoly like Adolf Hitler to commit crimes in the name of anti-Communism. The tool suited the method of operation. Then, the Nazis were defeated by "Democracy", (or by these "allies' financed and finally pushed over the brink of victory by U.S. finance capital). For "the Greatest Democracy on Earth" then to pick up the dirty anti-Communist mantle where vanquished Hitler had dropped it should have opened the eyes of the world's masses. Should have but, by and large, did not.

On the contrary, lies about Communism have never had greater success, including among so many of its colonial victims, pushed further along this road by racialist rooted errors made by white people from socialist countries, as discussed at length above.

How did anti-Communism become so widespread? Why did romantically-admired America pick up where despised Hitler left off?

The answer lies in world history since 1917. In that year, the capitalist system had been breached by Russia's successful socialist revolution. Despite massive intervention, despite the weakness of the new Russian economy, the "ignorance" of her masses, and all the factors which convinced "sensible" people that "it couldn't last", nothing was able to dislodge this first victorious revolution by a majority subjugated class. Within a short time, all Central and Eastern Europe were aflame with similar revolutions. These were temporarily defeated. The revolutions themselves were put down.

But it had been just the beginning. Despite these defeats,

> "The issue of the revolution was not averted. It returns today with added force in a world under the shadow of reaction and war...
>
> "From the outset the dominant concentration of all the leading statesmen of imperialism after the war was directed to the defeating of the revolution... The clearest and most conscious expression of this outlook was given by Lloyd George in his Memorandum to the Peace Conference in March 1919. He stated:
>
>> '. . . Bolshevik imperialism (sic!) does not merely menace the States on Russia's borders. It threatens the whole of Asia and is as near to America as it is to France. It is idle to think that the Peace Conference can separate, however sound a peace it may have arranged with Germany, if it leaves Russia as it is today.'
>
> "Hoover, in charge of American relief in Europe, expressed concisely the aim in a letter to Oswald Garrison Villard on August 17, 1921, quoted in Louis Fischer, The Soviets in World Affairs, vol. I, p. 174:
>
>> 'The whole of American policy during the liquidation of the Armistice was to contribute everything it could to prevent Europe from going Bolshevik or being overrun by their armies.'"[1]

Even as such words were being uttered, armies of fourteen capitalist nations were invading the infant socialist state. The Soviet had to fight a war on twenty-three fronts – yet, survived!

Russian workers, peasants and soldiers, guided by the incomparable Lenin and the monolithic Bolshevik Party he had forged in two and a half decades of struggle, defied the whole capitalist world, cleared their native soil of invaders and set about the historically-imposed chore of pulling themselves up by their own boot-straps.

The capitalist world answered with an economic blockade. It set up the "cordon sanitaire", anti-Communist states, in most of which revolutions had been defeated, which were to "contain Russian communism".

In the West, the kept press hooted, jeered and lied: Russia's "collapse" was "imminent"; she "lacked resources"; her economy was "inefficient". But the owners of the imperialist machinery who sponsored the lies knew better. They saw a socialist economy begin to advance at development rates hitherto unprecedented in world economic history.

At any cost – this must be stopped! If the intervention of the 20s had failed, that must be only because the Powers had been a bit exhausted by World War I. NOW, they would recover – and try again.

In the defeated, prostrate post-war German monster created at Versailles, the victorious "Allies" saw the instrument they sought – and picked up the option. Nazism and its inspired wild man Hitler became the darlings of international finance capital. The German war machine was supported, financed, and in desperate haste, built to enormous size. Hitler began boasting of "invincibility".

During two decades, the stages was set; the puppets, prepared. All that was missing was The Deed. The world hovered at the brink of explosion.

What was the real issue? Why such "insane" hatred of a single allegedly "weak" socialist country? What was at stake?

A lucid explanation of anti-Communism has been offered by two writers frequently cited in these pages:[2]

Britain, by her victory over Napoleon in 1815 had achieved "a decisive victory", following which the need for armaments seemed to fade. Even the young and lusty US had become Britain's ally — at a price. The famous Pax Britannica had prevailed until the first decade of the 20th century. But this temporary martial lull was due only to

> "one unchallenged leader sitting on top and stabilizing the whole system through its own strength and a flexible system of alliances."[3]

These, of course, lasted only until the German and Japanese challenges to British hegemony, after which arose a new militarism among capitalist countries that resulted in World Wars I and II.

The United States had entered the world scene relatively late. Until after the Civil War, her comparative insecurity led her to operate mainly through "alliances and deals designed to take maximum advantage of the needs and conflicts of the leaders". Through such means,

> "during the nineteenth century, Washington built up a large, if still secondary, empire and staked out a claim to a still larger one (especially in the Monroe Doctrine) without ever experiencing the need for a commensurately large military machine."[4]

By the end of World War II, the United States had attained in the international arena a position fully as commanding in the new epoch as Britain s had been after her victory of 1815. For this reason alone, the US would at first have needed an unusually large military build-up. Moreover, when older empires began breaking up, the US managed by fair means and foul to secure for herself large chunks of them. This would have increased her military needs for "defense" purposes still further.

But now, something new happened. Though now far more powerful in the size of and her control over this modern empire than Britain had been after 1815, the United States was unable to relax militarily:. there was NO "Pax Americana". Visibly and compulsively, the US continued to this day building up its armed might to undreamed-of heights. Far from stabilizing the situation through its position as undisputed leader of the imperialist world today (as Britain had done in the 19th century), the US hangs onto an international empire that is like a sackful of hedgehogs – full of prickles and struggling to get loose.

What has caused this difference?

> ". . . the rise of a world socialist system as a rival and alternative to the world capitalist system."[5]

Even so, why, specifically, should this cause such a military build-up?

The official US stance has been "the need to protect the 'free world' from 'communist aggression'". This alleged need is "justified" by the myth of "Soviet aggressiveness", usually inferred from the "fact" that, since Nazism was a totalitarian state and was aggressive, and since the Soviet Union is another "totalitarian state", therefore it "must be aggressive," too.[6] (It must be borne in mind that this argument applies to early USSR.)

But out of the mouths of American ideologues themselves, it has been shown that even some of the most belligerent enemies of the USSR, like Walter Lippman, do not believe in the aggressiveness of Soviet policy. For such men, facts prove that Soviet foreign policy has been

> "essentially defensive and bears no resemblance to the aggressive war policies of Nazi Germany and its Axis partners."[7]

How, then, explain the enormous US military machine? On what particular phenomenon does it rest? On

> "the same implacable hatred of socialism, the same determination to destroy it, that has dominated the leading nations of the capitalist world from the time the Bolsheviks seized power in November 1917. The central purpose has always been the same: to prevent the expansion of socialism, to compress it into as small an area as possible, and ultimately to wipe it off the face of the earth. What has changed with changing conditions are the methods and strategies used to achieve these unchanging goals."[8]

Thus, when the infant Soviet Union, often with the assistance of workers in capitalist countries, beat off counter-revolution, a "cordon sanitaire" was set up to "contain" it. When the socialist land nonetheless forged ahead, the military machines of Germany and Japan were built up and shoved into headlong attack on it. When this tactic in turn boomeranged, the US itself had to make common cause with the intended victim. Not only did the USSR survive World War II; a whole series of new socialist countries now replaced the hostile cordon around her periphery: the socialist world expanded.

And colonial countries, too, began to stir in revolt:

> "Clearly, world capitalism was facing an unprecedented crisis."[9]

Such were the circumstances under which the US ruling class stepped forward and appointed itself leader of a great imperialist counter-offensive. And the form that counter-offensive took was intense anti-Communism as preparation for eventual war. Even so, it took a full year from the opening gun of this campaign – Winston Churchill's famous Fulton (Missouri) speech on March 5, 1946 – before the American people were deemed ready to back the international anti-Communist crusade. Not till February 1947 did the US take its first step: intervention in Greece and Turkey, where revolutionaries were close to success.[10] The famous Truman Doctrine set up a protectorate over Greece and Turkey and proclaimed the US "right" to do so whenever a situation warranted.

Yet this was but the negative side of American policy: the announced US intention of preventing the spread of socialism even an inch.[11]

There was also a positive side to that policy. It was enunciated in two major speeches by Secretary of State Dean Acheson in March 1950 (i. e., before the Korean War).

In the first, Acheson had stated that the aim of the US Was to establish "situations in strength."[12] In the second, he defined in detail what that meant. Declaring that, if capitalism and socialism were to co-exist, certain points of difference would sooner or later have to be settled, he listed seven:

> "First Point: The German, Austrian and Japanese peace treaties must make those countries 'free' – in other words, capitalist countries allied with the US against the Soviet Union.

"Second Point: 'Orderly representative processes' must be introduced into 'the whole group of countries we are accustomed to think of as the satellite area' – in other words, the Soviet Union must stand aside while the United States organizes counter-revolutions in Eastern Europe.

"Third Point: 'The Soviet leaders could drop their policy of obstruction in the United Nations' – in other words, the Soviet Union must acquiesce in the UN's becoming an instrument of American policy.

"Fourth Point: The Soviet Union must accept 'realistic and effective arrangements for the control of atomic energy and the limitations of armaments in general' – in other words, the Soviet Union must place her work in the field of atomic energy under the control of an American-dominated agency and submit her military apparatus to outside inspection.

"Fifth Point: The Soviet Union must 'Desist from, and co-operate in efforts to prevent, indirect aggression across national frontiers' – in other words, since 'indirect aggression' is the usual pseudonym for social revolution, the Soviet Union must not only agree to United State counter revolutionary actions but actually aid and abet them.

"Sixth Point: The Soviet Union and its allies (as long as it has any) must give American official representatives the run of their countries.

"Seventh Point: The Soviet leaders must stop criticizing the United States and its allies."[13]

Instructive or appalling as hindsight makes these seven points, an American professor immediately dubbed them "a United States foreign policy" with "only one possible objective: . . . the destruction of Communist power."[14]

To implement such a policy, three things were needed:

> a) a world-wide military alliance dominated by the US (witness, the Marshall Plan, SEATO, NATO, and the rest);

> b) a network of military posts and bases to surround the socialist areas of the world:

>> "By 1959, the United States had . . . a total of 275 major base complexes in 31 countries and more than 1,400 foreign bases, counting all sites where Americans were then stationed and sites designed for emergency occupation."[15]

> c) above all, "Arms of all kinds (and) ... the men to use them".[16]

These are some of the reasons why the capitalist system is so hostile to the existence of a rival world socialist system.

But some people say that hostility is caused by irrational fears. If so, then could one but present proper rational arguments, one could presumably win these "mad" rulers over and make them "see the light." Indeed, this is the basic, stated or tacit, underlying premise of pacifist peace groups in the West as a whole, not to mention the revisionists.

In fact, however, "rational argument" only emphasizes the problem.

For example, the advance of socialism is said to constitute a threat to the foreign trade of capitalist countries, which cannot exist without such trade.

REPLY: Capitalist countries do require foreign trade. But socialist countries are more than ready, willing and able to enter such trade and have done so. The advance of industrialization in European socialist countries enhances their potential as a trading partner.[17] Of late, even President Johnson had waxed enthusiastic over the possibility of "trade bridges to the East".

At the same time, foreign trade is rarely conducted between themselves by governments, but by private business, mainly huge corporations.

> "What these corporations are interested in is not trade as such but profits: the reason they and the governments they control are opposed to the spread of socialism is not that it necessarily reduces their chances of importing or exporting (though of course it may), but that it does necessarily reduce their opportunities to profit from doing business with and in the newly socialized areas."[18]

And the source of the highest such profits has always been and remains the "less developed and under-developed countries." Hence their defection would be "the last straw".

Today, US need to police its global empire is inseparable from its need to fight socialism. For,

> "the threat to the empire comes from revolutionary movements which, like the American Revolution two hundred years ago, are sparked by a deep-seated yearning for national independence and are fueled by and increasingly urgent need for economic development, which experience is proving cannot be achieved by underdeveloped countries today except on the basis of public enterprise and comprehensive planning – in short, only if their nationalist revolutions are also socialist revolutions."[19]

So! Here, at last, is bedrock: clearly, the continued growth of the American military machine is inseparable from world anti-Communism spearheaded by the US. The intended effect is to implement the grand strategic aim of the US ruling class: "to contain, compress, and eventually destroy the rival world socialist system."[20] The existence of socialism, in turn, is feared by imperialism not only for its own dangers, but also because it was threatening the colonial system, where profits are from two to four and more times the domestic rate. It does this both by removing its own areas from the capitalist world and by suggesting an alternative to colonial peoples.

Freedom for colonies, were it to spread to include their economies, would mean the additional loss of monopolist control over foreign sources of supply, another major benefit to imperialism of the colonial system. Moreover, such control must include the ability to force political and legal concessions from subject governments.

These are all reasons why the defection of even a single colonial area today causes such panic in, and such brutal and immediate response by, imperialism: it disrupts the world-wide total control network threaded through all exploited lands and peoples. No longer can capitalism which once ruled the whole world support even the slightest deviation from its own needs. Rather, if it is to survive, it must if possible recoup a considerable portion (preferably, of course, all) it has lost. The "development" of Eastern Europe thus far must be peculiarly gratifying to Uncle Sam.

Now, imperialism had been forced to use colonial subjects in large numbers as soldiers in its anti-Nazi war, once its Hitler creature had proven "untrustworthy." Such soldiers brought home with them, from overseas duty, concepts of equality and comradeship. Many of them had, despite imperialist precautions, met real socialists and communists. The "independence" yeast began to work; it had to be counter-acted.

In curtailing contact between Africans and socialists, from the Bolshevik Revolution in 1917 on, the international ruling class had acknowledged their own clarity about what such contact might accomplish: they felt that any massive interchange between these two groups would be fatal to themselves. Massive contact might enable the two groups to overcome individual errors on either side, and permit news of the success and significance and structure of real socialism to get through to Africans. Successful relationships of this type, they also suspected, could destroy racism and its effectiveness: if white people could come into Africa and get past the first stage where they are seen as "acting white", the Color wall would have been branched; the structure of imperialism would be placed in great danger. The international ruling class did not dare to take a chance on any massive socialist presence in "its" "under-developed" areas.

When Ghana gained independence in 1957 and promptly announced that she was going socialist, the imperialists had to work fast. First, they stepped up their pressure against exactly such contact between the socialist world and Africa; and in this they were largely successful. Then they went all-out for the anti-Communist theme song.

So, when socialists did finally come into Africa, it was into the midst of an anti-Communism so intense that no Eastern European who had been raised under up-to-50 years of socialism could possibly imagine it. They came, trailing their ideological left overs behind them, and as we have seen in previous Chapters, the individual and/or collective errors they made – which at any other time or place might have been easily handled – proved grist to the imperialist mill in that context of anti-Communism and racism combined which is the African scene.

What, then, has been the effect on Africa of this concentrated anti-Communist campaign? As a matter of fact, there has been a resultant increase in the effectiveness of RACE and COLOR in braking the revolutionary movement.

It works like this: racism is imperialism's major tactical ideological weapon for frustrating anti-colonial liberation; liberation today is the key to any further advance in world revolution. But the existence of any considerable reservoir of colonial labor power super-exploitable by any metropolis guarantees the continued existence of that metropolis.

Furthermore, anti-Communism is the major strategic ideological weapon in the overall, imperialism-vs-socialism world struggle, its implement being unprecedented metropolitan military strength supplemented by pre-financed and ideologically-controlled colonial armies – all this permitting the ruling imperialists to maintain a bony hold on the system's current existence. Inside this sequence, militarism shelters anti-Communism, which in turn prevents the demise of racism.

The combined result, of course, has been that thus far the African continent as well as Latin America and large segments of Asia have been maintained in subjugation.

Yet – and here is the point of this section of the discussion – because of basic socialist POLICY; because of the basic mutual interests between Africans and socialists, it might have been possible to reverse the existing situation. But this could ONLY have taken place had the socialists accepted criticism and dealt sharply in self-criticism; that, and that alone, would have cut the ground out from under the neo-colonialists.

Not only could this have been done fairly simply; but every agent provocateur, European or African, could have been exposed and isolated. It did not come to pass; nor will it as long as socialists persist in ignoring real factors in the African milieu, especially as long as they refuse to study and understand how many African grievances have their roots in "Color" troubles; nor, as long as they refuse to see their own Color-based ideological left overs of imperialist ideology and practice. The sooner a public start is made in correcting such attitudes, the sooner the real conflict can come to the fore and be fought in concert.

In a word, because of racism and anti-Communism, together with errors made in Africa and/or toward Africans by real people accepted as socialists, the advent of socialism in Europe or elsewhere in and of itself has been no guarantee of the automatic evaporation of old prejudices and wrong ideas. This truism has long been accepted – but not applied.

Such attitudes can be changed only by courageously facing them and taking positive steps to root them out. Up-rooting cannot occur short of bold, difficult and surely painful criticism and self-criticism. But the stakes are high. Socialism has shown in other connections that it has the strength to make such a bold uprooting. The question is: WILL Socialists do it IN TIME to affect colonial casualties materially?

41. Anti-Communism, Racism and Social Democracy

One of the greatest obstacles to eliciting either in the Western Left or in Eastern European socialist lands the type of criticism and self-criticism envisioned at the end of the previous Chapter is the malevolently persisting Social Democracy of our time.

Its obstruction to revolutionary advance has become double: first, its activities – as before – inside colonial areas; and second, its appearance inside a section of the socialist world in a modern but recognizable form.

This Chapter will be concerned with the first factor: Social Democratic activities inside a colonial area. (The second is to be the subject of a separate study, Anatomy of Revisionism, AURORA edition, 1978.)

A most striking example of how Social Democracy utilizes the connection between racism and anti-Communism to defeat anti-colonial revolution is the case of British Guiana (now Guyana). There it was revealed how anti-Communism tries to block liberation alone; how, by itself, it is today inadequate to the task; how to its rescue, reinforcing and extending it, comes racism in the hands of a metropolitan labor aristocracy; and how this combination has so far succeeded in turning back the struggle for freedom.

It will also be noted that, despite all differences between them – and these are serious – European Social Democracy must now work hand-in-glove with American racism in US labor ranks wherever a colony threatens genuine revolt.

Guyana is about the size of Great Britain: 83,000 square miles. Situated on the mainland of South America, it is wedged between

Brazil along 500 miles of its south and southwest; Venezuela on its west; and Dutch Guiana, called Surinam, on its east. Ninety percent of the population, and most of the economy, are located in a narrow coastal land strip 50 miles wide comprising four percent of total area, located below sea level but protected by sea defences and drained by a complex canal system. The capital and chief port, Georgetown, contains 25% of population.

The economy is typically colonial: almost entirely agricultural, it depends on sugar, bauxite, rice, diamonds, hardwoods and rum. Only half of one percent of the land is cultivated. Processing sugar and distilling rum are among its oldest industries. Sugar exports in 1960 were valued at £26.5 million. In 1961, its mines produced 2.374 million tons of bauxite. Under Cheddi Jagan's pro-socialist regime, rice production more than doubled, and there were set up margarine and soap-making plants, breweries, factories making wallboard, cigarettes and aluminum ware, as well as boat-building yards.

In 1966, the UN estimated the population at 662,000. Inside the country, the 1960 census counted 558,769 Guyanese, of whom 279,460 were East Indian in origin, while 256,460 were of African or mixed descent; all others numbered only 16,190.

Until 1803, the Dutch controlled the area. Using mainly slaves from West Africa (with names suggesting specifically the old Gold Coast), the Dutch cultivated land along such broad rivers as the Essequibo, Demarara and Berbice. Their plantations extended miles upstream, and the soil's natural fertility was soon depleted. But they could not move into the rich savannah grasslands in the interior because the rivers were navigable only for short distances, while tropical rain forests made road-building expensive. Moreover, life in the hot humid interior was unhealthy; malaria, yellow fever and other tropical diseases were rife. The Dutch settlers, having found the clay of the coastal area suited to sugar cane, developed the drainage system which allowed them to grow that crop.

Plantation slaves suffered typically: cruelty, inhumanity and endless forced labor under a tropical sun. By the beginning of the 19th century, the colony had been swept by at least two slave up risings of serious proportions. For this reason, the British, who in 1803 had taken over from the Dutch, soon found slave labor unprofitable. Accordingly, in 1833, they abolished slavery. The freed slaves left the plantations and began forming small communities and. peasant villages, some even becoming small business men. This is how Guyanese urban areas, notably Georgetown, came to have a predominantly African-extracted citizenry.

Starting in 1851 and lasting until 1917, the British answer to their own need for a new source of cheap labor power was to import thousands of East Indians as indentured laborers. This eventually resulted, over the country, in East Indian population slightly out numbering that of African descent.[1]

What was the relationship between these two peoples?

A government-favored publication from British Guiana's London office in late 1963 described it as follows:

> "Race has never been a serious problem in Guiana. Indians and Africans have for many, many years played, worked and lived amicably together. Underlying the superficiality of racism is the basic problem of the class struggle and the struggle for land and jobs. Prior to the 1955 split in the People's Progressive Party, the Africans and Indians, who constitute the backbone of the working class and peasantry, were united in their struggles against the capitalists and landlords. On every front — sugar plantations, water front, mines, mills, quarries — the

workers battled (together) for improved wages and working conditions."[2]

A similar estimate was made by even so biased an authority as the former British judge, Mr. Wynne-Parry, who chaired a Commonwealth Commission sent to British Guiana in 1962 to investigate the "February disturbances" there. Said the honorable judge:

"We found little evidence of any racial segregation in the social life of the country and in Georgetown. East Indians and Africans seemed to mix and associate with one another on terms of the greatest cordiality . . . the disturbances of February 16th did not originate in a racial conflict, nor did they develop into a trial of strength between the East Indians and Africans.

". . . we are merely drawing attention to the circumstances mentioned above to show that there is no clear-cut division between the races and that, although broadly speaking Dr. Jagan's supporters are for the most part East Indian and the supporters of the P.N.C. are drawn mostly from the African race, the difference is not really racial, but economic and vocational."[2]

Concerning the racial makeup of the PPP itself and its governments, the following are the facts:

". . . persons of Indian descent comprise 50% and those of African origin only 34% of the population. But the PPP has won seats where the majority of the electors are of African origin. In the 1961 elections the PPP had 14 candidates of Indian origin and 11 of African descent. In the Legislative Assembly, the PPP had 11 Indian and 7 African members. . . . In the Government administration, those of African descent have 30 key positions in the police force and Indians have only 4. In the police ranks there are more than 1,000 of African origin and only 248 of Indian descent."[2]

The political result of this cooperation and harmony between two super-exploited sectors of a colonial people was that both British and American imperialism were frightened out of their wits: in April 1953, in the first General Elections under Universal Adult Suffrage held in British Guiana, Dr. Cheddi Jagan, an East Indian Guianese trained as a dentist in the US, led his avowedly-socialist People's Progressive Party (PPP) to victory. Out of a total of 24 seats, the PPP contested 18 and won them all. Mr. Forbes Burnham, an attorney of African extraction, later in Opposition and currently neo-colonial prime minister, was then Chairman of the PPP and Minister of Education in the new administration.

This parliamentary success brought consequences:

1. Generally.

> "Since 1953 . . . foreign intrigue has aimed at the destruction of (British Guiana working class) unity and militancy. Their actions were principally: the 'terror' rule which followed the 1953 suspension of the Constitution; the 1955 Burnham-engineered split in the PPP and the subsequent alliance of Mr. Burnham and his working class supporters with those reactionary elements who were opposed to the PPP before the 1953 suspension."[2]

2. The response of the British empire: first, via the kept press of the colony itself, it alleged "a Communist conspiracy", led, of course, by Dr. Jagan and the PPP. This was the prelude. Then, an "arson plot" was added, in which even the British government, to judge by its remarks in a White Paper following investigation, did not believe. Nevertheless, within 133 days,

British battle-ships had reimposed direct colonial rule, which lasted till 1957, followed

> "by all the trappings of a police state: assemblies and demonstrations were banned and persons were detained for months without trial."[2]

The first election having been nullified by British troops and warships, Britain followed through in typical style by setting up the usual British Commission of Inquiry to blow smoke in the public eye. One of the Commissions's members was George Woodcock, an Assistant General Secretary of Britain's T.U.C.

3. A campaign got under way inside the British Guiana T.U.C., under the direction and prodding of its British counterpart, to disrupt the unity of the Guayanese working people. By February 1962, this campaign had blossomed in the "disturbances" alluded to by the British judge above.

The excuse was a new Labor Relations Bill proposed by Jagan's Government (after his third election in 1961) which would have permitted the Guayanese sugar worker to choose by secret ballot his own labor union instead of being, as was then the case, forced into the Company union called the Manpower Citizens' Association (MPCA).[2]

4. In 1955, the Chairman of the PPP, Forbes Burnham, defected from the Party to form his own, the PNC or People's National Congress, which came out in opposition to "the communist aims" of the PPP.

5. The cry of "Communism" arose in British circles other than those of the T.U.C. and government: A Social Democrat (the British Labour M.P., Fenner Brockway), head of the English "Movement for Colonial Freedom", discussing British Guiana, and speaking of the 1955 split in the PPP, had said:

> "The split was fanned by the pro-communist leanings of Dr. Jagan ... As the ideological controversy grew, Forbes Burnham declared himself a Social Democrat and now heads the Opposition under that name. "[3]

Thus, anti-Communism was used by (a) the ruling imperialists to nullify an anti-colonial parliamentary victory; and (b) by a section of the international working population, pushed, prodded and guided by the metropolitan labor aristocracy, which now began combining racism with its usual anti-Communism.

By 1957, the PNC having weathered two years of existence, the British decided that the time was ripe for new elections. They felt reasonably sure that PNC had done its divisive work well enough to ensure the "desired" result.

Accordingly, in August, new elections were held. But again, the PPP scored decisive victory at the polls. Mr. Burnham then had no choice but to join Dr. Jagan in constitutional talks in London, both demanding independence of the British in 1961. The British, while forced to agree to the principle of independence, replied by scheduling still other elections, this time for August 1961.

Before then, however, a new element entered the Guayanese picture: a party calling itself the United Force (UF) had been organized by one Peter d'Aguiar, a businessman owning breweries and a newspaper. Helped along by open and lavish US funds, the UF joined forces with Burnham's PNC.

Nevertheless, when August rolled around, the PPP took 20 out of 35 seats. Jagan again became prime minister – but the police remained under British control. New constitutional talks were announced: first, for January; then, for May, 1962.

By now, it had become obvious that neither racism nor anti-Communism alone would be able to save this territory for imperialism. So, at this point, specifically in September 1961, the metropolitan labor aristocracy (i.e., Social Democracy itself) intervened in British Guiana. The active part it played there finally and successfully got rid of Jagan (meaning, of the immediate threat to colonialism in British Guiana).

The Social Democratic unions of England, through their T.U.C., working with their Guayanese affiliate, the British Guiana T.U.C., had already fomented "trouble" which led in February 1962 to the cited "disturbances" over the proposed Labor Relations Bill (some times likened to the US Wagner Labor Act).

Immediately after Jagan's third successful candidacy, in August 1961, the AMERICAN trade unions, representing racism in the metropolitan working class, took a direct hand in Guayanese union and political affairs:

> "US citizens, agencies and institutions – the American Institute for Free Labor Development, the Christian Anti-Communist Crusade, the International Congress of Free Trade Unions (ICFTU), and its Latin-American Regional Committee (ORIT) – have been actively engaged in subversion. Without the funds supplied by these organizations, the strike of 1963 would have collapsed in a couple of weeks."[2]

Instead, it lasted 80 days – nearly 12 weeks.

According to a corroborating statement,

> "The last twenty months, (i.e., from September 1961 - H.E.) have seen a massive effort to bring the trade union movement in British Guiana under the control of the United States trade union movement."[4]

An avenue for such a venture already existed: most important British Guiana unions were already affiliated either to US counterpart unions and/or to their international-controlled sections, starting with the B.G. TUC, which was tied to the ICFTU, international labor arm of Social Democracy; and including at least eight others with organizational bonds to American or ICFTU unions and/or their Regional Organizations.

Contrary to the usual stance of metropolitan trade unions, which want colonial unions to be NON-political in order to qualify for their "aid", the preoccupation of B.G. unions under British and American "stimulation", was with political rather than economic questions:

> "Notwithstanding the low rates of wages and poor conditions of work in certain commercial undertakings, the omission of certain employers to pay rates in excess of the minimum . . . prescribed by Government for certain categories of workers, and the failure of many employers to comply with provisions enshrined in protective labor legislation, there has been no strike to remedy these conditions since the 1961 General Elections by the Trades Union Council or its affiliates. Instead, the Trades Union Council has called two general strikes for obviously political reasons."[4]

This judgement had been supported by the aforementioned 1962 Commission appointed by the Secretary of State for the Colonies. Its report also attributed political motives to at least three leading B.G. trade unionists (Ishmael, Jackson and Sankar) all deeply involved in the "disturbances" because "they had personal grievances against Dr. Jagan and his Ministers".

US Unions took three general types of interfering action in British Guiana:[4]

1. They sent large sums of money into B.G. for special meddling;

2. Guayanese trade unionists were "trained" in the US In growing numbers;

3. A steady stream of US union officials began visiting B.G.

Part of the "large sums of money" consisted of scholarships for Guayanese unionists: eleven local unionists were named who either had already been trained in the US or were undergoing such training under scholarships said to have amounted to $44,000. At the same time, trade unionists sent on scholarship to the US were each paid "for full-time services in the Trades Union Movement", $250 per month for a period of nine months "with expected extensions". For the unextended nine months alone, this added up to a cool $18,000.

Eight of these scholarships came from the Institute for Free Labor Development, a project launched in 1962 with a quarter of a million US dollars under the Alliance for Progress, the organization which runs interference for Wall Street in Latin America; the launchers had been business tycoon J. Peter Grace, who became first President and Chairman of the Board of Trustees; and George Meany, President of the AFL-CIO, the Institute's Vice-Chairman.

All in all,

> "On the basis of union membership and population of the colony, British Guiana has had the highest proportion of scholarships in Latin America to the Institute of Free Labor Development."[4]

As to other money, one top official in the B.G. TUC and MPCA allegedly said that the ICFTU between 1958 and 1961 had – through its Regional branch ORIT and the Caribbean Labor Congress (CCL) – given local B.G. trade unions some 5,000 B.G. dollars (59c each, US money; about $3,000) plus an additional 8,500 (or about $5,000 US) between October 1961 and May 1962 "to assist the local movement in a special organizational crash program."[5]

These amounts, however, were only partial; there were at least nine "omissions" from the confession, involving well over a million dollars of which the following were typical:[4]

— During 1961, out of a total expenditure of $15,429.02 by the B.G. TUC, about $11,786 came from "overseas sources".

— Officers of B.G. unions had their salaries paid monthly by ICFTU affiliates.

— Unions acquired property, purchased with money advanced by outside, American-controlled organizations.

— Delegations of Guayanese trade unionists were sent abroad to various Labor conferences within the 18 months following the 1961 elections, with all passages and hotel expenses paid for them by the AFL-CIO or ICFTU outfits.

— Some of the heaviest outside financing of the B.G. Labor movement came in April 1963 when a general strike was instigated by these outside agitators against a Government Tax Bill made necessary by the refusal of financial aid by all Western sources. American and ICFTU unions sent in an asserted $125,000 per week for "strike relief and other assistance." The strike lasted eleven weeks and four days, making a total sent in for this purpose alone no less than $1,500,000.

— In addition, motor vehicles, cinema projectors, films, books and office equipment were sent to B.G. unions by US Trade unions.

As to the visits of American union officials, in the 18 months following the 1961 elections, more of them visited the colony than in the 18 preceding years. They organized five "sample courses" for local unionists, in addition to which,

> "Certain of the visiting US trade unionists also attended and participated in meetings of the Executive of the British Guiana Trades Union Council."[4]

When the California magazine RAMPARTS early in 1967 exposed extensive CIA penetration into allegedly progressive student organizations, it also implicated a number of US unions. Victor Reuther, international affairs director of the huge United Automobile Workers Union, commented that

> "there is a lot bigger story in the CIA's financial and other connections with the AFL-CIO than with students."[6]

As if in corroboration, a staid New York daily a few days later carried a story about CIA funds channeled through a New York Foundation to the American Federation of State, County and Municipal Employees (AFL-CIO). How AFSCME used such money to help bring about the downfall of the popularly-supported Jagan government was reported in detail: first, these funds supported the 1963 Georgetown general strike designed to overthrow Jagan by force. The strike in turn successfully caused a racial split between black and East Indian Guyanese along political lines. It also paralyzed the Guyanese economy, paving the way for US domination over the once-British colony. (Nevertheless, as we have seen, in the 1964 elections, Jagan again gained an electoral plurality, bigger than those which had sufficed to keep him in office previously; the British simply booted him out.)

AFSCME was said to have used CIA cash in the following specific ways:

> 1. "to set up in Washington an Inter-American Affairs Branch" of a London-based international confederation of public employees, the Public Service International. This outfit reportedly was administered by "two CIA aides with the knowledge of the union's leadership".

2. These CIA aides, using AFCSME as cover, advised Guyanese unions "how to organize and sustain" the anti-Jagan strike.

3. They provided funds, food and medical supplies to ensure its success.

4. One CIA aide "even served as a member of a bargaining committee from a Guiana dike workers union that negotiated with Jagan".[6]

Nor was this the first or only instance of union betrayal of colonial freedom – even in Guyana. In 1961 at New York City's Commodore Hotel, a secret meeting had taken place between an anti-Communist leader of the British Guiana Trades Union Council and AFL-CIO President George Meany with several other top AFL-CIO officials. This had been mere weeks after the August 1961 elections in which Jagan, despite British – and American – supported maneuvers, had again been voted into office.[7]

The AFL-CIO, either in its own name or via the ICFTU which it had helped found, had

> "channeled $20 million of their members' dues between 1949 and 1965 to support foreign trade unions which follow the US line in foreign policy."[8]

All this outside interference bore fruit in British Guiana in still further elections, held in 1964 under a protested Proportional Representation system imposed by the British. In that election, the PPP – with Jagan still prime minister – won 46% of the vote, increasing its total by 3.3% (the only party to register a gain). Burnham's PNC culled 40%, while d'Aguiar's UF got 14%. Using the PR voting system as excuse, the British thereupon forced Jagan out. A coalition was formed by the PNC and the UF with Burnham as prime minister.

THEN – at long last – the British set May 26, 1966, as the date of "independence" for Guyana. And that is how Guyana's present plight came to be.

The results of Burnham's first year as prime minister were described by Dr. Jagan in an analysis of the Guyana situation. Among other things, Jagan said:

"With the departure of the British, the United States will move into the vacuum created. A new stage of neo colonialism will thus be launched ...

"In its first 12 months in office, the Burnham-d'Aguiar government has strengthened the hold of imperialism ... It is moving also to denationalize the Guyana Electricity Corp., which my government nationalized and has embarked on a program to aid foreign firms at the expense of the people of Guyana. Taxes which my government imposed in 1962 on the wealthy have been abolished or modified drastically – property, gift, turnover, capital gains and prestige advertising taxes. On the other hand, taxes on consumer goods, against which Burnham campaigned . . . are now being imposed . . . on a large variety of items consumed by the working people . . . there would be no need of consumer taxes at all if the capital taxes against the wealthy had not been abolished in 1965."[9]

In this way, the reversion to and maintenance of factual colonialism became assured in British Guiana under the name "independence". It was ensured because Social Democracy had joined hands with "its" Government AND with RACIST union officials of a rival imperialist power, the United States of America. In concert, this unholy alliance had succeeded where no separate maneuvers of anti-Communism alone, racism alone or Social Democracy alone had been able to.

The lesson in this is that, faced with possible colonial liberation, imperialist rivalries and the differing class interests between the ruling class and "its" labor aristocracies fade into insignificance and can be utilized by anti-colonial revolution only if properly evaluated – not if they are expected to operate automatically. The tendency is for the major contradiction to take over at such times.

The British Guiana example was, of course, clear-cut. There are others, more complex; many of them, in Africa. At the same time, it is no news when Social Democracy resorts to anti-Communism. Its application of this ruling class weapon was not even, or ever, confined to colonies: it began in the West and continues there as well:

> ". . . the principal way in which Social Democracy assists the advance of Fascism to power (is) by disorganizing the working class front, by breaking strikes, by denunciation of the class struggle, by preaching legalism and trust in capitalism, by expulsion of all militant elements and splitting of the trade union and working class organizations

> "The war on Communism is placed in the forefront by Social Democracy. The German example has shown to what lengths of direct alliance with the militarist and White Guard Social Democracy will go in order to crush the revolutionary workers. But the slogan of the war on Communism is the slogan of Fascism. Social Democracy and Fascism offer, in effect, rival services to the bourgeoisie for the slaving of Communism."[10]

That was written in 1935. Today – 34 years later – Social Democracy has not yet abandoned (nor will it ever while it lasts) its use of anti-Communism. A recent example was the case of the progressive weekly (then) NATIONAL GUARDIAN, which published a "Report to Readers: Bitter Harvest of anti

Communism", [11] wherein it named itself a victim of red-baiting and "misrepresentation" by NEW AMERICA, "a twice-a-month tabloid newspaper published by the Socialist Party-Social Democratic Federation". This was related to an earlier NATIONAL GUARDIAN report on the connections between the CIA and certain national student unions. NEW AMERICA accused the GUARDIAN of "a McCarthy-like attack on an individual it implies is being a CIA agent . . . without . . . any evidence to back up these charges."[11] Apparently, it hoped in this way to lay the basis for a costly court suit against the progressive weekly. This is just one case among many.

The point is that anti-Communism is and has always been one major stock-in-trade of Social Democracy.

Another is and has always been racism in one form or another:

> "The overwhelming impression from these essays is of the dismal state of the socialist movement almost everywhere today. Largely responsible for this is Western socialists' failure to take the colonial masses' condition into account as a dominant factor in their own social and economic patterns; in fact, Western socialism has continued to be poisoned by racism."[12]

In summary, the linkage between Social Democracy, anti Communism and racism, when the three act in concert, is usually. detrimental to the cause of liberation; it is an inevitable result of the growth of liberation forces, both politically and organizationally. This is not to suggest that the combination is unbeatable. Armed with FACTS and a fact-guided, scientific leadership, only the masses of the exploited of this world are that. What seems to have been missing up to now is the willingness to deal on the Left in the West with – precisely – facts; and especially, about the West itself.

As to why the "romantically-admired" Americans picked up where the despised Hitler left off, we can now answer this question: the US as chieftain of world imperialism, today stands, of all imperialist countries, to lose most if there is any real defection among colonial peoples. With the socialist world as a solid bulwark for these peoples, the US ruling class rightly judges that, unless and until it can destroy that world, its entire empire remains in jeopardy. This has been true ever since 1917. Hence, the huge US military build-up, its all-or-nothing bid to "stop Communism" and its use of every conceivable ally – the labor aristocracy, racism, etc. – in attempting to prevent any new anti-colonial revolution from succeeding.

42. And So What?

The main concern of the foregoing restudy of Social Democracy since 1914 has been to expose and document the existence within the imperialist system of a subsidiary – currently principal – international contradiction: between the working class in the main capitalist countries and peoples in colonial areas.

To perform that exposition and documentation, it was necessary to return to Lenin's Imperialism, the Highest Stage of Capitalism. Based on it, an attempt was made to show that, to a far greater degree than when he first called attention to it, imperialism is an integral system wherein metropolitan areas exercise world hegemony through subjugating, oppressing and super exploiting world hinterlands. In this, its greatest ally has been Social Democracy.

The restudy has revealed what may be considered the central fact of this era: That, in its metropoles, imperialism is able to, and does (except for "pockets") with Social Democracy's help, bring prosperity to its own majority. But it does so ONLY at the expense of constantly worsening conditions for peoples in subjugated world areas like Africa, Asia and Latin America. This has been demonstrated as the general expression of the fact that imperialism is today, as Lenin described it yesterday, still primarily parasitic.

Imperialist parasitism finds particular expression via the growth in metropolitan areas to majority status of a once-tiny labor aristocracy, which Lenin called "the principal social . . . prop of the bourgeoisie". Concomitantly, there has arisen in the world's super-exploited areas a new, completely parasitic elite, which works with the metropolitan labor aristocracy in helping the international ruling class to stave off revolution in colonial areas.

It has been insisted that examination and exposition of the majority status of parasitic labor aristocracies in the West constitute neither "slander of the proletariat" nor denial of its long-run, major contradiction with its home bosses.

If, then, the demonstrated subsidiary contradiction between the Western Labor aristocracy and the subjugated colonial peoples is currently the main one operating on the world scene, genuine revolutionaries have to deal with IT now. How?

There is a choice:

1. The existence of such a contradiction can be denied. This, it has been shown, is how the situation is met by Social Democracy; by the modern revisionists; by self-styled anti-revisionists; and, lately, by the Chinese.

a) Modern revisionist headquarters are in the USSR. Their position, including at present, was set forth in Chapter 21:

"The capitalist world is shaken by class struggles with the working class in their center. Strikes – a school of struggle as Lenin called them – assume wide scope and deal heavy blows at monopolies….

"It is significant that the strike movement is growing fastest in the imperialist states ... and more frequently grew (there) into big political clashes between the working class and state monopoly capitalism ... demonstrating the immense force, staunchness, solidarity and determination (of the working class) and compelling the monopolies to make important concessions."[1]

b) Self-styled anti-revisionists concur:

> "...It is not the white workers in Britain who dominate and exploit the people of African countries; it is the wealthy finance capitalists who, through international concerns like Unilever, exploit not only the people of Nigeria but also the workers of Britain – white and black . . . It is true that the great majority of black people of the world are oppressed by imperialism – but so are the great majority of white people."[2]

c) The Chinese have now joined this segment of opinion:

> "Wages of the working people in the United States are not sufficient to maintain the minimum standard of living. . . The American people are suffering exploitation in all its forms from monopoly capital and are living an extremely hard life. . . . The persecution and exploitation of the working people by the US ruling clique serve only to further awaken the broad masses of the working people. . . A growing number of working people among the whites oppose racial discrimination and support the Black people's struggle against violent repression."[3]

In assessing such positions, it must be remembered that Lenin had predicted that, as revolution approaches, Social Democracy may be expected (whatever its form) to flare up. Never will it die out of itself.

2. The existence of such a contradiction can be faced, attempts being made to deal with it in the interests of real revolution. Happily, growing numbers (though still a tiny minority) in the West are showing in action that they are sick and tired of fairy tales that lull to sleep the world working class in all its sections while its pockets are picked and its throat slit:

a) Among American whites, there is a growing awareness of the vanguard role of the real proletariat, where to find it, what to do about it:

"The most important aspect of (the history and political development of the new left in this country) for white radicals to grasp and grasp firmly is the VANGUARD ROLE played by oppressed peoples in general and the most oppressed sectors of the international working class in particular.

"Take a look at our own history. At almost every turning point in our development from a left-liberal movement to an anti-imperialist and anti-capitalist movement, the decisive factor has been the exemplary action and leadership of the black liberation movement and, although indirectly, the example of the Cubans and the Vietnamese."[4]

b) In London, a few honest Leftists are groping toward the same position:

"Can we expect a class to reject the fruits of exploitation simply on theoretical or moral grounds? A class, for example, schooled in British bourgeois morality, steeped in bourgeois attitudes that seem essential to survival as individuals in a bourgeois society?

"On the other hand, can we fail to oppose exploitation, of any kind, whoever benefits from it?

"Those of us who don't take a clear-cut line on these questions will turn into pretty dubious revolutionaries. We'll probably find it convenient to drop the slogan about US-headed imperialism as the main enemy, since US imperialism is the main prop helping us to maintain exploitation. Then we can concentrate on a reformist-type struggle for a larger share in the loot (doomed to failure because the other side holds the strings that manipulate the economy). Or we might resort to a kind of jingoistic anti-Americanism: British capitalism is best!

"It doesn't seem that a truthful line is going to win us easy popularity. But how can we usefully be anything but truthful? Otherwise, we put the working class into the power of confidence tricksters.

"In the long term, a class that allies itself with the exploiters will go down with the exploiters . . . for example . . . the South African white working class.

"By making the situation crystal clear, by pointing to the inevitable downfall of the exploiters, as emphasized by every blow struck by the Liberation forces in Vietnam – only thus can we help the British working class to extricate itself from the actual, if passive, alliance with the exploiters."[5]

There are other examples, such as "Communist ORIENTATION" in Denmark.

As between these two choices, this text has taken its stand with the second: to face the real situation and work from there.

This approach requires first that the truth be documented. For, without the facts, a revolution has nowhere to go: the only hook on which to hang theory so the masses can grasp it is on WHAT THEY KNOW BY EXPERIENCE. Currently, however, the tendency is to try to use other's conditions and fit them into one's own situation. This has led revolution to fail!

This text has merely started the work of marshalling facts; it is hoped that the job will be picked up and carried on. Truth, however, must be dug for:

— What sums are actually involved in colonial robbery?

— What is the metropolitan-colonial wages discrepancy worth, for example, to the bourgeoisie? To the Western labor aristocracy?

— What is the essential – i.e., socially-necessary – cost of producing labor-power today, world-wise? What real difference, if any, exists due to geography (for instance, the relative ease of cutting down a tree as against pushing an automated button)?

— What factors inflate the prices of metropolitan commodities, including labor-power? Which constitute cheating when the ruling class buys colonially-produced goods, including colonial labor-power?

— What are other facts today about colonialism? Relations must be spelled out between "old" and "neo" ways whereby imperialism gathers its harvest; the complete size of that harvest; its future.

— Are there new facts today about imperialism? Certain modern studies in this field have been cited. (See Section B., Chapter 10, page 98, Above). But terms used in some quarters, like "neo-imperialism" or "neo-capitalism", are to be decried. If a man ages, and so alters his appearance with wrinkles, lost hair and a stoop in walking, has he ceased to be the man we've known all along? Is he now a "neo-man"?

These are a few questions in need of answers – answers still hidden under the bourgeoisie's manner of selecting its data.

At the same time, in thus assessing the world situation, account must be taken of ALL factors. Above all, the role of RACISM will have to be rescued from criminal neglect: it will have to be studied and documented so as to expose it as the material force it actually is in today's world. Until this is done, anti-Communism cannot be conquered; and so, world revolution will remain an unfinished task. To this truth, History stands witness!

If the racism growing in the world's cities today proves anything, it proves that workers (who, there, are mainly a labor aristocracy) know EXACTLY where the MAIN conflict will be joined. And the labor aristocracy thus gives ample warning of the side on which it intends to fight.

Having documented, or while documenting, the background FACTS with which revolution must deal, it is also necessary to work out the practical tasks which follow from the facts:

—First, to carry out any tasks, an orientation is required.

—Second, work started by men like Harry Magdoff in New York, studying imperialism in detail, must be continued. Care must be taken to ensure that, as orientation, it serves always only the primacy of anti-colonial struggle! This will influence what facts are gathered and how they are presented.

For example, it is imperative to refute factually the current Chinese contention that "US imperialism is falling apart". On the contrary. Uncle Sam can still fall back on 2,000 million human beings: all Latin America (except perhaps Cuba); all Africa; the Caribbean; Western Europe; and a good hunk of Asia – and to all these for the same purpose he is now adding more and more areas of Eastern Europe. Out of these at present, he squeezes his well-being. As long as such a condition persists, imperialism can – and will – continue to solve its inner and growing contradictions at the expense of deepening misery for colonial peoples. THEY MUST REMOVE THEMSELVES FROM IMPERIALISM'S REACH!

—Third, it is urgent that "the working class in the main capitalist countries" be widely exposed as NOT "the proletariat" of the world (acknowledging its inevitable but minority poverty pockets), but at present as a world labor aristocracy. Crystal clarity is needed about its actual political stance and its real material conditions. The object is to expose the FACT that today IT HAS NO CURRENT INCENTIVE TO MAKE REVOLUTION.

As this text has shown, the Western labor aristocracy in its overwhelming majority lives off the backs of colonial peoples. In this way, an antagonism, clearly demonstrated, has been created by imperialism between metropolitan workers and those in colonies. Today, it is this antagonism which, unfortunately, decides the way events turn out. The Western worker, therefore, is NOT NOW an ALLY of revolution. At THIS historical moment, he is a reserve of imperialism.

World revolutionary attention must be focused on this subsidiary contradiction till it can be utilized in moving the situation forward to new levels. Here, above all, the purpose must be to help pin down and kill the myth of "the poverty-stricken, revolution-oriented Western worker". The "Sweetness and Light" approach to revolution must be smashed as well.

— Fourth, for this purpose, it is necessary further to study the conditions which actually lead to revolution. A main one of them will be found to be the ideological and material need for a vanguard party: where and how is a vanguard party built? Does one exist today?

Material in the text has strongly suggested that it does not. A vanguard party cannot and will not be, and has not yet been, built in the West because all such attempts can be based only on current enemies of revolution. In France during May 1968 this inevitable absence of a vanguard party in the world's cities clearly and irrefutably revealed that struggles, no matter how violent, undertaken without such a party result – and CAN result – ONLY in a reformist outcome. In general, the world labor aristocracy demonstrably works against its so-called class ally in colonies because, today far more than in Lenin's time, the "working class in the main capitalist countries" is handed ITS SHARE of systemic sustenance out of those same 2,000 million human beings whom the ruling class brutally super exploits. THESE PEOPLE MUST BE REMOVED ALSO FROM THE LABOR ARISTOCRACY'S REACH!

—Fifth, if, as has been shown, imperialism's supply lines remain intact (neo-colonialism), and its mercenaries (the Western labor aristocracy) are still under its control, then it becomes necessary somehow to disrupt those supply lines; to throw confusion and doubt into the ranks of the mercenaries; but to win over any tiny minority among them who, despite years of receiving stolen goods, are still honest enough to recognize truth when they hear it.

—Finally, A VANGUARD PARTY MUST BE BUILT AMONG THE VANGUARD. As Lin Piao showed, that vanguard today resides in the world's hinterlands. But, today, aside from China (and even that becomes doubtful in the light of its current line about how "excellent" the world situation is for revolution), it would appear that NO VANGUARD PARTY EXISTS. Here is a formidable task, indeed!

Since, moreover, the vanguard from which such a party must be forged is made up of people from or in colonies, there is also a minority reserve of revolution inside the West, because of increasing numbers of colonial migrants there. Activity of a revolutionary nature has already begun emanating from them in some places, like the US

The world proletariat ALSO has 2,000 million human beings on which to rely for revolution. Let this fact, too, be considered in all decisions on tactics; LET IT NEVER BE FORGOTTEN!

A question confronting revolutionaries today is this: is it too late now to reverse the anti-revolutionary trend in the world Left? NEVER! United, the working class is stronger than the politically depraved, moribund ruling class.

We have been told that, if this book did not call for UNITY OF THE WORKING CLASS, it would be "no good". Well, let's set the record straight on this:

—There is NO "unity" if there is no vanguard party to steel people ideologically and guide the struggle to victory!

— It is NOT "unity" to hold Western workers up as "leaders of world revolution" by denying that they live off colonial peoples.

— Nor is it "unity" to appoint Western workers, with their stolen Good Life, as "revolutionary leaders" just because here and there they fight tenaciously for a bigger share in colonial loot. The struggle over stolen swag is NOT class struggle; just because one is a participant in it, that does NOT constitute credentials for leadership of revolution.

UNITY, to be viable, can be based ONLY on principle. Principle can subsist ONLY on FACT. This book is a small first step toward such – honest, real – working class unity because it calls for, and documents the sanity behind, HEGEMONY OF OPPRESSED AND SUPER-EXPLOITED PEOPLES IN MAKING REVOLUTION. It is primarily a call for FACTS as the METHOD eventually to achieve that UNITY in the WORLD WORKING CLASS which history requires.

— Colonial workers! You are the world's overwhelming majority! The metropoles cannot exist without you. BUT YOU CAN EXIST WITHOUT THEM! TAKE YOUR DESTINY INTO YOUR OWN HANDS! DO NOT EXPECT HELP WHERE NONE MAY BE EXPECTED! INSCRIBE ON YOUR BANNERS THE SOBER, COSTLY BUT EFFECTIVE WATCHWORD: Self-Reliance! ! !

This – and this alone – will eventually bring unity to the world working class, thus enabling world revolution at last to succeed! Meantime, the rest of us must find ways effectively to support colonial liberation struggles!

REFERENCE NOTES

Labor Aristocracy

Reference Notes

Introduction

1. V. I. Lenin, Chapter VIII, "The Parasitism and Decay of Capitalism," Imperialism, the Highest Stage of Capitalism (Moscow. Foreign Languages Publishing House. First published 1916) and "Preface to the French and German editions," 1921. (Hereinafter referred to as Imperialism.)

2. Lenin, Imperialism.

3. Lenin, Imperialism, in "Preface to the French and German editions."

4. Lenin, Imperialism.

5. Polemic on a General Line for the World Communist Movement (Peking. Foreign Languages Press. 1963), p. 6.

Chapter 1

1. London TIMES, April 22, 1968. Lead editorial.

2. Roy Perrott and David Haworth, "Fears behind White Workers' Backlash," London OBSERVER, April 28, 1968.

3. Ibid.

4. Ibid.

5. Ibid.

6. Ibid.

7. Ibid.

8. Ibid.

9. Mao Tse-tung, "On the Correct Handling of Contradictions among the People." Reprinted in PEKING REVIEW, June 23, 1967.

10. A proposal concerning the General Line of the International Communist Movement, Central Committee, Chinese Communist Party, letter in reply to one from Central Committee, Soviet Communist Party on March 30, 1963 (Peking. Foreign Languages Press. June 14, 1963), p. 6.

11. Ibid.

12. Ibid., pp. 12-13.

13. Ibid., p. 13.

14. Ibid., p. 14.

Chapter 2

1. R. Palme Dutt, Fascism and Social Revolution, (New York; International Publishers. 1935). (Hereinafter referred to as Fascism.)

2. Palmiro Togliatti, Social Democracy and the Colonial Question, speech before the Sixth Congress of the Communist International (Comintern) in 1928. Reprinted in AFRICA LATIN AMERICA ASIA REVOLUTION, January 1964. English edition (Paris, France). (Hereinafter referred to as Colonial Question.)

3. Lenin, Imperialism, 'Preface to the French and German editions," 1921.

4. Michael Kidron, Western Capitalism since the War (Weidenfeld and Nicolson. 1968), pp. 117 ff.

5. Lenin, The Proletarian Revolution and Renegade Kautsky. Selected Works, Vol. 7 (London; Lawrence and Wishart), p. 173.

6. Lenin, Bourgeois Democracy and Proletarian Revolution, ibid., p. 229.

Chapter 3

1. Lenin, Imperialism, "Preface to the French and German editions," p. 11.

2. Ibid., pp. 15, 16 and 17.

3. Lenin, Imperialism, Chapter VIII, "The Parasitism and Decay of Capitalism," pp. 171-2.

4. Ibid., p. 173.

5. Ibid., p. 174.

6. Ibid., p. 175.

7. Ibid., p. 178.

8. Ibid., pp. 175, 176.

9. Ibid., p. 176.

10. Ibid., p. 179.

11. Ibid., p. 181.

12. Ibid., pp. 181-2.

13. Ibid., p. 182.

14. Ibid., p. 184.

15. Ibid., p. 185.

Chapter 4

1. Jack Woddis, "Africa and Mr. Wilson's Government," AFRICAN REVIEW, May 1965 (Ghana).

2. J. R. Campbell, "The Incomes Policy of the Labour Government," PROBLEMS OF PEACE AND SOCIALISM, May, 1965 (Prague).

Chapter 5

1. Togliatti, op. cit., passim.

2. Victor Perlo, Militarism and Industry," (Marzani & Munsell), p. 70.

3. Pierre Jalde, The Pillage of the Third World (English translation, Monthly Review. 1968), pp. 2-3. (Hereinafter referred to as Pillage.)

Chapter 6

1. George Dimitroff, The United Front against Fascism (New York. International Publishers. 1937).

2. Dimitroff, op. cit., Section, "The Role of Social Democracyand Its Attitude toward the United Front of the Proletariat."

3. Palme Dutt, Fascism, pp. 79 ff.

Chapter 7

1. Palme Dutt, Fascism, p. 155.

2. Ibid., p. 79.

3. Lenin, Imperialism, "Preface to the French and German editions." Requoted.

4. Lenin, "Social Democracy and the Split in the Working Class," Address to Stuttgart Congress, December 1916. (Hereinafter referred to as Stuttgart Address.)

5. British TUC, The ABC of TUC, 1 966, pp. 10, 11, 23 and 24. Cited in Kidron, op. cit. Also see Chapter II, Reference Note 4.

Chapter 8

1. Dr. Wong Lin Ken, "Democratic Socialism, Marxism and the Intellectual Left," 1USY SURVEY (official organ, International Union of Socialist Youth), March 1965.

2. Ibid.

3. Ibid.

4. O. Timashkova, "Sweden Today," INTERNATIONAL AFFAIRS (Moscow), No. 2 (February), 1963.

5. London TIMES, October 18, 1966.

6. WORLD ALMANAC, 1960 (New York WORLD TELEGRAM).

7. Ibid.

8. Lenin, Imperialism, Chapter VI, p. 138.

9. Kidron, op. cit., p. 84.

10. COMMUNIST ORIENTATION (Copenhagen, Denmark). English edition. Vol. 5, No. 18, October 2, 1968, pp. 10 and 11. (Hereinafter referred to as C.O.)

Chapter 9

1. Lenin, Imperialism, Chapter VIII, "The Parasitism and Decay of Capitalism."

2. Howard Selsam, Socialism and Ethics (International Publishers. 1943. Second edition, 1945), pp. 33-34.

3. Survey of Current Business (monthly), April 1, 1962 (Office of Business Economics of the U.S. Department of Commerce), cited in Labor Fact Book No. 16 (New York. Labor Research Association), (annual), pp. 16, 21 ff.

4. Chapter II, Footnote 2.

5. Victor Perlo, op. cit., p. 63.

6. Harry Magdoff, "Economic Aspects of Imperialism." Lecture, September 11, 1966, at Socialist Scholars' Conference, New York. Reprint, MONTHLY REVIEW, November 1966, p. 14.

7. Survey of Current Business, May 1965, "Foreign Trade of the United States."

8. Ibid., "Foreign Transactions in the National Income Account," p. 6.

9. Victor Perlo, op. cit., p. 64.

10. Jerome Pakula, first of two featured articles about U.S. balance of payment deficits, NATIONAL GUARDIAN, June 25, 1966.

11. NEWSWEEK, August 30, 1965, p. 47.

12. Survey of Current Business, June 1965, p. 12. U.S. Statistical Abstract, 1961, p. 865 (and see Footnote, p. 70, text).

13. Paul A. Baran and Paul M. Sweezy, Monopoly Capital, Chapter 4 (Monthly Review Press. 1966), p. 105.

14. Ibid., pp. 105, 106.

15. Ibid., p. 107.

16. Ibid., p. 108.

Chapter 10

1. Magdoff, op. cit.

2. Leland Hazard (Vice-President of the Pittsburgh Plate Glass Co.),"What Economists Don't Know about Wages," HARVARD BUSINESS REVIEW, January-February 1957, p. 56. (Cited in Baran & Sweezy, op. cit., p. 33.)

3. Perlo, op. cit., p. 65.

4. FORTUNE Magazine, October 1956 (cited in Perlo, op. Cit., p.67).

5. David Michaels, "The Growing Financial Crisis in the Capitalist World," MONTHLY REVIEW, December 1966, p. 12.

6. Magdoff, op. cit., p. 20.

7. Ibid., p. 18.

8. Perlo, op. cit.

9. Magdoff, op. cit., p. 22.

10. Ibid., passim.

11. Baran and Sweezy, op. cit., p. 214.

12. Kidron, op. cit., pp. 48 et passim.

Chapter 11

1. Labor Fact Book No. 16, p. 16. U.S. Statistical Abstract, 1966, Table, p. 327 and see Footnote, p. 70, text).

2. Compiled from information in Billionaire Corporations, Their Growth and Power (New York. Labor Research Association. 1954), pp. 7-9 passim.

3. Dr. Boguslaw Jazinski (lecturer, Winneba Ideological Institute, Ghana, during Nkrumah regime), "Why Developing Countries Cannot Go Capitalist Way," first of two articles, THE SPARK (Accra), June 11, 1965.

4. Sekou Touré, Guinean Revolution & Social Progress, p. 116.

5. Jalfie, op. cit., Table III, p. 12.

6. Magdoff, op. cit., p. 28.

7. Fenner Brockway, "Basis of Imperialism is Economic Exploitation," GHANAIAN TIMES (Accra, Ghana), November 7, 1964.

8. Time Essay: "The Technology Gap," TIME Magazine, January 13, 1967.

9. K. Nkrumah, Neo-Colonialism , the Last Stage of Imperialism (Nelson. 1965).

10. Magdoff, op. cit., p. 41.

11. WORLD CONSTRUCTION, July 1967.

12. Baran and Sweezy, op. cit.

Chapter 12

1. Magdoff, op. cit.

2. Ibid., passim.

3. Time Essay: "The Technology Gap," TIME Magazine, January 13, 1967.

4. Nkrumah, op. cit., p. 42.

5. Magdoff, op. cit., p. 39.

6. Nkrumah, ibid., p. 44.

7. "The Capitalist Economy in 1963," Accra EVENING NEWS,November 6, 1964. (A reprint. Source not given.)

8. VOICE OF AFRICA, May-June, 1964 (Accra, Ghana).

9. Truman Materials Policy Commission, "Resources for Freedom," cited in Magdoff, op. cit., pp. 17 ff.

10. Nkrumah, ibid., pp. 84 ff.

11. Ibid., p. 85.

12. Ibid., p. 43.

13. VOICE OF AFRICA, loc. Cit.

Chapter 13

1. Accra EVENING NEWS, November 6, 1964, loc. cit.

2. MONTHLY REVIEW, October 1966, p. 4.

3. Lenin, Marxism and Revisionism, in Against Revisionism, pp. 117-118.

4. Baran and Sweezy, op. cit., p. 178.

5. MONTHLY REVIEW, December 1966. Leading editorial.

Chapter 14

1. Dimitroff, op. cit.

2. Nkrumah, Speech at the Cairo Conference of Non-Aligned Nations, September 1964.

3. Peter Kai, "West Germany: An 'integrated' Working Class Movement," in AFRICA-LATIN AMERICA-ASIA REVOLUTION. English edition (Paris, France).

4. Baran and Sweezy, op. cit., pp. 192 193.

Chapter 15

1. Lenin, Imperialism and the Split in the Socialist Movement, SBORNIK SOCIAL-DEMOKRATA, No. 2, December 1916.

2. Lenin, Imperialism, Chapter VII.

3. U.S. Statistical Abstract, 1961, Table, p. 209.

4. Baran and Sweezy, op. cit., p. 115.

5. Ibid., p. 138.

6. Time Essay: "Union Labor: Less Militant, More Affluent," TIME Magazine, September 17, 1965, p. 21.

7. C. Wright Mills, "The New Middle Class," White Collar (Oxford University Press. 1951. Paperback), p. 71.

8. Ibid., p. 65.

8a. Ibid., pp. 113, 118, 129.

9. "The Disappearance of the Working Class," THUNDER (official theoretical monthly organ of People's Progressive Party (PPP) in Guyana), June 1967.

10. Mills, op. cit., p. 63.

11. Ibid., Chapter 4, Section on "Industrial Mechanics." pp. 65 ff.

12. U.S. Statistical Abstract, 1966, p. 2(>i>.

13. Ibid., p. 216.

14. Baran and Sweezy, op. cit., p. 246.

15. U.S. Statistical Abstract, 1966, Table, p. 218.

16. Ibid., Table Heading, p. 218.

17. TIME Magazine, November 18, 1966, p. 52.

18. U.S. Statistical Abstract, 1966, p. 311.

Chapter 16

1. Baran and Sweezy, op. cit., pp. 77-78.

2. Karl Marx, Wages, Price and Profit (Moscow. Foreign Languages Publishing House, n.d.), pp. 73 ff.

3. Marx, Wage Labor and Capital (Moscow. Foreign Languages Publishing House, n.d..), pp. 56 ff.

4. Baran and Sweezy, op. cit., Chapter 7, "The Absorption of Surplus: Militarism and Imperialism," p. 178.

5. Marx, Wage Labor and Capital, pp. 40 ff.

6. Horowitz, review of Monopoly Capital by Baran and Sweezy, MONTHLY REVIEW, January 1967.

6a. U.S. Statistical Abstract, 1961, p. 26.

6b. Ibid., p. 28. 20,490,000 of U.S. population were non white, including Negroes.

7. "What the Negro Has — and Has Not — Gained," TIME Magazine, October 28, 1966.

7a. U.S. Statistical Abstract, 1961, p. 316.

8. Mao Tse-tung, On Contradiction (August 1937). Selected Works, Vol. I, p. 335. In his discussion On the Chungking Negotiations (October 1945), Selected Works, Vol. IV, pp. 59-60, Mao makes some remarks so pertinent to this

discussion that, at the risk of offending some of our readers, we quote herewith virtually their entirety: "We should carry on constant propaganda among the people on the facts of world progress and the bright future ahead so that they will build their confidence in victory. At the same time, we must tell the people ... That there will be twists and turns in our road... The Seventh Congress of our Party ... preferred to assume there would be more difficulties rather than less. Some comrades do not like to think much about difficulties. But difficulties are facts; we must recognize as many difficulties as there are and should not adopt a 'policy of non-recognition'. We must recognize difficulties, analyse them and combat them. There are no straight roads in the world; we must be prepared to follow a road which twists and turns and not try to get things on the cheap. It must not be imagined that one fine morning all the reactionaries will go down on their knees of their own accord."

9. Baran and Sweezy, op. cit., Footnote 4, above.

10. Andre Gunder Frank, "The Development of Underdevelopment," MONTHLY REVIEW, September 1966, p. 20. Frank was then Visiting Professor in Economics and History at Sir George University in Montreal, Canada.

Chapter 17

1. Sekou Touré, op. cit., p. 116.

2. U.S. Statistical Abstract, 1961, p. 921. ibid., 1964, pp. 50, 51.

3. J. H. O'Dell, "The Southern Power Structure," FREEDOMWAYS, First Quarter, 1964. (Reference covers entire paragraph.)

4. "What the Negro Has - and Has Not - Gained," TIME Magazine, October 28, 1966.

5. U.S. Statistical Abstract, 1961, p. 31.

6. Ibid., pp. 56, 57. ibid., 1964, pp. 55, 57.

7. Baran and Sweezy, op. cit., Chapter 9, "Monopoly Capital and Race Relations."

8. Ibid., p. 258.

9. Ibid., p. 257.

10. Ibid., p. 258.

11. U.S. Statistical Abstract, 1964, p. 300. U. N. Statistical Yearbook, 1966, p. 531.

12. Marx, Wages, Price and Profit, pp. 88 ff.

Chapter 18

1. Lenin, Stuttgart Address, December 1916.

2. Palme Dutt, op. cit., sub-section on "Parliamentary Democracies," p. 78.

3. Palme Dutt, "British Labour and Africa," AFRICAN COMMUNIST (official quarterly, South African Communist Party), First Quarter, 1966.

4. Lenin, Stuttgart Address.

5. Ibid.

6. Lenin, Speech at the Second Congress of the Comintern, 1920.Collected Works, Vol. 31 (Moscow), pp. 230-231. Cited in C.O., Vol. 5, No. 19, October 17, 1968. English edition (Copenhagen, Denmark).

7. Lenin, Imperialism and the Split in Socialism (December 1916), BOLSHEVIK Magazine (Moscow), No. 1, 1949.

8. Lenin, Imperialism, 'Preface to the French and German editions.

9. Ibid., Chapter VIII, "The Parasitism and Decay of Capitalism."

10. U.S. Statistical Abstract, 1961, pp. 347, 360.

11. Ibid., pp. 349, 360.

12. Ibid., pp. 10, 307.

13. Ibid., p. 203. Labor Fact Book No. 15, pp. 78 ff.

14. "The New Militancy of Labor," NEWSWEEK, September 26, 1966.

15. Lenin, Stuttgart Address.

16. U.S. Statistical Abstract, 1961, pp. 483, 639.

17. Kidron, op. cit., p. 84.

18. U.S. Statistical Abstract, 1966, pp. 210-211.

19. Ibid., 1961, pp. 42-44.

20. Ibid., from data reported to U.S. Bureau of Census for its "Census of Religious Bodies, 1955 to 1959."

21. TIME, January 14, 1966. Small item under Religion.

22. U.S. Statistical Abstract, 1961, pp. 42-44.

Chapter 19

5. Historical Statistics of the United States, Colonial Times to 19 57, pp. 165, 186. U.S. Statistical Abstract, 1961, pp. 85, 317.

5. Ibid., 1964, pp. 86, 338.

5. Ibid., 1967, pp. 333, 650.

6. Leiter by Elizabeth Briesberg, a "student in California," SANITY, June 1965 (organ of pacifist CND in England).

7. Baran and Sweezy, op. cit., Chapter 7, "Militarism and Monopoly."

8. NATIONAL GUARDIAN (New York), July 30, 1966.

Chapter 20

1. U.S. Statistical Abstract, 1961, p. 457.

1. Ibid., 1966, p. 466.

1. Ibid., 1967, p. 465. Survey of Current Business, October 1965, p. S-17.

1. Ibid., November 1968, pp. S-l, S-17.

2. U.S. Statistical Abstract, 1961, pp. 12, 196, 457, 516, 547, 558, 560.

3. Ibid., pp. 821, 830.

3. Ibid., 1964, p. 811.

3. Ibid., 1967, pp. 565, 729.

4. Baran and Sweezy, op. cit., footnote, p. 245.

5. U.S. Statistical Abstract, 1961, pp. 821, 830.

5. Ibid., 1964, pp. 811, 820, 826.

5. Ibid., 1967, pp. 776, 783, 784.

6. Survey of Current Business, November 1968, p. S-ll.

6a. Time Essay: "Union Labor: Less Militant, More Affluent," TIME Magazine, September 17, 1965.

7. "The New Militancy of Labor," NEWSWEEK, September 26, 1966. Section on Automation.

8. "The Perils of Prosperity,? TIME, April 9, 1965. Under "Labor" in Section on "U.S. Business."

9. U.S. Statistical Abstract, 1961, pp. 303, 329.

9. Ibid., 1964, p. 326.

9. Ibid., 1967, pp. 324, 349. Survey of Current Business, November 1968, pp. S-2, S-9.

10. Horowitz, op. cit., see Chapter XVI, Reference Note 6.

11. "U.S. Labor Is Being Conned," NATIONAL GUARDIAN, October 22, 1966.

12. VIETNAM COURIER, January 30, 1967. Discussion of President Johnson's State of the Union Message to the U.S. Congress, same month.

13. TIME, November 11, 1966. Section on "World Business: Western Europe," first part; sub-title: "The Wages of Prosperity."

14. Sekou Touré, Guinean Revolution and Social Progress, pp. 172, 173.

Chapter 21

1. U.S. Statistical Abstract, 1961, p. 347.

2. C. Wright Mills, op. cit., pp. 55, 56, 57.

3. M. Ivanov, "The Strike Movement in the Capitalist Countries,"a reply to readers' questions, INTERNATIONAL AFFAIRS (Moscow), May 1965.

4. KOREA TODAY, May 1964 (Pyongyang. Foreign Languages Publishing House), pp. 5, 6.

5. Labor Fact Book No. 8, p. 152. ibid., No. 16, p. 88. U.S. Statistical Abstract, 1961, pp. 230-231.

5. Ibid., 1964, p. 249.

5. Ibid., 1966, p. 247.

5. Ibid., 1967, pp. 5, 221, 249.

6. "The Perils of Prosperity," TIME Magazine, April 9, 1965. Under "Labor" in Section on "U.S. Business."

7. "The New Militancy of Labor," NEWSWEEK, September 26, 1966. Section on Automation.

8. U.S. Statistical Abstract, 1966, p. 246 (compares 1962 and 1964).

9. Karl Marx and Friedrich Engels, Selected Correspondence, (Moscow. 1965), 'p. 320. Cited in C.O., Vol. 5, No. 22, December 10, 1968. English edition (Copenhagen, Denmark).

10. C.O., December 10, 1968, pp. 3, 4.

11. Lenin, Our Immediate Task, 1899. Collected Works (Moscow), Vol. 4, p. 215. Cited in same issue, C.O.

12. C.O., same issue, p. 4.

13. Lenin, op. cit., "further on." (See C.O., same issue.)

14. C.O., same issue, p. 5.

15. Lenin, The Tasks of the Third International, in On Britain (Moscow), pp. 413-414. Cited in same issue, C.O.

16. C.O., same issue, p. 5.

17. Baran and Sweezy, op. cit., pp. 274, 277.

18. Frank Huscroft, "What is Economism?" THE MARXIST (London), Spring 1968.

Chapter 22

1. USSR Embassy Bulletin (Accra, Ghana), May 10, 1964.

2. Simone de Beauvoir, Force of Circumstances, pp. 338, 339, 366.

3. Adam Schesch, "Vietnam: victim of power politics," GUARDIAN (New York), February 10, 1968.

4. Jack Woddis, "Africa and Mr. Wilson's Government," AFRICAN REVIEW, May 1965 (Ghana).

5. Palme Dutt, "British Labour and Africa," AFRICAN COMMUNIST, First Quarter, 1966.

6. All-African Trade Union Federation (AATUF), "ICFTU — Subversion in Africa: THE FACTS," October 1965, p. 3.

7. Baran and Sweezy, op. cit., p. 210.

8. MONTHLY REVIEW, Vol. 15, No. 12, April 1964, p. 652.

9. AATUF, op. cit., p. 2.

10. Ibid.

11. TIME Magazine, September 17, 1965, loc. cit.

12. VIETNAM COURIER, June 30, 1967.

13. U.S. Statistical Abstract, 1967, p. 341.

14. Ibid., pp. 392-393.

15. Ibid., p. 324.

16. Marx, Wage Labor and Capital, pp. 56 ff.

Chapter 23

1. U.S. Statistical Abstract, 1966, p. 36.

1. Ibid., 1961, p. 38.

2. Labor Fact Book No. 16, p. 21.

3. Lenin, A Caricature of Marxism and 'Imperialist Economism', section on 'Monism and Dualism' in Against Revisionism, pp. 307-308.

4. KOREA INFORMATION BULLETIN, February 1964, (Pyongyang. Foreign Languages Publishing House), p. 33.

5. Pat Sloan, "Apartheid is only a particular case in imperialism," ACCRA EVENING NEWS (Ghana), December 2, 19G4.

6. Robert L. Allen, "Vietnamese experience needed here," NATIONAL GUARDIAN, October 28, 1967.

7. U.S. Statistical Abstract, 1967, p. 3.

8. Ibid., p. 36.

9. Ibid., p. 5.

Chapter 24

1. Time Essay: "Union Labor: Less Militant, More Affluent," TIME Magazine, September 17, 1965.

2. "Two Lines (5)," C.O., Vol. 6, No. 1, p. 6, January 14, 1969. English edition (Copenhagen, Denmark).

3. Marx, Wage Labor and Capital, pp. 64 ff.

4. Mao Tse-tung, Tribute to Norman Bethune (Peking. Foreign Languages Press). Footnote, J. V. Stalin, Foundations of Leninism.

5. Lenin, A Caricature of Marxism, August to October 1916, in Against Revisionism (Moscow. Foreign Languages Publishing House. 1959), p. 311.

6. Ibid., in ibid., p. 312.

Chapter 25

1. Togliatti, op. cit.

2. "Down with Colonialism," a reprint of the British CommunistParty's policy statement for the 1964 elections in England, GHANAIAN TIMES, January 31, 1964.

3. Ibid.

4. Lenin, Stuttgart Address.

Chapter 26

1. Togliatti, op., cit.

2. Fuad Nasser and Aziz Al-Hajj, "The National Movement and the World Revolutionary Process," abridged text, NEWS FROM THE SOVIET UNION (Embassy Bulletin), May 10, 1964, p. 3 (Accra, Ghana).

3. Jack Woddis, Africa - The Roots of Revolt," p. 186.

4. U.S. Statistical Abstract, 1961, p. 220.

Chapter 27

1. N. Kaloudis, "Trade Union Unity is the Key to Unity in theGreek Working Class," PEACE, FREEDOM AND SOCIALISM, March 1964 (Prague).

2. Lester Morris, "The Communists and the National Question: National and Democratic Revolution in French Canada,"

2. Ibid., September 1964.

3. Andre Gunder Frank, op. cit., Part V.

4. "Let Us Fight Japanese Imperialism," PYONGYANG TIMES, Supplement, January 13, 1966.

5. Philip G. Altbach, "The Suicide of the Indian Left," PEACE NEWS (London), August 20, 1965.

Chapter 28

1. Lenin, Stuttgart Address, December 1916, cited.

2. Philip S. Foner, The History of the Labor Move ment in the United States (New York. International Publishers. 1947).

3. Ibid., Vol. I, pp. 448-449, 450.

4. Ibid., p. 395.

5. Marx, "The Future Results of British Rule in India," July 22, 1853. From the New York DAILY TRIBUNE, August 8, 1853. In Karl Marx and Friedrich Engels, On Colonialism, (Moscow. Foreign Languages Publishing House, second impression. n.d.), p. 88.

6. Foner, op. cit., Vol. I, p. 278.

7. Ibid., p. 268.

8. Ibid., p. 281.

9. Ibid., p. 285.

10. Ibid., p. 398.

11. Ibid., p. 394.

12. Ibid., p. 394.

13. Ibid., p. 270.

14. Ibid., p. 271.

15. Ibid., p. 276.

16. Ibid., p. 281.

17. Ibid., p. 401.

18. Ibid., p. 401.

19. Ibid., pp. 401-402.

20. Ibid., p. 399.

21. ibid.. p. 399.

22. Ibid., p. 400.

23. Ibid., Vol. II, p. 196.

24. Ibid., p. 196.

25. Ibid., p. 196.

26. Ibid., p. 204.

27. Ibid., Vol. Ill, p. 238

28. Ibid., p. 239.

29. Ibid., p. 240.

30. Ibid., p. 240.

31. Ibid., p. 254.

32. Ibid., pp. 254-255.

Chapter 29

1. Andre Gunder Frank, op. cit.

2. African Socialism and Its Application to Planning in Kenya (Nairobi, Kenya. Office of Economic Planning and Development, c. 1964). Foreword by Jomo Kenyatta.

3. Kwesi Armah, Africa's Golden Road (London. 1965).

4. Tony Cliff, reviewing a book on The Sino-Soviet Rift, PEACE NEWS (London), October 26, 1964.

5. Lee Kuan Yew, "Why Has Asian Socialism Failed?" S.I.I., SOCIALIST INTERNATIONAL INFORMATION, Vol. V, No. 14-15, July 10, 1965. Extracts from opening address at the Bombay Conference of Young Asian Socialist Leaders, May 6 to 9, 1965.

Chapter 30

1. Togliatti, op. cit.

2. Sekou Tourfi, op. cit., p. 109.

3. Ibid., p. 176.

4. Togliatti, op. cit.

Chapter31

1. Z. Nkosi, "Bending the Colour Bar," AFRICAN COMMUNIST, Third Quarter, 1966.

Chapter 32

1. Lenin, Imperialism, "Preface to the French and German editions.

2. Z. Nkosi, loc. cit., combining two of his tables.

3. Quoted in Lorraine Hansberry, A Matter of Color, p. 68.

Chapter 33

1. Time Essay: "In Defense of Waste," TIME Magazine, November 18, 1966.

2. H. M. Basner, "Does Africa Need Foreign Aid?" Public lecture, March 14, 1965 (Kumasi, Ghana). Basner is a South African white socialist lawyer and quondam columnist for the pro-Nkrumah Ghanaian TIMES, in which this lecture was reprinted shortly after its delivery.

3. All-African Trade Union Federation (AATUF), "ICFTU - Subversion in Africa: THE FACTS," October 1965 (Accra,Ghana).

Chapter 34

1. Lugo Taguaba, article in FREEDOMWAYS, Fall 1962.

2. Bill Bland, Chairman in "Marxist-Leninist Organization of Britain (MLOB), "Does the Phenomenon of Black Racialism Exist?" Closing address to The Congress of the Nigerian Left, October 5, 1968 (London).

3. Robert F. Williams, speech at Peking Rally, reprinted in PEKING REVIEW, No. 33, August 12, 1966.

4. John Killens, Youngblood (London. 1956), pp. 242 ff.

5. Robert F. Williams, loc. cit.

6. Article by Do Xuan Sang, Deputy Secretary of Vietnam Lawyers' Association, VIETNAM COURIER, July 14, 1966.

Chapter 35

1. Ghanaian TIMES, February 16, 1963.

2. Accra EVENING NEWS, February 14, 1963.

3. H.M. Basner, Column, Ghanaian TIMES, February 18, 1963.

4. Anonymous (by demand), personal letter from a leading Marxist authority on Africa.

Chapter 36

1. Program of the then-newly-formed People's Party of Nigeria,May 1, 1961.

Chapter 37

1. Article by Professor D. Olderogge (Chief of the Department of African Studies, Institute of Ethnography, USSR Academy of Sciences), NEWS FROM THE SOVIET UNION (Embassy Bulletin), January 12, 1964 (Accra, Ghana).

2. Ibid.

3. "Problems of African Students in Moscow," PEACE NEWS, December 27, 1963.

Chapter 39

1. N. Numade, "The Working Class and the African Revolution," AFRICAN COMMUNIST, October-December, 1962.

2. A. Lerumo, "Showdown in Kenya," ibid., Third Quarter, 1966.

3. A. Zanzolo, "Crisis in Africa," ibid., same date.

4. WORLD MARXIST REVIEW, August 1962.

5. Nkrumah, op. cit., p. 247.

Chapter 40

1. Palme Dutt, World Politics: 1918-1936, pp. 45 ff.

2. Baran and Sweezy, op. cit., Chapter 7, "Militarism and Imperialism," pp. 178 ff.

3. Ibid., p. 180.

4. Ibid., p. 182.

5. Ibid., p. 183.

6. Ibid., p. 184.

7. Ibid., p. 186.

8. Ibid., p. 187.

9. Ibid., p. 187.

10. Ibid., p. 188.

11. Ibid., p. 188.

12. Ibid., pp. 188, 189.

13. Ibid., pp. 189, 190.

14. Ibid., p. 190 (referring to Professor Frederick L. Schuman of Williams College).

15. Ibid., p. 191.

16. Ibid., pp. 190, 191.

17. Ibid., p. 192.

18. Ibid., pp. 192, 193.

19. Ibid., p. 206.

20. Ibid., p. 191.

Chapter 41

1. WORLD ALMANAC, 1968 (New York. Doubleday), p. 496. Also, Reference Note 4, below.

2. Brochure by British Guiana Freedom Association (BGFA), 1963. Distributed by London Embassy of British Guiana.

3. Fenner Brockway, "The Problem of British Guiana, Ghanaian TIMES, May 17, 1963.

4. "What is ORIT?" British Guiana Embassy publication, June 1963 (London).

5. Statement by Richard Ishmael, President of B.G. TUC, GUIANA GRAPHIC, May 3, 1963. Quoted in Reference Note 4, above.

6. Press conference, February 16, 1967.

7. New York TIMES, February 22, 1967.

8. NATIONAL GUARDIAN, March 4, 1967, reprinted from ibid., issue of June 27, 1963.

9. Cheddi Jagan, article on British Guiana, NATIONAL GUARDIAN, May 21, 1966.

10. Palme Dutt, Fascism, p. 185.

11. NATIONAL GUARDIAN, March 18, 1967.

12. Cedric Belfrage, review of The 1 966 Socialist Register, edited by Ralph Miliband and John Saville, NATIONAL GUARDIAN, November 12, 1966.

Chapter 42

1. SOVIET NEWS (London Embassy), March 4, 1969, p. 63, Column 1.

2. The Marxist-Leninist Organization of Britain: Address to the Congress of the Nigerian Left, October 5, 1968 (London),pp. i and ii.

3. Hung Tsai-ping, "Clumsy Performance," PEKING REVIEW, February 28, 1969.

4. Carl Davidson, "From the New Left," GUARDIAN (N.Y. weekly), March 22, 1969.

5. Camden Newsletter No. 1, April 1968. Camden Marxist-Leninist Group, London.

Preface by H.W. Edwards

Seven years have passed since this book was completed. No one can accuse me of rushing into print with it! Its contents, therefore, have been put to that acid test: time. I think, on the whole, they passed the test. However, it is only natural that some factors on the scenes which I was describing should have changed. What sorts of changes? Have they affected my conclusions? How?

In the "Background" section of the book, I set forth the Western Left's miscalculations and underestimations of imperialist parasitism insofar as they related to its inability to build the great working class United Front which they saw as the answer to fascism. Today, through Chinese experience, I see further light on this subject. If the USSR-directed United Front failed, it was because it was not – certainly, not in practice – based on the "dialectical policy of both unity and struggle."

"Struggle" within whatever developed of that United Front was kept in abeyance and then dropped. This adds a bit of additional depth to my explanations as to why Social Democracy devoured the "real Left," and not, as the latter planned, vice versa. Time has also vindicated my analysis of Scandinavian realities. An article in NEWSWEEK for August 22, 1977, reported the rapid erosion of the antiseptic wall of "exceptionalism" between Scandinavia and the rest of Western Europe: 12% inflation, balance of payments deficits, foreign borrowing, devalued currency, loss of competitive "edge" in European markets; threat of unemployment while taxes continue rising beyond wage gains; and, above all – yes! – "race riots" between Swedes and Turks in Swedish streets. Time has begun filling in the outline of my own diagnosis of Sweden as no exception to European capitalism.

As to the nature of class collaboration, since 1971 the "Sweetness and Light" phase ("all buddies together") is becoming harder and harder for imperialist rulers to sustain. Thanks to the divisive role and confusion-sowing effect of modern Social Democracy in the form of Social Imperialism (notably in Africa), "middle men" are beginning to take actions which, in proletarian hands, could be decisive for revolution.

In Chapter 16, I refer to "abnormally cheap" prices for staples "such as tea, coffee, sugar, tobacco and others." Today, in the United States at least, some of these have advanced notably in price.

At first, this development brought forth anguished screams from the monopolies ruling the West, especially those in the U.S.; lately, these screams have diminished notably in volume: an adaptation has been accomplished; a "middle level absorbent" has been created. Once again, imperialism has had to make a new division of its loot. Some of the system's Frankenstein monsters – the imperialist-spawned ruling class elites in neo-colonies (especially in "Araby" and certain Latin American countries) – having learned in a good school, are now applying their lessons.

They discovered what a whip they hold in their position inside neo-colonies as buffer against colonial revolution. Accordingly, they have begun raising formerly ridiculously low primary product prices. Oil, coffee and sugar are harbingers.

In so doing, these neo-colonial elites have reduced the maneuverability of their own major customers (the big Western imperialist powers) vis-a-vis those customers' internal problems; namely, the amount of swag available for the monopolists' "crumb factory," "at home."

Imperialism's anguished screams died down when they realized that they were being held to ransom by people of their own ilk. The ruling class fully understands that primary product price rises in the hands of people's governments would signal the start of collapse for them. Instead, the actual price rises merely, thus far, open avenues for incredible benefits to internal neo-colonial oppressors.

These buffer elites in neo-colonies become richer and more powerful; they move into the U.S. economy, buying up banks, real estate and other assets. The monopolists sigh in relief: this is a ploy they understand – they believe they will "get to" these upstarts later. Once again, the brunt of super-exploitation can continue being absorbed by the proletariat and peasantry of the Third World.

And this happens mainly because the world – especially the Western – Left continues to overlook, ignore and even deny Lenin's warning about the primacy of parasitism in the makeup of Western imperialism.

The writer sees this development as evidence of how, in the absence of clarity on a key factor in the world situation, a good thing is turning into a bad thing.

My Chapter 28 on "Reformism and Racism in U.S." describes certain phenomena which were beginning in England; these are now full-blown racist "blossoms," outspoken, outright, undisguised. Furthermore, to the not-unexpected slobberings of the Margaret Thatchers and Enoch Powells are, this time, added the definitely unexpected blessings of at least one section of the quondam "real Left:." The Finsbury Communists actually beat both Conservative leaders to the punch in denouncing immigration into England of "foreign nationals," that is, in effect, of blacks. Social Democracy develops according to inexorable law.

Chapter 31, "Racism as the Least Common Denominator of Social Democracy" touches briefly on Social Democratic ideology in Latin America: that much touted "democratic path" to (alleged) socialism. Events in Chile, which occurred after completion of my manuscript, should leave no doubt about the validity of "socialism" so achieved.

But such lessons are always paid for in blood; the blood of revolutionaries who misjudge the nature of imperialism. That this happened in a land whose value to imperialism is that of inexhaustible well for super-profits should give particular pause: here, indeed, was a case where imperialism's parasitism was invisible to its own greatest victims. The latter, rather, dreamed that the Colossus would yield as much of its powerfully entrenched advantages as "the people's will" requested. Such are the results of being lulled by Revisionism's fairy-tales! (See LONDON TIMES, February 20, 1978: "Face reality or keep quiet, Mr. Powell tells politicians. "The only way is a positive outflow' of New Commonwealth immigrants"").

My Chapter 32, "Racism – Major Tactical Ideological Factor in Imperialism's Superstructure" comments briefly on why socialism had, to 1970, been unable to "overtake and surpass" its vaunted U.S. rival: it forgot that the amazing productivity of American labor was mainly a product of imperialist parasitism, which allowed that country's monopolies to invest in more "R & D" (Research and Development) than any other power.

'Socialism," I stated then, ". . . does not, . . . will not, . . . Cannot super-exploit. When it starts trying to, it is no longer socialism."

This remark now seems to me a prophetic spotlight on the present role of Social Imperialism in Africa and elsewhere (Indonesia, for example).

In my discussion of racism in Eastern Europe (Chapter 36), it will undoubtedly be noticed that I did not specify my sources of information. "I was told . . .", etc. This was made mandatory by the February 24, 1966, military coup in Ghana, following which many known Ghanaian supporters of the fallen Nkrumah regime were under constant, strict surveillance. To have used their names – even to use them now – would have, and could still, place them in jeopardy.

In Chapter 42, I touched upon "the demise of imperialism." Now, it is time to amplify those remarks. U.S. imperialism is being challenged by other imperialisms; many of these challenges will inevitably cut into American super-profits. Still, it is not yet the ruling class which will suffer; rather, a section of the American labor aristocracy, studied in such detail in my pages, will be called upon to cough up some of its earlier gains.

Nonetheless, in 1978, as staple prices rise, the U.S. Labor aristocracy – grumbling as it does so – still has the money to pay the increased prices for its luxuries – and pay it does. All the same, these price hikes are signs. First, as labor aristocracies begin to suffer cut-backs, a possibility exists for new allies for colonial revolution. However, this is true only if attention is paid to that contradiction among the world's peoples which my book examines.

The Western labor aristocracies have shown that they intend to defend their present position to the death: this has given rise, in the U.S., to Hell's Angels, storm troopers on motorcycles; and of outright, self-proclaimed Nazi groups, forming, drilling, meeting secretly in the dead of night in "cowboy" cafes in the valleys of California, and no doubt elsewhere. Such ominous developments auger a different conclusion to anti-colonial struggles than revolutionaries wish.

Yet, knowing something means having the potential to apply knowledge. It strikes me as exceedingly important that this particular development receive intense scrutiny with the aim of testing tactics and strategy by Western Leftists who genuinely wish to act in a revolutionary manner.

If not, imperialism can totter on indefinitely, sucking the blood and marrow of its neo-colonies; it cannot be expected to fall of its own weight.

My remarks about what I thought unity within the world working class ought to embody should evoke loud screams among the Sweetness and Light Brigades of the "left." All the same, I stand by them: leadership for world revolution does not reside in the West. The most that Western revolutionaries can or should expect is to play a supportive role in the central struggles of colonial peoples to destroy colonialism and neo colonialism. That is, the well from which imperialism draws its major super-profits must be destroyed. Their source remains the same as ever: the qualitatively greater, and still increasing, misery of Third World peoples.

If this book does nothing else but bring sharply into the lime light the parasitic nature of imperialism and the real size and role of that parasitism's major outgrowth, the Western labor aristocracy, it will, in the author's opinion, have served a valuable purpose. Let the controversies rage; they are the mills wherein clarity can be achieved.

Revolutions have never been made out of wishes. Rather, they are rooted in hard, cold and usually dreary facts. It is only by facing all the facts in any situation that a realistic and workable solution can be reached.

I would, therefore, be pleased if this book could become the basis for far more extensive and detailed investigation into the nature of super-exploitation, including exact measurement of the very real, very substantial benefits it still brings – as well as those it has already brought – to Western workers.

I wish this, not (as critics will leap to say in order to avoid – as before – facing unpleasant realities) to show that "imperialism is not so bad." Rather, I want my facts to reveal the full extent of its real badness. It is necessary to face the fact that we cannot hope for imperialism's spontaneous demise; we must understand and measure the true extent of its disease and how that affects us. We have to look boldly and clearly at the remnants of vitality upon which it can still draw.

I consider it a hindrance to basic change that a decisive section of the world proletariat can allow itself to enjoy, and will defend to the death, privileges which (a) hide its own exploitation and (b) derive from the blood, sweat and tears of proletarian brothers and sisters in the Third World.

LABOR ARISTOCRACY
MASS BASE OF SOCIAL DEMOCRACY
First Edition Back Cover

In his great classic, Imperialism, the Highest Stage of Capitalism, Lenin described the labor aristocracy of that time as "a tiny minority of the working class." Ever since, with out relating current statistics to Lenin's guide-lines, the world Left, especially in the West, has continued mouthing: "The Labor aristocracy is a tiny minority of the working class."

This book undertakes to apply official U.S. and other data to the criteria for a labor aristocracy which Lenin set forth in his "Preface to the German and French editions" of the cited source. Supported by a resulting 43 statistical tables, it proves that, today, the entire working class of the West constitutes a labor aristocracy on a world scale; that its former "crumbs" from the capitalists' table have, due to the escalation of imperialism's parasitism, augmented greatly; that the labor aristocracy's acceptance of this kick-back, which Lenin called "imperialist bribery," has created for them in the West a "Way of Life" such that a serious internal contradiction now exists within the international proletariat: the one between workers in the West and those of the "Third World;" that Social Democracy is and always has been the political mouthpiece of the labor aristocracy; and that the Least Common Denominator of Social Democracy is racism. The author contends that, if not seriously studied and fought against, this internal contradiction can and will harden, if it hasn't already, into an antagonistic one within the international working class, in a world of which the imperialist section is now ruled by transnational corporations rather than by nations, as in Lenin's day. If such political sclerosis is allowed to set, it can only postpone further the arrival of the necessary "final conflict."